Recreation Leadership

Recreation Leadership

Maryhelen Vannier, Ed.D.

Professor and Director, Professional Preparation
Department of Health and Physical Education,
Southern Methodist University, Dallas, Texas

Third Edition

Lea & Febiger

Philadelphia 1977

Health Education, Physical Education, and Recreation

RUTH ABERNATHY, Ph.D.
Editorial Adviser

Professor Emeritus, School of
Physical and Health Education,
University of Washington,
Seattle, Washington

Library of Congress Cataloging in Publication Data

Vannier, Maryhelen, 1915–
  Recreation leadership.

  Previous editions published under title: Methods and
materials in recreation leadership.
  Includes bibliographies and index.
  1. Recreation Leadership. I. Title.
GV181.4.V36 1976   790   76-9783
ISBN 0-8121-0548-6

Published in Great Britain by Henry Kimpton Publishers, London

Printed in the United States of America

Print Number: 3 2 1

This book is dedicated to the blind children with whom I worked as a volunteer recreation leader in gratitude to each one for helping me to see more fully the beauty, joy, and wonder of life.

Preface

This book contains a wide range of activities that should be found in a creative, modern, and meaningful recreation program. It is also a book of leadership techniques and teaching methods for conducting a successful recreational program in community centers, schools, churches, industry, hospitals, prisons or detention centers, and on playgrounds.

It has been written mainly for three groups: (1) college recreation and physical education majors who are preparing to become professional leaders; (2) beginning paid or volunteer leaders who want to learn how to become effective leaders; and (3) experienced leaders who seek new and better ways to guide and instruct people of all ages through recreation.

The book contains over 1000 program ideas and ways to teach a wide range of activities including music, dramatics, arts and crafts, dance, nature and camping, athletic sports and games, and social recreation.

A chapter is devoted to techniques for teaching special groups, including children, teen-agers and the aged, as well as those who are handicapped, including the orthopedically atypical, the mentally retarded, as well as the gifted. Other chapters contain techniques for successfully conducting club activities and for evaluating the results of the program and its leaders.

The opening chapter of the book is entitled, "Free Time, Work, and Leisure in Changing America," and points out the role recreation can play in helping to solve these pressing problems. Throughout the text I stress that the recreation program must be far more than a means of helping others to fill a free time vacuum or to find mere entertainment, but rather recreation must be concerned with improving the quality of life. Throughout the text, emphasis is placed upon the need for the recreation leader to help people discover true leisure, positive free time use, and to achieve a happier, more cultured, and morally sensitive life.

This book is a text intended for use in such college courses as Recreation Leadership, Introduction to Recreation, or Community Recreation.

Maryhelen Vannier

Dallas, Texas

Contents

chapter 1

Free Time, Work, and Leisure in Changing America

To use leisure intelligently and profitably is the final test of civilization.   Jay B. Nash

We are living in a time of drastic change, violence, and uncertainty—in a distance-shrunken world. Ours is the age of hot and ever threatening cold wars. In spite of our present economic difficulties, due largely to inflation and the oil shortage crisis, our nation is one of the most prosperous in the world. Yet at the same time, our country abounds with internal strife, hatred, fear, violence, and moral indifference. Most people living in our consumer-oriented, highly-mechanized, and youth-centered society now have to struggle harder than ever to become or remain unique individuals. The goal of many people now is to *surpass* the Joneses. Duped by clever advertisers, many believe that they can do so mainly by acquiring more *things* and consuming the right products rather than by the means our ancestors honored to gain status.

The average American now has the potential of between 8 and 10 hours of free time daily for off-the-job living. If he lives a well-balanced life, he works 8 hours, sleeps nearly 8 hours, and has a large part of the remaining time to do as he pleases. If he is foolish, he works all day and worries most of the night, or he "moonlights" by taking on an extra job to survive in this time of rapidly rising costs, or to buy more "things," or get ahead. On the weekend many play too much and too hard. Their yearly hard-earned vacation is an exhausting experience from which they often need another holiday in order to recover from the one just had. The wife is on a merry-go-round, too, increasing her original role as a wife and mother to that of a full- or part-time employee outside the home, as the family chauffeur, shopper, gardener, and community do-gooder. Even the children are caught on a treadmill of routinized after-school activities of ballet and music lessons, scout and church activities, plus organized sports—all to be followed by hours of increased homework assignments to be completed before bedtime. No wonder our

1

foreign friends scoffingly call Americans fast travelers but poor loafers, speedy runners but insipid ramblers.

In our push-button, mechanical age we tend to snatch at fleeting pleasures, grab and gulp at life endeavoring to cram as many thrills into our lives as possible and seemingly prefer watching others perform rather than taking part in activities, and have mistaken the "good life" for the soft life. Medical specialists, criminologists, educators, and a host of other experts warn us to slow down, and learn how to live joyfully before we destroy ourselves and others. They warn man that he is God's creative masterpiece. As a human being he is composed of a body, mind, and soul and is driven by basic emotional, social, and physical drives. Included in the latter is the need for daily creative and re-creative activity, which builds, repairs, relaxes, and refreshes his mind, body, and spirit from the many draining experiences of life.

Our Work-Oriented Society

Our early American ancestors, the majority of whom lived on farms or small villages, worked from sunup to sundown struggling against the forces of nature to provide food, shelter, and clothing for themselves and families. Greatly influenced by the strict and somber Puritans, who claimed that "the devil made work for idle hands to do," many went to an early grave from overwork and lack of proper medical care. Although we today owe a great debt in many ways to these early Puritans for the many successful things they did accomplish, as a group they greatly failed in their vigorous attempts to stamp out man's natural urge for play, laughter, and joy.[1] Thus, there are those among us now who view the shortened work week with its resulting increase of free time and leisure as great threats which will weaken the moral fabric of our society. Certainly, too, there are those today who believe so strongly in this old Puritanic "work ethnic" that they, in their quest for more status and money, become "workaholics" and too often neglect their families, wreck their health, in that they never take a vacation, work 7 days a week, and thus, like our pioneering ancestors, literally kill themselves from overwork combined with overworry. Such individuals lack balance in their lives and rarely find joy or happiness of life itself.

As America changed from being an agricultural nation to an industrial one and the majority of people moved from the country to the big city, Americans became a nation of clock watchers.

Today less than 5% of all Americans live on farms. Our economy is now based upon the output of mass labor and big business, which is found in many forms. The time clock, the computer, along with many other kinds of machines have taken over. The individual worker no longer speaks for himself to management, for this is now the task taken over by an all-powerful union leader. Human dignity once found through work, along with the pride of creating something beautiful with one's own hands, are rapidly becoming a thing of the past. Man himself has come to think of himself too often a helpless victim caught in a vicious trap. Those working in factories especially feel that they are but a tiny part of a huge production line. Some add nuts, screws and bolts to the car being manufactured when it comes to them momentarily before passing on to the next worker standing near the conveyor belt. Others are can stuffers and pattern stampers. All are victims of boredom, resulting from dull, routinized work. Meaningless, mechanical work is fast becoming a major problem to thousands of Americans.[2]

In a recent survey done through lengthy recorded interviews over a 3-year period, the writer Studs Terkel heard many of these workers make statements like these:

> " 'I'm caged,' says the bank teller,' 'I'm a mule,' says the steelworker.' 'A monkey can do what I do,' says the receptionist. 'I'm less than a farm implement,' says the migrant worker. Blue collar and white call upon the identical phrase, 'I'm a robot.' Nora Watson may have said it most succinctly, 'I think most of us are looking for a calling, not a job. Most of us, like the assembly worker, have jobs that are too small for our spirit. Jobs are not big enough for people.' "[3]

Some people, of course, as Mr. Terkel found, do enjoy their work. These are the lucky ones among us, for like Theodore Roosevelt, the former United States President, they have found that one of the greatest prizes found in life comes from working hard at work worth doing.

TRENDS

In our society technology has advanced more rapidly in the past 50 years than in the past 5000. In this period of rapid change, the 40-hour-work week is now a reality for many Americans except for those who are on the executive level and those who moonlight by working at one and a half or two jobs. In this type of schedule, the individual works only 4 days a week for a period of 10 hours each, instead of following the traditional pattern of the 40-hour work week spread over a 5-day period.

Another significant new trend is retirement with pay for those who are 55, instead of the older pattern of retirement at the age of 65.

The third major trend is that many more women are working than ever before in our history. Although the vast majority of these employees are not on the managerial level, increasingly but slowly this pictured fact is beginning to change.

The fourth trend is the longer and more frequent paid vacation for workers. Before 1940 only those in managerial positions got paid vacations. By 1970, however, two-thirds of all nonfarm workers had at least 2 weeks paid vacation. As Daniel Bell, a sociology professor at Harvard University has pointed out, if one includes paid holidays and sick leaves, the actual work year has shrunk more than 3 weeks in the past 3 decades.[4]

FUTURE FORECASTS

Some researchers in the work-leisure field believe that by the end of this century our present 40-hour work week will be reduced to being 28 hours of work.[5] Others believe that these figures are incorrect and that by the end of this century our society will become so mechanized that only a small majority of all people will work and that the vast majority will be paid to remain idle.

Startling as these above predictions may seem, and should they come true, they are cause for much alarm, contemplation, study and the revamping of our cultural patterns and values.

The Meaning of Work

Work and play are like the two sides of a coin: each is an integral part of the other. We work so we can play or enjoy life during our free time, but we play so that we can work more productively. For work one receives a monetary reward, whereas play carries its own reward. Work today in America is becoming more playlike—the coffee break, business deals made on the golf course, and the piped-in soft music. For some, play becomes work. Watch an adult struggle to learn golf or a teen-ager to learn to water-ski. No longer is there a wide separation between work and play, and some kinds of work of yesterday, such as hunting and fishing, have become the major play activities of today. Work for the adult is responsibility rewarded by a wage, and if one has chosen his vocation wisely, he receives deep satisfaction as well. For youth, work is school responsibilities and his reward is a grade. Work for some is hated drudgery. Some look forward to the end of the work week as eagerly as Lindbergh searched for the coast of Europe. The TGIF Club (Thank God It's Friday Club) has a large membership, as does the OGIM (Oh, God, It's Monday Club). Others, like Thomas Edison, who declared that he never worked a day in his life, feel work has a greater importance than free time.

According to an old folk saying, "those who do not enjoy their work are like men carving statues with hatchets." Every society scorns idleness and refusal to work, although each has a different concept of what is work and how it ranks on a scale of values. Although we jokingly say "don't just stand there, do something," we really mean it. Walt Whitman would have us "loaf and invite our souls," but those who do so in our work-oriented, materialistic society would fast become social outcasts.

To Americans, the long Mexican siesta, the extended leisurely lunch hour of the French, and the afternoon closed shops and markets of the Spanish represent sinful waste. It is the belief of many that those who do not work are shirkers, for only through work can one find wealth, status, purpose, or an antidote for loneliness. The philosophy of Samuel Smiles, Benjamin Franklin, and Horatio Alger's heroes that the best way to advance economically and socially is through thrift, hard work, and virtue is now being replaced by modern man's concept that work is something to endure in order to do what he really wants to do, namely, to play and enjoy life. To such people, work is regarded as spinach and play as the desired ice cream.

Play and Its Importance

Play is becoming less of a dirty word among adults and is now rapidly gaining an increasingly important place in our society and in our national economy. Play is voluntary activity, which has its own reward of joy, satisfaction, or diversion. It springs from free time and can be negative (stealing, raping, or excessive drinking—all detrimental to society and the individual) or positive (playing a game of softball according to the rules through a cooperative team effort or watching a ballet program—all beneficial to society as well as the individual). Play is a balance wheel of life and is one of the great physical needs of man. All work and no play makes Jack, regardless of how old he is, not only a dullard but a maladjusted person. Finding challenging, adventurous, and positively refreshing activities to do through recreation can add meaning, luster, and beauty to life.

What is one person's work can be another man's play. The manual laborer lays bricks as a means of livelihood, whereas Winston Churchill, during England's wartime crisis, laid bricks for fun and re-creation of his spirit and energy. The main differences between work and play lie mainly in attitude, the reward received, as well as the degree of challenge found in either. Play need not be always vigorous; it may be passive, spontaneous as well as planned, regularly or irregularly consistent, and engaged in as a change of pace or a refresher.

There are three types of play: motor (physical activities such as swimming or ice skating); sensory (watching a sunset or listening to music); and intellectual (going to a lecture or reading the current best seller). Frivolity, gaiety, and joy have a vital role in helping people find balance in life. Happy people add to life; they contribute, appreciate, as well as create beauty. Through play, such individuals find socially accepted ways to work out stored up feelings of aggression, to fulfill needs to dominate, destroy, excel, create, and to improve themselves physically, mentally, and culturally. "Play for the child is the gaining of life, play for the adult is the renewal of life." This is a concept held by Joseph Lee, known as the Father of the American playground movement. It carries much educational merit.

Play is one of the great physical needs of man, along with food, rest, elimination, and sex. It is leisure-time activity voluntarily selected and done in free time that brings satisfaction and re-creation to the individual. It is also part of the rhythm of life of work-play, energy breakdown-energy buildup, sorrow-joy, health-sickness, life-death. Leisure is not self-indulgence—it is a basic human need.

The difference between work and play is determined by the attitude of each individual and the amount of pleasure which comes from each. We work so we can play (along with other reasons), but if we play well we can both work more productively and get more joy out of life. Those with re-creative leisure usually are the most creative and productive workers.

Determining factors of free time use are: geographical location, cultural conditioning which has already labeled activities as positive or negative, sex, age, amount of depth of education, existing opportunities, economic and social status, religion, personal drives and desires, race, life-styles, and leadership.

All races culturally condition their members through play. Although play is universal, each child in each culture (whether he is an Eskimo, Pygmy, or a freckle-faced American boy or girl) is taught by adults the approved activities and games of the clan, tribe, race, city block, plus the most favored ones of his own sex, race, and religion. A boy is taught games thought to be best for boys. Little girls are given dolls and baby carriages. Today, largely due to the "women's lib" movement, toys are becoming less "boy" or "girl" centered (stuffed lions, rabbits, etc.).

The Meaning of Free Time

Free Time. Free time is those hours remaining each day after work or school responsibilities are completed. Every individual has the same 24 hours each day as long as he lives. What he does with this time is a different matter. Although we try to kill time, this is an impossibility. However, we might waste it, for in reality, time destroys us. Or to put it another way, time stays but man goes. The average American wage earner now has approximately 3,700 free hours a year—the equivalent of 250 full 16-hour days off from work. This is only the beginning of the age of expanding free time. It is not enough, however, for people to have this opportunity. They need to learn how to use their added work-free hours for their own development.

There is an abundance of evidence that many people are using their free time in self-destructive ways, searching for fun, thrills, and sensuous pleasures. Many, on the other hand, use their free-time hours moonlighting, commuting to and from work (which takes an average of 8½ hours a week), performing "do-it-yourself" projects, and wasting their time on poorly planned household chores. Few Americans have discovered ways to use added free time sensibly. They are not well-organized and self-disciplined enough to do their work with the least effort in the shortest amount of time. Learning to separate the really important life tasks from those which are trivial is basic not only to self-discovery, but to gaining an extra time bonus.

The Meaning of Leisure

Leisure. Leisure can only be defined in terms of what it does for a person. In its narrowest sense it is mere diversion; in the highest it is a developing, creative, and re-creative experience. The word comes from the Latin *licere*, meaning to be permitted freedom or opportunity to do something of value. Education, leisure, and freedom have the same common root. In the fullest sense all three mean far more than just freedom from. They mean, rather, freedom for. Through leisure we can find ways to upgrade and improve ourselves and society. It can help us raise our cultural levels. It can also assist us to become more uncommon and less common and to be human individuals of integrity and humane value.

It can help us find quality in life. Such leisure is based upon Socrates' belief that "the unexamined life is not worth living," for it largely is concerned with time used for inward growth and the discovery of joy, beauty, and meaning of life. Although free time is for all men, only the elite minority will find true leisure. Such fortunate ones will live creatively.

The ancient Greeks held that leisure was much more than just free time. Rather, it was an earned bonus resulting from work needed by all men in order to develop finer values through aesthetic, psychological, religious, and philosophical contemplation. Jay B. Nash of New York University, one of our foremost philosophers in the leisure field in the 1960's, along with Charles Brightbill of the University of Illinois, claimed that leisure time was far more than mere fun and frolic but, instead, was an opportunity for man to improve the *quality* of life. Sebastian de Grazia, in his classic book, *Of Time, Work and Leisure,* as well as other more recent authorities in the leisure field, such as Robert Lee, Max Kaplan, James Murphy and others, support the concepts held by Nash and Brightbill by writing that leisure time is, indeed, a period man needs for rediscovering the meaning and purpose of life and for the development of the mind, body and spirit.

The first widely adopted concept that leisure is discretionary time which parallels the economic concept of discretionary money, was that advocated by Marion Clauson, whose book, *Resources For The Future,* influenced many others. Ott Romney, who also had great influence upon other writers in the leisure field, believed that leisure time is a "choosing time" left over after time spent for existence (sleeping, eating, etc.) and subsistence (working or school) in which man could choose what he wanted to do in that period.

The antiliterarian view that leisure is time to be spent finding real joy and pleasure in life was first expressed by Walter Kerr, the former drama critic for *The New York Times,* in his widely-read book, *The Decline of Pleasure.* Many modern day sociologists believe that whether or not what a person does in his free time can be defined as leisure depends on the subjective meaning he attaches to his leisure activity rather than what he does.

I believe that leisure time is a cultural opportunity enjoyed by only a few people who, in their quest to find joy, beauty, and meaning in life, do a wide variety of activities, dependent upon their own unique individuality and lifestyles. Only these few who use free time in creative and re-creative ways make precious hours meaningful. These are the fortunate ones who have learned to budget their free time wisely, to separate the important things in life from the trivial, and to say "No" to those who would infringe too much upon their "golden hours" of freedom away from work. Such people make up an elite minority in our society. They are inner-directed, well-disciplined people who seek beauty, meaning, and joy in life. They are the creative ones who have found the true meaning of the word "leisure." They contribute the most to our present culture and will help chart the destiny of America.

It is they who have learned that leisure can provide man with his greatest opportunity to gain self-expression, self-understanding, and self-development. To increase their numbers is the challenge educators must face if we are to become a cultured nation which values beauty and creativity more than it does the cheap, the tawdry, and the "quickie."

The Meaning of Recreation

Recreation. There are many definitions of recreation. To many professionals, recreation is not a matter of motions but rather a matter of emotions; it is an attitude and a way of life. To still others it is any activity which is performed for its own sake during free time which offers man joy and satisfaction and an outlet for his physical, mental, and creative powers.

Recreation, in its purest sense, has the following characteristics:

1. It is both a creative and re-creative activity.
2. It may be passive or active.
3. It occurs mainly during free time.
4. In its finest aspects it can become leisure through which one can learn how to live a creative, happy, and meaningful life.

Problems of Modern America

America is rapidly changing geographically, socially, economically, and morally. The population explosion, rising juvenile delinquency and adult crime, the increase of working mothers coupled with the increase of the number of marriages which end in divorce, increased mental illness among adults and emotional disturbance among children, a longer life span and shorter work week, earlier retirement, the threat of automation upon the individual, increased mobility of families uprooted by busing or unemployment, inflation, and rapid urbanization are but a few of our most pressing and interwoven problems. Bigness, with its resulting smothering of the individual, is but one of the many prices (along with the breakdown of morals and shifting values resulting from more open permissive and daringly erotic lifestyle) that we pay for being basically a nation of wealth and diversity of our population.

Geographic Change. By 1980 approximately 90% of our population will be living in large cities or their nearby suburbs. Experts predict that by the end of this century most Americans will be crowded into ten major districts of merged suburbs. One such big area will extend from Buffalo, New York to Alexandria, Virginia and include Philadelphia, Washington, D.C. and New York City. People will live in large apartment houses clustered around their own schools, department stores, markets, hospitals, etc. Each large apartment complex will be a miniature modern city built next to other such sub areas. As more and more people are crowded into fewer and fewer places, such problems of individualism, employment and providing recreational outlets will become of even greater concern than they are today. Not only will we be faced with increased crime due to the increased density of population, family mobility will become even greater than it is now. Thus, we are greatly threatened into becoming what the writer, Vance Packard, has called "a nation of strangers," who look away from criminal acts, social, economic or physical problems which affect others, because we are relieved someone unknown was the victim, not us. In short, we will not be our brother's keeper because we do not know who he is and besides he is a threat to our survival anyway.

Social Change. Today it is the blue collar worker, thanks to powerful labor unions, who is making the fastest financial and social gains. Clear-cut lines, which once separated men from women, the highest, middle, and lowest class, are becoming blurred. Those seeking status go increasingly into debt to gain such status-yielding symbols as the third family car, the backyard swimming pool, the big, powerful motor boat, the large house with its terraced lawn. The greatest social mobility exists within the middle class, for those highest on the social totem pole still remain aloof, while those on the lowest level mostly remain trapped there because of lack of salable vocational skills and adequate education, and because they come from a minority group. Over a million youth, largely from these minority groups, drop out of our public schools each year, and these soon are forced to join the vast numbers of the undereducated and unemployed. Literally more, made up of hundreds of youth, attend school but have dropped out mentally. In many states our schools have become jungles because of forced busing and high school students, who can barely read or write, live in a dream world of the souped-up car or the glamorous life of a TV or movie star as they sit in chemistry, French, or other classes in our desegregated schools.

It is the "in" group that sets the pace in the status climb, the "out" group that remains the most stationary, and the "we want in" group that struggles hardest to gain as many pleasures and possessions as they struggle upward for social and economic gain. What a person does for work and play, how and where he lives, what is the color of his skin, what his religion and race are, the amount of education he has, and where he got it—all quickly classify and place him in our stratified society.

Today more women are seeking entrance into law, medicine, and other vocations once primarily labeled "for men only" than ever before. At the present time 51% of all mothers are working and ⅔ of them have full-time jobs. Furthermore, 1 in every 3 working mothers have children at home or in day care centers who are below the age of 6.[7] The "women's lib" movement triggered thousands of women into leaving their homes to enter the world of work, return to college, or run for political office.

At the present time many parents, both of whom work, are too busy to spend time with their children. It is estimated that many fathers now are spending on an average of only 15 to 20 minutes a day playing or being with their children on a face-to-face or one-to-one basis.[8] Child abuse is becoming a serious national problem. Research discloses that the battered child usually becomes the parent who beats up his own children.

Economic Change. In spite of inflation, far too many Americans are on a credit card spending spree which leaves them heavily in debt. Like our government, they are greatly in debt and slashing away at one part of their budget only to spend another part of it lavishly. People from all economic levels now buy many luxuries once reserved for the very rich, even though they may have to mortgage themselves to the hilt in order to get them. Others, like Nero, fiddle while Rome burns, declaring that they must live it up today, knowing that death and perhaps even disaster looms ahead. Teen-agers, who spend an exorbitant amount of money for free-time fun, seemingly have an insatiable appetite for records, motorcycles, cars, cheap liquor, and food. Manufacturers are now busily planning ways to carry their expensive tastes over into adulthood and to snare thousands of pre-teens into becoming well paying customers of their products as well.

The Population Explosion and Implosion. Population is increasing in the so-called backward countries (India, China, parts of Africa and South America) at such a rapid rate that this trend is referred to as "the population explosion." In America, in spite of the pill, illegitimate births among teen-agers are increasing at an alarming rate, as is alcoholism. The average size American family is composed of 3.48 persons per household. Over one million newly married couples live with their parents instead of in their own households. Many others go heavily into debt in order to live in swanky apartment resort-type apartment complexes and to take advantage of the many recreational outlets planned for them therein. Still others live in "for singles only" resort villages and have a wild, swinging, great time of fun, frolic and sex.

The divorce rate is also rising rapidly among young teen-agers and middle-age couples. Today nearly one out of every two marriages ends in divorce. Increasingly, children are being raised by a single parent and more fathers are being given the custody of their child. Many thousands of children below school age are being parked at day care centers daily, with neighbors or hired babysitters during their own formative years. Children today rarely have aunts, uncles, and grandparents around to help teach them values, nor can these be taught via periodically made long distance telephone calls. Such brief voice contacts are then, indeed, the second best thing to actually being there in the life of a child most needing the physical presence of loved ones.

Proportions within our population are changing also. It is estimated that by 1980 half of our population will be under 25 years of age and one third will be under age 15. There will also be an increase in those over 65. It will continually become more difficult to find employment in certain fields, if one does go on to college. At the same time, the span of life will gradually increase. Thus, in the near future we will have not only more older people but those who want to work will have to strive much harder to find satisfying work, forge stronger family ties, and gain meaning, happiness, and joy in life. The health and welfare problems to arise from the dense packing of human beings into our rapidly shrinking world are almost beyond comprehension.

Rising Delinquency and Crime. Our present 20 million teen-agers have created a sub-culture of their own, which has set up a chain reaction often resulting in tyranny against the values of the mature world. Although juvenile delinquents actually make up only 3% of the total number of teen-agers, this is a startling number of people, for many crimes are committed by youth who elude the police. Today one out of every ten youths becomes an arrested delinquent. Legally, a delinquent is any youth caught and taken into custody for breaking a law. Arrests of juveniles in America have increased more than three times as fast as has their population. Delinquency is a social cancer which is spreading at an alarming rate. It results from multi-causation factors, including lack of parental acceptance, love, and discipline as well as maladjusted personality, improper use of free time, and even indirectly by prosperity. Reformatories and prisons are not the preventive answer to this social malady, for it costs the public around $3000 a year to keep a child in a reformatory, far more than it does to keep him in a public school. Approximately 80% of all youths sent to such correctional institutions return as repeaters and later enter the adult criminal world.

Newspapers, movies, paperback books, television, and other media of communication have made us a crime-centered nation. Emotionally unstable youth and adults are greatly affected by what they see and hear. Such individuals are ripe for learning more about how to revolt against law and order. Inconsistent value and behavior patterns of adults, who can gain status quickly through materialism, do much to confuse youth further as to what is right or wrong.

At the present time there are thousands of jobless youth as well as older people who are no longer looking for work. These are the drifters seen in the streets, parks, and bars of every city. These are our uneducated, unskilled, and most vulnerable youth, and their numbers are increasing.

Juvenile Delinquency. The sharp increase in juvenile delinquency in America during the past decade has been considered by many experts in the fields of sociology, psychology and education to be our most alarming, dangerous and puzzling social problem. Research discloses that this social malady is due largely to:

1. Emotional disturbance caused by frustrated and thwarted drives.
2. Faulty environmental conditions, including slum areas and/or an unhappy home life among any income group.
3. Psychopathic personalities who cannot distinguish between right and wrong.
4. Poor use of leisure time.

Sheldon and Eleanor Glueck of Harvard University have concluded from their studies of hundreds of young criminals that the antisocial belligerent behavior of those who get into serious enough trouble to be arrested is due to many interlaced factors and that no single cause can be isolated. They have discovered the following definite traits and characteristics of delinquents.[9]

Physical—Mesomorphic (average) in build and constitution
Temperament—Restlessly energetic, impulsive, aggressive, destructive
Attitude—Hostile, defiant, resentful, suspicious, stubborn, socially assertive, adventurous, unconventional, nonsubmissive to authority
Intellect—More understanding of the direct and concrete rather than symbolic, less methodical in their approach to problems
Socioculture—Reared in homes of little understanding, affection, stability or moral fiber, most usually by unstable, unfit parents
School adjustment—Truant, disobedient, defiant, hatred toward school
Companions—Extreme gang loyalty, frequent companionship with those older.

Legally, a juvenile delinquent in most states is usually one between the ages of 7 and 18 who has broken a law and has been arrested for doing so. The most common offenses are auto theft, burglary, running away, sex offenses, truancy and incorrigibility. Of late, more thought and financial support have been given to prevention of, rather than to punishment for, youth crime. Numerous community authorities throughout the entire nation have been shocked into action upon learning that at the present time four out of every ten juvenile delinquents become hardened adult criminals. All experts agree that an attack on this rapidly spreading social cancer in only one or two areas will surely fail. More neighborhood parks, community centers or increased athletic competition for younger children will neither solve nor eradicate the problem. In fact, Los Angeles, Dallas and other cities have painfully discovered that gangs often used a new center as a clubhouse where future crimes were plotted and gang membership easily increased. Certainly a concentrated effort on the part of all leaders close to youth can do much to spot and save predelinquents. Since frequent and increased truancy is an early but sure symptom of serious socioemotional maladjustment, these leaders and teachers should increase their efforts to help each student succeed, belong to groups, and find adventure and recognition in legitimate ways. In addition to school skipping, other signs easily detected among those most vulnerable for delinquency are:

1. Hatred of school because of
   a. Failure to succeed
   b. Lack of intelligence, aptitude or real interest
   c. Repeating a grade or grades
   d. Being put back a grade or grades
2. Failure to belong to any supervised recreational character-building group.
3. Bad home conditions
   a. Alcoholic parent or parents
   b. Broken home; a foster parent
   c. Employment of both parents
   d. Inconsistent home discipline ranging from indifference to extreme harshness
   e. Home in a high delinquency area
   f. Overcrowded living conditions
   g. Frequently changed family residence
4. Signs of hatred or deep resentment toward others
   a. Has extreme prejudices and shows violent dislike for others
   b. Lacks security, belongingness, and cannot identify with any socially approved group
   c. Face and posture show strain and stress marks; child looks much older than he is
   d. Shows extreme withdrawal or aggressiveness; shows fight or flight reactions toward life and society

Certainly the wisest preventive measures of all are in helping all children to succeed according to their capabilities in assigned tasks at school, at play, and especially in the home, protecting those most vulnerable, and eradicating evil home and community influences. The school, church, home and state must unite to destroy costly social evils and to help youth have a real and meaningful place in society at all times—not just in time of war or when in serious trouble.

THE STREET CORNER LEADER

A number of recreation departments throughout the nation and other youth-serving agencies have found that the best way to make contact with troubled youth and adults who are the most vulnerable to crime is through using the roving leader approach. These leaders often are themselves from minority groups living in ghetto areas. Thus they have firsthand knowledge of the many problems these teen-agers and adults face. Although most of these "street corner" leaders are therapeutic recreation or activity specialists or social workers, many of them are also volunteers living in or near inner-city areas. They hang around those places attractive to youth—beer joints, pawnshops, rundown movie theatres, and cheap restaurants, and they dress in the same kind of a sloppy or flashy garb as those around them. Some pose as drug pushers, ex-cons, or pimps. Gradually they form a small cluster of followers. By working through and with the assistance of the natural leader within this cluster group, the adult helps his newly found followers in many ways. These include: (1) the discovery and use of available community resources for positive rather than negative use of free time, (2) helping keep potential school dropouts from leaving school by working cooperatively with school authorities, (3) assisting those who are on trial for criminal acts, (4) becoming a trusted friend and behavior model for those who are troubled, unhappy and lack positive models to emulate in their own home or community environment.

Working Mothers and the Changing Role of Women. Ours is a job centered society and with both parents working, home for many merely means a family filling station and rest stop. The greatest increase of all working mothers (83%) has been among those with children under 6 years of age. Never before have so many children been placed in day care centers nor have we had so many "latch key" children. These youngsters let themselves into an empty home after school and sit waiting for their working parents to return there. Many are street roamers and soon become the victims of sex or other crimes. Many women are returning to college to finish work toward a degree. Many others in the 45 to 70 age bracket are making precious use of their free time now that their children are raised. These people are contributing to their community through volunteer services as well as to our economy by becoming employed. On the other hand, many adult women remain empty, frustrated, and bored. These are the all-day bridge players, the alcoholics, and the lonely. Many lack purpose as human beings, while still others live in a four-ring circus of feverish activity, fearing to be alone. As Betty Friedan has pointed out in her provocative book, *The Feminine Mystique,* many American women have refused to grow up, have no real identity, and have failed to pursue a meaningful career or find fulfillment as a human being largely because of our cultural myth that a woman's place is in the home.

Although women in our society have more potential free time than ever before, due largely to labor-saving devices, many are guilt laden when they do take time out to read in mid-afternoon or to take part in other leisurely activities. This guilt complex regarding the use of time is inherited from a belief that play is evil, a concept inherited from the Dark Ages and our Puritan ancestors.

Increased Mental Illness. One of every ten Americans becomes mentally ill. Over 52% of all people hospitalized are emotionally disturbed or mentally ill. Such illness is due to many factors; chief among them, however, is the failure to cope successfully with problems which exist in our present complex society. Signs of emotional maladjustment usually appear early in life. This connotes that we need our most skilled and understanding leaders working with youth. It is estimated that 10 to 14% of all school children are emotionally disturbed today.

A Longer Life Span and Shorter Work Week. Americans are not only living longer, but more babies survive birth and early childhood. By the end of this century the average length of life for the female will be 76.8 years and for the male 71.2. Even today, more Americans are reaching the ages of 70/80/90. Our present college students have almost two-thirds of their lives ahead of them. Since women live longer than men do, most of them will be widows before death. Although in our society women control most of our economic wealth, it is the male who will work harder and longer and is more apt to become mentally ill or die from a heart attack. Women, however, who enter the world of work will pay the price for doing so by having an increased number from their ranks become ulcer, pychosis, or heart attack victims.

Although the shortened work week coupled with a longer life span sounds wonderful, the thrill of living must now be added to increased years, and a place of value must be made in our society for the growing number of nonworkers.

Increased Automation. Automation results in increased productivity and new job opportunities, which ultimately will raise our living standards and bring greater national wealth. Many regard it as a disguised curse. Numerous employees today are losing pride in their work, for too few ever see their contributed part in the finished product or are able to control where, when, and what kind of work they will do. These questions are answered by a remote boss or union leader. There is no doubt that automation will give man more free time than he ever had before and more money with which to buy more things. However, man in reality must find ways to spend his expanding free time doing things of real value.

Although man himself is in danger of becoming insensitive to the needs of others, he is far more than a mere machine and is more than a rectangular hole in a computer card.

TEENAGE DRINKING AND ACCIDENTS

More and more teenagers are learning to drive at the same time that they are beginning to drink, now that the age for both has been lowered to 18 or 19 in 27 states, a law that had previously been in effect in 6 other states. The percentage of automobile accidents involving 18- to 20-year-old drinking drivers has increased drastically ever since. In Michigan this has meant a 112% increase in car accidents involving teenagers and drinking, with a corresponding percentage increase in the number of teenage fatalities. In Wisconsin in 1971, 72 accidents involved people 18, 19, and 20 years of age. In 1972, after the drinking age was lowered, this number increased to 94 and is rising sharply at the present. In Nebraska and elsewhere throughout the nation the problem of teenage drinking is becoming increasingly serious. A recent statewide survey in Massachusetts showed a 92.7% increase in the use of alcohol, and 59.4% of the students questioned said they had been drinking within the past year. Students from all over the nation in other recent surveys have said that alcohol is increasingly becoming the favorite drug of teenagers. Many parents are so relieved that their children are not on "hard drugs" that they tend to look the other way at alcohol indulgence. The sales to teenagers of "pop" wines have also increased rapidly, rising from 3 million gallons in 1968 to 33 million gallons in 1973. Even junior high and elementary schoolers are often getting drunk in some areas of the country. In America car accidents involving drunken teenagers in the 13- to 17-year-old age group are also increasing. Alcoholics Anonymous has reported a sharp rise in teenage membership as well as the fact that some of its youngest members are 10-year-olds who are trying to remain sober.

Alcoholism is also increasing among adults and especially so among women.

CHANGING STANDARDS OF VALUES AND CHOICE

We are rapidly becoming a thrill-seeking, hedonistic culture wherein anything goes and the more shocking that is, the better. Our movie and television programs largely evolve around crime or those who commit it and like our cheap, brightly packaged magazines prominently displayed in all airports and elsewhere, are full of shock and sex. Each citizen is urged to do "his own thing" and the race is on to become the most perverse and most revolting in actions, as well as looks. The cheap, the tawdry, and the quickie are destructive elements found in the blowing winds of change which are threatening to distort the vision of us all.

The Role of Recreation in Helping to Solve These Problems

Recreation is far from being an answer for solving the many problems we face as a nation. It must, however, become a more important one of many ways to eradicate them.

To live is to change, for without change life does not exist. Some of the major changes mentioned above will help advance society, others will deter it. Above all, we cannot return to the good old days. To become concerned or to care enough is basic to finding the solution to any problem. Knowledge, it has been said, is knowing that a problem *does* exist. Wisdom is knowing *how* to solve it. Virtue is *doing* it or finding *how* to solve it. As adults, citizens, and leaders we can, through our trial-and-error learning attempts, find ways to solve our many complex problems—but only if we capitalize upon our mistakes. We *can* individually do much to end human waste, moral decay, and deterioration.

As individuals and as professional members in the field of education, recreation, health, physical education, safety, or the humanities, we have never had such a challenge as exists today. Never have our opportunities for raising the level of human society been greater. We can and must help people find ways to spend their time profitably and to find joy in their lives by engaging in meaningful, happiness-filled activities.

Recreation has a special role to play in helping us to solve these national problems. It is the task of all recreational leaders, as a vital part of their profession, to work toward solving these major issues within their own areas. Some suggested approaches and activities for doing so are as follows:

Geographic Change. Since more and more people are living in crowded metropolitan areas, the programming of small-group activities must be stressed so that those who are socially isolated may be included, and especially those who live in crowded, decaying inner cities, most of whom are of minority groups. New techniques should be devised to reach and assist each person within these smaller units so that each may feel a sense of belonging and security. The more the leader learns about each individual, the greater will be his understanding and the greater will be his chance to assist others. Increased efforts should be made to provide creative outlets for individual self-expression through arts and crafts, dance, and dramatic activities.

Since many people are losing contact with the land, programs in nature, camping, and conservation should be emphasized. One of the greatest contributions any recreation leader can make toward helping people appreciate nature is to provide beautiful parks, gardens, and nature trails within the community and to encourage people to discover and use them fully.

Social Change. Because our concepts of values are shifting, the recreation leader must make a greater effort to stress such ethical concepts as good sportsmanship, courage, fair play, honesty, and consideration for others. Although these values are inherent in all activities, they are especially prevalent in sports and games. However, they will remain untapped unless they are stressed by the leader both verbally and nonverbally through his actions. Throughout these activities, emphasis should be placed upon character development, the relationship between playing according to game rules and obeying laws, and the development of leadership and followship traits. Greater effort should be made to provide opportunities for all people to participate in these activities regardless of skill level, age, or sex. If such activities as Little League baseball have value for boys as well as girls, more youngsters through homogeneous grouping should be provided with opportunities to be on a league team and compete against others of similar skill.

Through a well-directed sports and games program for all people, each individual can be aided to gain improved health, vigor, and coordination. They will also be given an opportunity to develop social and physical skills and find legitimate ways to let off steam and relieve feelings of aggression and hostility. Many watchers will become doers only when they discover the thrill of participating for themselves. Greater endeavor must be made to reach these spectators and provide ways for them to take part in physical activities. This can only be accomplished when more people are provided with an opportunity to learn increased skills in physical activities.

Economic Change. In spite of inflation, more people today have more money to spend, even though many are heavily in debt, than ever before and are seeking happiness through buying more and more things. The recreation leader can, through planning increased creative program activities, guide these persons to find the joy in making things with their own hands, whether this be through metal crafts, rug weaving, or whatever. Now is also the time to bring more of the fine arts into the lives of more people through such activities as oil painting or sculpture. Increased efforts should be made to utilize cultural storehouses within the community through planned trips to such places as art museums and public libraries. Children as well as parents in culturally deprived areas will profit greatly from such excursions, for studies show that the vast majority of these individuals rarely, if ever, go to these places. Many need encouragement. Once there, some find beauty, as they often do in church, to brighten up their lives. One of the benefits received from the Head Start Program for Culturally Deprived Children, which began in the summer of 1965, was that parents as well as children went on field trips to the local zoo, art museum, library, and air terminal for the first time. Such experiences are both recreational and educational and are far-reaching in effect.

Teen-agers, most of whom are idealistic and want to serve, can assist in such trips and follow-up programs.

At the present time most recreation departments are being forced to reduce their staffs and program offerings. At the same time, because of inflation, the oil crisis and gas shortage, more people are coming to recreation centers and playgrounds to use their costfree or inexpensive recreational outlets. Thus, it is imperative that more programs be included for families and that these programs remain as inexpensive as possible. Staff members must be more carefully selected in an endeavor to find those who can lead a wide variety of activities so that full-time leaders can replace many part-time specialists.

The Population Explosion. Often the most under-serviced group in recreation is the one made up of young married couples with youngsters. Greater effort should be made to draw these people into community recreation and service programs. Many organizations wisely provide free baby sitting services for young parents so they may participate in such co-ed activities as bridge or such individual activities as slimtrim classes for the wife and weight lifting for the husband.

Increased effort should be made to provide recreational and service outlets for senior citizens, also. Although many communities do offer programs for these people, actually they are reaching only a small proportion of those living in many localities. Many need to be sought out and guided into recreational activities. Some recreation departments are enlisting the aid of young and middle-aged couples to provide transportation and leadership for these oldsters, taking them not only to the center itself but into available camping and picnic areas, historical and art museums, or to other types of recreational areas. Through such planned activities young couples, middle-aged adults, and senior citizens can all be successfully serviced through recreation.

The Rise of Juvenile Delinquency. Recreation will *not* solve the problem of delinquency or crime, nor is recreation in its present form an effective deterrent or counter-measure to it. Leaders must not assume any custodial role. It is important, then, that the leader be far more than a policeman or baby sitter. Both educational and community service agencies should work more closely together to help solve this problem. Studies show that most troubled youths rarely take part in community recreation programs, for to them such activities are thrill-less kid stuff. As long as recreation leaders keep on offering routinized programs, which do not interest these adventure-seeking youths, the more they will find that this group will not take part in organized recreation. Greater effort must be made to (1) reach the potential delinquent and (2) plan youth program activities to reach their interest, skill, and intelligence levels. Likewise, greater opportunities should be provided for this group to find good adult leaders. These leaders, to be successful, should work on a one-to-one basis with the delinquent and teach him the physical and social skills he needs. By becoming a substitute father or mother image and by giving encouragement, the leader can inspire some to stay in school. Some recreation departments are successfully using older youths to reach these youngsters through sports and games. Others are placing street or block recreation leaders in culturally deprived areas to work with gang children.

Working Mothers and the Changing Role of Women. More mothers are now working than ever before. Many school-age children come home to an empty house or roam the streets looking for someplace to go and something to do after school hours. Many of these unsupervised children often get into serious trouble, and almost all are vulnerable to delinquency. Many schools and recreation departments are working together to provide school-centered recreation programs during after-school hours for these youth. Physical education, music, art teachers, and community volunteers are often used to provide recreational programs for them. Such facilities as the school gymnasium and library are opened on Saturdays to provide safe, wholesome places for children to play under the direction of adult leaders. Older students can be drawn into such extended programs and serve as leadership assistants. Day care and nursery play schools also can be organized at recreation centers. Senior citizens can be drawn into this type of program, thus supplying substitute grandparents for many children.

Increased Mental Illness. The role of the recreation leader in this area is twofold: (1) working with those who are mentally ill and (2) preventing those who are emotionally disturbed from becoming victims of mental illness. The field of therapeutic recreation is a specialized one, requiring a special kind of experience and professional preparation.

Much can be done through recreation to help prevent this increasing malady. Children who display extreme fear, anxiety, aggression, or cruelty, who act out or are withdrawn, are in need of additional guidance. Dr. Fritz Redl, a psychiatric specialist working with emotionally disturbed youth, believes that the first function of programmed recreation for these children should be to help them release tension and aggression through active sports and rugged games. The program should be carefully supervised and geared to give each child immediate satisfaction and a reward of some kind, whether this be in the form of praise or a blue ribbon. Dr. Redl recommends, also, that the program should expose the children through adult and group pressure to challenging experiences such as creative crafts. This, he believes, will enlarge their interest in things outside of themselves. He suggests, furthermore, that the leader stress sportsmanship and game rules so the defiant child can gain respect for authority and life rules.

Above all, the recreation leader who works with emotionally disturbed children must be highly sensitive to the needs and moods of each individual within a group. He must be able to use skillfully a wide variety of methods in order to reach all within a group. He must realize that each person has his own degree of specific needs. Another leader in this area, Bert Kruger Smith, found that the best programs planned for these youth are those based on the following principles:[10]

1. Any activity, whether of small or great social significance, should be of genuine interest to the group.
2. The activity should be specific and known to be within the capacity of the group, thus providing opportunity for immediate satisfaction and evident progress.
3. The activity should be a stimulation for further related activity.
4. The activity should help the members to be participating citizens in the world of today and tomorrow.

A Longer Life Span and Shorter Work Week. In their free time, people voluntarily seek joy and satisfaction. They take part in recreational activities only when they feel the need and when they have enough skill or desire to participate successfully. Such facts are a tremendous challenge to all recreation leaders. They must make a greater effort to get more people interested in recreation. They must create more attractive programs and conduct them in appealing settings. They must also help all within the community to realize the value of play and its relationship to working more productively and living more joyously. All recreation leaders, in order to reach the potential that is inherent in any recreational program, must help those who participate in it to realize that recreation is far more than just a time filler or a means of escaping boredom. Program offerings for those in the senior age group should evolve around physical, creative, social activities through which individuals in this group can gain or retain a better state of total fitness, find ways to creatively improve their own homes and the community in which they live, as well as provide them with opportunities to meet and have fun with other people of all ages.

Increased Automation. One of life's great joys is found in learning how to make beautiful things with your own hands. A well-planned and well-conducted arts and crafts recreational program can lead to lifelong enjoyment. However, it is not enough to offer just a simple crafts program for those of beginning or average skill. Highly skilled people should also have an opportunity to learn how to make lovely things of artistic worth, quality, and beauty. The fine arts have often been ignored in the recreation program largely because of a lack of leadership. Some communities are solving this problem by enlisting the help of experts, who volunteer their services or are paid from a collected fee from the participants.

Creative experience for children should be of wide range and include painting (finger, watercolor, sand, and oil), stenciling and printing, paper crafts, wood carving, clay modeling, woodwork, making rhythmical instruments, and all forms of nature crafts.

Adults and older youth engaging in a fine arts program will enjoy activities in paper decorating, paper sculpture, book binding, weaving, decorating fabrics, leather work, pottery making, mosaics, enameling, silk screen painting, lapidary work, and metal work.

One of the outstanding fine arts programs is found in Richmond, California. Over 8000 persons come to the center every month to take part in their fine arts and crafts program, which is housed in a modern, superbly equipped, million-dollar center. The building contains adequate classrooms, permanent art collections, galleries, display facilities, and exhibition programs. Classes are held in all phases of art. The center conducts a yearly art festival in which the work of the participants is displayed. Attendance at the permanent art gallery and for the exhibits is over 40,000 yearly.

Although few communities have their own art center, most cities do have an art museum. Guided tours and art appreciation classes conducted by art experts can help bring beauty into the lives of people.

For the adult working in a world of machines, such visits can be of great value. Those who learn to appreciate beauty are most likely to create lovely things themselves.

CHANGING STANDARDS OF VALUES AND GOALS

Youth today greatly need heroes to emulate. Recreational programs must be greatly altered for them to ever combat crime and delinquency. Leadership is the key and it is important that the leader be of the highest caliber, but it is also important that he be assisted by employees and volunteers who may have a sparse formal education but because they come from the same background can communicate and more often effectively deal with people of all ages, especially youth. Teen-agers in the inner-city are greatly in need of places to go and things to do that are constructive rather than destructive and antisocial. Many of the program activities at teen centers in different kinds of minority groups and poor neighborhoods should center around self-development, job training and placement, educational skills and health services. They should be conducted on an informal basis and not be like school but rather be geared to provide youth with pleasurable experiences aimed at helping them master skills in many things, including themselves.

Those planning recreation programs must do far more than provide activities most popular among those who take part in them, for they should gradually introduce new and more worthwhile activities into the program. This connotes that one task of the leader is to help people learn to do more challenging and finer things in their free time. For example, program planners can schedule only dances for teen-agers or they can also include activities on a higher cultural level such as Listening to the Classics or Learning to Appreciate Art Through Visits to Museums. Unfortunately, many who have cheapened their program offerings in an attempt to reach the masses have fallen victim to the old folk saying, "If you can't lick them, join them." To illustrate the folly of this argument, one then logically could say, "Since you can't stop crime, you should become a criminal."

We must, through the combined efforts of recreation and education, help all individuals and, thus, our society to find longed-for beauty, happiness, and meaning in their lives. The prospect for Americans to attain a newer and higher civilization plateau *can* become a reality. Reaching that new level will take much effort on the part of many people.

Suggested Readings

Bucher, Charles and Bucher, Richard: *Recreation for Today's Society.* Englewood Cliffs, N.J., Prentice-Hall, Inc., 1974
   The authors discuss modern philosophy of recreation upon which worthy goals should be based, the many services recreation renders to people of all ages in a variety of settings, and presents valuable principles by which programs should be organized and administered.

Carlson, Ray, Deppe, Ted, and MacLean, Janet: *Recreation in American Life.* Belmont, California, Wadsworth Publishing Company, 1963
This textbook, still being used in Community Recreation classes, is a valuable addition to every recreation leader's library. Part IV, "The Recreation Program," has many fine suggestions for improving each of the many areas on which a well-planned balanced recreation program should be built.

Ellis, Michael J.: *Why People Play.* Englewood Cliffs, N.J., Prentice-Hall, Inc., 1973
The author discusses recent theories regarding the meaning of play written by our most competent present behavioral scientists and compares these new views with our older, traditional ones. This book is especially valuable to advanced students and their teachers, for it should stimuate both thought and needed expanded research regarding the significance and meaning of play.

Hormachea, Marian and Hormachea, Carroll: *Recreation in Modern Society.* Boston, Holbrook Press, 1972
This fine book of readings is a compilation of many of the best articles which have appeared in current periodicals about expanding recreation and leisure in America. Part V, "The Future of Recreation," is especially valuable.

Kraus, Richard and Curtis, Joseph: *Creative Administration in Recreation and Parks.* St. Louis, The C. V. Mosby Co., 1973.
Many sections of this book were developed from original manuals gathered from Recreation and Park administrators throughout the nation. The sections on budget procedures and practical everyday problems of administration are thoroughly discussed.

Kraus, Richard: *Recreation and Leisure in Modern Society.* New York, Appleton-Century-Crofts, 1971
This book contains an analysis of the total recreation field and discusses ways in which recreation can become an even more vital base for our cultural growth. The author stresses that every recreational service provided nationally as well as by local agencies must become more purposeful in order to achieve greatly needed, more significant outcomes.

Murphy, James: *Concepts of Leisure—Philosophical Implications.* Englewood Cliffs, N.J., Prentice-Hall, Inc., 1974
This valuable book is destined to become a classic, along with Jay B. Nash's *Philosophy of Leisure and Recreation.* The author projects a futuristic look at society and discusses the impact more meaningful recreational pursuits can have upon the improvement of society.

Murphy, James: *Recreational Leisure Service: A Humanistic Perspective.* Dubuque, Iowa, W. C. Brown, 1975
In this book, the author stresses the need for viewing leisure opportunities through a humanistic perspective and the need for recognizing the interrelationship of the social, psychological, and organizational components of community life., His predictions of the future expansion of increased free time and leisure, and of rapidly changing work patterns are worth much careful consideration.

Parker, Stanley: *The Future of Work and Leisure.* New York, Praeger Publishers, 1971
In this book the author stresses the point that present social and political changes will bring work and the prerequisites for a good life closer together.

Stanley, Edwin and Miller, Norman, Editors: *Leisure and the Quality of Life.* Washington, D.C., American Association for Health, Physical Education and Recreation, 1972.
This book is a report of the conclusions made by the delegates and papers presented at a national conference on the problems of expanding free time and leisure. Topics include man and his leisure, quality environment, the quest for a leisure ethic, alternative future for leisure, and national goals for leisure as an added dimension in the quality of life.

Talamini, John and Page, Charles: *Sport and Society, An Anthropology of Readings.* Boston, Little, Brown, 1973
  This interesting collection of articles on the sociology of sport includes sections on the role sport plays in our culture, race and sport professionalism, sport as work versus sport as play or recreation, and sport and the mass media. This is an eye-opener.

Terkel, Studs: *Working.* New York, Pantheon Books, 1974
  Based upon tape-recorded interviews with a number of people in a wide variety of jobs, the author of this fascinating book discovered that most of these workers hated their jobs. In their own words, they describe their fruitless search for meaning in their work and their desperate quest for far more than just a paycheck received for their efforts.

References

1. Dulles, Foster Rhea: *A History of Recreation, Americans Learn to Play,* 2nd Ed., New York, Appleton-Century-Crofts, 1965, pp. 3–21.
2. Bell, Daniel: "The Clock Watchers: Americans at Work," *Time Magazine,* Sept. 8, 1975, pp. 55–57.
3. Garson, Barbara: *All The Livelong Day: The Meaning and Demeaning of Routine Work.* New York, Doubleday, 1975, pp. 1–30.
4. Terkel, Studs: *Working: People Talk About What They Do All Day and How They Feel About What They Do.* New York, Pantheon Books, 1972, pp. 1–2.
5. Op. cit: *Time Magazine,* Sept. 8, 1975, p. 56.
6. Kaplan, Max.: *Leisure: Theory and Policy.* New York, John Wiley & Sons, Inc., 1975, p. 100.
7. "Who's Raising The Kids," *Newsweek Magazine,* Sept. 22, 1975, pp. 48–56.
8. Op. cit.: *Newsweek Magazine.*
9. Glueck, Sheldon and Glueck, Eleanor: *Delinquents In The Making.* New York, Harper Brothers, 1948, p. 141.
10. Smith, Bert Kruger: *Children of the Evening.* Austin, Texas, The Hogg Foundation for Mental Health, 1961, p. 12.

chapter 2

Leadership for Recreation

*The truly great leader is not simply
a technician highly skilled as an
organizer, teacher, and director of
leisure activities. He must care
deeply about life and destiny.*
                    Howard Danford

Recreation is a new profession with many challenging and different kinds of employment possibilities. It is also a profession which will increase both in prestige and membership as the hourly work week decreases and more people have more free time. Employment possibilities are exceptionally good and the predicted future growth of this field is truly remarkable. Cities and communities are sponsoring public recreation programs in astonishingly increasing numbers. Voluntary and private organizations such as the Girl Scouts, summer resident and day camps, hospitals, industry, and the Armed Forces are all expanding their programs, as are other types of privately supported clubs and recreational centers. Large apartment complexes, condominiums, and resort villages are also increasingly seeking trained recreational personnel. New community-centered schools and junior colleges are looking for recreation leaders to work with people of all ages in their many facilities which often are open almost 24 hours 7 week days. Church-sponsored recreation programs are also increasing throughout the nation and leaders skilled in working with the aged as well as teen-agers are much in demand.

Other types of jobs are:

> *Public Administrator*
>> Superintendent of parks and community centers
>> Director of community centers
>> Recreation specialty leader

Music	Athletics
Dance	Camping
Arts & crafts	etc.

Therapeutic Recreation
> Crippled (postpolio, cerebral palsied, etc.)
> Mentally retarded
> Mentally ill
> Inner city recreation leaders
> Working with delinquents
> Prison recreation

Industrial Recreation
> Director
> Activity specialists

Semi-Public Agencies
> YWCA, YMCA, YMHA, YWHA
> Boy Scouts, Girl Scouts, Campfire, etc.

College Campuses
> Professor of recreation
> Director of student centers
> Director of intramurals
> Director of special events

Armed Forces
> Director of recreation for each branch of the service
> Activity specialist (athletic director, social hostess, USO, librarian)

Church Recreation
> Director of the entire program
> Activity leader
> Leader of a specific age group (teen-age or senior citizen)

Private
> Director of country clubs
> Recreation director for large condominiums
> Activity director
> Social director for large steamship companies

Recruitment and Selection

Although more than thirty thousand persons are now employed as full-time recreation workers and over sixty thousand are employed on a part-time basis yearly, there is a great gap between the supply and demand of professional leaders. It is estimated that if every present full-time recreational worker were to recruit ten more new persons to enter this fast-growing field, there would still be a wide difference between the number of positions to be filled and the number of students professionally prepared to become recreation leaders. Some citizens still believe that no special talents are needed to teach others how to play or have a good time. Fortunately, the number holding this erroneous view is rapidly diminishing. Like any new profession, recreation is hampered by growing pains and faulty practices, which often include low salaries, poor working conditions, long hours, and the ineffective utilization of present leadership and facilities. The whole problem of recruitment and selection of personnel, improved professional preparation, and the upgrading of professional standards can best be solved by those preparing leaders for this profession. This can be done best in our colleges and universities if they work closely with agencies sponsoring recreation programs and the leaders of professional recreation societies.

Essential Personal Qualities

Since recreation is a need of all people, it is imperative that the recreation leader be a person who cares about the rights and the human dignity of people. Such a leader receives his greatest satisfaction from working with other human beings instead of working with machines. The essential personal qualities that a recreation leader should possess are:

1. A love for people plus an understanding and sensitivity toward them.
2. Personal integrity coupled with skills in how to work with other human beings of all kinds—the unskilled as well as the skilled, the uncooperative as well as the willing, the group scapegoat or the group leader.
3. Enthusiasm and a dedicated desire to raise professional recreation standards as well as to help people find meaning, purpose, and beauty in life.
4. The courage to try something new. The ability to start as well as to improve existing recreation programs. And the enthusiastic drive to make better programs for more people the year round.
5. The intelligence and cultural background to work with people from all walks of life as well as the skill to help others raise their own personal and cultural levels.
6. Good judgment, dependability, and flexibility.
7. Personal attractiveness and that magical unknown "X" quality that draws people to a real leader.
8. A sense of humor and zest for life.

Needed Special Abilities and Knowledges

If by taking part in recreational activities people are to find self-fulfillment, physical as well as intellectual challenge, and a higher cultural level, the recreation leader in charge of a program must be a person of the highest caliber. Such an individual must know a great deal about people and how to motivate them to want to take part in activities. He must also possess the ability to help others improve themselves. He must realize that it is more important for a person to learn to do for himself than it is to have something done for him. He must also realize that the learner teaches himself but that the role of the teacher-leader is largely to (1) demonstrate skills to be learned, (2) diagnose faulty trial-and-error learning attempts, and (3) direct progess around learning snags. Such a teacher-leader should be well aware of the fact that how the learner *feels* about him and what she is learning is as important as what she learns. The teacher's presence, encouragement, patience, and faith in the learner's desires and ability to master what he sets out to do helps longed-for goals become a reality.

Special abilities, knowledges, and skills that the recreation leader must possess include:

1. The skill to see himself realistically, to judge his strengths and weaknesses, and to improve his leadership effectiveness by capitalizing upon his trial-and-error attempts.
2. The organizational skill to plan and carry out a well-balanced recreation program that periodically includes new kinds of activities to learn and new challenges to be met.
3. Skill in organizing and directing a wide variety of recreational activities, including crafts, drama, music, sports and games, dramatics, and others.
4. The ability, patience, and skill to work with volunteer leaders so that they profit from their experiences and grow both in leadership skill and in understanding of people and the value of recreation.
5. The ability to use democratic methods of working with others so that each individual within the group feels he is an important part of a united team working toward the attainment of worthwhile goals.
6. The ability to accept responsibility, make decisions, and draw up both long- and short-range plans, objectives, and goals. Such a leader grows with the job and gains his greatest satisfaction from watching the program grow and the participants benefit.
7. The ability to sell the value of recreation to others as a balance wheel necessary for living a healthier, happier, and more productive life.
8. The ability to get a recreation program started in any community by having needed skills to find and develop local leadership so that a program is set up for the benefit of all people within the community.
9. The ability to gain community support for the program, utilize all media of communication necessary for its growth, and evaluate the results realistically.
10. Needed energy, drive, job devotion, and personal ambition to make a significant contribution to human happiness and the betterment of mankind through the recreational approach.

Any leader having these and other needed special ability and skills can

Theorize, analyze, organize, improvise, deputize, synthesize, harmonize, supervise, summarize and, if necessary, compromise. He has vision to create ideas, intelligence to investigate possibilities, logic to assemble a plan, ingenuity to make substitutions in his plan, common sense to delegate authority, personality to integrate group action, human understanding to observe what his group is accomplishing, executive ability to tie up loose ends, and the wisdom to be flexible, if the tension of the situation makes his plan undesirable.[1]

Professional Preparation

Approximately 2000 college students major in recreation yearly. At the present time 78 institutions for higher learning are offering a separate undergraduate recreation major degree, 35 the M.A. degree, and 9 the doctorate. Although the curriculum on both the undergraduate and graduate levels closely relates to health and physical education, recreation is a separate field of specialization. Only those colleges and universities should offer a recreation major which have a qualified faculty experienced in recreation, adequate facilities, and can provide field work experiences for major students in local recreation departments, hospitals, or other public, private, or voluntary agencies primarily concerned with recreation.

The chief aim of the undergraduate professional preparation curriculum should be to provide students with a broad background in the humanities. At least 50% of the course content should be devoted to cultural education, 37% to specialized professional preparation, and the remaining 13% should be concerned with related fields. The curriculum for the undergraduate major should help the student develop competence in the following fields:[2]

General Education

1. Understanding the biological and social sciences, which will contribute to an awareness of the changing social and physical environments and their effect on man and society.
2. Understanding and awareness of man as an individual and as a social being, including his needs, desires, and capabilities at all age levels and for a variety of physical and mental abilities.
3. Understanding how man thinks.
4. Understanding and knowledge of the nature and function of groups and individuals and the settings in which interaction takes place.
5. Understanding and appreciation of the historical view of man's achievement—social, intellectual, and artistic.
6. Understanding skill and practice in the basic tools of effective communicative arts.

Related Areas of Professional Recreation Education

1. Understanding human growth and development.
2. Understanding the processes of how man learns.
3. Understanding the principles and skills in the use of group processes.
4. Ability to use the tools of public and human relations.
5. Knowledge of and skill in health and safety practices and procedures with regard to recreation programs, facilities, and personnel.
6. Understanding business procedures related to the operation of recreation programs and park services.

SPECIAL PROFESSIONAL RECREATION EDUCATION

1. Understanding the concepts of leisure, the philosophies of recreation, and the development of a personal and professional philosophy of recreation.
2. Knowledge of the nature, history, and development of the recreation movement, including factors influencing the origin and the continuing progress of the movement.
3. Knowledge of the place, scope, and importance of recreation in the community setting.
4. Knowledge of the interrelationships and relationships to the recreation profession of social institutions such as government (local, state, federal), hospitals, business and industry, schools, religious organizations, home and family, armed services, youth-serving organizations—public and private, institutions— penal, correctional, etc.
5. Knowledge of the roles of the leader and his function in the guidance and counseling of the individual in social, personal, and leisure concerns.
6. Personal experiences, practical application, and skill in the following program areas: aquatics, arts and crafts, camping and outdoor recreation, dance, dramatics, mental and linguistic activities, music, service activities, social recreation, sports and games, hobbies, special interests, and special events, with respect to:
   Scope (breadth and program)
   Possible rewards and values
   Methods of organization
   Resources
   Safety procedures and practices
   Acquisition, use, and care of equipment
   Leadership needs and techniques
   Program planning and promotion
   Practical experiences

(It is understood that one individual will not be proficient in all program areas, but it is desirable that he be adept in at least two and that he have knowledge concerning the scope, values, and program opportunities in all.)

7. Knowledge of those principles which guide recreation program development and execution in a variety of settings, including hospitals, playgrounds, parks, churches, community centers, and camps, under the auspices of governmental, private, and voluntary agencies or organizations and schools.
8. Knowledge of the planning and operation of park and recreation facilities.
9. Ability to train, supervise, and utilize both volunteers and professionals.
10. Ability to interpret the role of the recreation profession to colleagues, community groups, and participants in recreation programs.
11. Knowledge of professional, service, and related recreation organizations—their development, structure aims, objectives, services, values, and problems of interrelationships.

Those seeking advanced degrees might well consult the *Directory of Professional Preparation Programs in Recreation, Parks and Related Area.* This publication lists all colleges and universities offering the Master's degree or a doctorate in the field of recreation. It is available from the American Alliance for Health, Physical Education and Recreation, 1201 16th St. N.W., Washington, D.C. 20036 or from the National Recreation and Park Association, 1601 N. Kent St., Arlington, Va. 22209. Also available from the AAHPER is a new publication, *Graduate Education in Health Education, Physical Education, Recreation Safety, and Dance.*

The Junior College Program

At the present time around 100 junior colleges throughout the nation offer a 2-year major in recreation. Such programs prepare students for a position as either a program specialist or program leader for both community recreation programs or those sponsored by other agencies, private organizations, or youth-serving agencies. Many students enrolled in 2-year junior college programs transfer to 4-year schools to complete a degree in recreation.

Certification in Recreation

Many states now require recreation personnel to be certified before employed to work in that state, just as all states required teachers to be state certified before teaching. Other states are now in the process of developing certification standards. Such certification plans will do much to raise professional standards in recreation.

The Graduate Program

For those who wish to advance in recreation to the executive policy-making level in large cities or agencies, work beyond the bachelor's degree is often required. The graduate program should help students gain a deeper understanding of the philosophy and principles of recreation, administration of recreation programs, research and evaluation, personnel management, and public relations. It should also provide for specialization in such areas as therapeutic recreation, park and recreation administration, camping, outdoor education, or related areas such as group dynamics, landscaping of recreational areas, community planning, adult education, audio-visual education, sociology, public administration, cultural anthropology, public relations, recreation education, and business. Above all, the graduate program should continually encourage students to grow professionally, to conduct meaningful research, and to contribute to the growth of recreation. The graduates of such educational programs must do their utmost to recruit outstanding youth for recreation, for the shortage of well-prepared leaders is one of the most pressing problems in the entire recreation field. Willard Sutherland, Director of the National Recreation Association's Personnel Service, estimated as long ago as 1970 that there would be nearly thirty thousand vacancies in the recreation field and that unless more leaders are recruited for the recreation profession only one sixth of these available positions will be filled by well-prepared personnel.

In order that the graduate program be of recommended quality it should meet the following guiding principles:

1. At least half of the graduate courses must be in recreation.
2. Graduate students who have not had successful professional recreation experiences should be advised and encouraged to participate in professional laboratory experiences.
3. Only institutions of higher education with qualified staff and available outdoor areas and facilities should offer specialization in camping and outdoor education. The major portion of this field of study should take place in the out-of-doors.
4. Since outdoor education is an interdisciplinary field, the varied resources of the institution should be utilized.
5. A program of therapeutic recreation should be offered only in those institutions of higher learning that are associated with a medical center or have direct access to similar opportunities for education.
6. Hospitals are required to give clinical practice in the therapeutic recreation curriculum offerings, but a hospital should not attempt to operate or administer a curriculum for recreation specialists independently of a college or university.
7. If a curriculum is offered in therapeutic recreation, at least one of the faculty members should have had direct, practical

experience in dealing with recreation in the medical setting prior to the assignment of teaching responsibilities in this subject area.[3]

Types of Positions Available

Full-time employment in recreation is usually found on the administrative, supervisory, and organizational levels both in public, private, and semiprivate organizations. Such positions are being filled increasingly by those with advanced degrees in recreation. Part-time positions are usually available during the summer for persons seeking to become camp counselors, playground leaders, lifeguards or swimming instructors, or settlement house workers. Although these positions are usually filled by students from various major fields, increasingly those employing such leaders are requiring that applicants have had at least one course concerned primarily with recreation leadership skills.

Types of positions available for those professionally prepared in recreation include:

Generalist and/or specialist in the following program areas:
Arts, crafts, and the fine arts
Dramatics, puppetry, and storytelling
Dance, music
Athletic sports and games
Aquatics and water safety
Nature activities
Camping and outdoor education
Social recreation
Special groups (the handicapped, senior citizens, young children, teen-agers)
Special activities and events

Other types of positions available are:

Superintendent of municipal or community recreation
Director of city parks and playgrounds
Supervisor of various types of recreational activities (sports, music, crafts, etc.)
Camp director (school, private, or agency)
Executive field representative, or recreation director of such agencies as the YWCA or YMCA, Boy Scouts, Girl Scouts, Camp Fire Girls
Director of student centers or campus recreation in colleges and universities
College instructor or professor of recreation
Recreation activity specialist (gymnastics, choral groups, dramatics, etc.)

Director or leader of hospital recreation
Armed service recreation director or program activities leader
Park or playground designer
Rural recreation specialist
Director or coordinator of church recreation
Program director or activity leader in industrial recreation
Country club director
Social director on ships

The Volunteer

An outstanding leader has the magnetic power to draw others to him. The recreation director will need the services of volunteers if he is to provide a well-balanced program. Although it is wiser to select a few assistants rather than to try to train a large number of amateurs, the leader should find work for everyone who is willing to donate his time, energy, and talents to the program. The businessman might best serve as a director of money-raising campaigns, the secretary as a receptionist, the professional coach as an athletic advisor, the housewife as a canteen hostess, the teen-ager as a messenger. The alert director will utilize the services of all willing helpers and will impress upon each one the importance and value of his unique contribution.

The recreation leader, also, should be on the lookout for outstanding potential leaders, rather than accept the services of anyone willing to try to direct others. Talks to civic groups, college clubs, and announcements of the need for a leader of a particular activity in the local newspaper often attract desirable recruits.

A definite training program for all volunteers is desirable but should be required for activity leaders. This training program might include: (1) the meaning and importance of directed recreation; (2) leadership do's and don'ts; (3) understanding people of all ages; (4) the procedure for handling discipline problems and accidents; (5) necessary reports to be made; (6) skills in as many cultural-creative, social, camping and outing, and physical activities as possible; (7) techniques of teaching people through activities; and (8) techniques of evaluating the results.

Each volunteer leader should first be an assistant before leading his own group. In-service training and wise supervision will add to the security and the effectiveness of the inexperienced leader. Staff meetings, films, resource materials, and observational visits to other recreational groups are valuable training aids.

A real leader makes more leaders. This "multiplication of doers" is basic to good leadership, for the more others are involved in helping to make a group project successful, the more so it will become. The volunteer can gain much from working closely with such a professionally prepared leader.

Leadership Do's

Leadership skills in recreation can be developed. The leader should:

1. Be enthusiastic. Enthusiasm is contagious.
2. Develop leadership within the group. A real leader becomes progressively unnecessary by developing more leaders.
3. Plan the complete program carefully as well as each subdivided part. Keep objectives in mind.
4. Improve skills by capitalizing on mistakes. Learning means changed behavior.
5. Encourage people to take part, praise attempts as well as success, inspire self-confidence, develop a spirit of fun.
6. Build skill upon skill. Help others grow as individuals and group members.
7. Introduce new activities that are enjoying current popularity elsewhere. Include old favorites at scheduled intervals.
8. Be sincerely interested in people.
9. Recognize your position as an opportunity to lead others to higher goals.

Principles of Leadership

Qualified democratic leadership is a must if a recreation program is to be of value. It is the face-to-face program leader who adds the personal touch to the program. The successful activity leader will be one who provides equally for all who take part in the activities, helps all participants develop a keener zest and appreciation for life and other people, and aids each individual to develop a wide variety of skills for free-time use. Such leadership is based upon the following principles:

1. *A real leader makes more leaders.* The leader should establish, explore, and extend opportunities for the development of natural leaders he may find within each group. Every individual should be helped to find opportunities for leadership among his peers. A leader who cannot delegate authority is not worth his salt.
2. *A true leader gets his lead from someone or something greater than himself.* The leader must be a follower of an idea or ideal that embodies religious concepts and democracy. These guiding stars should chart his course of action, aid him to progress through troubled waters, and beach him on the shore of accomplishment.
3. *A real leader has a high degree of expectancy in each group member.* The leader must hold each group member in high regard, believe in him as a unique personality, and be able to forgive and forget petty misdemeanors, because his eyes are on far-reaching goals.

4. *A true leader must support and believe in his group and each member in it.* It is difficult, but necessary, for a leader to maintain a social distance between himself and the group. Aloofness, though, can end in disaster as can an attitude that is too familiar. The leader must be able to enjoy each group for its own uniqueness. When working with children, he must be able to delight in their games, speak and understand their language, share with them, and become an ideal to them. He will, if wise, establish unity within all groups early by such techniques as singing, symbols, and frequent use of the words "ours" or "we" instead of "mine" or "I."

5. *The best leader uses the positive approach.* The leader must be able to recognize and satisfy the personal interests and needs of each group member. The approach should be largely a positive one and appeal to each individual's own sense of personal worth, reinforce and stabilize confidence, and work toward self-direction.

6. *The true leader is skilled in working with people and objects.* Dexterity in using objects, especially in sports and games, proficiency with things, and skill in human engineering is vital if one is to become a potent, positive influence upon others.

7. *A real leader looks and acts the part of a leader.* The leader must be the embodiment of good character, cleanliness, health, and neatness.

Professional Organizations

Any professional worker should support his own professional organizations through membership, subscription to professional publications, and attendance at local, state, regional, and national meetings or conventions. The National Recreation and Park Association, 1601 North Kent Street, Arlington, Virginia 22209, provide their members with valuable service and publications. Other related organizations are:

American Camping Association
Bradford Woods
Martinsville, Indiana

American Association for Health, Physical Education and Recreation
1201 16th Street, N.W.
Washington, D.C.

National Industrial Recreation Association
203 North Wabash Avenue
Chicago, Illinois

Suggested Readings

AAHPER. *Professional Preparation in Health Education, Physical Education and Recreation Education*, a National Conference Report. Washington, D.C.: American Association of Health, Physical Education and Recreation, 1974. This report contains valuable recommendations for the professional preparation curriculum on the undergraduate and graduate levels.

ARS. *Code of Ethics*. Washington, D.C.: American Recreation Society. All recreation leaders should become familiar with the guiding principles and ethical concepts found in this material.

AAHPER. *Journal of Health, Physical Education and Recreation*, "Leisure Today," January, 1973. This issue contains four fine articles in the area of expanding free time use. These include Leisure and Environment, Environmental Education for Teachers, Environmental Resource Center for the Handicapped, and The School Site as an Educational Resource.

Careers in Recreation and Parks. Michigan Recreation and Park Association, Box 896, Lansing, Michigan 48904 Various career opportunities are included in this booklet, along with qualifications needed, salary range expectations, and other valuable information.

Hjelte, George and Shivers, Jay: *Public Administration of Recreational Services*. Philadelphia, Lea & Febiger, 1972. This book is primarily a text for use in professional courses preparing recreational personnel at the administrative level. The chapters on Personnel Management in Public Recreation Service, Supervisory Functions of Management, and Recreational Service and the Public Schools are especially recommended readings in conjunction with this chapter in this book.

Lewith, H. Douglas: "Certification," *Parks and Recreation*, Vol. VI, (January, 1971) In this article the author discusses various certification programs including leadership qualifications for certification.

Stein, Thomas and Sessoms, H. Douglas: *Recreation and Special Populations*. Boston, Holbrook Press, 1973. This book contains 14 contributions by 11 recreation authorities concerning leadership qualifications and program materials for working with the mentally retarded, those in prisons and detention homes, the mentally ill, alcohol and drug addicts, the crippled, blind, the deprived, senior citizens, and racial minorities. This book is a must for all recreation leaders working with the disadvantaged and/or handicapped.

Shivers, Jay: *Leadership in Recreational Service*. New York, The Macmillan Co., 1963. The author discusses in detail the various kinds of leadership positions available in the field of recreation, qualifications and duties.

Stevens, Ardis: *Fun is Therapeutic: A Recreation Book to Help Therapeutic Recreation Leaders by People Who are Leading Recreation*. Springfield, Illinois, Charles C Thomas, Publisher, 1973. The many leadership suggestions found in this book will be of value to students especially.

Weatherford, Allen: "Field Services, an Essential Phase of Professional Preparation," *The American Recreation Journal*, September-October, 1965. The author suggests various types of field-service internship experiences to improve the quality and breadth of professional recreation education.

References

1. Reynold Carlson, Deppe, Theodore, and MacLean, Janet: *Recreation in American Life*, Belmont, California, Wadsworth Publishing Company, 1963, p. 332.

   2. AAHPER: *Professional Preparation in Health, Physical Education and Recreation*, a National Conference Report, Washington, D.C.: American Association of Health, Physical Education and Recreation, 1962, pp. 87–95.
   3. AAHPER: op. cit., p. 91, Sec.(2).
Bartholomew, Warren J.: "Recreation Education in Selected Junior or Community Colleges," *Parks and Recreation*, Vol. II (January, 1967).
Careers in Recreation and Parks. Michigan Recreation and Park Association, Box 896, Lansing, Michigan 48904.
Cosgrove, Francis E. and Kraus, Richard: "The Role of Civil Service," *Parks and Recreation*, Vol. VI (June, 1971).
Lewith, H. Douglas: "Certification," *Parks and Recreation*, Vol. VI (January, 1971).
"Recreation Program Leadership—A Suggested Two-Year Post High-School Curriculum," Department of Health, Education and Welfare, Office of Education.
Recreation As Your Career. American Association for Health, Physical Education, and Recreation, 1201 16th Street N.W., Washington, D.C. 20036.
Sarkisian, Sevan: "Career in Recreation," *Parks and Recreation*, Vol. VI (February, 1971).
Verhoven, Peter J.: "Associate Professional Recreation Programs," *Parks and Recreation*, Vol. IV (April, 1969).

chapter 3

Understanding
Human Behavior

*In vain we build the world, unless
the builder also grows.*
　　　　　　Edwin Markham

Although all people are basically alike, each is as unique as a snowflake. Thus, a successful leader must know as much as possible about each individual with whom he works. He should know the characteristics of age groups and each person's developmental level, family background, home environmental conditions, as well as his special interests, needs, problems, and desires. Likewise, the leader must know how to motivate best each individual with whom he works, realizing that motivation is an individual thing and that what will cause one person to react favorably may cause an opposite reaction in another.

The Basic Needs of All People

Needs that are basic to all human beings are: (1) physiological, (2) social, and (3) ego or self-needs. If people are to find security, challenge, and happiness as they take part in recreational activities, these inward pressures, or needs, must be fulfilled. When such basic drives are thwarted, people become disturbed and unhappy. Since recreation is a voluntary activity, attendance, whether regular or spotty, is an indicator that an individual feels secure in the group he has voluntarily joined and feels he has something both to give to and gain from this group endeavor.

PHYSIOLOGICAL NEEDS

Food, elimination, rest, activity, and fresh air are all basic physiological needs. Proper balance between rest and activity produces improved health and zest for life. In our automated society people are increasingly sitting and watching others and riding instead of going places on their own steam. We are becoming a nation of softie on-lookers. The problem of physical weakness, obesity, and boredom exists among many children as well as adults. It is important from the standpoint of growth that especially children should take part in vigorous big-muscle activities that include running, jumping, and skipping. It is also vital that they have some hours weekly of unscheduled time in which to explore, roam, wander, and create their own fun, instead of constantly being entertained. It is imperative that they learn the give-and-take of peer play and good sportsmanship. Those who can play together away from the watchful eyes of adults grow socially as individuals and as group members. One real test of the effectiveness of the leader upon them is their behavior when playing among themselves and away from supervising adults.

SOCIAL NEEDS

These needs are especially strong among all people, regardless of age. We all need to (1) belong, (2) feel secure, (3) gain recognition, (4) love and be loved, and (5) have adventure. Atypical behavior is usually a symptom that one or more of these basic drives is being thwarted.

All behavior patterns are formed early in life. Crowd-fringers, bullies, shy and withdrawn individuals are all in need of helpful guidance and understanding. Often these persons need extra help and the utmost of patience on the leader's part. Many lack physical and social skills. The recreation leader is trained to detect early signs of abnormal behavior and is in an ideal position to help prevent serious personality maladjustment.

Steadying kinds of relaxed day-to-day relationships between all individuals and the recreation leader can do much to help those who feel unwanted, unpopular, and unhappy. Since behavior patterns change slowly, it is impossible for the leader to undo in a few weeks or even months undesirable personality traits that have been years in the forming.

All normal people crave to be noticed, to be the "best" in some areas. Those who fail to gain recognition legitimately do so by negative actions. Delinquent gang leaders are often the most skillful thieves, or the most daring. Adults need to be recognized for their achievements and actions the same as children do and should receive earned praise from their leaders and peers. Photographs on bulletin boards can do much to publicize the recreation activity program and give participants needed recognition for their contribution.

Psychologists have discovered that the need to love or be needed is stronger than is the need *for* love. Everyone needs to feel close to at least one human being and that he is a person of value, is trustworthy, and that others do care about his welfare and safety. Expressions of genuine love for others are far beyond the Hollywood version of the word "love" and are a basic factor in successful leadership.

Love and hate needs constantly clash within every person. The need to build has as its counterpart the need to destroy. One often-unrecognized value in physical activity is that it gives a person a chance to work out feelings of hostility and aggression. Boxing, a favorite sport of many in minority groups, is an ideal activity for those who are frustrated or are mad at the world. We all need to find legitimate ways to express aggression, frustration, and anger. Collecting stamps, for example, is far superior to collecting scalps. Hitting a golf ball is better than hitting a person.

The need for adventure is ever present, but its potency varies with age. Youth craves it and shuns safety, whereas adults, especially after marriage and parenthood, feel the need for safety and the need to avoid unnecessary risks. Many people, in spite of an urge to seek greener pastures and to find excitement, live dull, drab, and routine lives. Thus it is wise to add new program ideas to any recreation program and also to include some of the old familiar and favorite activities.

Age Groups

The recreation leader must understand people and how to work with each age group successfully. Children thrill to simple games that often fail to interest the advanced adult; teen-agers delight in adventuresome play that causes the aged to turn pale over their quiet table games. Knowledge of the differences in roles the two sexes play in games, although these are not so many as was formerly believed, is also important. Because of cultural conditioning, boys tend to favor more rugged activities, whereas girls select less dangerous ones. As much as possible, co-recreational activities should be stressed.

Children Ages 6 through 9. These children are in love with life. They crave activity but tire easily. Although they are awkward, boastful, and eager to show off, many have hidden fears of being left alone or of displeasing adults. Their favorite pastimes revolve around a make-believe world, which they copy in imitative play. Fairy stories, simple games that require little skill but much physical exertion, myths, nature, comic characters—all bring delight to those in this age bracket. By the end of the eighth year many children temporarily regress and become dependent upon parents or other adults again. However, this behavior soon changes, and they become increasingly interested in others of their own sex. Gang life becomes a vital part of living. In spite of being aggressive and argumentatively sassy to adults, these children favor adult-led activities. Many go through the pack-rat stage, and their collections range widely. Special needs of the 8-year-old center around adult praise and encouragement. Creative outlets in crafts will help these youngsters develop the coordination of the small intricate muscles of eyes and hands.

Most 9-year-olds have a fairly accurate knowledge of the difference between right and wrong. Although they may argue over fairness in games and accuse others of cheating, many of them cheat themselves in order to win or blame others through rationalization when they fail to catch a ball or fail in crucial game situations. Love for country becomes intensified at this period, and much of their gang discussions are on war, honor, bravery, and loyalty. Vigorous horseplay among peers often results in frequent fist fights. Gang rivalry is strong and often violent.

Children in this age group need frank answers to their questions about sex and increased responsibilities for their own behavior and the welfare of others. Their leaders should place increased emphasis upon skill development in physical activities, and praise should be given liberally for improvements made.

Children Ages 10 through 12. Authorities in the field of growth and development of children refer to this developmental period as the "golden period" and believe that those working with this age group can have their greatest impact upon the character development and value systems of children. This is the time of emotionalized hero worship. Although many individuals in this age bracket resent being treated like children, often their social behavior regresses, is experimental and unsure. This is also the age of deepening loyalties to the gang, team, or a chosen ideal. Although most in this group are awkward in their movements, their motor coordination is rapidly improving. These children especially need challenge, guidance, and opportunities to refine hobby and physical activity skills. Above all, they should have an opportunity to be under the guidance and direction of outstanding leaders worthy of their emulation.

The Adolescent. There is a wide range of individual differences in maturity levels among this age group. However, certain generalizations can be made. The adolescent prefers his gang to his girl friend and will often be more loyal to this group than to his own parents. There is a marked interest difference between the sexes, yet both tend to prefer team games, pets, television shows, radio programs, and comic books. Teasing and other forms of antagonism between boy and girl groups is a favorite pastime. Although the majority of adolescents tend to be overcritical, rebellious, and have an "I know it all" attitude, some do not display these characteristics. Nail-biting, daydreaming, and often impudence are evidences of a regression to the habits characteristic of younger children. Fear of ridicule and of being different becomes a nightmare.

The adolescent needs to know about and understand emotional and physical changes happening within him. A sense of belonging to a peer group and increased opportunities for independence are paramount. Adult guidance that is friendly and unobtrusive enough not to threaten his need for freedom is necessary. Increased opportunities for the adolescent to earn and spend his own money, pick out his own clothes, and set his own daily routine should be provided. Membership in clubs that work toward a worthy cause should be encouraged.

Skill mastery is one of the great desires of youth. They long to surpass others in strength, speed, and accuracy. Strict physical training to gain team membership is willingly accepted and should be encouraged.

Atypical and Exceptional Children. The majority of children attending recreational centers are normal. However, there is a small percentage who suffer from physical, emotional, and mental handicaps. These children require additional attention. The social values of play are greater than adults have formerly believed. A neurotic, psychotic, or disturbed child first shows evidence of emotional illness when he withdraws from the crowd and refuses to play. Yet psychiatrists tell us that, oddly enough, the first sign of recovery from emotional involvement is the sudden desire to be active and to play with others. Physically handicapped children can profit, often even more than normal youth, from the social aspects of physical activities. The crippled child needs to be accepted. His chances for being taken into groups will be increased through the play approach. Every child can and should be taught to master some type of physical activity. An individual program should be tailored to fit his physical case should he deviate from normal.

All atypical persons fall into two groups: (1) those physically handicapped, and (2) those socially handicapped. Within each of these classifications each person differs greatly, for no two are alike, just as no two normal persons are identical.

Types of physical handicaps are:

Postural	Speech
Crippling	Respiratory
Visual	Cardiac
Hearing	Nutritional

Types of social handicaps are:

Mental retardation
Delinquency and/or deep emotional difficulties

Techniques for successful activity leadership with atypical persons are largely the same as those used with the normal. The leader, however, will need increased patience, knowledge of what is the cause of difficulty and how to help the individual work around his handicap, and a real desire to work with each individual to guide him to a world of new interest.

The Young and Middle-Aged Groups. Studies show that people in these groups are the most neglected of all from the standpoint of recreational service. Early adulthood is usually a time of getting settled in marriage and a profession. Many women in the 20–25 age bracket are seeking both a career and a mate. They change residence often and share glamorous apartments with other career girls. Their unwed male counterparts likewise flock to such types of dwellings and also pool funds in order to live in the best section of the city and in the apartment with the largest swimming pool. Often these young adults take little part in community affairs and are rootless seekers. Although churches and public recreation departments offer them some few kinds of recreational outlets, they seldom take part, believing that such programs lack excitement or thrills.

Many in early adulthood are married, have limited funds, and are involved in school, home, and civic responsibilities. Many of these are young parents needing two kinds of recreational outlets—those which give them opportunity to get away from their offspring and those which the whole family can enjoy together. As Danford has pointed out, "While the stated purpose of a recreation department seldom includes the promotion of successful marriages, nevertheless, this is one of the desirable by-products of an effective program for young adults."[1]

Too often young married couples are neglected in organized recreation programs. In reality, this group greatly needs outside interests and stimulating social contacts with others. A Newcomer's Club and a Young Married Couple's Club sponsored by the YMCA in Dallas, Texas, last year drew a surprising number of eager participants.

Adult recreation is a relatively new field for Americans. Today, more than ever before, however, adults everywhere are coming to regard play as a necessary emotional, mental, and physical cathartic. The adult seeks more than just fun during his leisure time; he searches for activities with meaning and purpose to them.

Types of activities appealing to this group (ages 24 to 35) include:

1. Physical activities—swimming, volleyball, handball, tennis, badminton, hiking, skating, golf, archery, sailing and boating, horseback riding.
2. Social recreation—dinner parties, folk and square dancing, social dancing, social games.
3. Dramatics—play acting and production, minstrel and stunt shows, play reading, fashion shows, going to plays or making it possible for other groups to go, collecting hobbies.
4. Music appreciation clubs—participation in glee clubs, choral groups, orchestras, and bands; listening to and discussing radio, television, or "live" concerts; collecting hobbies related to music.
5. Literary and general cultural clubs—collecting and discussing such material as rare books or poetry; current events, debates, public forums, guest speakers.
6. Art appreciation clubs—china painting, woodcraft and machine shop activities, water color and oil painting, metal craft, photography, collecting hobbies.
7. Table games—bridge, canasta, hearts, poker, checkers, dominoes, Scrabble, ping pong.
8. Outdoor recreation—picnics, outdoor cooking, hiking, nature lore, gardening, collecting hobbies.

9. Family fun—picnics, family trips, at-home nights, birthday and other parties.

Techniques for successfully leading recreational activities with this group stress:

1. Basing the initial program upon an interest finder chart.
2. Working with a small committee of four to six persons to set up a sample program.
3. Forming other committees and giving as many people responsibilities as possible. This leads to individual identification with and support of the group.
4. Introducing new activities in the program gradually.
5. Forming hobby clubs. (Toy Makers Club, Fly and Bait Casting Club, etc.)
6. Creating new interests. A hobby show, demonstrations, visits to community centers, etc., will help groups see the vast number of recreational activities possible.

Young adults continue to take part in sports such as swimming, volleyball, golf, or tennis, if they have previously developed skill in these activities. The majority have learned from experience how to fill their free time with entertaining, diverting, and relaxing activities. Those who are beginning to sag and bulge physically flock to such courses as "Fashion Your Figure" or "Body Building." Informal self-improvement courses especially appeal to this age group. Many use their own free time as volunteer leaders, helping others find happiness in such activities as Cub Scouts or Camp Fire Girls.

Although aging is a continuous process, it is usually only when middle age approaches that people realize their body functions are slowing down and there is a general dulling of their senses. As one grows older, family-centered fun gains in both importance and popularity. Volunteer civic duties continue to attract those in this age bracket. Popular recreational activities include mother-daughter or father-son dinners, shuffleboard, swimming, fishing, gardening, and dancing. Game rules often need slight modification so that sports activities still can be enjoyed without physical harm being done to the body.

It has been said that the family that plays together is the family that stays together. Increasingly, churches, agencies, and community centers are recognizing their responsibilities to provide recreation for families in their groups. Home and neighborhood parties are long cherished in the minds of children and parents.

The purpose of Family Fun Night is to help the family develop stronger bonds of unity through play and discover the vast number of activities available, ones they can continue to do in their own home. The community center, church, school, or city playground can profit greatly by providing a game library. Cards, checkers, balls, and other kinds of equipment may be checked out overnight for a family party or evening of fun at home and be returned the next day. This is not only ideal publicity for the institutions but may draw many more people of varying ages into the program. Unfortunately, agencies (including the school) too often decry spectatoritis and the misuse of leisure time and too rarely make their buildings and equipment available when people have free time.

In directing family recreation at a church, center, or elsewhere the leader should:

1. Start with an icebreaker type of activity in which all family members take part. (Song, Scramble, etc.)
2. Provide for father-son, mother-daughter, father-daughter, and mother-son couple activities.
3. Have several games in which only one family member competes to represent the group. (A cracker-eating, whistle-blowing contest for mothers, a button-sewing contest for fathers, a balloon-blowing contest for brothers, a nail-driving contest for sisters, etc.)
4. Separate all the adults for some games at one end of the room and direct this group in the games while all the children are directed in games at the opposite end of the room. Exchange leaders and activities so that eventually the entire group plays the same games.
5. Provide some time for everyone present to join a group and some activity of his own choosing. (The son may want to play ping pong, the daughter to throw darts, the parents to play bridge.)
6. End the evening's activities at a successful climax with a game in which all the family take part and have everyone feel that the evening went all too fast.

Teaching activities that can be played at home should be the ultimate goal of family recreation conducted by any agency or institution. Home recreation possibilities include:

Yard games—croquet, badminton, horseshoes, etc.	Gardening
	Informal dramatics
Table games—dominoes, snap, canasta, rummy, etc.	Puppetry
	Puzzles
Astronomy and homemade telescopes	Reading aloud
Birthday and seasonal parties	Storytelling
Book and daily news discussions	Tricks
Clay modeling	Weather forecasting
Entertaining guests	

The Aged. In early Roman times the average life span was only 23 years. By 1850 it had extended to 40 in the United States. During this century it has increased to 65 years for men and to 68 for women. By 1945, over 11% of all Americans were over 60 years of age. This means that over 28 million persons will be 65 years old or more. However, many people are now living to be 90 years old or more. Today one in every ten Americans is 65 years of age or older. It has been estimated that 20% of all Americans will be beyond the age of 60 by 1980. Thanks to scientists, doctors, physical educators, and other professional groups we have more people living longer and, consequently, have more new problems—housing, unemployment, and an increase in certain diseases. Our success in adding years to life must be now coupled with a concentrated, united drive to add life to years, add breadth and joy to lengthened life. Although there are many wealthy aged people (most of whom are widows), the older group is largely a low-income one. Although almost two thirds of the aged own their own homes, increased taxes, inflation, and other economic problems have struck hard in this group.

The problems of aging are largely sociological, psychological, financial, and physical. The older group needs less labeling such as "old and discarded" and more recognition as one who is a vital part of the community—the church goer, the voter, family member, potential volunteer and above all, a valued *human* being.

Providing stimulating activities for the aged is a community task and responsibility. Agencies and institutions should work together in this program. A survey should be made of how many aged people reside in the area, who and where they are, what they do during a 24-hour period, and what they would like to do in the way of recreation or fellowship with others. A program based upon these data should be made available. Factors to consider in starting such a program are: organization, personnel, budget, facilities, program, publicity, and community relations. A full- or part-time director is necessary for success. His qualifications should include:

1. A genuine interest in and understanding of older people.
2. The ability to plan and carry out a program that will benefit and stimulate all members.
3. A belief in and knowledge of how to direct programs leading to interest, growth, and happiness among this group.

The meeting place for the group, when organized, should be centrally located, easily accessible, attractive, well lighted and heated, and if possible, it should have a kitchen where the members can make tea, coffee, or sandwiches.

Program areas are:

1. Card games—bridge, canasta, pinochle, cribbage, hearts, whist, rummy.
2. Table games—checkers, chess, billiards, others.
3. Outdoor games—croquet, bowling on the green, shuffleboard, archery, horseshoes, others.

4. Dancing—ballroom, folk, square, waltz, and contests.
5. Instruction in handcrafts—sewing, knitting, millinery, jewelry making, violin making, junk crafts, toy making, others.
6. Classes in charm, current events, Americanization, dramatics, music, china painting, others.
7. Picnics, camping, and outings.
8. Birthday and seasonal parties.
9. Hobby groups—poetry lovers, stamp and coin collectors, picture postcard collectors, others.
10. Trips to historic landmarks, county fairs, rodeos, state parks, others.
11. Service projects—knitting and sewing for welfare groups, toy repairing, others.
12. Visits and conducted tours to places of local interest (to a bakery, the zoo, the automobile factory, others).
13. Travel films, free and rented movies. Homemade slides and travel films.
14. Guest speakers.
15. Dramatics, music, and art activities.
16. Fishing, hunting, hiking.
17. Gardening, flower arrangements, transplanting, others.
18. Nature activities—bird walks, care and training of animals, weather forecasting, hobbies, others.

Suggested techniques for successfully leading this group are to:

1. Realize that the best approach is through fellowship and service. Organize clubs around hobby interests and service projects.
2. Use volunteer leaders from the group or outside oldsters of the same age.
3. Plan a program with officers the group elects.
4. Develop new hobbies that are easily done and inexpensive. (More than 70% of all people over 65 live on investments, savings, pensions, charity, or family support.)[2]
5. Arrange for transportation to and from the meeting place.
6. Provide opportunities for each person to take part in organized recreation as well as in leisure time activities of his own choice. (For example, toy repairing and reading a magazine, both done at the center.)
7. Serve refreshments at every party and meeting if possible. Food brings much pleasure to this age group.
8. Observe all birthdays and seasonal occasions with colorful parties.
9. Help provide a recreational program for shut-ins by using volunteers from the group. Capitalize upon their desire to serve others.

10. Avoid discussions of controversial issues, such as religion, sex education, racial prejudice, and politics.
11. Work toward health and happiness as worthy goals to be realized at any age.
12. Provide opportunities for the group to be with young people and children.
13. Give everyone a feeling that he has found real friends and that he is very much needed in the club and community.
14. Personalize the program to the utmost.

Social or Emotional Maladjustment

Most recreation leaders have, in their recreation programs, a few children and adults with behavior problems. Those needing special assistance and often professional help will show the following signs of maladjustment:[3]

Overtimidity; seclusiveness.
Overaggressiveness; constant rivalry and quarreling with others.
Excessive daydreaming; persistent inattentiveness not due to any discoverable physical cause.
Extreme sensitiveness to criticism expressed or implied; feelings hurt easily; cries easily.
Difficulty in reading or reciting not due to any discoverable physical cause.
Failure to advance in school at a normal rate in spite of good physical health and adequate intellectual capacity.
Extreme docility or anxiety to please.
Excessive boasting or showing off—anything to attract undue attention.
Resistance to authority; constant complaints of not being treated fairly, of being discriminated against, "picked on."
Poor sportsmanship; unwillingness to engage in group activities that might result in losing and so in loss of face; not playing fair, or cheating in group games.
Undue restlessness; habit tics, stammering, nail-biting, or lip-sucking not due to any discoverable physical cause.
Frequent accidents or near accidents.

The Leader's Role in Helping Individuals

It is imperative that every skilled recreation leader know how to (1) teach individuals *through* activities and (2) teach skills effectively so that each participant feels self-satisfaction and self-benefit from having learned how to do an activity well. The leader must have the ability to draw others to him. This should come from his evident love for people, certain aspects of his personality or appearance, or his love of life.

Furthermore, he must be sensitized to the needs of others. He must know how to read meaning into behavior by listening to what others say or do not say and by observing meaningful characteristics in movements and speech. He must also have a fundamental belief in the basic goodness of people. He must continually observe the reactions of the group as a whole and the individuals in it. Also, he must know how to communicate with others and how to gain from and give to the group mutual respect, admiration, and understanding. The leader must know how (1) to build group unity, (2) to help each individual feel a vital and contributing part of the whole, and (3) to give recognition for a person's worth. He must do these things by filling the basic needs of each group member. *Esprit de corps* is basic to guiding the group to reach *their* desired goals through *their* devised plans and efforts. This can only be accomplished through effective leadership.

One way to recognize the worth of each individual taking part in an activity is to remember that:

1. First impressions are often misleading.
2. Some people are on guard and do not show their real needs, feelings, or selves quickly.
3. Each person is truly an individual; the more you can discover about each one, the more you will recognize this remarkable individuality and be successful in working with each individual.
4. All people have many sides and many parts; yet only when the leader can put these together in a right pattern can he really know and understand another person.
5. All people react differently in different situations and all will be affected in different ways and degrees by what they experience in any situation.
6. See below the surface of every person, remembering that the word "personality" comes from an ancient word meaning mask.
7. The more you talk, the less you will learn about another person. Learn how to listen.
8. All people speak through their behavior.
9. The most skillful leaders in recreation know far more than mere activities. They know what it means to be a human being and how to become a positive force for the improvement of mankind.

Suggested Readings

Berne, Thomas: *I'm OK—You're OK—A Practical Guide to Transactional Analysis.* New York, Harper and Row, Publishers, 1969.
This book is a fresh approach to understanding the problems human beings face in relationship to themselves and others. It distinguishes the three elements in each person's makeup: the Parent, the Adult, and the Child (P-A-C) and shows how to work with people more effectively.
Blishen, Edward, Editor: *The World of Children.* London, Hamlyn Publishing Company, 1966.

This is one of the most beautiful books ever written about children. The exquisite photographs in color used are of children throughout the world. The book is so beautiful, and the text written by experts in the field of children so valuable, that most readers rush out to buy their own copy of it.

Buck, Pearl: *The Joy of Children.* New York, The John Day Company, 1964.

Written by a world famous author, this book is in itself a joy. Both the photographs and text will help sensitize the leader to the uniqueness and value of children in society.

Cratty, Bryant: *Learning About Human Behavior Through Active Games.* Englewood Cliffs, N.J., Prentice Hall, 1974.

Although the materials contained herein pertain to the behavior of children while playing, many clues are included in this book which will aid the reader to better understand adults too through their actions.

Humphreys, Alice: *Heaven in My Hand.* Richmond, Virginia, The John Knox Press, 1950.

This is a small, sweet book every leader, teacher, and parent should read. Written by a first-grade teacher, it is made up of character-sketch stories about various six-year-olds she has taught. To the author each child is so precariously unique that to work with each one in a group of children is, indeed, like holding a bit of heaven in your hands.

Nesbitt, John, Brown, Paul, and Murphy, James: *Recreation and Leisure Service for the Disadvantaged.* Philadelphia, Lea & Febiger, 1970.

This valuable book is designed to improve recreational and other programs for people of all ages living in urban ghettos through better understanding, planning, and united action. Stress is placed on gaining insight concerning the problems especially of black people, the majority group of most urban inner-city areas. Especially informative are the sections entitled, "The Inner City Clientele: What They are Like," "The Family," and "Recreation and Delinquency."

Smith, Bert Kruger: *Aging in America.* Boston, Beacon Press, 1973.

All recreation leaders should read this book, for it is about human beings. For those who work with the aged, it is a must, for it is beautifully written and contains much valuable information. Bert Kruger Smith is the Director of the Hogg Foundation for Mental Health at the University of Texas and is a nationally recognized leader in this field. The index contains resources for gaining additional information about aging as well as the addresses of various departments to contact in each state for needed help for those working with this group.

Time and Life Books: *Human Behavior.* Chicago, Illinois, 1975.

This is a series of six volumes ($7.95 each) designed to help the reader gain greater understanding of himself and others and covers the whole gamut of human behavior from childhood to old age. Titles of the separate volumes in this series are: *The Individual; The Family; Man and the Organization; How We Learn; Men and Women;* and *Man: The Social Animal.*

Vannier, Maryhelen: *Teaching Health in Elementary Schools, 2nd ed.* Philadelphia, Lea & Febiger, 1974.

Of special value are the chapters entitled, "Children, Their Growth, Development and Characteristics" and "The Challenge" which stress techniques for gaining increased understanding of children and the many problems encountered in working with them successfully. The chapter on Mental Health will help the reader gain insight upon many emotional problems people of all ages face in our modern society.

References

1. Danford, Harold: *Creative Leadership in Recreation,* Boston: Allyn and Bacon, 1964, p. 47.

2. State of California Recreation Commission: *Recreation for Older People in California*, p. 4.
3. *What Teachers See*. New York: Metropolitan Life Insurance Company, 1959, p. 15.

chapter 4

Teaching and Leading Participants

Blessed is the leader who knows
where he is going, why he is going,
and how to get there.
from the NEA Manual
for Locals

There is learning wherever there is life. Teachers by no means have an option upon educating others. Human beings learn from other people as well as from things in their environment. All of our various kinds of communicative media are also concerned with education. Television, especially, has a powerful impact upon the behavior and purchasing habits of its viewers as well as upon our national economy. The recreation leader is in a choice seat, educationally speaking. In contrast to the teacher whose primary role is that of motivating students to *want* to learn, the recreation leader works with those who come to him voluntarily. The very environment of a recreation center differs widely from that of the school. The people there seem relaxed and active because they are not bell-herded from one place to another.

In its broadest sense, education means to lead forth. Teaching is a magical process of guiding, inspiring, influencing, and sharing with others so that they learn, grow, and become more sensitive and better thinking, feeling, and performing individuals.

The recreation leader is a teacher specialized in the play approach to learning. His objectives resemble those of the educator—to develop values, skills, knowledges, appreciations, attitudes, and good citizens. His approach to doing so is different, his success is often greater. People voluntarily take part in his program and are not required by law to do so. Freedom to choose, move, make noise, talk, laugh and tease, be with one's own friends, come and go as one wishes are great learning incentives. One learns best, retains information longer, traces behavior patterns deeper when he feels secure, enjoys what he is doing, and can have a voice in planning what he is going to learn. Pleasure and success spur learning on to a gallop; the pain of failure slows learning to a hesitant, stumbling gait. Insistence upon skill mastery or perfection often leads the learner to an unrewarding experience or negative attitude. Education seeks perfection; recreation obtains it through pleasure or the play approach.

Learning goes on wherever there is life. However, it may be negative or positive, depending largely upon leadership. The child learns at an early age how to shoot craps, puff discarded cigaret butts, or steal toys from a store with his gang. He could learn how to snap a carom ring into the corner pocket, hang by his knees in a set of swinging rings, or steal home in a ball game at a supervised play center with his same street gang friends. His basic needs for adventure, recognition, love, belonging, and security are fulfilled by both sets of activities. It is the leader who makes the difference, because he is concerned about his role in molding plastic youth. Youth copies its chosen models. Children will choose the playground in preference to the alley and adults will prefer the community center to a smoke-filled dive as long as they find there pleasure, release, adventure, security, others they enjoy being with, and someone they admire.

We do the things we enjoy in our free time. We enjoy most the things we can do well. The leader's goal is to help people find what they want to do and gradually guide them to want something better for themselves and others. If the leader is to reach the greatest number of people through the best possible activities he should have a program that is:

1. Based upon the needs and interests of all. It must have variety to meet the basic urges of everyone. The leader should be aware of the unique needs of each participant and guide each one through activities for the fulfillment of these basic needs.
2. Geared to help others develop in new interests, skills, appreciations, and knowledges. Familiar activities are the springboard leading to new and better ones. In educational circles this is known as going from the known to the unknown.
3. Planned and conducted to make the best use of available space, facilities, equipment, professional and volunteer leadership. This connotes that one hundred should not sit and watch a few play with the only volley ball but that, instead, the entire group should be directed in playing mass activities suitable for a small space. (Team relays, square dancing, play party games, etc.)
4. Developed with desired goals and objectives in mind of the group as a whole and of each individual within it. If the main objective is only to entertain, easy-to-do activities should be included. If it is to enlighten, book review clubs or discussion groups of current political affairs could be stressed. If the goal is character building, then overnight camping or competitive team games might be featured and led by a person who has a high sense of values and is skilled in helping others grow as human beings.

How People Learn

Learning comes largely through our senses of hearing, tasting, touching, and seeing. The more the different senses are combined to help others to learn, the faster will learning occur. There is no such thing as only using your head in learning or in learning only through your body or by merely getting the feel of any movement skill. Learning involves the entire self—the physical, mental, and emotional interwoven inward parts of every human being. Man's mind is a central clearing house, a transfer station or a switchboard, which can only function when messages come to it and are received, filed, clarified, and sent back out again. As a famous educator has said "we learn what we live," meaning that where we live, with whom we live, toward what ends we strive, and what we do through our actions as a living person all determine what and how we learn.

In reality, the learner teaches himself through his own trial-and-error attempts. It is an individual matter, and every person learns at his own rate of speed. The teacher's role is to guide the learner around sure-to-fail attempts, encourage him to keep on trying, and to capitalize upon his mistakes as well as to lead him to new and more difficult challenges. Repeated failure is a wet blanket to learning, success an eagerness flame-fanner that results in quicker mastery. Past experiences, goals, and drives are the foundation upon which learning attempts are built.

TYPES OF LEARNING

We all learn when we:

1. Can understand words and symbols.
2. Can communicate with others.
3. Develop new skills.
4. Form new habits.
5. Develop new attitudes.
6. Gain new understandings.
7. Build new interests.
8. Can make generalizations from learned facts.
9. Develop social skills and can contribute to group endeavor.
10. Become concerned about our environment and the rights and happiness of other people.
11. Have a fairly accurate view of ourselves—our strengths as well as weaknesses.

MOTIVATION—THE KEY TO ALL LEARNING

We have all heard the old folk saying that "we can drive a horse to water, but we cannot make him drink." Few, except educators, realize the accuracy of this simple statement. We all learn only what *we* want to master. We all, however, can be motivated to learn new things as well as how to accomplish desired goals faster. Motives that can spur or check a drive to learn include:

Wants and needs	Interests
Attitudes	Individual behavior traits
Habits and previously	Purposes
learned skills	Rewards
Emotions	Group recognition
Punishment	Self-satisfaction

The recreation leader should capitalize upon children's natural curiosity, eagerness to do new things, and need to be active. The purposes, ambitions, needs and values of each should be channeled to help him develop along his own natural potential lines. Since you can catch more flies with honey than you can with vinegar, praise for most people motivates better than reproof. Care must be taken, however, that it be given in just the right amounts, for if everything is good, all things become equal but also of lesser value.

Teen-agers can be motivated primarily by capitalizing upon their natural desire to master new skills, gain recognition for being the best of the group, and eagerness to learn how to dance, play, and be with the opposite sex. Youth is also idealistic and wants to serve, a fact any leader should recognize when working with this age group especially, for this desire is a built-in motivator.

All people can be motivated best to learn when they:

1. See meanings—the values of and relationships in what they are learning.
2. Are trying to learn tasks that are not too far beyond their capabilities.
3. Know what is expected of them in the way of behavior and in other areas.
4. Take part in activities *they* deem important to learn.
5. Are carefully guided through a step-by-step learning process and are able to see the why as well as the how for correcting their own mistakes.
6. Gain earned praise from their instructor and peer group recognition for their accomplishments.
7. Like or admire and respect their teacher and, in turn, feel secure and needed as a group member working with him.
8. Can use what they learn in their everyday life at home, school, and community.

Adults are motivated far less by tangible awards, such as cups or ribbons, than are eager youths. Time, with an awareness that life is slipping away, is a great motivator among adults, especially those beyond middle age. Those in their mid-fifties suddenly seem to awaken to the fact that there are just so many remaining sand grains left. Although each reacts to this startling discovery differently, the majority decide to have a final hell-bent-for-pleasure fling or else to cram into their dwindling future time all kinds of activities they have longed to do for their own or society's betterment. Cruise ships and vacation resorts are filled by those of retirement age and beyond.

Money is a great motivator in all age groups except among very young children. Each individual in each group values it differently, whether it be to go on to college, start a family, store up to leave behind, or to spend lavishly. Interest also plays an important role in motivation. Changes in interests reflect a variation in abilities and energy, outlets for sex drives, and vocational advancement. Both interests and attitudes are more closely related to occupation, social class, and cultural background and appreciation than to chronological age. The older a person becomes, the less active he tends to be and the more likely he will engage in more passive recreational activities such as reading, talking, or watching television. Attendance and interest in movies drop off sharply after the age of 25 and many 60 or beyond never go to the cinema.

LEARNING OTHER SKILLS

Although skills are taught more informally by the recreation leader than by a professional educator, the method of helping students, regardless of their age, to learn new skills with average or above mastery are the same. In order to teach skills to others the teacher must be able to help learners: (1) set up desired goals (to play tennis, the guitar, etc.), (2) select the materials to be learned (the basic tennis strokes or musical chords), (3) guide learning progression so that skill is built upon skill (learning how to place the ball with a spin on it or the abstract fingering used in "picking" a melody instead of strumming it), and (4) evaluate the results (how well did you reach your desired goals?). The best teaching is that which is concerned with teaching far more than mere skills. It is also centered around helping others develop finer attitudes, deeper and more lasting appreciations, and more meaningful knowledge.

In teaching skills to others, the instructor should (1) briefly explain what is to be taught, (2) demonstrate how the skill is done, (3) have the group practice it by imitating the demonstration given and gaining an understanding of the verbal explanation of it, and (4) have each evaluate his progress made. All movement skills should be integrated into a game or larger whole as quickly as possible—the lay-up shot in a basketball game, the soccer dribble in a team relay, etc. The group should understand that accuracy of movement is far more important than speed or force, for it is *where* the ball is hit that counts in a tennis game, not how hard it is sent back across the net.

The leader's presence, encouragement, patience, and faith in the learner's desire and ability to master what he sets out to do help longed-for goals become a reality. Every skillful instructor knows how to demonstrate well, diagnose learning snags, and direct new movement patterns so that the learner *does* hit the archery target or does the swan dive, or whatever skill he is trying to perfect.

HELPING OLDER PEOPLE GAIN MORE FROM THEIR FREE TIME

Although ours is a culture that stresses youth and the present (nowness), we are rapidly becoming a nation filled with older people. A longer life span coupled with forced retirement presents thousands of Americans with the problem of time on their hands. To some, retirement means a marked decrease in income, isolation, and feelings of being put out to pasture as a non-productive member of society with its subsequent loss of self-esteem. Many face financial as well as physical and emotional problems of great magnitude.

Although most workers live approximately 15 years after retirement, merely adding *length* to life must now be coupled with adding *breadth* to their existence. Most people over the age of 65 do have physiological losses and need to do things at a slower pace. However, the vast majority of them can still take part in challenging, intellectual, and cultural activities. Some communities are recognizing the recreational needs of these senior citizens. The more aggressive oldsters soon begin searching for vocational and educational experiences. Some are even enrolling in college for the first time. Others are going back to complete a once started degree.

The line is thin between adult recreation and adult education. It is evident that these oldest students, who are flocking in large numbers to such non-credit college courses as world government, philosophy, or Spanish, seek far more meaningful activities than such educational tidbits as How To Use Your Camera or Flower Arranging. However, there is a need for both types of activities in a well-balanced recreation program.

Suggested techniques for successfully leading this older group are to:

1. Realize that the best approach is through fellowship and service. Organize clubs around hobby interests and service projects.
2. Use volunteer leaders who love and respect older people to help work with this age group.
3. Plan all programs *with* officers the group elects.
4. Develop new hobbies that are easily done and inexpensive. (More than 70 percent of all over 65 live on investments, savings, pensions, charity, or family support.)
5. Arrange for transportation to and from the meeting place.
6. Provide opportunities for each person to take part in organized

recreation as well as leisure time activities of his own choice. (For example, toy repairing and reading a magazine, both done at a center.)

7. Observe all birthdays and seasonal occasions with colorful parties.
8. Provide a recreational program for shut-ins by using volunteers from this older group.
9. Avoid discussion of controversial issues, such as religion, sex, racial prejudice, and politics.
10. Work toward increasing the health and happiness of each individual.
11. Give everyone a feeling of belonging and that he is very much needed in the club and community.
12. Personalize the program to the utmost.

The Role of the School in Recreation

George Bernard Shaw once declared: "Youth is a wonderful thing. What a shame to waste it on children." An increasing number of American taxpayers are wondering why schools are being used exclusively for children. Many adults are aware of and are concerned that school buildings, gymnasiums, and coliseums are too frequently locked up when the majority of people are free to use them for recreational purposes—on weekends, after work, and during the summer months. Yet in some communities school authorities, urged into action by a few persuasive physical education teachers, are either working cooperatively with an already existing recreation department or are establishing community school recreation councils to develop an area-wide, year-round recreation program for all people in the community. Outstanding programs that are attracting national attention are now being conducted in Flint, Michigan; Milwaukee, Wisconsin; and Tyler, Texas. In other regions, community leaders have developed an extended after-school recreation program wherein boys and girls, regardless of their degree of skill, are taking part in a well-planned recreation program that ranges in activities all the way from sports and games to arts and crafts. Still other localities are conducting summer day camps and/or a sports program in an earnest and sincere effort to increase youth fitness. As fine as many of these programs are, they still are not good enough. There are not nearly as many of them as there should be. Youth and adults who are *not* being reached tremendously outnumber the few who are being served by an after-school program for students or by a school-centered recreational program for all people in the community. Far too many schools still cater only to good athletes. These few often receive the most and best of everything, including training and instruction, equipment, uniforms, and almost exclusive use of the gymnasium, tennis courts, or playground areas. It is no wonder, then, that most American school children and college students cannot even meet the lowest acceptable standards of physical fitness. Often they use their leisure time in negative and in physically and socially destructive ways. It is no wonder, then, that many adults are below physical par and are tragically wasting their leisure hours watching mediocre television programs and cheap movies or frantically pursuing new thrills and happiness.

Increasingly, school administrators and teachers are becoming convinced that they must be concerned with all aspects of human living and that they should conduct an enriched educational program that includes both adults and youngsters not yet old enough to enter school. Experts claim that the role of the modern school is to improve both the *quality* and *quantity* of the culture of which it is a part. Therefore, if schools are to raise the cultural level of the people, they must educate for the whole of life, for leisure as well as labor, and for the enjoyment of the good life as well as for the earning of an adequate living. Responsibilities of school in the area of leisure and recreation are in: (1) educating for leisure throughout all subject areas offered in the curriculum, whether this be history, science, physical education, or in any other field, (2) supplying both leadership and the use of school facilities for a school-connected recreation program for the entire community, (3) acting in cooperation with other public agencies in order to provide a widely diversified and positive leisure-time program for all people, and (4) interpreting to the citizens in both the school and community the significance, purpose, and value of recreation to the life and happiness of each individual, and, thus, to the community itself.

GETTING STARTED

The local board of education should first set up an advisory committee made up of outstanding and influential people in the community who are interested in the welfare of people, know something about recreation, and are concerned about what people locally do with their leisure time. A representative of the board of education, the school superintendent or principal, the director of physical education or a physical education teacher, along with a male and a female student leader should also serve on this group. The committee should be made up of around eight people; but each one should be a recognized and respected leader. Who is on this initial planning group is of the utmost importance, and who is elected chairman can be of vital importance.

Since the success of any recreational program rests almost entirely on leadership, great care should be taken in selecting the person who will be placed in charge of planning and overseeing the overall program. Utmost caution should also be taken in selecting those who will work as paid and volunteer activity leaders. Not just anyone can be a good recreation leader. Physical education teachers tend to overstress sports and games. The average school teacher in other subjects tends to use the more formal classroom techniques rather than the more relaxed recreational approach. The volunteer hobbyist tends to know his specialty and to be carried away with enthusiasm for it; but often he cannot teach its skills to others. Consequently, there should be a leadership training class for all who work in the program. This should be conducted by someone who has had some professional training in recreation and has had recreational leadership experience. Such people can often be found at nearby colleges and universities or through such agencies as the YWCA, YMCA, Boy Scouts, Girl Scouts, FFA, or the 4-H Club. The training program for selected paid and volunteer leaders should contain these topics: (1) the meaning and importance of directed positive recreation pursuits to health and happiness, (2) leadership do's and don'ts, (3) understanding people, (4) procedures for handling discipline problems and accidents, (5) necessary reports to be made, (6) skills in as many different kinds of activities as possible, (7) techniques for teaching people through activities, and (8) how to evaluate the results.

Although it is better to select a few assistants wisely rather than try to train large number of amateurs, the leader should find an activity for every person who is willing to donate his time, energy, and particular talents to the recreational program. The alert director will utilize the services of all willing helpers, regardless of age, and impress upon each one the importance and value of his unique contribution.

THE PROGRAM

To have real merit, a recreation program must be based upon the present and future needs, interests, and development of all participants. Consequently, there is no one program which can be used as a set pattern for all communities to use. Rather, a broad program should be developed for the people that is based upon sound recreational, educational, and democratic principles. Such a program should:

1. Be varied in activities for all people.
2. Be established for the basic purpose of physically and morally bettering those who take part in it.
3. Provide participants with opportunities to share in planning and conducting activities.
4. Be adaptable and usable in all available facilities.
5. Be in accordance with local customs, mores, and traditions.
6. Be established for all people in the community, ranging in appeal from the pre-schoolers to the older retired adults.
7. Be designed to serve the community 12 months a year, during the day, after school, in the evening, during holidays, and on weekends.

8. Consist of a wide range of activities under each of these headings:

Arts, crafts, creative arts	Music
Sports and games	Dance
Camping, outing, and nature activities	Dramatics
	Special events
Social recreation	Cultural activities
Family recreation	Special holiday celebrations

9. Include an expanded intramural sports program made up of as many teams for girls as for boys and provide for co-ed teams in as many activities as possible.
10. Include city- or community-wide competition in sports in leagues and tournaments organized for men and women in business, industry, service clubs and other groups.

THE USE OF SCHOOL FACILITIES

The use of school buildings and playground areas for community recreation purposes should be guided by written joint-working agreements. Such devised policies should include provisions for supplying needed equipment, its care and repair, rules governing the use of the entire plant or part of it, means for underwriting expenses, and custodial services. Dual use of school buildings requires good working relationships and an understanding of each agency's role and responsibility in providing school-community recreational programs. Since many school buildings are not designed for recreational purposes, many adaptations may be needed. The use of portable gates will help restrict and zone usable areas. Portable storage cabinets, bulletin boards, and other needed supplies that can be easily moved and stored are recommended. Since the misuse of various school facilities and the destruction of equipment are the major problems found in dual use of school buildings, each area to be used for recreational purposes should be carefully studied so that this facility can be given optimum use.

Outstanding school-centered community programs in existence for many years are found in Los Angeles, California; Flint, Michigan; and Milwaukee, Wisconsin. The public response to these programs has been tremendous. What these cities have accomplished serve as models for other recreational departments and school systems throughout the nation.

FINANCE

There are many ways in which such a recreation program could be financed. These range all the way from state aid granted on the average daily school attendance basis to state grants (as in Pennsylvania), special excise tax (as the tobacco tax in New Mexico), to permissive legislation (as in California and Ohio). Possibilities for sources of money to supplement tax money are from foundations and corporations (such as the Mott Foundation, which pays the cost of the outstanding program in Flint, Michigan), contributions, gifts and grants of land, fees and charges, dues, and special assessments.

Granted, any such a program will cost money. Yet each community has a choice to make—whether to invest in educating people or in building facilities to house juvenile offenders and adult lawbreakers. If the old adage that an ounce of prevention is worth a pound of cure is still true, intelligent citizens will choose to put their money into efforts that will make and keep people healthy instead of into bigger and better mental institutions, hospitals, and jails for those who are unfit physically, socially, and morally. They will likewise study to find out for themselves just what there is that is constructive, recreative, and wholesome for themselves and others to do in their community.

Suggested Readings

Bannon, Joseph: *Problem Solving in Recreation and Parks.* Englewood Cliffs, New Jersey, Prentice-Hall, Inc., 1972
  This book contains a series of 100 case studies in recreation, illustrating the many kinds of problems the recreation leader will have as he works with people of all ages. These cases cover such problems relating the teaching and leading participants in the inner city, vandalism, drug use, and many more.
Bucher, Charles and Bucher, Richard: *Recreation in Today's Society.* Englewood Cliffs, New Jersey, Prentice-Hall, Inc., 1975
  The chapter entitled "Services Rendered by Recreation" is especially recommended to the student to read in conjunction with this chapter. It will enable the reader to understand better the many skills the leader must have in order to reach effectively each individual taking part in any recreation program, so that his learning attempts and participation in the program be both successful and enjoyable.
Cochran, E. V.: *Teach and Reach That Child.* Palo Alto, Peek Publications, 1971
  The author explores herein techniques for reaching each individual child in a large or small group. These suggestions are both practical and can be easily applied by any teacher-leader in both a school or recreational setting.
Vannier, Maryhelen and Fait, Hollis: *Teaching Physical Education in Secondary Schools,* 4th Ed., Philadelphia, W. B. Saunders Co., 1975
  In Chapter 4 of this text, "The Teaching Process," the authors give concrete suggestions of many ways to produce greater learning results. Especially valuable is the section on teaching motor skills through both direct and indirect methods and techniques for teaching large groups successfully.
Vannier, Maryhelen, Gallahue, David and Foster, Mildred: *Teaching Physical Education in Elementary Schools,* 5th Ed., Philadelphia, W. B. Saunders Co., 1974
  Chapter 7, "The Techniques of Successful Teaching," clearly informs the reader of the importance of goal setting in relationship to learning mastery. The materials in this section also cover many kinds of teaching approaches which should be used to enhance learning attempts.
Vannier, Maryhelen: *Physical Activities for the Handicapped.* Englewood Cliffs, New Jersey, Prentice-Hall, Inc., 1976
  The many suggestions given to the readers for teaching and leading the handicapped successfully are also applicable to working with normal people of all ages, if tailored to meet the specific interest and needs of these individuals as well.

Wees, W. R.: *Nobody Can Teach Anyone Anything*. New York, Doubleday and
Company, 1971
The author stresses that the learner teaches himself, and that the role of the
teacher is largely that of motivation and the correction of learning attempts.
Unlike many books in the fields of education and recreation, this one is a joy
to read. Although written in a breezy style, it contains many pearls of wisdom
relative to the actual facts regarding how people learn. It is true, indeed, that
the learner teaches himself. Since educators too often express this basic truth
in educational jargon confusing to would-be successful teacher-leaders, all
readers of this book will profit from having done so.

Suggested Management Booklets

From The National Recreation and Park Association

No. 40 *Creative Playground Equipment*
No. 46 *Budgeting for Parks and Recreation*
No. 49 *Swimming Pool Management*
No. 63 *Personnel Policies*
No. 65 *In-Service Training Manual*
No. 72 *Administering Admissions to Events and Programs in the Park and
Recreation Field*
No. 79 *Publicity Handbook*
No. 82 *School-Community Park and Recreation Operations*

chapter 5

The Recreation Program

*Recreation should be more than
something we can do when we have
nothing else to do; it can fulfill
emotional and spiritual needs.*
Hugh B. Masters

To be of value, recreation must be more than mere entertainment or a time filler. The program should be carefully planned with definite objectives in mind so that the participants as well as the leader know what is to be accomplished, what the main purpose is, and how each activity relates to the total program. Likewise, recreation should be primarily concerned with helping others find joy, beauty, and meaning in life.

The recreation leader must care deeply about people, their present welfare, their possible future, and the destiny of humanity. The program is the magic wand with which people can be touched and receive lasting benefit. The leader's primary role is to help each participant grow as a unique individual and become a contributor of positive gains in our society. His primary concern should be to teach people *through* activities and not merely to direct games. What a person learns about human relations and life through the program offerings is vastly more important than the relief he gains from boredom.

Principles of Program Planning

Principles are truths or basic beliefs that are action guidelines. As professional leaders of integrity, those in charge of planning recreation activities should strive to provide a program that has value, is of the highest quality, and will benefit all those taking part in it. There are times, however, when program changes must be made and compromises devised due to political or social pressures. As long as the leader can operate upon such basic principles as "the greatest good for the greatest number," or "the community recreation program should be for all the people all of the time, instead of just for children in the summer," he is on the right track.

One authority said:

> Expediency and compromise of principles are always fraught with danger of personal integrity. One may give way on a minor principle in order to gain a major one, or one may accept a present defeat in view of a promise of a later victory. The ultimate test, however, is a professional rather than a personal advantage; a cause served rather than a profit gained.[1]

Every recreation program should:

1. Provide equality of opportunity for all, regardless of sex, age, race, or religion.
2. Be based upon the age, sex, needs, capabilities, and interests of all individual participants.
3. Serve co-recreational and fellowship needs.
4. Provide for family participation both as a unit and separately for all individuals within it.
5. Be planned in light of the desired goals and objectives sought by the sponsoring group, the instructor, and each individual participant.
6. Be devised to make the best possible use of all available community facilities and other resources, available equipment, and the leader's various leadership skills.
7. Be wide enough in scope to be of present and future value to the individual, community, state, and nation.
8. Be one which every person can engage in safely and one which will lead to improved health and total finess (physical, mental, and emotional).
9. Be planned for the betterment of social and moral behavior.
10. Be flexible, with provisions made for instructor-group planning and modification.
11. Be planned to develop degrees of skill among the beginners, intermediates, and advanced participants in each activity.
12. Provide outlets for self-expression and creativity.
13. Include carefully planned activities for the ill, handicapped, and aged in such places as prisons, hospitals, and institutions.
14. Be well balanced with both active and passive activities.
15. Help build recreation patterns and hobbies of lasting value.
16. Be modified and improved upon as the results of continuous evaluation by all who plan, take part in, and administer it.

The Need for Goal-Setting and Devising Objectives in Programming

Recreation programs must increasingly become concerned with improving and enriching the *quality* of each participants's life. Such programs must become far more than just fun and games or used to stuff a vacuum of time. Such activities as arts and crafts projects which are, as one leader has said, neither artistic or craftsmanlike must be replaced by those which are and other such mediocre program offerings must be replaced with activities more suitable for every age group.

Establishing goals and objectives is basic to good program planning. Goals are statements of broad direction, purpose, or intent based upon the needs of the community. Objectives are ways in which goals can be reached. Goals should be challenging, long range, and established for each specific community, agency, group, or individual.[2] For example, a long-range goal for a community might well be to provide more parks and recreational areas; for an agency to provide recreational outlets for all people all year round rather than just for children and teen-agers during the "long, hot summer;" for a musical group meeting in a recreation center to enlarge its membership and for an individual leader to help Johnny become a better sportsman in athletic contests.

All goals and objectives of leisure service agencies must be consistent with the basic psychological needs of good citizenship, the enlargement of interests, character development, total fitness and health. All overall goals should be broken down into obtainable, measureable, and realistic objectives. Every YMCA worker is aware that the goal of this agency is to develop the mind, body and spirit of all members. All activities are planned with this in mind and all leaders and all participants are striving to develop themselves and others in each group according to this triangled concept of mind, body, and spirit. Likewise, each recreation leader, as well as each participant in any recreation program should be keenly aware of the overall goals he and his team members are striving to achieve, each must plan and conduct his program activities in such a way that will lead to the attainment of these goals. Next, the leader should make a list of the specific objectives he hopes to achieve with each group taking part in each program offering he leads. For example, if he is teaching a class in gymnastics, his objectives might well be to teach:

(1) As many basic skills as possible, including
    a. free exercises
    b. the balance beam
    c. side horse vaulting
    d. the even and uneven bars
    e. the trampoline and mini-tramp
(2) the safety procedures to be followed in each sport
(3) free exercise routines
(4) advanced skills in all of the above-mentioned areas to individuals when they are ready to master them

GOAL SETTING BY THE INDIVIDUAL

Each participant in the program should also set his own goals and objectives he hopes to attain through taking part in each activity he chooses to do. Sometimes it is difficult to know exactly what each person hopes to accomplish. Children, as well as adults, when asked why they wanted to join any recreational activity, would likely say "to have fun." It must be remembered, however, that what is fun for a child or an adult often is far from fun to an adult leader. Thus, the leader needs to help any person, regardless of age, define what she means by the word "fun." Some adults join a class in weight and figure control or weight lifting, for example, hoping to have a good time there but specifically each wants to shed a few pounds or become more physically fit. Others sign up for swimming classes in order to learn how to have fun swimming.

It is vastly important for the recreation leader to realize that, unlike the school teacher who has a captive audience because it is a law that every child must go to school, those who take part in his program come into it because they want to. They will continue to attend *only* as long as they feel that the experience they are having there is worth the effort to come.

Influences on Program Planning

The success of any recreation program depends upon the ability of those in charge of it to (1) draw up daily, weekly, monthly, and seasonal program offerings according to established goals and objectives and (2) carry these plans out successfully. In small community centers or playgrounds where only one person is in charge of the program or where one male and one female leader are responsible for the entire program, ideas can be gathered from many sources. These include the individuals or groups to be served, other recreation specialists, periodicals, and books. Recreation specialists, especially, welcome the opportunity to educate others in the nature, purpose, scope, and value of programs. Some of the best ideas for program improvement, however, often come from those who take part in it. Leader-group planning helps others to gain democratic leadership skills and an understanding of their importance, increases interest and personal identification in the program, helps others gain increased responsibility for their own choices and actions, and aids in the development of stronger leader-group rapport, with resulting friendlier group relationships.

All programs to be of value must be based upon the interest, needs, and abilities of the group. When involved in group planning, the poorest approach is to ask the groups what they want to do, for the majority will cling to old favorites, rebel against anything new, or will follow the suggestions made by the most persuasive person in the group. The use of an interest finder, such as the one found below, has merit for discovering the real recreational interests of each individual.

After these questionnaire results have been tabulated, the recreation leader and group-selected representatives should plan a program that will reach the needs and interests of the majority. For such planning the group should be composed of the leader and not more than 5 or less than

3 persons. Minor matters, such as how to choose teams for tournament play and voting procedures, can be settled by the entire group. This concept of leading with the assistance of elected sub-leaders is real leadership. It can be used most successfully and is a learning laboratory for democracy.

Interest Finder of Activities for Program Leaders

Directions: Check those activities you most like to do in your leisure time. Double check new activities you would like to learn how to do. Write in any omitted activities you would like to learn to do.

Activities	Activities You Like to Do	Activities You Would Like to Learn How to Do
Sports and Games		
Baseball	_____	_____
Basketball	_____	_____
Box hockey	_____	_____
Boxing	_____	_____
Bowling	_____	_____
Handball	_____	_____
Horseback riding	_____	_____
Horseshoes	_____	_____
Kickball	_____	_____
Lifesaving	_____	_____
Roller skating	_____	_____
Skiing	_____	_____
Sailing	_____	_____
Swimming	_____	_____
Other	_____	_____
Social Activities		
Bridge	_____	_____
Canasta	_____	_____
Party leadership techniques	_____	_____
Pencil and paper games	_____	_____
Social dancing	_____	_____
Square dancing	_____	_____
Other	_____	_____
Table Games		
Checkers	_____	_____
Chess	_____	_____
Dominoes	_____	_____
Other	_____	_____

Interest Finder of Activities for Program Leaders—continued

Activities	Activities You Like to Do	Activities You Would Like to Learn How to Do
Music Activities		
Glee clubs	_____	_____
Harmonica playing	_____	_____
Mandolin, guitar or ukulele playing	_____	_____
Opera groups	_____	_____
Orchestra (dance)	_____	_____
Rhythm band	_____	_____
Singing games	_____	_____
String quartets or ensembles	_____	_____
Symphony orchestra	_____	_____
Whistling groups	_____	_____
Other	_____	_____
Arts and Crafts		
Basketry	_____	_____
Beadcraft	_____	_____
Carving wood, soap, brick, bone	_____	_____
Ceramics	_____	_____
Costume design	_____	_____
Etching	_____	_____
Finger painting	_____	_____
Home decorations	_____	_____
Jewelry making	_____	_____
Millinery	_____	_____
Model airplanes, cars, trains, villages	_____	_____
Painting—oils, water colors	_____	_____
Photography	_____	_____
Woodwork	_____	_____
Other	_____	_____
Drama Activities		
Costume design	_____	_____
Fashion shows and modeling	_____	_____
Marionettes	_____	_____
Mask making	_____	_____
Minstrel shows	_____	_____
Puppetry	_____	_____
Radio and television plays	_____	_____
Storytelling	_____	_____
Other	_____	_____

Activities	Activities You Like to Do	Activities You Would Like to Learn How to Do
Dancing Activities		
Ballet	------------------	------------------
Folk	------------------	------------------
Modern	------------------	------------------
Social	------------------	------------------
Square	------------------	------------------
Other	------------------	------------------
Nature and Camping Activities		
Astronomy	------------------	------------------
Bird walks	------------------	------------------
Campcraft	------------------	------------------
Caring for and training of pets	------------------	------------------
Explorations	------------------	------------------
Fishing	------------------	------------------
Gardening	------------------	------------------
Hiking	------------------	------------------
Hunting		
Mountain climbing	------------------	------------------
Nature study	------------------	------------------
Tent pitching and ditching	------------------	------------------
Other	------------------	------------------

INTERESTS OF THE PARTICIPANTS

Learning the real interests of any group or of any individual is fundamental to good planning. The role of the leader is to recognize the development level of a person and to guide him to learn new and challenging activities and make richer discoveries. Several ways to discover the interests of the majority are to use an interest finder, make door-to-door surveys, and observe where people usually go for their recreation and what they do there. The use of publications can also be of help.

Some organizations have a policy to start a new club if ten people express an interest in an activity. The use of volunteers and hobbyists for such clubs as model airplane making or flower photography enables the professional leader to plan for and provide new program activities. Since the success of any recreational offering depends upon leadership skill and participant interest, both old favorites and the latest craze, whether it be sidewalk surfing or dancing the Freddie, will help gain new and retain previous participants.

AGE

Every age has its own unique characteristics, interests, needs, and favorite things to do as well as the necessary skill needed for accomplishment. However, grouping of certain ages can be used successfully, too, whether this be by children, teen-agers, young adults, the middle-agers, or senior citizens. The majority within such classifications will fit generalized characteristics. Recognition of the play and other interests of each developing group as well as their readiness or ability to learn sports and games is of paramount importance.

Planning for adults often is harder than planning for other groups, for unlike children, many are afraid to lose face among their peers. Likewise, it is more difficult to help grown-ups gain movement mastery, such as in dancing, unless they have had experiences in earlier childhood in rhythmical response and moving to rhythm. Adults also tend to be more routinized than youth in their recreational patterns and often are less eager to do something entirely new. Adults playing in sports and games should be classified largely according to age and sex. Youngsters and older people, however, can belong to the same hobby club or take part in activities such as music, crafts, nature, or dramatics.

SEX DIFFERENCES

Recent studies show that differences between the sexes in ability to excel in sports are not as great as once believed. Girls and boys differ in play interest largely because of cultural conditioning, which begins soon after birth. Little boys are given balls to play with. Girls are given dolls. And each copy in play the habits and roles of the adult male or female. Actually women have the same potential to excel in sports and games as males; yet throughout history boys and men have had a greater opportunity to take part in sports and have thus gained more mastery and interest in them.

It is often best, because of variance in acquired interest and strength, to plan highly competitive sports events separately within each sex group for boys and girls who have reached puberty. Competition for girls and women should include events that stress skill and form, such as tennis or synchronized swimming. Competition for boys and men should include sports that call for strength and speed, such as weight lifting or handball. During adulthood, co-recreational sports such as mixed volleyball, bowling, and swimming are popular. However, opportunities should also be provided for both sexes to play among their own group, as in men's golf or in an archery tournament for women. Music, crafts, dancing, and camping are ideal co-recreation program activities.

Older adults seemingly favor co-recreational activities such as dancing, cards, or dramatics. Men, however, enjoy such craft activities as woodworking or metal craft; women prefer activities that center around the household acts, such as interior decorating or sewing.

FACILITIES

Ideally, the program should determine the facilities. Unfortunately, few leaders are fortunate enough to be able to start a program from scratch and then plan a building or other type of facility in which to conduct it. Rather, most leaders are stuck with what facility is available and must modify their program accordingly, regardless of where the program is conducted, whether this be in an industrial or camp setting, in a hospital or church recreational building or elsewhere.

Leadership is the key to the successful recreation program. It is far more important than any impressive facility. Ingenious leaders learn to utilize fully available community resources. Some conduct early morning bowling classes or leagues in commercial alleys. Others conduct a splendid program in schools during the summer months or during the evenings. Still others use store parking lots for Sunday afternoon or evening programs. Where there is a will, there is a way, and any leader truly believing in this folk saying *will* find facilities in which to conduct a well-planned program.

Multiple-purpose tennis courts can also be used for handball, roller and ice skating, dancing, volleyball, basketball, goal shooting, and shuffleboard. The use of lighting alone will bring many participants to a recreational facility, thus reducing the cost of a program when determined by the number of people serviced.

Public community recreation facilities often include play lots, a zoo, various kinds of museums, neighborhood playgrounds, large centrally located parks, fishing, boating and water skiing areas, a golf course, tennis courts, picnic and camping areas, athletic fields, game areas, as well as pools of varying size for all age groups. The latter usually includes wading and small instructional pools for youngsters and olympic size pools with diving wells for older age groups.

The chart shown below shows a variety of the various types of facilities needed for a variety of community recreation programs.

TIME

If recreation is of value, then in a democracy all should have opportunity to receive its benefits. Industrial recreation specialists have learned to provide activities before and after work hours as well as during the noon hour. Schools have been doing this for a long time through their intramural competitions, club programs, and recess activities. Many communities now have bowling alleys and other facilities open all night in order to accommodate people who work at odd hours.

Special events, such as pet shows and parades, an old settlers' reunion, Santa Claus visit, or a local fair, add variety to any planned year-round program. Seasonal sport activities, whether they be swimming and baseball in the summer months or ice skating and skiing in the winter,

Needed Community Recreation Areas

Type	Size	For	Location	Needed Areas
Playlot	2000–5000 square feet	Pre-school children mainly	Located near housing projects or densely populated areas	1. Simple play area including swings, etc. 2. Open area 3. Benches, paths, and walks
Neighborhood playground	4–7 acres	For children 6–14 mainly, but could be used by all ages	Not more than ¼–½ mile from most homes in the neighborhood	1. Assigned areas for youngest children as far away as possible from athletic areas and courts 2. Apparatus area 3. Open space 4. Fields and courts 5. Shaded areas 6. Wading pool and shelter house
Playfield	12–50 acres. One acre for each 800 people	For use by all ages	Within one mile of the majority of homes	1. Children's playground 2. Game courts and lawn games 3. Athletic game areas 4. Swimming pool 5. Recreation building 6. Wooded area 7. Special facilities

Facility	Size	Age use	Location	Facilities
Large park	100 or more acres. One park for every 50,000 population.	For use by all ages	Usually within city limits	1. Large wooded area 2. Water area 3. Picnic areas 4. Boating and winter sports 5. Bicycle paths 6. Comfort stations 7. Refreshment facilities
Reservation	1000 acres or more	For use by all ages	Located outside city	1. Camping and picnic areas 2. Hiking area 3. Water sports area 4. Refreshment facilities and comfort stations
Special recreation areas	Size depends upon activities included	For teen-age groups and adults primarily	Located at various places within city	1. Tennis, handball, platform tennis courts, skeet shooting and archery ranges, ice skating, sledding and skiing areas, etc. 2. Fishing, boating and water skiing areas, etc.
Athletic fields	Size depends upon sport	Teen-age and adult groups primarily	Centrally located	1. Baseball 2. Football 3. Track and field 4. Etc.
Pools	Size depends upon use	All age groups	Preferably smaller pools in several locations with one or two larger olympic size pools available in widely separated geographic areas	1. Separate wading and instructional pool for young children 2. Olympic size pools with diving boards and separate diving well area with boards

help to stimulate and maintain interest among all age groups. Timeliness is good program planning. Also important is a sense of timing. The wise leader is one who recognizes that some events are more successful when planned on a short-term basis: for example, a model airplane club; others, such as a tennis class for beginners, are more successful when carried on for several weeks. The type of activity, coupled with the skill required to master it, is a major determining factor in all program planning.

SIZE OF THE GROUP

Although it always impressive to have a large number of people taking part in any recreational activity, what *happens* to each individual within the group is vastly more important than how large the group is. Many activities are best for not more than ten people, especially if it is a hobby club or a class of beginners in, for example, golf or swimming for handicapped children.

The size of the group should also determine how it can be serviced best. A baseball or bowling league may be organized on a city-wide basis. Some large recreation departments, such as the one in Dallas, Texas, have one physical educator whose primary job is to set up all league and tournament play. Since many sports bring greater satisfaction to individual players when they are part of a team competing in a regular league and have scheduled times to play and practice, the development of league play is highly recommended.

THE SCOPE OF THE PROGRAM

In its totality, a well-balanced recreation program will consist of:

Creative-cultural activities
Social activities
Camping and outing activities
Physical activities including sports and games
Service activities
Special events

Under each of these separate parts are often found the following items:

Creative-Cultural Activities

Arts and crafts
  Basket making
  Bead craft
  Block printing
  Bookbinding
  Cabinet making
  Carving
  Ceramics
  Costume design
  Drawing
  Dyeing and coloring
  Embroidery
  Etching
  Finger painting
  Knitting
  Leather work

Metal craft
Model airplanes
Painting
Paper folding
Photography
Pottery
Reed and raffia
Rug making
Sand painting
Sculpture
Sketching
Tincraft
Toy making
Weaving
Wood carving
Collecting
  Antiques
  Books
  Buttons
  Coins
  Dolls
  Furniture
  Glassware
  Guns
  Indian craft
  Paintings
  Ships
  Stamps
Dancing
  Acrobatic
  Ballet
  Creative dance for children
  Clog
  Ethnic (folk) dance
  Jazz dance
  Modern dance
  Social or ballroom dance
  Tap and clog dance
Drama
  Charades
  Festivals
  Impersonations
  Informal dramatics
  Making scenery

Marionettes
Mask making
Masquerades
Minstrel shows
Movies
One-act plays
Pageants
Pantomimes
Parades
Play reading
Punch and Judy shows
Puppetry
Stage craft
Story plays
Storytelling
Three-act plays
Vaudeville acts
Mental
  Book clubs
  Debates
  Discussion groups
  Forums
  Guessing games
  Lectures
  Mental games
  Public speaking
  Puzzles
  Reading
  Study groups
  Television watching
  Tricks
Musical
  Bands
  Barber shop quartets
  Chamber music ensembles
  Community singing
  Glee clubs
  Jazz bands
  Instrumental instruction
  Orchestras
  Operetta companies
  Rhythm bands
  Rock-and-roll groups
  Symphony orchestras

Social Activities
Banquets
Basket suppers
Beach parties
Card games
  Bridge
  Canasta
  Hearts
  Pinochle
  Poker
Carnivals
Conversation

Dancing
  Folk
  Social
  Square
Dinners
Family reunions
Parties
  Birthday
  Block
  Costume
  Seasonal

Pencil and paper games
Potluck suppers
Scavenger hunts
Treasure hunts
Talent shows
Table games
  Anagrams
  Caroms
  Checkers
  Chess
Crokinole
Dominoes
Monopoly
Parchesi
Pick up sticks
Picnicking
Ping Pong
Treasure hunts
Visiting

Camping and Outing Activities

Bait and fly casting
Barbecues
Boating
Camping
Canoeing
Corn roasts
Clambakes
Crafts from native
  materials
Fish fries
Gardening
Hiking
Horseback riding
Hostelling
Making nature trails
Mountain climbing
Nature study
  Astronomy
  Bee culture
  Birdhouse building
  Caring for pets
Collecting
  Animals
  Birds
  Bugs
  Flowers
  Minerals
  Mosses
  Rocks
  Snakes
  Trees
Rifle shooting
Skeet shooting
Skiing
Snowshoeing
Snow tracking
Tobogganing
Trap shooting
Trapping
Walking
Wiener roasts
Visiting zoos

Physical Activities

Archery
Badminton
Baseball
Bicycling
Body conditioning, physical
  fitness, weight and figure
  control activities
Box hockey
Boxing
Bowling
Croquet
Darts
Deck tennis
Diving
Fencing
Field hockey
Fishing
Football
Golf
Handball
Horseshoes
Horseback riding
Ice skating
Jacks
Judo or karate
Kite flying
Lacrosse
Mass games
Mountain climbing
Ping pong
Raquetball
Roller skating
Rope skipping
Rope spinning
Scuba diving
Shinny
Shuffleboard
Sky diving
Skiing, water and snow
Soccer
Softball
Speedball
Squash
Stunts
Tennis
Track and field
Tumbling
Volleyball
Wading
Water ballet
Water polo
Weight lifting
Wrestling

Program Scheduling

Most community recreation and other recreational programs are broken down into the four seasons (winter, spring, summer, and fall) for scheduling purposes. What events to schedule in or outdoors, as well as available facilities and leaders, must also be taken into consideration. Usually most indoor programs are scheduled during the winter months, whereas during the fall and spring seasons events are scheduled fairly equally in or outdoors. In the summer, however, most of the events are scheduled to be held outside. In addition, more activities are included in the program in order to serve children free from school as well as many adults on vacation.

TYPES OF SCHEDULING AND PLANNING PITFALLS

After a seasonal program plan is drawn up, this usually is broken down into more workable schedules. These may include weekly programs which are often further broken down into daily programs wherein activities are scheduled hourly. Scheduling activities by age groups is also feasible.

A Sample Schedule of Activities By Age Groups

3–5 Year Olds
Arts & crafts
Pre-school classes
Dance classes
Tumbling
Special activities

6–9 Year Olds
After-school program
Ballet
Ceramics
Cooking
Drama
Football ladder
Judo
Tap dance
Tennis
Tumbling

10–12 Year Olds
Abstract drawing
Ballet
Cartooning
Ceramics
Cooking
Dodgeball
Drama
Football ladder
Judo
Leathercrafts
Modern dance

Tap dance
Tennis
Tumbling

13–15 Year Olds
Abstract drawing
Ballet
Ceramics
Dodgeball
Drama
Football ladder
Judo
Karate
Leathercrafts
Modern dance
Tennis
Tumbling
Youth advisory council

16–18 Year Olds
Abstract drawing
Bridge
Cartooning & drawing
Dodgeball
Fencing
Judo
Karate
Leathercrafts
Tennis
Youth advisory council

Young Adults
- Ballet (ladies)
- Basketball (men)
- Belly dancing (ladies)
- Book review club
- Bridge
- Ceramics
- Community advisory council
- Fencing
- Flag football (men)
- Indoor soccer (men)
- Karate
- Landscaping
- Leathercrafts
- Needlecrafts
- Oil painting
- Round dance
- Slimnastics (ladies)
- Tap dance (ladies)
- Tennis clinics
- Tennis leagues
- Tile painting
- Volleyball

Senior Citizens
- Reading club
- Community sing
- Square dance party
- Musical program—Record hits of yesterday
- Checker tournament
- Bird walk

Recreation programs should be planned for all people of all age groups. Often in most communities the 10–12 year group is over serviced and have too many recreational outlets to the detriment of older citizens as well as young married couples. Other pitfalls to avoid in programming planning are:

1. Establishing a summer recreation program for children only as a means of "keeping them busy and out of trouble," thus not planning programs for all groups in the community.
2. Repeating the same type of program offerings too often and failing to introduce new ones periodically.
3. Failure to provide equal time for girls and women to use facilities for sports and games or other activities.
4. Judging the success of the inclusion of any activity in the program solely on the basis of the number of participants rather than on the values received by those who do take part in it.
5. Organizing programs by age groups only, thus eliminating the possibilities of youth to participate in activities with senior citizens or family groups to enjoy doing activities at the recreation center together.

TRENDS IN PROGRAM PLANNING

Recreation programs throughout the nation are sprucing up with a bright, "new look." Greater emphasis is now being placed upon finding ways to attract participants to the many events planned for them at community recreation centers, playgrounds, in industry and elsewhere. Innovative program designers are increasingly:

1. *Using mobile materials and portable facilities.* These are transported in brilliantly colored buses, wagons drawn by decorated horses, and even by helicopters. Often these moving storehouses of fun are in the form of nature museums, zoos, or

science fairs, portable swimming pools, bookmobiles, or art displays.

2. *Providing day and overnight camping for people of all ages, including senior citizens.* In such programs ecology is playing an increasingly important role, and greater effort is being made to help those living in cities to discover nature firsthand in the country.

3. *Increasing program offerings for the aged.* More cities and communities now have senior citizens drop-in centers than ever before. Churches as well as nursing homes are also doing much more than ever before to add a wider variety of cultural and creative activities in existing programs, and a greater effort is being made through these programs to help the aged add depth and richness to life through the discovery of many new and exciting interests. Likewise, colleges and universities are increasing the number of courses in their evening classes through their schools of continuing education in order to attract older people to discover again the joy of learning.

4. *More schools are being opened for community recreation purposes.* Increasingly taxpayers are demanding that school building use be expanded in order that all people receive the most benefit from the invested public funds which have gone into the building of schools. Consequently, many schools are now opening their doors to the general public in each community for recreational as well as educational purposes. In such schools community-school swimming, tennis, and physical fitness programs are especially popular.

5. *The construction of more facilities and areas for independent individual, family, or small group use.* These include nature, hiking, and bicycling trails, lighted play areas and courts which people use in their free time. Lighted public tennis courts are now being used in some communities from dark to dawn, as well as from sunlight to sunset.

The Summer Playground Program

The summer neighborhood playground program should consist of a variety of activities for all age groups. These activities might well include the following broad classifications:

Nature crafts and nature study	Arts and crafts
Musical activities	Athletic games and sports
Square, folk, and creative dance	Story telling
Dramatics	Campcraft activities including
Quiet table games	cookouts
Pageants	Puppetry—stagecraft
Interplayground activities	Special events
Day camping	Pet shows

Family night programs
Playground circus
Summer learn-to-swim programs
Talent shows
Hobby interest groups
Instruction by specialists in the
    areas of hobbies, nature, sports,
    camping, astronomy, etc.

Animal obedience classes
Picnics—family and
    neighborhood
Community sings
Club activities
Excursions
Small tots activities
Swimming, diving, and other
    aquatic activities

Suggested age groupings are:

Pre-schoolers—3–6 years
6–9 year old youth
10–12 year old youth
12–14 year old youth
High school students
Adults
Senior citizens

Opportunities should be provided, however, for mixed age groups to do some activities together, for youth and adults have much to learn from each other. These activities might well include hobby interest groups, or such classes as in woodcarving, nature crafts, or archery, etc.

An ideal summer playground program provides a wide variety of activities for people of all ages that are fun and challenging to do. Youth as well as adults should have many opportunities for service as volunteer assistants in the program.

The three card files, "Find Your Own Summer Thing," "Kool Summer Fun," and "Getting Together is the Thing," available from the National Recreation and Park Association, Arlington, Virginia are packed full of new and exciting summer fun activities. Each file contains over 100 activities and covers a wide variety of program materials.

The Playground

Playground space should be planned so that there is opportunity for the greatest number to play safely at one time. At least five acres should be provided for children. A minimum of 100 square feet per pupil should be an absolute requirement. Separate areas should be set off for the youngest group for safety purposes, and this group should be assigned the space that is the furthest away from the oldest, most active group. Space should be planned for use by as many age groups as possible. For example, baseball diamonds may be used for kickball and for softball for older youth at different periods of the day. The area should also be enclosed by a metal fence.

Playground surfacing is usually of dust-treated dirt, hard cement, black top, grass turf, or sawdust combined with asphalt. Regardless of which type is used, the area should be a safe and healthful one for children's play. It should be well planned so that it can be adequately and easily supervised, fenced, well shrubbed and shaded. The youngest children should be assigned permanent play areas near the shaded side of the building where they will be well protected and safe at all times. Backstop fences for softball and enclosed swing and apparatus areas are highly recommended. Space should be provided for sandbox and creative play for the younger children. The entire playground area should be attractive, clean, and safe. It should look like and be a place for great adventures!

THE ADVENTURE PLAYGROUND

The old-fashioned playground is outmoded. The trend is to provide facilities which have creative possibilities and to provide equipment which can have many uses, such as giant Lincoln logs, rocket ships, climbable towers, old discarded boats, climbing nets, and "pretend" ships. Children need things to move, mold, and manipulate, as well as lots of tiny things they can use to build bigger ones that can easily be moved from place to place. One of the most popular newer pieces of equipment is the "stack sack," which is many cotton bags filled with dry cement.[3] The children stack them any way they like and then douse them with water. When hardened, these new child-created forms bring them much challenge and delight. Old car tires, wheels, metal poles, and other discarded objects thrill children far more than standardized equipment ever could, and can be used to help develop their own creative efforts for their after-school play.

Sixteen fourth and fifth grade children in the Quaker Ridge School of Scarsdale, New York, recently formed a Playground Design Club. From their models, a Space Platform resulted which is an 8' × 12' redwood platform, 8 feet from the ground, with bright red, yellow, and blue railings.[4] It is the most popular object on the school's playground and could be a model for a playground in any community.

As one authority on school playgrounds has said, "We really haven't taken full advantage of the only thing children offer us freely—their desire to play."[5] It is true that as children we had many more chances to create our own fun, to run at will, make treehouses, or to wander and explore. Consequently, playground designers of today try to put back into the child's environment such things as cages, nets, ropes, trees, and walls to climb; dirt hills and sandboxes; tunnels and crawl barrels; rockers; bar rollers and barrels; tire walks and jump pits; tire, boat, and rocket swings; all kinds of slides of varying heights: old cars; hills, flowers, and trees to look at; water to wade and even play in; and a lighted school play area for night use for children supervised by parents, if need be. In such play areas, vandalism has been a very minor problem in contrast to that found in traditional areas. These adventure playgrounds are loved by children and they flock to them. Like any good playground, the users can constantly rearrange it. Play to these children is not just physical activity; it is a rich learning experience! It influences the mind, emotions, and body of the child as he partakes in a learning adventure called play.

Outdoor play equipment should be chosen carefully from the viewpoint of safety and valued use. Jungle gyms and horizontal hanging bars should be provided which hang 36 inches from the ground for the youngest children and up to 54 inches for those who are older. Swings with canvas seats from 10 to 12 inches high, slides, monkey rings, parallel bars and merry-go-rounds are highly recommended. Some physical educators believe that, because seesaws do very little to develop physical fitness or coordination, they are unwise investments of public funds.

Other than the above-mentioned items, the following permanent playground facilities should be included:

Apparatus
Wood or pipe climbing apparatus.
Horizontal ladders.
Low graded to high circular traveling ring.
Hemp or Manila climbing ropes suspended from poles, or securely fastened to the building or trees.
Heavy rope giant stride.
Swings, frame 12' high in sets of six.
Slides, 8' high, approximately 16' long.
Balance beams of various heights from the ground.
Traveling rings.
Tether ball poles.
Horseshoe stakes.
Bicycle racks.
Automobile tires, suspended on ropes.
Several outdoor bulletin boards.
Suspended Manila climbing ropes.
Vertical climbing poles.

Play Equipment for Younger Children
Sandboxes and tools.
Wide and narrow horizontal planks and boards several inches off the ground for running and balancing.
Barrels, kegs, and hoops for rolling.
Inclined boards for running up and sliding down on.
Stairs built with varied step heights to climb up and over and jump from.
Wheelbarrows.
Small tables and work benches.
Large wooden boxes and cartons.
Telephone poles laid flat on the ground for climbing on and jumping from, and others holed securely in the ground for vertical climbing.

Numerous tires and wheels of varying sizes for rolling with hands
   or a crossed T-shaped board.
Pipe tunnels of reinforced concrete sewer pipe, arranged in units of
   three, set at different angles three feet apart.
A "Whatnot," or small platform of 9 × 6 feet, surrounded on three
   sides by a low wall and reached on the fourth open side by steps.
Tables and benches.
As many box hockey sets as feasible.

Serious consideration should be given to the following factors
regarding playground facilities and their use: location, arrangement for
the protection of all children but especially the youngest ones, regular
safety inspection forms and procedures, fencing and marking hazardous
zones, care of the ground underneath apparatus, instruction in its
correct use, and necessary safety rules.

Courts and playing fields laid north and south should be designated as
permanent play areas and marked with paint or whitewash. Dry slaked
lime or tennis tape markers can be used on turf or dirt areas. Fixed posts
are superior to moveable standards for paddle-type games. Iron nets are
better and cheaper in the long run than oil-treated ones, substituted
wire fencing, or ropes. Track and field facilities should be laid out
according to the recommendations made at the National Facilities
Conference sponsored by the Athletic Institute.[6]

Multiple purpose courts of cement or macadam should be laid and
marked on all permanent play areas. A tennis court can also be used for
paddle tennis, volleyball, badminton, shuffleboard, basket shooting,
hopscotch, ice and roller skating. Electric outlets, if provided, will make
it usable for dancing or showing films at night. Lighted courts and play
areas increase participation to such an extent that they are wonderfully
inexpensive investments.[7]

Standard game areas that should be established are:

Outdoor badminton courts	Softball and baseball diamonds
Basketball courts	Speedball court
Croquet courts	Speed-a-way fields
Handball courts	Tennis courts
Horseshoe pits	Touch football field
Shuffleboard courts	Volleyball court
Soccer fields	Paddle tennis courts
Lawn bowling courts	

Outdoor equipment, other than balls of varying size, includes:

Aerial darts	Individual and long jump rope sets
Badminton sets	Jumping standards and crossbar
Basketball or Goal Hi standards	Lawn bowling sets
Bat-O-Net sets	Marbles
Box hockey sets	Putting game sets
Croquet sets	Shuffleboard sets
Deck tennis rings	Tennis equipment
Horseshoe sets	Tether ball sets
Hurdles	

Activities for the playground should add to the pleasure of the moment and enrich the recreational life of the child. By teaching obedience to rules and regulations, games help teach children to get along with others. Activities should be selected that are suitable to sex, playing space, clothing and weather, as well as age level.

Some suggestions to assure proper conduct on the playground are to:

1. Provide a varied program appealing to all.
2. Have a few concise rules and enforce them.
3. Make frequent tours of the playground with pupils, looking for hazards and having the children paint these hazards bright yellow.
4. Always maintain a spirit of fairness and justice.
5. Foster a spirit of self-government by giving children a share in the making of conduct rules on the playground, and have them help supervise and officiate at activities.
6. Use game rotation plans so that all get equal use of the best facilities and equipment.

SUPPLIES AND EQUIPMENT NEEDED

The materials listed below are minimum essentials needed to conduct an adequate program for children. The amount and variety to be purchased will be dependent upon class size. Rubber balls are cheaper than leather ones and may prove to be just as serviceable.

Supplies

Balls:
  Basketball, official
  Basketball, rubber
  Football, official
  Football, rubber
  Indoor, 12"
  Rubber, 5", 6", 8", 10"
  Soccer, official
  Soccer, rubber
  Volley, official
  Volley, rubber
Baseball gloves, balls, bats,
  protective equipment
Beanbags, 6 × 6, and targets
Broomsticks of various lengths
Chalk

Deck tennis rings
Five-pin bowling sets
Hoops
Hula hoop rings
Indian clubs
Jump-off boxes
Jump ropes, 3/8" sashcord
  Individual, 6', 7', 8'
  Long, 12', 15', 20', 25'
Phonograph needles
Phonograph records
Shuffleboard sets
Squad cards
Tape measure, 50'
Tempera paint

Equipment

Balance beams of varying height
  from the floor
Ball inflator
Bases

Bats
Bicycle racks
Blackboard, portable and
  permanent

Bulletin board
Cabinet, steel
Canvas bags in which to
    carry balls
Chinning bars
Equipment box
Flying and stationary rings
Game nets
Hurdles, 12″, 15″, 18″, 20″
Jump and vault standards
Jungle gym
Junior jump standards
Landing nets
Lime and markers
Low parallel bars
Mats, 33″×60″, 3′×5′, 4′×6′
Microphone and speaker system
Net standards
Percussion instruments
Portable phonograph
Recreational games (checkers,
    horseshoes etc.)
Slides
Stall bars, vertical and
    horizontal bars
Stop watch
Storage cabinets or lockers
Surplus parachutes
Swim fins, unsinkable boards,
    hair dryers
Swings
Table hockey
Targets
Teeter boards
Tin can walkers
Traveling rings, vaulting buck and
    horse, Swedish box, springboard,
    parallel bars, climbing stairs
Wooden stilts of varying heights
Whistles, timers

All equipment should be carefully selected, kept, and repaired. The children can aid in oiling balls, repairing nets, and sewing ball rips. Sporting goods companies can usually provide better equipment for money spent than local department stores.

Creative Ideas in Programming

Albert Einstein once wrote that he considered ingenuity to be greater than knowledge. Certainly it is true that the most successful leaders in any recreation program are highly creative. They can see program possibilities and needed materials for carrying them out in discarded junk, waste products made of paper, wood, or wires, and even discarded automobile tires. Some are smart enough to capitalize upon the cultural backgrounds of certain communities or subgroups within them. The Spanish Cultural Night, held yearly in Albuquerque, New Mexico, grew out of someone's idea. The Tulip Festival, sponsored jointly by the Atlanta Recreation Department and the Atlanta Tulip Study Club, annually includes over 600 folk dancers dressed in Dutch patterned costumes who add color and rhythm to a program in which a beauty queen and her court are honored. Thousands of people in Atlanta enjoy watching this entertaining program. Such city-wide programs can lead to increased participation in other program activities sponsored by the community recreation department and foster good publicity and public relations.

Community service activities help people feel that they *do* have something of value to give to others. Many youth-serving organizations, such as the Camp Fire Girls or YMCA groups, receive assistance from volunteer parents, who help set up summer camps. Such worthwhile activities yield far more return than just money saving, for they help others gain a feeling for and identification with such places as camps, recreation centers, and sandlot play areas for children in a low-cost housing area.

Suggested similar community service projects include:

> Serving in fund-raising campaigns for health organizations or the Community Chest.
>
> Transporting handicapped people to recreation centers or the ill to hospitals.
>
> Taking children from depressed areas to visit such places as an airport, a local bakery, art museum, university, library, etc.
>
> Volunteering for leadership work in hospital recreation or in a local community center and being a scoutmaster or den mother or sharing recreation with shut-ins on a person-to-person basis.
>
> Serving on a planning council or recreation board.
>
> Taking part in community beautifying projects, such as tree planting or landscaping.

Such suggested planned volunteer activities will provide outlets for those who enjoy working with people. However, it is recommended that the professional leader who sponsors such a program have several orientation meetings, in-service briefings, and a final evaluation period with all taking part in the program. The purpose of such a program, it should be stressed, is to help people learn *how* to help themselves and that the program is not to be merely entertainment or transportation. As in the Peace Corps, only qualified volunteer leaders should be used, and those who are to work directly with children, shut-ins, or handicapped must be carefully screened.

Suggested Readings

Butler, George: *Introduction to Community Recreation*, 4th ed., New York, McGraw-Hill Book Co., 1967
    Chapter 16, "Organizing and Conducting Recreation Activities," is suggested supplementary reading in conjunction with this chapter. These materials include guiding principles of program planning and conducting playground activities, indoor activities, the athletic program, and special community events.

Carlson, Reynold, Deppe, Theodore, and MacLean, Janet: *Recreation in American Life*. Belmont, Cal., Wadsworth Publishing Company, 1963
    Part IV, "The Recreation Program" in this fine book has many suggestions for organizing and conducting activities in each of the many areas of a well-planned program.

Hjelte, George and Shivers, Jay: *Public Administration of Recreation Services*. Philadelphia, Lea & Febiger, 1974
    Since many tax-supported recreation departments are now conducting community recreation programs in schools and plants, the authors present in this chapter arguments for and against the use of school-operated recreational services.

Kraus, Richard and Curtis, Joseph: *Creative Administration in Recreation and Parks*. St. Louis, C.V. Mosby Co., 1973

Chapter 6, "The Recreation Program," is concerned with the many ways possible for developing a wide variety of recreational programs for all ages. The section in the chapter, "Innovative Activities and Trends," will give the reader insight into the latest trends nationwide for planning city-wide community recreation programs for all the people within the community.

Shipp, Robert: "Expanding Program Services," *Parks and Recreation*, Vol. III (November, 1968)

The author discusses in this article various helpful ways for expanding recreation programs through the fuller utilization of all community resources.

Staffo, Donald: "A Community Recreation Program," *Journal of Health, Physical Education and Recreation*, Vol. II (August, 1967)

Readers of this article will discover a fresh new approach to recreational program planning and content.

References

1. Williams, Jesse Feiring: *The Principles of Physical Education*, 8th ed. Philadelphia, W. B. Saunders Company, 1964, p. 24.
2. Murphy, James, et al.: *Leisure Service Delivery System*. Philadelphia, Lea & Febiger, 1973, p. 93.
3. Sanders, J.: "Swings and Sandboxes Are Out of Style." *Dallas Morning News*, March 16, 1972.
4. Holter, P.: "Playground Design Club." *The Instructor Magazine*, March 1972, p. 76.
5. Pennington, G.: "Slide Down The Cellar Door—The New Approach To Playgrounds." *The Instructor*, March 1972, pp. 74–76.
6. Athletic Institute: *A Guide for Planning Facilities for Athletics, Recreation, and Physical and Health Education*. Revised ed. Chicago, Illinois, 1970.
7. Vannier, M. and Fait, H.: *Teaching Physical Education in Secondary Schools*. 4th ed. Philadelphia, W. B. Saunders Co., 1975, p. 123.

Music

I will sing the song of companionship.
Walt Whitman

Music is a universal language unequaled in its communicative potency. Even primitive man knew of its power to stir men's hearts and satisfy his need for rhythm and beauty in life. As a recreation activity, a music program should receive major emphasis and provide people with an opportunity to listen, play, sing, or create. Combined with other activities such as synchronized swimming and roller or figure ice skating, it adds to enjoyment and completeness. Ideally, the program should be broad in scope, ranging from single rhythmic singing games to playing in a symphony orchestra. A recent study conducted by the National Recreation Association disclosed that there are 165 different types of program possibilities in the area of music alone, from accordion bands to variety talent shows.[1]

Those in charge of the music program should help people develop a keener, more knowledgeable appreciation of music at its best and gain a lifelong interest in music as a source of entertainment and artistic satisfaction. The leader, concerned with giving music a major role in a program, should be aware of its vast scope, secure needed professional and volunteer specialized assistants, provide necessary funds from the overall budget, and give direction to its growth in importance in the lives of people and of the community. Music is an art form. In our materialistic society it can bring, when fully shared and promoted, quality and beauty to the lives of many.

It is the leader's task to:

1. Provide opportunities for all ages and all levels of musical taste to experience the pleasure of listening to music through such media as recordings, radio, television sets, concerts, and recitals.
2. Encourage community singing in both small and large groups and stimulate the organization of all kinds of choral groups.
3. Sponsor the organization of instrumental ensembles through

provision of supervisory leadership and the necessary facilities, such as rooms for rehearsals and auditoriums for concerts.

4. Furnish instruction for those individuals who wish to learn to play an instrument or to sing and who have had no such opportunity previously.
5. Build a file of talented musicians in the community and encourage them to offer their services on programs of a civic service nature.
6. Help mobilize the musical resources of the community both human and physical.
7. Work harmoniously with other agencies in a common effort to conduct such city-wide activities as music festivals, operas, concerts, and show-wagon projects.[2]

The complete music program should include:

Singing Groups—A capella choirs, choruses, informal community sings, glee clubs, singing games, other.

Instrumental Groups—Rhythm bands, marching bands, chamber music groups, groups making and playing homemade instruments, special instrumental groups (ukulele, violin, saxophone, etc.), symphony orchestras, other.

Special Events—Band concerts, pageants, musical festivals, old fiddler's contests, square dance caller's contests, operas, operettas, original song contests, other.

Cultural Groups—Music appreciation clubs, study groups, musical composition groups, other.

Program Activities

Community singing	Harmonica playing
Community choruses	Easter music
Community concerts and recitals	Christmas music
Public school music	Social music activities
Glee clubs	Home music activities
Orchestras and bands	Community opera
Musical competition	Congregational singing
Vocal	Music in community celebrations
Instrumental	and patriotic holidays
Music festivals	Music in theatres
Toy symphonies	Music memory contests
Ukulele playing	Music weeks
	Oratories

Song Leading

One of the quickest ways to build group unity and raise spirits high is community singing. The leader should direct the group by counting out the tempo with his hands using the following patterns:

Two Beats (2/4 time).

Songs in this tempo include:
  Dixie
  Yankee Doodle
  Oh Suzanna
  I Want to Be Ready
  O Give Thanks
  Camptown Races.

Three Beats (3/4 or waltz time).

Songs in this tempo include:
  Let Me Call You Sweetheart
  The Tennessee Waltz
  Juanita
  The Blue Danube
  I Ride an Old Paint
  The Streets of Laredo.

Four Beats (4/4 time).

Songs in this tempo include:
  America, The Beautiful
  Go Down Moses
  The Twelve Days of Christmas
  Dear Lord and Father of Mankind
  Alouette
  Waltzing Matilda.

One or both hands may be used for directing. Some find it easier to count out the tempo with the right hand and to use the left one to control volume or draw in other singers at a given time. Others prefer to use both hands to count out the beat. Skill in doing either can be developed through practice objectively evaluated. The group can be taught to lead, too, by having everyone direct and sing while sitting in front of the director. Volunteers often enjoy taking turns leading the group.

Techniques insuring success are:

1. Start with a song the group knows and likes to sing.
2. Pitch the tune clearly in a distinct, steady tone. Start the song with the sharp command, "Sing," or with a decisive hand movement down.
3. Sing with the group.
4. Praise the crowd for having sung a song well. Sing another favored familiar one.
5. Introduce new songs gradually. Be sure you know them before trying to share them with others.

6. Announce each new song by telling a few brief well chosen facts about it. Explain that "She'll Be Coming 'Round the Mountain" was once a work song chanted by the men who laid the first railroad ties during the frontier days. Or tell that "Shenandoah" and "The Erie Canal" were originally sung by farmers as they poled their boats up and down our eastern waterways long before the Civil War.
7. Use piano, banjo, ukulele, guitar, accordion, or harmonica accompaniment. If you cannot play any of these instruments, teach yourself how to; instruction books are inexpensive and easily understood.
8. Be on the lookout for outstanding voices. Bring them in for certain verses or the chorus to add variety.
9. If you are to direct the singing at a banquet ask to be seated at the guest's table near the piano. Use only your designated time and include songs known to the majority present.
10. End with a favored familiar song. Close while group spirit is high. It is better to stop with a climactic third song than with a fifth one after spirit has dropped.

Variety adds to program interest. Have one group whistle while the rest sing, or have the women hum while the men sing. Try combining two familiar tunes such as "Solomon Levi" with "The Spanish Cavalier," "Tipperary" with "Pack Up Your Troubles," "Keep the Home Fires Burning" with "There's a Long, Long Trail," or "Humoresque" with "Sewanee River."

It is best to select a wide variety of songs. One round, patriotic, folk, and popular song would be superior to four popular ones. Above all, choose songs to fit the occasion. For example, "Peace, I Ask of Thee, Oh River," or "Witchcraft" would be a wiser choice for an inspirational campfire than "Go Tell It on the Mountain" or "Under the Spreading Chestnut Tree."

If the leader does not know how to play any musical accompaniment, the group will enjoy furnishing its own. Give everyone a small folded piece of wax paper. Have each fit his own comb in it and hum the tune. Divide the group by having half sing while the rest play, and vice versa. "Twinkle, Twinkle, Little Star" is an easy one to do for the initial attempt and will give all the desired feeling of success.

Increased group enthusiasm can be perked up if the leader, or someone in the group, can play an accompanying musical instrument such as an autoharp, uke, accordion, piano, or guitar. Playing can easily be learned singly or in groups. Since most songs for group singing are based upon a few, simple basic chords, once these are mastered each song leader could have an assisting helper of great value.

SONGS FOR ALL OCCASIONS

Pocket size song books add much to group singing. They are superior to mimeographed sheets or sheer memory and are inexpensive since they can be used many times. Four superior booklets available for a nominal fee are:

Sing It Again (SIT)[1]
Service Department
Methodist Church
810 Broadway
Nashville, Tennessee. Price 20¢.

Camp Songs 'n' Things (CS)[1]
1950 Addison Street
Nashville, Tennessee. Price 25¢.

Lift Every Voice (LIV)[1]
Service Department
Box 871
Nashville, Tennessee. Price 20¢.

Joyful Singing (JS)*
Cooperative Recreation Service
Delaware, Ohio. Price 50¢.

*These initials refer to the booklets in which the words and music of following listed titles are found.

Each booklet is a jewel. All can be purchased for less in quantity orders.

Listed below are songs that groups throughout the country will greatly enjoy sharing together:

Type	*Source*	*Page number*
Action		
Little Tommy Tinker	CS	50
One Finger, One Thumb, Keep Moving	CS	44
Under the Spreading Chestnut Tree	CS	42
Rounds		
Alouette	JS	7
Man's Life's a Vapor	CS	54
Kookaburra	SIT	3
Come Follow, Follow	JS	33
Oh, How Lovely Is the Evening	CS	103
Chairs to Mend	CS	5

Puffer Billie	CS	49
Hey Ho! Nobody Home	LIV	72
Sweetly Sings the Donkey	CS	39
Whipperwill	SIT	4
To Ope Their Trunks	CS	67
Grasshoppers Three	JS	19
We're On the Upward Trail	CS	63
White Coral Bells	CS	50

Folk Songs

The Keeper (English)	SIT	19
Walking at Night (Czech)	SIT	34
Twelve Days of Christmas (English)	LIV	44
The Alpine Song (Swiss)	JS	5
Sweet Potatoes (Creole)	SIT	18
Song of the Volga Boatman (Russian)	SIT	32
Marianina (Italian)	CS	66
Marching to Pretoria (South African)	LIV	47
Oh, Dear What Can the Matter Be? (English)	SIT	22
Zum Galli Galli (African)	JS	44
Cielito Lindo (Mexican)	JS	3
Waltzing Matilda (Australian)	SIT	26
The Ash Grove (Welsh)	JS	6
All Through the Night (Welsh)	SIT	31
Above a Plain (Czech)	LIV	62
Weggis Song (Swiss)	SIT	38
The Riddle Song (Kentucky mountains)	LIV	90

Blessings

Be Present at Our Table, Lord	CS	111
God Has Created a New Day	CS	107
O Give Thanks	LIV	64
Round of Thanks	JS	80
Morning Has Come	CS	111
For Health and Strength	CS	113
Praise for Bread	LIV	64

Camp and Campfire

The Far Northland	CS	59
Cowboy Lullaby	JS	13
Ol' Texas	SIT	2
Good News	LIV	33
The Call of the Fire	CS	104
Dying Cowboy	CS	110
Down in the Valley	CS	98

Camp Hymns	CS	110
White Wings	SIT	35
Home on the Range	CS	72
Walking at Night	CS	67
Witchcraft	CS	87
Oh Lord, I Want Two Wings	SIT	35
When the Moon Plays Peek-A-Boo	CS	97
Each Campfire Lights Anew	CS	53
Canoe Song	JS	18
Sarasponda	SIT	28
Now the Day Is Over	LIV	15

Spirituals

Lord, Make Me Holy	SIT	11
Dese Bones Gwine Rise Again	CN	18
Go Down Moses	CN	12
I Want to Be Ready	JS	48
Gwine to Lay My Burden Down	CN	11
Lonesome Valley	JS	63
You Can Dig My Grave with a Silver Spade	CN	17
I Know the Lord	LIV	32
I Got a Robe	JS	52

Excellent materials can also be found in:

> *Brownie Songs* (No. 23–386)
> *Girl Scout Song Book* (No. 20–191)
> *Sing High, Sing Low* (No. 23–468)
> *Sing Together* (No. 20–190)
> *The Ditty Bag* (No. 23–460)
> *The Saucey Sailor* (No. 23–414)
> *We Sing* (No. 23–464)

The above booklets may be obtained from the Service Department, Girl Scouts, New York, N. Y.

Other excellent sources of song materials are the following:

> *Music and Bugling* (No. 3336)
> Service Department
> Boy Scouts of America
> New York, N. Y.

> *The Golden Song Book*
> Simon and Schuster, Inc.
> 630 Fifth Avenue
> New York, N. Y. 10020

The American Songbag (Carl Sandburg)
Harcourt, Brace and Co.
383 Madison Avenue
New York, N. Y. 10017

Sing and Be Happy
Mills Music Company
1619 Broadway
New York, N. Y.

Community Songs
National Recreation Association
315 Fourth Avenue
New York, N. Y. 10010

Everybody Sing Book
Paull-Pioneer Music Company
1657 Broadway
New York, N. Y.

Cultural Clubs

Music appreciation clubs, composition classes, and study groups have much to contribute to a well rounded recreation program. Each club should be open to all ages. Here an 18-year-old boy can share more than just a deep appreciation for and interest in music with an old timer. If possible these clubs should have special rooms for meetings. A collection of good records, books, phonograph, radio, and television set will add richness to the activity. Special broadcasts of regularly scheduled programs such as the New York Philharmonic Symphony Orchestra's Sunday concerts will draw the club listeners together and provide an opportunity for fellowship.

Musical taste can be developed. The leader, after gathering interested participants, can best retain and nurture their interest by including lighter music at the initial meetings. Individual members should be encouraged to bring and share their own records with others. Every community has trained musicians or teachers who usually are willing to be in charge of an occasional program, if called upon.

Suggested recordings that music appreciation groups will enjoy are:

Orchestral

Beethoven, *Concerto for Piano and Orchestra No. 1, in C,* Opus 15	DM-1036
Brahms, *Concerto for Violin and Orchestra in D*, Opus 17	DM-581
Chopin, *Concerto for Piano and Orchestra No. 1, in E Minor*, Opus 11	DM-458

Mozart, *Symphony No. 35, in D*	DM-125
Shubert, *Symphony No. 8, in B Minor*	DM-1039
Tchaikovsky, *Symphony No. 4, in F Minor*, Opus 36	DM-1318

Instrumental

Casals, *Adagis*	DM-1302
Heifetz, *Concerto for Violin and Orchestra*	DM-1267
Landowska, *Treasury of Harpsichord Music*	DM-1181
Menuhin, *Concerts for Violin and Orchestra*	DM-1023
Rachmaninoff, *Prelude in C Sharp Minor*, Opus 3, No. 2	1326
Rubenstein, *Rhapsody on a Theme of Paganini*	DM-1269

Vocal

John McCormack, *John McCormack Sings Again*	DM-1228
Marian Anderson, *Songs and Spirituals*	DM-986
Richard Crooks, *Stephen Foster Album*	DM-354
Robert Merrill, *Songs You Love*	DM-1150
Robert Shaw Chorale, *Dramatic Scenes from Verdi Operas*	DM-1245
Susan Reed, *Folk Songs and Ballads*	DM-1107

Rhythm Band

A rhythm band or toy orchestra brings joy to children aged 3 to 8 and, in some instances, to others up to the age of 12. It has proved to be challenging to adults. Even a leader untrained in music can develop a band successfully by:

1. Having the children who are interested in joining such a group clap out the rhythm of any phonograph record in 4/4 time. A good one to use for this would be "The Parade of the Wooden Soldiers."
2. Giving out each instrument (with some ceremony) to the child as he selects the one he wants to play.
3. Having the group play together. After they have seen and heard that all must stay together in order to produce music they will next respond to training.
4. Giving the group a note or signal that means all instruments are to be taken up, put down, or played in unison.
5. Having the group listen to the record again, next clap out its rhythm, and then play the number together as directed.
6. Developing orchestra leaders from the group by having the children choose the two best ones to be leaders for two weeks. This will aid in developing leadership traits and interest in most children.
7. Helping the group develop a finer musical appreciation by gradually letting them select their own pieces to play

Drums, tambourines, triangles, and cymbals are adequate instruments for a beginning group. To obtain the best effect, have twice as many drums and tambourines as cymbals and three times as many triangles as drums.

Other instruments which can be added are:

bells on sticks	wood blocks
silver bells	sand blocks
clogs	piano
tone blocks	xylophone
beaters	bird whistles
castanets	bagpipe
maracas	finger cymbals
	snare drums

The leader should build skill upon skill. Twirling broomsticks or batons, marching, dancing, or a combination of any of these can be gradually included by having half of the participants perform to the musical accompaniment of the rest. Some leaders believe that special uniforms and public recitals are interest builders among the children and adults. Others, who scorn exhibitionism of any children's activity, believe that what has been called a child's natural love for display is a superimposed adult idea. However, with or without special uniforms or fanfare, the children should be allowed to play occasionally for some special person, group or event.

Ideal records to use with a beginning group are:

Classical

Haydn, *Toy Symphony*	Victor 20215
Grieg, *Anitra's Dance*	Victor 20245
Grieg, *Norwegian Dance*	Victor 45-5016

Popular

Here Comes Santa Claus	Under the Double Eagle March
For He's a Jolly Good Fellow	Parade of the Wooden Soldiers
Rudolph, the Red Nosed Reindeer	Stars and Stripes Forever
The Lollipop Tree	The Black Hawk Waltz

A desirable seating arrangement for a large orchestra of forty children follows:

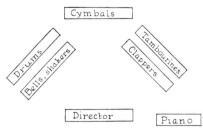

Homemade Musical Instruments

Homemade musical instruments are fun to make. There is real satisfaction received from playing a tambourine you have made for yourself. Scrap materials are abundant and the alert leader will be on the lookout for discarded junk from which useful articles can be created. Even very young children can make these musical instruments:

Drums

Obtain a large oil can from any gas station. Stretch large pieces of an old inner tube over either end and draw the ends together by heavy cord or a leather thong. Paint green. Make a beater from a heavy stick padded on one end and paint it red.

A drum can also be made out of a hollowed log, oatmeal box, wooden cheese box, or upturned wastebasket.

Tambourines

Sew two paper plates together front to front with yarn. Tie tiny bells around the sewed edge. Paint a bright color.

Tin pie plates can be used by nailing or pasting them together. Put tiny rocks or rice inside.

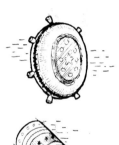

Wooden Shaker or Rattle

Partly fill a number two or larger can with rice, popcorn, or tiny rocks. Cut a hole in one end and insert a stick handle. Paint a bright color.

Sand Blocks

Cover two wooden blocks, blackboard eraser size, with emery paper. Rub together.

Wooden Sticks

Saw a broom or mop handle into six-inch lengths. Paint a bright color. Hit together.

Bottles or Glasses

Put varying amounts of water into glass tumblers or several kinds of bottles. Color the water in each a different color with tempera paint. Strike with a silver spoon.

Uke Box

Cut notches on the ends of a candy box parallel to the long sides and fit rubber bands into each notch. Paint the box a bright color. Strum with your fingers.

Roofing Disks

Loosely nail one or two roofing disks (available from any hardware store, three for five cents) to two tongue depressors glued together. Paint a bright color. Strike against the palm of one hand.

Bell Cake Rack

Weave brightly colored ribbons through a metal cake rack. Tie bells to the rack. Shake it.

Wash Board

Paint a metal scrub board in bright colors. Rub a spoon up and down on it.

Singing Games

Although singing games are primarily for young children, all ages seem to enjoy them. Perhaps this is because they provide a combination of ever-appealing drama with music and dance. The leader can best direct these games by:

1. Striving for wholehearted group enjoyment rather than skill perfection.

2. Showing the group how the whole game is danced before attempting to teach it to others.
3. Teaching all the words to the music as a whole.
4. Teaching the dance steps by having his back to the group and having them behind him in a straight line across the floor.
5. Calling out the steps as they are being done, for example, "Step, step, hop," and having the group join in. In this way each person tells himself what to do, then does it.
6. Praising the group and encouraging them to continue by saying, "That was fine," or in other similar ways.
7. Using phonograph records or the piano for accompaniment.
8. Starting each new meeting with the favorite singing game from the previous session.

Formations Used for Singing Games

Circle.
Boy, Girl, Boy, Girl, etc.

Double circle.
Boys inside.
Partners holding hands.

Double circle.
Boys inside.
Partners facing.

Two forming an arch.
Rest in a single line.
Move around behind one another.

Two lines.
Partners facing.

Square.
Boy has girl on his right.

Bingo (a mixer)   Record: Victor 45–6172

Words

A big black dog sat on a back porch
And Bingo was his name.
A big black dog sat on a back porch
And Bingo was his name.
B—I—N—G—O, B—I—N—G—O
B—I—N—G—O, B—I—N—G—O
And Bingo was his name.
B—I—N—G—O.

Action

All walk in a circle in partners, singing the first four lines: On B-I-N-G-O, grand right and left. On the final spelling, B-I-N-G-O, the boy lifts the new partner he meets high in the air. Each new couple continues marching around the circle.

A-Hunting We Will Go   Record: Victor 45–5064

Words

Oh, a-hunting we will go,
A-hunting we will go.
We'll catch a fox and put him in a box.
And never let him go.

Action

Players in two parallel rows in couples. Head couple slides four times down between the rows on the first line and back to place on line two. On lines three and four each skips back of his own row to the end. Second couple repeats.

Dance continues until all couples have done it. Then all join hands and circle left on the first two lines, back to right on the last two, and jump one step into center yelling "Ya!" at the end.

The Snail   Record: Victor 45–5064

Words

Hand in hand you see us well,
Creep like a snail into its shell;
Ever nearer, ever nearer,
Ever closer, ever closer,
Who'd have thought this little shell
Would have held us all so well?

Hand in hand you see us well,
Creep like a snail out of its shell;
Ever farther, ever farther,
Ever wider, ever wider;
Who'd have thought this little shell
Would have held us all so well?

Action

Dancers join hands in a semicircle. During the first verse all
walk to the left in time to the music following the leader around a
series of circles, each getting smaller, all resembling a snail
crawling into its shell.

During the second verse the line reverses and the one at the
end of the line leads the rest back to their original places.

Hippity Hop to the Barber Shop   Record: Victor 45–5064

Words

Hip-pit-y hop to the barber shop
    To buy a stick of candy;
One for you, and one for me,
    And one for sister Annie.

Action

Partners in double circle skip around the circle clockwise on
lines one and two. On "One for you, and one for me" they face
each other pointing to the opposite then to self. Each inside child
moves up one to a new partner on the last line.

The Needle's Eye   Record: Victor 45–5067

Words

The needle's eye, it doth supply
    The thread that runs so true;
There's many a beau I've let go
    Because I wanted you,
You, oh you,
    Because I wanted you.

Action

Played like London Bridge. The two players catch the last one going through the arch at the end of the song. After all have been caught and lined up behind the one of his choice, a tug of war tests the thread's strength.

Skip to My Lou   Record: Victor 45–5066

Words

Flies in the buttermilk, two by two,
Flies in the buttermilk, two by two,
Flies in the buttermilk, two by two,
Skip to my Lou my darlin'.
Little red wagon painted blue, etc.
Purty as a red bird, purtier too, etc.
She is gone and I'll go, too, etc.
Git me another'n as purty as you, etc.

Action

Form a circle in partners. One couple chooses another player and all three skip around in the center while outside circle goes the opposite way. On the word "Skip" the chosen player of the inside circle skips under formed arch made by the inside couple.

The original couple joins the larger circle while the odd dancer chooses another couple. She takes the new boy for her partner. They form the next arch and the dance continues as long as desired.

Sally Go Round the Moon   Record: Victor 45–5064

Words

Sally go round the moon,
Sally go round the stars,
Sally go round the chimney pot,
Every afternoon—bump.

Action

The circle moves clockwise. On the word "Bump," all squat. The last one down is out. The game continues with all moving in the opposite direction.

The Muffin Man   Record: Victor 45–5065

Words

Oh, do you know the muffin man,
    The muffin man, the muffin man?

Oh, do you know the muffin man
  That lives in Drury Lane?

Oh, yes I know the muffin man,
  The muffin man, the muffin man.
Oh, yes I know the muffin man,
  That lives in Drury Lane.

Two (four, eight, sixteen, etc.) of us know the muffin man,
  The muffin man, the muffin man.
Two of us know the muffin man that
  Lives in Drury Lane.

Action

Dancers form a circle around the "muffin man." On the first verse he skips around the circle and stops in front of one girl. He jumps up and down there in time to the music.

This chosen partner joins him in jumping up and down to the music in verse two.

On the third verse this couple skips around the circle with hands joined in skater's position. Both become "muffin men" and the dance continues until all have been chosen and become "muffin men," too.

The Playtime Record Company now has the Markel Splendid Singing Games for only twenty-five cents. These plastic records are well recorded and the words are sung clearly. A list of the best records available from this company is found at the end of the chapter.

For those who prefer to use the piano for accompaniment instead of records, the list at the top of page 50 of selected favorite singing games with their words, music, and dance directions will prove helpful:

Some children will enjoy creating their own singing games from records they own. They may do this individually or in groups of three. It is best to teach them the singing as it is supposed to be done. This gives each child a starting point and makes it easier for him to make up variations. They will enjoy finding new ways to do "Old King Cole," "Pop Goes The Weasel," "The Bear Went Over The Mountain," as well as many other of their favorite tunes.

Name of the Singing Game	Book Reference	Page
This Is the Way the Lady Rides	1	159
On the Bridge of Avignon	3	64
How D'ye Do, My Partner	2	85
Skating Away	1	162
The Swing	2	107
Pig in the Parlor	1	172
Diddle Diddle Dumpling	1	153
Captain Jinks	6	239
A-Tisket, A-Tasket	3	45

Chum, Chummy Lou	5	89
Go from Me	4	75
Ducks	2	82
Ach, Ja	5	495
Blue Bird	3	41
Six Little Girls A-Sliding Went	6	503
Sandy Land	6	271
Here We Go Round the Mountain	6	248

Inexpensive Singing Game Records
(Twenty-five cents apiece)

Available from Columbia Records, Inc., Bridgeport, Connecticut

305-PV Old MacDonald Had a Farm—Part I
Old MacDonald Had a Farm—Part II

331-PV Jingle Bells
Good King Wenceslas

333-PV The Three Bears
Parade of the Ducks

336-PV Hey Diddle Diddle; Goosey Goosey Gander;
Little Miss Muffet; Alphabet Song;
Ding Dong Bell; Diddle Diddle Dumpling;
To Babyland; Hickory Dickory Dock

337-PV Little Bo-Peep
Tom, Tom, the Piper's Son

338-PV Three Blind Mice; Higgilty Piggilty;
Lavender's Blue; Hobby Horse;
Peter, Peter, Pumpkin Eater; Jack Spratt;
Hark, Hark the Dogs Do Bark; I Had a Little Doggie;
Ring Around the Rosy

339-PV Farmer in the Dell
Mulberry Bush

340-PV London Bridge
Pop! Goes the Weasel

341-PV Jack and Jill;
Little Boy Blue; See Saw, Margery Daw

342-PV Mary Had a Little Lamb; Pussy Cat;
Sing a Song of Sixpence; Ten Little Indians

343-PV Old King Cole
Fiddle-De-Dee; Simple Simon

334-PV Looby Loo
Did You Ever See a Lassie?

345-PV Git Along, Little Dogies;
        Big Rock Candy Mountain

349-PV Skip to My Lou
        Buffalo Gals

350-PV Today Is Monday (Soup Song)
        The Bear Went Over the Mountain
        A-Hunting We Will Go

361-PV Lazy Mary
        A-Tisket, A-Tasket

362-PV Daddy Wouldn't Buy Me a Bow-Wow
        I Don't Want to Play in Your Yard

References

1. Frieswyk, Siebolt: "The Performing Arts as Recreation," *Recreation*, June, 1960, p. 257.
2. Danford, Howard G.: *Creative Leadership in Recreation*, Boston, Allyn and Bacon, 1964, p. 235.

RECORD SOURCES

Bowmar Records, Inc., 622 Rodier Drive, Glendale, Calif. 91201
Stanley Bowmar Co., Inc., 4 Broadway, Valhalla, N.Y. 10595
Children's Music Center, Inc., 5373 West Pico Blvd., Los Angeles, Calif. 90019
Custom Fidelity Record Co., 222 E. Glenarm St., Pasadena, Calif. 91101
Folkways Records, 701–7th Ave., New York, N.Y. 10036
RCA Records, 1133 Ave. of the Americas, New York, N.Y. 10036

**SUGGESTED SINGING GAMES AND OTHER MUSICAL RECORDS
WITH INSTRUCTIONS INCLUDED**

Dances of Hawaii, Bowmar Educational Records.
Dubka, Rashid Records, 191 Alantic Ave., Brooklyn, N.Y. 11201
Eighth 18th-Century Dances, Paxton Records PR 699 (Nos. 1–4), PR 700 (Nos. 5–88).
Festival Folk Dances, (Scottish Songs and Dances), RCA, (LPM-1621).
Folk Dances for All Ages, RCA (LPM-1622).
Folk Dance Records, (Singing Games for Children), Ruth Evans, Children's World, Inc., Box 433 Highland Station, Springfield, Mass. 01109.
Folkraft Records, 1159 Broad Street, Newark, New Jersey 07102.
French Game Songs, Bowmar Educational Records, M-107.
Latin-American Game Songs, Bowmar Educational Records, M-104.
Let's Square Dance, Richard Kraus, RCA Series 3000–3004.
Listn, Move, and Dance, Vols. 1 and 2, Capital Records, H-21006 and H-21007.
Play Party Games, Decca Records, AL278.
Play Party Games, Bowmar Educational Records.
Ring Around the Rosy and Other Singing Games, Allegro Records, JR-3.
Rhythms for Children (Call and Response). Ella Jenkins, Folkways (FC7308).
Singing Games and Folk Dances, Bowmar Educational Records.
   A series of albums (revised ed.) for young people.
   Singing Games, Albums 1 and 2.
   Singing Games and Folk Dances, Album 3.
   Folk Dances, (from around the world), Album 4.

Folk Dances, (American), Album 5.
Folk Dances, (Latin-American), Album 6.
Singing Square Dances, Bowmar Educational Records.
Sometime-Anytime Songs, Washington Records, (WC-303).
Songs and Rhythms from Near and Far, Folkways #7655 (LCR-64-343).

BAND UNIFORM AND CHOIR GOWN MANUFACTURERS

Collegiate Cap and Gown Company, 1000 No. Market Street, Champaign, Ill. 61820
The Fechheimer Bros. Co., 4545 Malsbary Road, Cincinnati, Ohio 45242
The C. E. Ward Company, New London, Conn. 44851

MUSICAL EQUIPMENT MANUFACTURERS

The Empire Music Company, Ltd., 934–12th Street, New Westminster, B.C., Canada
Magnamusic-Baton, Inc., 6390 Delmar Blvd., St. Louis, Mo. 63130
Mitchell Manufacturing Co., 2740 South 34th St., Milwaukee, Wisc. 53246
Pacific Music Supply Co., 1143 Santee St., Los Angeles, Calif. 90015
Rhythm Band, Inc., P.O. Box 126, Ft. Worth, Texas 76101
School Specialties, 48 W. Northfield Rd., Livingston, N.J. 07039
Trophy Music Co., Div. of Grossman Music Corp., 1278 West 9th St., Cleveland, Ohio 44113

Suggested Readings

Baird, Forest: *Music Skills for Recreation Leaders.* Dubuque, Iowa, Wm. C. Brown, Publishers, 1963.
  This book contains many fine suggestions for making music a more vital part of a recreation program in a wide variety of settings.
Batcheller, John and Monsour, Sally: *Music in Recreation and Leisure.* Dubuque, Iowa, Wm. C. Brown, Publishers, 1972.
  This valuable book should be in every recreation leader's library, for it is full of many program suggestions for musical activities in a variety of recreational settings. It also includes many instructional techniques and teaching resources in the areas of group singing and song leading, instrumental accompaniment, musical appreciation, choral speaking, and dancing.
Best, Dick and Beth: *The New Song Fest.* New York, Crown Publishers, 1963.
  This is the International Outing Club's collection of words and music for 300 songs: folk songs, work songs, college songs, drinking songs, chanties, and rounds.
Britten, Benjamin and Imogen Holst: *Wonderful World of Music.* Garden City, N.Y., David McKay Co., 1969.
Carabo-Cone, Madeleine: *The Playground as Music Teacher.* New York, Harper and Row, 1959.
  The author interprets fundamentals of music through the medium of make believe, using terms and activities familiar to children. She gives instructions for playing over 100 games on a music staff drawn on a playground or indoor center floor.
Cohn, Nik: *Rock From the Beginning.* New York, Stein and Day, 1969.
Dykema, Peter: *Twice 55 Community Songs.* Boston, C.C. Birchard and Company.
  This well-known collection of favorite songs will liven up any community sing.
Eisenberg, Helen and Larry: *How to Lead Group Singing.* New York, Association Press, 1955.
  This book gives special attention to folk songs and is particularly good for plannng and selecting music, teaching the song, learning how to accompany, and acting out songs.

Fox, Lilla: Instruments of Popular Music. New York, Roy Publishing Company, 1969.

Hood, Marguerite: *Teaching Rhythm and Using Classroom Instruments*. Englewood Cliffs, N.J., Prentice-Hall, Inc., 1970.

Keene, Laura: *Sing and Play a Ukulele*. Far Rockaway, N.Y., Carl Van Roy Co., 1957.

Kraus, Richard: *A Pocket Guide of Folk and Square Dances and Singing Games for Elementary Schools*. Englewood Cliffs, N.J., Prentice-Hall, Inc., 1966.

Latchaw, M.: *A Pocket Guide of Games and Rhythms for the Elementary School*. Englewood Cliffs, N.J., Prentice-Hall, Inc., 1970.

Lomax, Alan and Elizabeth Preston: *The Penguin Book of American Folk Songs*. Baltimore, Penguin Books, 1965.
    This book contains 111 ballads, sea chanties, love songs, lullabies, reels, work songs, cowboy songs, and spirituals from Colonial days to modern times. It includes piano arrangements, guitar chords, and illustrated methods for learning to play guitar accompaniments.

Machlis, Joseph: *Music Adventures in Listening*. New York, W. W. Norton & Co., Inc., 1968.

Nye, Robert and Vernice; Neva Aubin; and George Kyme: *Singing with Children*. Belmont, California, Wadsworth Publishing Company, 1962.
    More than 170 songs children will like to sing, many of them familiar, others not so well known, are included. Excellent suggestions are given for the uses of songs and how to enjoy them.

Taussig, Harry: *Folk Style Guitar*. New York, Oak Publishing Co., 1967.

Timmerman, Maurine and Griffith, Celeste: *Guitar in the Classroom*. Dubuque, Iowa, Wm. C. Brown Co., 1971.

Ulanov, Barry: *Handbook of Jazz*. New York, Viking Press, 1967.

Vannier, Maryhelen; David Gallahue and Mildred Foster: *Teaching Physical Education in Elementary Schools*, 5th Ed. Philadelphia, W. B. Saunders Co., 1973.

chapter 7

Dramatics

"I would rather be the children's storyteller than the queen's favorite or the king's counselor."
Kate Douglas Wiggin

Informal

Informal dramatic activities include verse speaking choirs; finger and hand puppets made from fruits, vegetables, or scrap materials; shadow plays; charades; storytelling; dramatic stunts; and play production. Although many of these appeal primarily to youngsters, adults also enjoy participating in them or watching others perform. We are all magically drawn to the land of make believe where we can escape our routinized daily lives.

In presenting these activities the leader should:

1. Strive for enjoyment instead of perfection.
2. Offer a wide variety of them for all ages.
3. Make the best use of available space, materials, and talent.
4. Be creative. Help others become more aware of people, places, and of the abundance of useful articles in their own environment that can be used in dramatics for shared enjoyment with others.

The leader should ever be on the alert for costumes, stage props, and new materials. Scraps of cloth, discarded furniture, cardboard boxes, and other junk can, if one knows how or will try to learn, transform a bare room into a wonderland, a freckle-faced 5-year-old into a dashing prince. Tin cans make wonderful stage jewelry, old socks interesting hand puppets, used cardboard boxes clever shadow play figures.

VERSE SPEAKING CHOIRS

Charles Laughton, the famous character actor, did much to revive interest in reading aloud individually or in groups. Many recreational directors are now experimenting with choral groups throughout the nation. The steady growth in popularity of this activity is proof of its appeal.

Children during their spontaneous play chant simple jingles and slogans. Jump rope ditties, although puzzling to grownups, seemingly are meaningful to children. They find sheer joy in imitating animal sounds such as "cock-a-doodle-doo," the "chug-chug" of a car, or repeating queer nonsense syllables such as "tiddledy-tiddledly-dum." These favorite rhymes and jingles should be the first ones the leader uses with a beginning children's verse speaking group. Simple poems full of repetition, swinging rhythm, and imitative sounds should constitute further program selections. Excellent materials for children's choirs can be found in:

> Batcheller, John, and Monsour, Sally: *Music in Recreation and Leisure.* Dubuque, Iowa, Wm. C. Brown Co., 1972.

A beginning adult group might well try saying aloud together popular advertising slogans. Nursery rhymes spoken in unison will aid them to see the fun and skill inherent in this activity. The leader should help the members find a deeper satisfaction by selecting material from the beautifully written masterpieces of literature. Readings from the Bible, the sonnets of Elizabeth Barrett Browning or Edna St. Vincent Millay, the poems of Carl Sandburg, Sara Teasdale, Robert Frost, Christina Rossetti, Vachel Lindsay, and Walt Whitman are recommended. Individuals will, if encouraged, bring their favorite poems to the group. This is one way to build a desired "we" feeling as well as to help each develop an awareness of and appreciation for the beauty found even in everyday words and sounds.

No special seating arrangement is necessary for success in leading choral groups other than placing all those with high or low, soft or loud voices together. The members will enjoy giving a recital for some special occasion or persons. Tryouts should be used for classifying all those interested in joining the choir and not for the purpose of selecting only those with the best voices.

PANTOMIME

This is an especially fine activity for young children. However, it can also be used successfully with older groups in the form of charades. It can be a fun approach used to help those who are too self-conscious and is a good activity to use to introduce children to characterization.

Suggested activities are:

> *For young children*
> A fat man attempting to sit on a small chair
> A cowboy roping steers
> Going grocery shopping

Helping prepare the family dinner
A visit to the amusement park
Walk on all fours imitating an animal

For older groups
Buying a new Easter outfit
Characters seen on a walk in the park
Your first date
Taking your dog on his first visit to the vet
Repairing a flat tire
Your first job interview

PUPPETS

The young enjoy finger plays and wall shadows in the form of bears, rabbits, dogs, or other animals. These are simple to master and even the amateur leader can teach himself how to do them.

DRAMATICS

Homemade puppets fashioned from discarded materials are fun to make and use. The following ones are so simple that even young children can make them:

Paper Bag

Paint a face on a paper sack with tempera or draw it with crayons. Make braids or hair from red, yellow, or black yarn and sew on. After blowing it up insert your hand and tie the sack around your wrist or use a stick instead of your hand. Make up a poem or recite a known one for the puppet.

Make twins, married couples, grandma and grandpa to act out a clever dialogue.

Divide a party into groups of five. Each person in a group makes a puppet for a group show. Little Red Riding Hood, The Three Bears, or Hansel and Gretel are easy ones to act out.

Sock Puppet

Cut a large anklet or man's sock as shown and stuff it with silk stockings, rags, cotton, or kapok. Sew on a face made with colored buttons and braid the top for hair or use yarn. Use it to act out a nursery rhyme.

Tennis Ball

Cut two finger holes into a tennis ball or hollow rubber ball. Paint or color on a face. Cover your arm with a cloth, insert your fingers into the holes, and act out a poem or sing a song.

Light Bulb

Paint a face on a light bulb with tempera. Make a paper hat, cover your hand with cloth and put the puppet through his paces with your right thumb, first finger, and hand.

Make a whole family by using bulbs of varying sizes. These puppets can best be made by adults. Only heavy bulbs should be used.

Papier Mâché

Cut newspaper into strips or small pieces. Soak in water and wheat paste. Fashion a figure around a round object on a stick. Paint with tempera. Cover your hand and arm with cloth and give a skit.

Vegetable Puppet

Cut eyes, mouth, mustache, hair, rouged cheeks, etc., out of colored paper and paste them on vegetables. Cucumbers, potatoes, tomatoes, eggplant, squash, carrots, etc., can be used. Insert a stick, conceal your hand with a cloth, and give an impromptu skit.

Make a whole family of these puppets and act out popular fairy tales.

Oranges, lemons, apples, plums, bananas, and other fruits can also be used with success.

Hedge Apple Puppet

Paste on parts of the face made from colored paper, or pin them on with straight pins. Insert a stick, use a concealing cloth for your hand and recite nursery rhymes.

Box Puppet

Paint a round ice cream carton or square half pint milk carton red. Paint on a face and paste on crepe paper hair. Cover your hand and arm with cloth. Insert your hand in the open end of the box. Act out a song or poem.

Brush Puppet

Cut a face out of colored paper. Draw ears and paste them on a vegetable brush. Use a hat pin for a nose. Paste the face on so that part of the brush becomes hair. Cover your hand with cloth and recite a nursery rhyme.

Suggestion: Make a whole family by using toothbrushes, nailbrushes, shoebrushes, etc.

Sawdust Puppet

Mix one pound of sawdust with a solution of wheat paste and water. Form a head on top of a bottle with the sawdust mixture. Let it dry overnight. Paint on a face and shellac it. The bottle becomes the body of the puppet. Cover your hand with cloth and act out a song.

Spoon Puppet

Paint a face on a metal or wooden spoon, using either side. Make hair or a hat from paper and Scotch tape it on. Cover your hand and act out a skit.

Suggestion: Make a whole family of these from spoons of varying sizes: a small sugar spoon, a teaspoon, a tablespoon, a gravy spoon, etc.

Hair and Beards for Puppets

Make these from yarn, cellophane, wood shavings, metal pot cleaners, chenille thread, or soft leather cut into strips. Make curly hair by twisting the material around a pencil. Paste or Scotch tape it on.

Puppet and marionette shows are most effective when properly presented. Each should be given on a stage that is well lighted. Upturned tables, card boxes, scrap lumber, and flash lights or electric lights are the required equipment for a homemade one. A curtain and miniature props add to the effectiveness of a show. All participants should make and use their own puppets and be encouraged to write their own plays.

Flannel Board Cutouts

Tack a large piece of heavy colored flannel over a board. Cut figures of animals, people, etc., from colored construction paper. Place them on the board and move them about as you refer to each in a story you read or tell. The Old Testament is a rich source of materials, as most Sunday school teachers know.

Shadow Plays

Cut figures of animals, people, birds, houses, trees, etc., out of heavy cardboard. Paste each on a separate stick. Have a bright light behind a bedsheet screen. Hold each performing figure close to the screen and take it down below the table when its part is finished. Act out fairy tales. Use phonograph records for accompaniment.

STORYTELLING

We all like to hear and tell stories. Throughout the ages man has thrilled to their spell. From times long before Christ, who was the master storyteller of them all, down through the wandering minstrels and the pilgrims walking to some holy shrine, out to the far-flung borders of new lands, around every campfire, and in each home, word weavers have spun tales of magic, enchantment, and wonder.

Each age group has its favorite stories.

1. *Very young children* like best stories revolving around their own daily lives. They enjoy hearing about everyday things such as clocks, trees, dogs, cats, etc. They respond readily to rhythms, jingles, and repetitions of words and sounds.
2. *Elementary school children* like best stories of make believe and of dangerous places. Their heroes are about their own age, such as Tom Sawyer or Heidi. The appeal of folk stories is strong, as is that of Greek myths and stories of early pioneers.

3. *Junior high school children* like best stories that appeal to their developing power to reason and see hidden meanings. They are beginning to enjoy the way in which a story is told almost as much as the story itself. Daring heroes and heroines, folk tales, and great leaders such as King Arthur, Florence Nightingale, or Abraham Lincoln strongly attract this group. It is often harder to tell stories to them than to younger children, for they are more critical of the story and the storyteller. However, they can be reached and won over.

4. *High school students* like best stories of adventure, famous people, customs of other lands, and romance. By this time most of them have developed strong individual story preferences best suited to their own developmental stage.

5. *Adults* like best stories of adventure, humorous incidents that happen to others, romance, jokes, travel, heroes and heroines who emerge from problem backgrounds similar to their own.

In selecting a story to tell the leader should consider the age, sex, and background of the group with whom it will be shared. The setting in which the story will be told is a most important factor. A group of children sitting around a campfire at night will respond to legends full of idealism more than a spontaneously collected group of youngsters at noon on a playground. Camp experts long ago discovered that a low embered fire is superior for such stories than a large roaring one.

Techniques for telling stories successfully are to:

1. Get the audience's attention with your first sentence. Young children want you to get to the heart of the story. Older ones will let you set the stage verbally before introducing the characters or plot.

2. Tell the story from memory but not necessarily word for word except for magic phrases such as "Hokus-pokus, open fast," or "Then I'll huff, and I'll puff until I blow your house down." As one expert storyteller has said, "Tom, Tom, the Piper's Son" is quite a different fellow from the Piper's son, Tom.

3. Believe in the story yourself and identify with the characters so that you become Billy Goat Gruff, Cinderella, or Jack, The Giant Killer.

4. Keep your group small and be aware of each one in it. Seat the group in a semicircle. Watch your audience and be on the lookout for lagging interest. Develop techniques for keeping interest and for recapturing wandering attention.

5. Talk on the experience level of the group. Young children will not understand big, unfamiliar words, nor will older children respond to an oversimplified story from a collection of tales for tiny tots. Likewise, a boy from Cape Cod, whose life is spent near the sea, will not be as interested in hearing about gang life in

the slums of Harlem as will a city child living close enough to this kind of environment to understand it.

6. Pause at just the right moment. This whets curiosity's appetite. For example, "The boy opened the door and there stood— (pause)—a tiny gray rabbit wearing a large black hat," is superior to "The boy opened the door and there stood a tiny gray rabbit wearing a large black hat." A pause *can* heighten interest as well as refresh.

7. Master the art of telling one story well at a time rather than repeating five poorly told ones in order to fill a half hour story hour.

8. Become acquainted with a wide variety of carefully selected stories to tell (see p. 125). Develop an art for storytelling by experimenting with people of all ages. Keep those of the same age grouped together.

9. Help others become skillful storytellers. Suggest reference readings and guide preparation.

10. Form a storyteller's club and keep informed on new techniques and materials.

DRAMATIC GAMES

The following informal games are simple, easily directed, and bring quick enjoyment. In leading them, keep directions to a minimum.

CHARADES

Divide the group into two teams. Each takes a turn acting out a word, song, movie or book title.

Keep time and the team wins that guesses in the shortest time what the other one acted out.

Suggestions: Gone with the Wind, Mississippi, Georgia, The Moon Is Blue, etc.

Variations: Each team sends a representative to pick up and act out the written directive.

Act out mottoes, nursery rhymes, fairy tales, slogans, famous people.

IMPROMPTU DRAMATICS

Give each player on each team a situation to act out. Each one from each team takes turns. The group chooses the best person.

Suggestions:

A wooden soldier in a parade.

A woman buying a new hat.

A driver getting a ticket for speeding.

A boy's first day at school.

An opera star singing from *Tristan and Isolde.*

ANIMAL DRAMATICS

Show at the same time to each representative from the divided teams an animal's name you have written on a piece of paper. Each goes back to his team and without a sound acts out the animal shown. Score one point for the team that guesses first correctly. Play for ten points.

Suggestions: A pig, donkey, possum, etc.

Variations: Use famous people, book characters, professions.

HISTORICAL EVENTS

Divide the group up into teams of six. Allow five minutes for all groups to prepare to pantomime a famous event from ancient, modern, or current history. Award one point to the group first identifying it correctly. Play until one team wins five points.

Suggestions:

A participant in the ancient Olympics.

The signing of the Magna Carta.

The Korean truce talks.

BABY

Divide the group up into four to six on each team. Give each group props such as diaper, pin, rouge, milk bottle, etc. After 5 minutes' preparation, each group presents one member as its baby. Award a prize for the best one or for the one who both looks and acts the most like a baby.

Variations:

1. Provide ribbons, hats, skirts, etc., for a spring fashion show.
2. Provide long skirt, hat, shawl, etc., for a grandma.

AMBITIONS

Each in turn pantomimes the thing which as a child was his life's ambition.

Variations: Each portrays what he wanted to look like when grown up.

RESOLUTIONS

Each in turn pantomimes his New Year's resolution while the rest guess what it was.

SPRING FLOWERS

Divide the group into teams of four. Give each group the name of a flower for all to act out, such as a rose (rising to tiptoe from bended knees, etc.). All guess what flower each group represents.

STICK BURN

Give each a small stick to throw into a burning fireplace when his turn comes. He acts out poems, mottoes, or book titles while his stick burns but can only go on to a new one when each one is guessed. The winner acts out the greatest number.

Suggestions: Excellent for teen-age campers.

GUESSING GIFTS

Wrap several inexpensive toys individually and place on a table together or under a Christmas tree. Each selects his gift and pantomimes what he thinks is in the box. Those who are successful keep their gifts.

Suggestions: Wrap up an airplane, toy mule, ball, etc.

PERFORMING ANIMALS

Each person draws the name of an animal out of a hat and acts it out while the others guess what animal he represents.

TAKE-OFF

Assign couples to take off in pantomime well known people or types (the henpecked husband and his wife, a salesman and a cautious buyer, two people gossiping, etc.). Choose the best.

THE WORD GAME

Divide into groups of four to eight. Give each team one word around which they make up a skit. Award a prize to the best group.

Suggestions: A fifty dollar bill, a rope, a shovel, a book, the ocean, etc.

Variations: Give each group the name of a place around which they build a skit such as jail, mountain, New York, Paris, etc.

Formal

PLAY PRODUCTION

Plays given purely for recreational purposes should be short and simple. It is best to use one-act productions with a beginning group. After the play has been chosen by the director an announcement of tryouts should be posted and well publicized. During the first meeting of those interested in being cast, the time should be spent largely in reading the play aloud and describing its mood, theme, and plot. All who wish to have parts should try out for the roles they most desire. Each should be judged for his diction and ability to speak clearly, his physical characteristics, and his ability to act the part. Rehearsals should begin as soon as possible for those selected. The director ought to:

1. Encourage all to learn their parts by the second rehearsal.
2. Provide the necessary props and costumes as soon as possible and train each to use them properly.
3. Hold a full dress rehearsal two days prior to the production with all players in makeup and costume.
4. Give all interested persons a job of importance to do. Needed committees include:
   a. Stage crew—building, painting, striking and stacking all scenery.

    b. Costume crew—making of and caring for all costumes.

    c. Publicity crew—making necessary posters, handbills, writing newspaper announcements.

    d. Prompter crew—(not more than two) assist with prompting.

    e. Prop crew—collecting, returning, and being responsible for all props.

    f. Usher crew—assisting all to their seats, acting as hosts or hostesses.

    g. Ticket crew—making, selling and taking tickets.

    h. Clean up crew—performing janitorial duties.

5. Have few rules of conduct but enforce them. Rules should include:

    a. No gum chewing.

    b. No curtain peeking.

    c. No visitors behind stage until after the performance.

6. Use folk tales or simple plays for young children. Use more advanced materials for adults (see p. 127).

7. Organize a dramatic club as soon as possible and keep alive a sparked interest by producing carefully selected and well performed plays periodically.

Hints for staging amateur productions include:

COSTUMES

1. Make jewelry from junk or ten cent store oddities such as curtain rod rings for ear screws, etc.
2. Use brightly colored scarves, head bands, sashes, etc.
3. Make riding boots by covering shoes with black oilcloth.
4. Use old curtains for veils, trains, wedding dresses, angel robes, etc.
5. Make mustaches, wigs, beards out of old mops, yarn sewed together, colored crepe paper, or raveled rope.
6. Make hats, dresses, trousers, etc., out of scrap goods.
7. Use blankets, cardboard, pillows, etc., for animals.
8. Make oriental costumes from dyed muslin, Turkish towels, bathrobes.
9. Use crepe paper or tempera paint to make flowers, jackets, skirts, etc.
10. Make Indian costumes from burlap bags.

SCENERY

1. Make simple props.
2. Label a funny substituted prop. (A park bench could be two chairs close together with a large printed sign on them.)
3. Use color generously.
4. Make a curtain from blankets, sheets, large bath towels pinned together.

MAKE-UP

1. Determine whether the person is to look like himself or someone else and work from there.
2. The amount of make-up used depends upon amount and kind of light. Test this out for yourself.
3. Wash the face thoroughly with soap and warm water. Apply about a quarter of an inch of grease paint and rub in, spreading it over the whole face. Apply eye shadow, rouge, and lipstick. Use grey liner for eye shadow for grey eyes, blue for blue, etc.
4. For old age—paint in a few forehead, neck and cheek wrinkles. Rouge lower cheeks. Powder hair white.
5. For beards—paint on mustaches and sideburns with black or brown pencil or burned cork. Make a beard from finely shredded crepe paper sewed together, trimmed. Paste it on with spirit gum.
6. For scars—paint on with lipstick or nonflexible collodion.
7. For large noses—use nose putty, cover with grease paint and powder.
8. For missing teeth—block out with black tooth wax.

LIGHTING

1. Comedies should be brilliantly lighted, tragedies shown more in shadow.
2. Use 10- or 20-watt bulbs in stage prop lights such as lamps, a fireplace, or street corner lights.
3. The stage should always appear to be lighted from natural sources such a windows, open door, etc.
4. Light the center of the stage more brightly than the corners.
5. Use white lights for sunlight, magenta for a sunrise or sunset, blue for moonlight.
6. Use white, amber, and a few blue or green bulbs for the footlights.
7. Use gelatine mats obtained from any motion picture supply house for spot light. Popular colors are blue, amber, green, and red.
8. Mark exit doors with red lights.

References

STORIES TO TELL

FOLK STORIES

Chase, Richard: *Grandfather Tales*. Boston, Houghton Mifflin Co., 1948.
Field, Rachael: *American Folk and Fairy Stories*. New York, Charles Scribners' Son, 1929.
Fillmore, Parker: *The Mighty Mikko*. New York, Harcourt, Brace and Co., 1950.

Finger, Charles: *Tales From the Silver Lands*. New York, Doubleday and Co., 1943.
Grinnell, G. B.: *Pawnee Hero Stories and Folk Tales*. New York, Charles Scribners' Sons, 1932.
Harmon, Humphrey: *Tales Told Near a Crocodile*. New York, Viking Press, 1967.
Jacobs, Joseph: *English Fairy Tales*. New York, G. P. Putnam's Sons, 1949.
Lucas, Mrs. Edgar: *Fairy Tales of the Brothers Grimm*. Philadelphia, J. B. Lippincott Co., 1952.
Nusbaum, Aileen: *Zuni Indian Tales*. New York, G. P. Putnam's Sons, 1946.
Smedley, A. C.: *Tales from Timbuktu*. New York, Harcourt, Brace and Co., 1931.
Steel, Flora Annie: *English Fairy Tales*. New York, The Macmillan Co., 1962.
Stern, James: *Grimm's Fairy Tales*, Complete Edition. New York, Pantheon Books, 1944.
Whitney, Thomas: *The Story of Prince Ivan; The Firebird; Grey Wolf*. New York, Charles Scribners' Sons, 1968.

STORIES OF FANCY AND MAKE BELIEVE

Byfield, Barbara: *The Haunted Spy*. New York, Doubleday & Co., 1969.
Brown, Abbie: *In the Days of the Giants*. New York, Houghton Mifflin Co., 1949.
Housman, Laurence: *A Doorway in Fairyland*. New York, Harcourt, Brace and Co., 1946.
Kipling, Rudyard: *Just So Stories*. New York, Doubleday, Doran and Co., 1932.
Leamy, Edmund: *The Golden Spears*. New York, Longmans, Green and Co., 1949.
Lightner, Alice: *Doctor to the Galaxy*. New York, W. W. Norton & Co., Inc., 1965.
Lucas, Mrs. Edgar: *Fairy Tales by Hans Christian Anderson*. New York, E. P. Dutton and Co., 1951.
Potter, Beatrix: *The Tailor of Gloucester*. New York, Frederick Warne Company, 1950.
Sandburg, Carl: *Rootabaga Stories*. New York, Harcourt, Brace and Co., 1936.
Stephens, James: *Irish Fairy Tales*. New York, The Macmillan Co., 1932.
Stockton, F. R.: *Ting-A-Ling Tales*. New York, Charles Scribners' Sons, 1941.

ANIMAL STORIES

Anderson, Clarence: *High Courage*. New York, The Macmillan Co., 1941.
Graham, Kenneth: *The Wind in the Willows*. New York, Charles Scribners' Sons, 1953.
Harris, Joel Chandler: *Uncle Remus, His songs and His Sayings*. New York, D. Appleton-Century Co., 1928.
Hawthorne, N.: *Tanglewood Tales and The Wonder Book*. Boston, Houghton Mifflin Co., 1931.
O'Hara, Mary: *My Friend Flicka*. New York, Charles Scribners' Sons, 1941.
Lawson, Robert: *Rabbit Hill*. New York, Viking Press, 1944.
Shedlock, Marie: *Eastern Stories and Legends*. New York, E. P. Dutton and Co., 1935.
Waldeck, Theodore: *Lions on the Hunt*. New York, Viking Press, 1942.

TALES OF HEROES AND HEROINES

Alexander, Rae Pace: *Young and Black in America*. New York, Random House, 1970.
Bontemps, Arno: *Famous Negro Athletes*. New York, Dodd, 1964.
Buckmaster, Henrietta: *Women Who Shaped History*. New York, The Macmillan Co., 1966.
Freedman, Russell: *Teen-Agers Who Made History*. Chicago, Holiday Press, 1968.
Grinnell, G. B., and Company: *Pawnee Hero Stories and Folk Tales*. New York, Charles Scribners' Sons, 1941.
Judd, M. C.: *Wigwam Stories*. New York, Ginn and Company, 1942.
Kennedy, Howard: *The Red Man's Wonder Book*. New York, E. P. Dutton and Co., 1931.

Marvin, F. S.: *The Adventures of Odysseus.* New York, E. P. Dutton and Co., 1929.
Pyle, Arthur: *King Arthur and His Knights.* New York, Charles Scribners' Sons, 1931.
Pyle, Arthur: *Stories of Champions of the Round Table.* New York, Charles Scribners' Sons, 1932.
Sherwood, Merriam: *The Tale of the Warrior Lord.* New York, Longmans, Green and Co., 1948.
Tietjens, Eunice: *The Romance of Antar.* New York, Coward-McCann, Inc., 1946.
Young, Ella: *The Tangle Coated Horse.* Philadelphia, David McKay Co., 1949.
White, Hilda: *Truth Is My Country.* New York, Doubleday, 1971.
Zimmern, Helen: *The Epic of Kings.* New York, The Macmillan Co., 1941.

MYSTERY STORIES

Byers, Betsy: *Go Hush the Baby.* New York, Viking Press, 1971.
Chrisman, A. B.: *Shen of the Sea.* New York, E. P. Dutton and Co., 1937.
Jacobs, Joseph: *English Fairy Tales.* New York, G. P. Putnam's Sons, 1942.
Kipling, Rudyard: *Puck of Pook's Hill.* New York, Doubleday, Doran and Co., 1931.
Poe, Edgar Allan: *Tales.* New York, D. Appleton-Century Co., 1932.
Stevenson, Robert Louis: *Island Night's Entertainment.* New York, Charles Scribners' Sons, 1941.
Thomas, Dawn: *Mira! Mira!* New York, J. B. Lippincott Co., 1970.
Turkle, Brunton: *The Sky Dog.* New York, Viking Press, 1969.

POETRY BOOKS

FOR THE LEADER

Arbuthnot, May Hill and Root, Shelton: *Time for Poetry.* Chicago, Scott, Foresman & Co., 1968.
Brandon, William: *The Magic World: American Indian Songs and Poems.* New York, William Morrow & Co., Inc., 1971.
Colum, Padraic: *Roofs of Gold: Poems to Read Aloud.* New York, The Macmillan Co., 1964.

FOR CHILDREN

Armour, Richard: *All Sizes and Shapes of Monkeys and Apes.* New York, McGraw-Hill Book Co., 1970.
Barnstone, Willis: *A Day in the Country.* New York, Harper & Row, 1971.
Holman, Felice: *At the Top of My Voice.* New York, W. W. Norton, 1970.
Swenson, May: *More Poems to Solve.* New York, Charles Scribners' Sons, 1971.

PLAYS FOR CHILDREN

Burack, Isabel: *100 Plays For Children.* Boston, Plays, Incorporated, 1949.
Connor, J. Hal: *Stunts and Features for Carnivals.* Franklin, Ohio, Eldridge Entertainment House, 1937.
Hackett, R. D.: *Radio Plays for Young People.* Boston, Plays, Incorporated, 1950.
Horowitz, Caroline: *A Child's Treasury of Things to Do.* New York, Hart Publishing Co., 1945.
Jagendorf, Moritz: *Penny Puppets, Penny Theatre, and Penny Plays.* Indianapolis, Bobbs-Merrill Co., 1941.
Mackay, Constance: *Children's Theatres and Plays.* New York, D. Appleton-Century Co., 1927.
National Recreation Association: *Eight Plays and Pageants for Children.* New York, 1936.
Watson, Katherine: *Radio Plays for Children.* New York, H. W. Wilson Company, 1947.

PLAYS FOR ADULTS

Bacon, Josephine: *Snaps, A Collection of Stunts and Short Sketches for Every Occasion*. Des Moines, Iowa, Ivar Bloom Hardin Press, 1935.
A Catalog of Plays and Entertainment Material. Minneapolis, The Northwestern Press.
Cohen, Helen: *One-Act Plays*. New York, Harcourt, Brace and Co., 1937.
Eisenberg, Helen and Larry: *The End of Your Stunt Hunt*. 2403 Branch Street, Nashville, Tennessee, 1947.
Kozlenko, William: *One Hundred Non-Royalty One-Act Plays*. New York, Greenberg, Publisher, Inc., 1941.
Williams, Bertha: *Hail! Stunt Night*. Franklin, Ohio, Eldridge Entertainment House, 1935.

Suggested Readings

Arbuthnot, May Hill and Zena Sutherland: *Children's Books*, 4th ed. Chicago, Scott, Foresman & Co., 1972.
Baird, Bill: *The Art of the Puppet*. New York, The Macmillan Co., 1965.
Carlsen, Robert: *Books and the Teen-age Reader*. New York, Harper & Row, 1971.
Dorson, Richard: *Folk Tales of the World*. Chicago, University of Chicago Press, 1969.
Fader, Daniel and Elton McNeil: *Hooked on Books*. New York, Putnam, 1968.
Huber, Miriam: *Story and Verse for Children*. New York, The Macmillan Co., 1965.
Joseph, Stephen: *The Me Nobody Knows: Children's Voices From The Ghetto*. New York, Avon Books, 1969.
Lanes, Selma: *Down The Rabbit Hole*. Boston, Mass., The Macmillan Co., 1971.
Perrault, Charles: *Perrault's Complete Fairy Tales.*, New York, Heath Robinson Dodd Press, 1961.
Wenzel, Evelyn and May Hill Arbuthnot: *Time for Discovery*. Chicago, Scott, Foresman & Co., 1971.

ANTHOLOGIES

Arbuthnot, May H., comp.: *The Arbuthnot Anthology of Children's Literature*. (Includes: *Time for Poetry; Time for Fairy Tales; Time for True Tales*), rev. ed. Glenwood, Ill., Scott, Foresman & Co., 1961.
Hollowell, Lillian, ed.: *A Book of Children's Literature*. New York, Holt, Rinehart & Winston, Inc., 1966.
Martignoni, Margaret E., ed.: *The Illustrated Treasury of Children's Literature*. New York, Grosset & Dunlap, Inc., 1955.

PAMPHLETS

Following Folk Tales Around the World. Reprint from *Compton's Pictured Encyclopedia*. Chicago, Ill.: F. E. Compton Co. (free)
For the Storyteller. Ed. by National Recreation and Park Association Committee, New York: National Recreation Association.
How To Tell A Story by Ruth Sawyer. Reprint from *Compton's Pictured Encyclopedia*. Chicago, Ill.: F. E. Compton Co. (free)
Let's Read Together: Books for Family Enjoyment. Children's Services Division. Chicago, Ill.: American Library Association.
Light the Candles! ed. by Marcia Dalphin. The Horn Book, rev. ed. Boston, Mass.: Horn Book, Inc.
Once Upon a Time. Rev. ed. by Picture Book Committee of the Children's & Young Adult Section of the New York Library Association. New York: The New York Public Library.

Stories: A List of Stories to Tell and Read Aloud, edited by Ellin Greene, new ed. New York: The New York Public Library.

Stories to Tell, edited by Jeanne Hardendorff, 5th ed. Baltimore, Maryland: Enoch Pratt Free Library (Publications).

Stories to Tell to Children, edited by Laura Cathon *et al.,* 7th ed. Pittsburgh: Carnegie Library of Pittsburgh.

Storytelling by Sara I. Fenwick. Lake Bluff, Ill.: The American Educ. Ency., Publishers House. (free)

Storytelling and Stories I Tell by Gudrun Thorne-Thomsen. New York: The Viking Press, Inc.

Tell Me Another by Arlene Mosel. Reprint from Wilson Library Bulletin, October 1960. Bronx, N.Y.: H. W. Wilson Co.

chapter 8

Arts and Crafts

"The love of beauty lies close to religion. All through the centuries men have laboured bit by bit to build cathedrals and in so doing have built themselves, have become what they were not before. ... Slowly we learn — but surely — that our wealth in this world is not what we have bought, but in what we have created, in what we have really and truly made our own."
— Howard Braucher

Arts and crafts make up one of our richest and most satisfying recreational areas. It can also be one of our most inexpensive ones, for discarded materials such as old tires, tin cans, and box crates can be had for nothing. Most of the projects included in this chapter can produce something useful or even beautiful from salvaged or inexpensive materials.

A purposeful arts and crafts program provides more than just busy work. It is more than gluing or assembling packaged parts together. The program will be of value only if it is built upon worthy goals and objectives. These might well be to develop:

1. An appreciation for beauty, good workmanship, tools, color, and design.
2. Skill in working creatively with materials and tools.
3. Good habits of carefulness, patience, and stick-to-itiveness until a project is completed.
4. Desirable relaxation patterns through learning to use the hands creatively.
5. Legitimate outlets for basic needs for destruction, recognition, belonging, security, affection, construction, and adventure.

The program must be well directed. The teacher-leader should know how to do many crafts as well as how to teach them to others. He should be keenly aware of each group member and help everyone accomplish desired goals. If he is enthusiastic about creating beautiful things, the group will be, for high interest is as contagious as measles.

The director must direct. This connotes that the leader must have a well-planned graded program. It is best to start with a few recruits and help them make useful articles in a short time. Avoid herding a reluctant group together with the promise that "Crafts are really lots of fun and I'll let you make anything you want to." The rank beginner does not usually know what he wants to make and even less how to go about it. A satisfied customer is the best possible kind of advertising. An initial nucleus of four or five will increase if they have a satisfying, worthwhile experience.

It is wise to start with simple projects requiring the use of only a few tools. All that is needed to get a program going is a skilled leader, a room, a few tables, and a minimum of materials and tools. Easily completed short term projects made from scrap will help the group be more creative since they will see that the raw materials are of no real value. Although later everyone should be allowed and encouraged to make what he wants to, a beginning group should be started on the same project. As each develops skill and interest he should be given increased freedom to make what he desires from any of the available material. The leader's role then changes. He then should be concerned primarily with guiding the learner into becoming more creative and in turning out a more beautifully finished product. One expert craft teacher expresses this by saying:

> The arts and crafts program should be directed as a man driving a wagon. He gives the mule his head and, with the reins firm but relaxed, puts the mule on his own, except for a few "gees" and "haws" here and there. It is indeed a rare thing to see a man leading a mule and wagon and an even rarer one to see them being *driven*. With the same delicacy of touch, the counselor guides his artists and craftsmen to see and use the materials they find in their environment.[1]

Other methods for best conducting an arts and crafts program are to:

1. Show the group what the finished product will look like. This serves as a great motivator to beginners.
2. Make useful articles from native materials.
3. Project fun into the program but at the same time gradually raise perfection standards.
4. Give clear-cut and definite instruction while demonstrating what you mean, for people learn mostly through imitation.
5. Develop both individual (such as wood carving) and group projects (such as making a parade float).
6. Focus the program around each person's development of skill

and appreciation rather than upon yourself as a skilled craftsman. Nurture originality and creativeness in each individual.

7. Divide groups according to interest rather than age.
8. Have a display or show of all articles made by the group. Award prizes, if possible. Obtain newspaper publicity and pictures of winners.

Buy only a few tools at first. Gradually increase the number in proportion to group interest in the program. Initial materials should include:

coping saws	scrap lumber	charcoal drawing pencils
scissors	thread	and paper
modeling tools	yarn	finger paints and paper
construction paper	scraps of cloth	wheat paste
water colors and paper	vise	whittling knives
glue	handsaws	paint brushes
crayons	tin shears	clay
scrap leather	hand drill	buttons

Developmental stages of interest in arts and crafts are somewhat similar to those of play interest. Both tend, like a wheel, to be circular and return to a starting point. The child moves from simple patterns to the more complex ones of the adult, but regresses to beginning patterns when old. This is seen in the chart below:

Age	Play Interests	Arts and Craft Interest
1–3	Isolated solitary play.	Scribble stage.
4–6	Parallel play with one or two others.	Symbolic stage. Draws a queer looking blob which to him is a cow.
6–18	Group play. Number with whom he plays successfully gradually increases. As he grows older he becomes more selective in number of playmates and close friends.	Realistic stage. Draws a cow that looks like a cow.
Adulthood to Old Age	Gradually returns to individual and small group play centered around his family, mate or self as in parallel and isolated play.	Return to symbolic stage. Draws a heavy, awkward animal that could be a cow but draws man as a graceful figure. Gradually returns with increased age to crafts requiring use of large muscles, as in scribble stage.

Suggested recreational crafts most appropriate for each age group are:

Children — Age 1–3. Scribble Stage.	Children — Age 4–6. Symbolic Stage.	Children — Age 6–18. Realistic Stage.	Adulthood to Old Age —. Gradual Return to the Symbolic Stage.
Unguided imaginative drawing, finger painting, coloring, clay modeling, hammering, cutting out pictures with dull scissors. Color books best that contain big pictures.	Crayon drawings. Clay modeling of animals. Finger painting done freely. Paper dolls. Paper cutouts from colored construction paper. Pastings things in scrapbook. Simple rhythmical homemade toys and instruments. Simple cross stitch embroidery. Boat making from scrap lumber. Spatter painting. Use of hammer, saw, nails. Wood puzzles.	Doll clothes and furniture. Stick printing. Weaving. Photography. Clay modeling. Simple pottery using glazes. Felt craft. Cartooning. Plaque and wood carving. Papier mâché figures of animals, people, puppets, and birds. Model airplanes. Marionettes. Hand puppets. Block printing. Junk crafts. Copper tooling. Knot craft. Simple sketching and water coloring. Tree houses. Gang shacks. Boats and paddles. Kites.	Useful household articles. Block printing. Knitting. Metal craft: candle sticks, jewelry, bowls. Editorial cartooning. Copper tooling. Book binding. Leather tooling: belts, wallets, book covers. Advanced junk crafts. Charcoal sketching. Oil painting. Refinishing antiques. Photography and home movies. China painting. Poster design and lettering. Plastic craft. Silk tie painting. Mural painting. Woodwork.

Junk Crafts

Objects made from salvaged materials provide a satisfying creative experience for all ages and comprise our simplest crafts. Everyone responds to the challenge of making something useful or attractive from practically nothing. The following articles are both simple and satisfying to make:

BOOKMARKS

Cut designs from felt and cement them to another piece of felt cut into the proper shape for a bookmark.

Type lines of famous poems, mottoes, or quotations on pieces of ribbon and use them as a marker.

Cut the corners of envelopes for page markers.

Mount colored pictures from magazines on heavy construction paper.

Crochet a marker from colored materials.

LETTER OPENERS

Whittle the desired shape from a tongue depressor. Sandpaper it and rub brown wax shoe polish into it or paint it.

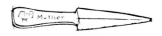

Whittle driftwood in the shape of an opener. Sand and wax or paint it.

PINS

Cut a large bottle cork in half lengthwise. Use colored thumb tacks for eyes and glass beads for mouth, yarn for hair, paper clips for earrings. Fasten a safety pin on the back and wear it as a lapel pin.

SCRAPBOOKS

Collect poems, stories, cartoons, etc., and paste them into a scrapbook. Collect or take pictures of sunsets, hands, women, men, babies, birds, rocks, stars, clouds, trees, etc., and paste them into the book.

Make a scrapbook diary of everything funny or beautiful, or things you think about each day and illustrate it with matching cartoons, pictures, or your own sketches.

PENNANTS

Tear discarded felt hats into pieces. Steam press each piece flat. Cut into desired shapes and cement with airplane glue. Make animals, birds, shields, flags, awards, pennants, or scenes.

Small blocks of felt may be obtained from the Handicrafters, Waupun, Wisconsin.

MILK BOTTLE TRAIN

Cut windows into a milk carton. Use bottle caps for wheels. Paint each coach and the engine in different colors. Join them together with wire or string.

Make trucks from round or oblong milk or ice cream cartons. Cut into desired shape, use bottle caps for wheels, and paint in bright colors.

Make doll beds from round ice cream cartons. Cut into desired shape and glue in mattress. Paint in a soft color.

OLD SOCK DOLLS

Split the sock foot and sew up each half to make legs. Stuff with old rags or cotton. Tie a ribbon around the middle for a waist and one around the top for a head. Sew on buttons to make eyes, nose and mouth. Attach two stuffed pieces for arms.

OLD JAR FLOWER POTS

Enamel old bottles, jars, or glasses with a dark basic color. Paint on designs of flowers, fruit, or scenes in contrasting colors. Use for flower pots.

Paint old tea kettles, coffee pots, or dishes and make a varied set of pots.

SOAP CARVING

Use a sharp knife, razor blade or regular carving tool to carve figures of animals, birds, or people out of Ivory soap. Rough out the desired shape first and follow with finer details by drawing the knife slowly towards you.

Carve from wood, brick, and coal as you become more expert.

WIRE SCULPTURE

Shape thin wire with metal cutters or pliers. Attach to a wooden base. Add construction paper, cloth, yarn, etc., for color and effect.

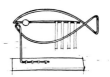

PIN BOXES

Paint pill boxes with enamel and paste on braided gold or silver cord, making an attractive design. Use as a pin box.

STUFFED TOYS

Cut scraps of cloth or oil cloth into the shape of an animal. Stuff with kapok, socks, or cotton. Sew on button eyes, cloth for mouth, and fringe other pieces for tails, eyebrows, etc.

PIPE CLEANER ANIMALS

Bend two cleaners into inverted U shapes. Add another for tail, backbone, uplifted neck, and head. Wind a third one around for the body, joining the neck piece and tail. Glue to cardboard or wood for place cards.

BRICK BOOK ENDS

Clean each brick and apply two coats of shellac on all sides. Wrap cloth tightly and neatly around the brick and glue heavier cloth or felt to the bottom. Paint the cloth with enamel or oil paints, adding stripes or figures as desired. Use for book ends or door stop.

LAPEL ORNAMENT

Use eight wool strands 6 inches long, five that are 4 inches long, and have colored thread for tying. Group longer strands together and fold in the center over the grouped shorter strands. Tie off head, arms, body, legs, hands, and feet with colored thread. Wear as a lapel pin.

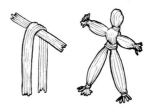

PAPER BEADS

Cut magazine covers into long triangular strips three-fourths of an inch wide at the base. Glue the colored side of the paper. While the glue is still wet, place a kitchen match along the base of the triangle on the dry side of the paper and roll the paper on to the match from the base to the tip of the triangle. Remove the match. Allow the beads made this way to dry and then string them together to make a necklace or bracelet. Shellac the beads after they have been strung. Make matching sets.

PIN CUSHION

Paint the bottom part of a round powder box and decorate with designs cut from a magazine. Pack it with cotton until it is three-fourths full. To make the cushion cut a circle of cloth slightly larger than the box and gather with a running stitch about one-fourth to one-half inch from the edge and around the entire cloth. Gather material to size to fit the box and fasten the thread. Fill it tightly with cotton and put into the box. Then glue the cloth to the inside edge of the box to hold in place.

Woodcraft

Useful and beautiful articles can be made from wood including:

pins	scrapbook covers
wall plaques	mail boxes
toys	bird houses
picture frames	cigarette cases
furniture — miniature and real	book ends
buttons	carved objects
buckles	letter openers
lamp bases	

When using large pieces of wood it is best to trace or draw the original design on the wood, then cut it out with a coping saw or power saw. Next, smooth out all rough edges using varying grades of sandpaper. Finally, finish it by waxing, staining, varnishing, or painting.

BUTTONS

Cut branches, wood chips, window shade rollers, mop handles or broom sticks into discs. Sandpaper and decorate in harmonizing or contrasting colors. Drill the necessary holes with a brace and small bit or burn through with a hot nail.

JIGSAW PUZZLES

Paint or paste a scene or animal picture on a large piece of thin wood (plywood is excellent). Saw out pieces of various shapes and sizes, according to the age group for whose fun the puzzle is being made. Keep the pieces simple and few in number for young children. (See sketch.)

CIGAR BOX TOYS

Make a wagon by using the box for the body. Use wooden spools for wheels and make axles of wood. Use bent nails for holding the wheels on. Make houses, barns, churches, garages and other buildings, using the wooden boxes or parts of them. Paint each in bright colors.

Make shelves, lamp shades, baby beds, book covers, book ends, and wall brackets. Decorate by wood burning or varnish.

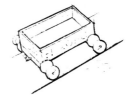

LAWN ORNAMENTS

Use plywood or thin scrap lumber. Cut out the desired design with a coping saw. (First practice following a curved as well as a straight line.) Paint your ornament and mount it on a pointed piece of wood to stick into the ground.

CURTAIN PULLS

Use a pencil to draw a design within a double or rimmed circle. Cut out the design inside the small circle first, then cut around the outer circle. Use show card colors to decorate the figure, leaving the rim in natural finish. Shellac the entire piece.

KITCHEN REMINDER

Mark off desired design on a square piece of thin wood. Cut it out with a coping saw. Sandpaper both sides and all edges. Paint the cutout figure in bright colors. Cement it to the top quarter or third of a rectangular board, which is left in natural finish. Glue a pad of note paper to the center of the board. Tie a string to a pencil and fasten the loose end of the string to the bottom of the boards by means of a thumb tack.

KNIFE CRAFT OR WHITTLING

The best woods for beginners to use in knife craft are white pine, sugar pine, spruce, poplar, white wood, cypress. Advanced whittlers can carve red cedar and harder woods with success. The material used by either group should be seasoned, milled, or dressed and finished lumber.

The knife should be sharp and may be a common pocket knife or a commercial carving tool. The commonest is the full hand grip. The thumb or first finger can be extended along the back of the blade to guide it.

Canes, paper knives, eating utensils, lapel pins, as well as many other useful articles can be whittled out of tree sapplings and decorated by bark whittling (cutting part of the bark away in a desired design). Let the branch dry a few days before starting and have the object you want to complete clearly in mind before starting.

Advanced whittlers can make a ball in a cage, laced hearts, or a chain from a single piece of wood.

CARVING

Although the knife can be used for straight or chip carving, it is best to use a chisel and other wood carving tools. In using these let the left hand guide the blade while the right hand pushes it through the wood.

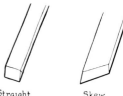

Straight Chisel　　　Skew Chisel

Chip carving is used to decorate flat wooden surfaces. Start by experimenting with pine, gumwood, or poplar. Basic figures to use include the triangle with straight or curved sides. Make slightly slanting cuts about one-eighth inch deep into the wood and remove the chip. Stop cuts will make the work easier. These are made by the left hand cutting into the wood on one side to stop the second blade used by the right hand from cutting beyond a bordered line. Mallets may be used to drive the blade deeper into the wood when needed.

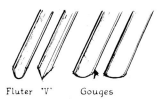

Fluter   'V'   Gouges

Incising, a process for decorating wood below the surface, can best be done by gouges, V tools, or veiners. Use one hand to guide the tool and the other to push it. Where two grooves intersect, cut the one running against the grain first to avoid splitting the wood.

Finishing carved wooden objects properly is important. Sand off with the grain using 4/0, 6/0, or 8/0 sandpaper. Use three coats of wax and polish or use water stains from cloth dye, or water colors in two coats followed by one of wax.

Leather Craft

Leather craft offers a pleasurable as well as profitable leisure time activity. Improvised tools can help make it an inexpensive hobby. Ice or nut picks, sharp knives, and hammers can be used almost as well as costly tools. Vegetable and bark tanned leathers are best for tooling. Skins most commonly used are: cowhide, calfskin, steerhide, sheepskin, goatskin, pigskin, deerhide, horsehide, and elkskin.

Cut out the desired design first or rip apart an old object of the same kind for a pattern. Place the pattern on the leather, finished side up, and hold it down with heavy objects on the corners. Outline the pattern with an awl or modeling tool. Place the leather on heavy linoleum and cut out with scissors or a sharp knife. Dampen the leather slightly and transfer the design on it. Press or trace it on with a modeling tool. Trace it deeper when the leather dries.

Flat tooling, or lowering the background around an initial or figure, is done as above by using the broad end of the modeling tool. Work out from the designed edges with short circular strokes. A pebbled surfaced can be added by tapping the top of the tool or tracer.

Embossing, or raising the design higher, is done from the back of the dampened leather by pressing out the part to stand out with the blunt end of the tool. Keep the pressure uniform. Hold the leather in your hand or place it face down on a heavy pad. Fill the hollowed parts with tissue paper strips or string coated with rubber cement.

Lace through holes punched by machine or hand using leather thongs. Stiffen one end of the thong with shellac and pass it through corner edges two or three times. Finish off by tapping the lacing lightly with a mallet to remove irregularities and create smoothness. Types of stitching include the running, over and under, cross, and loop.

Use snap fasteners, taking care to place the two pieces so that they will come together correctly to close the article when it has been completed.

Leather purses, pocketbooks, wallets, key cases, billfolds, cigaret cases, boxes, gloves, and moccasins are satisfying things to make.

Tin Craft

The common everyday tin can has unusual craft possibilities. It is not a dangerous material to use if the instructor first teaches skills in cutting and handling it. Smaller children can paint and decorate two pound coffee cans for canister sets or flower containers. Older ones will enjoy making the following articles:

RECIPE BOX

Use a Spam can or one of a similar shape. Cut out one side. Cut down each end of an adjacent side and across the center for an opening. Fold back the rough edge with a wooden mallet. Punch two nail holes in the back for hanging it on a wall. Polish with steel wool, enamel and paint on a design or paste on colored pictures cut from magazines.

LETTER HOLDER

Cut the bottoms out of two tin cans at least six inches in diameter. Fasten them to the ends of a wooden base by means of small flat-headed nails. Decorate with painted designs.

BILL FILE

Cut the bottom from a number two coffee can. File or grind off the sharp edges. Drive a long thin nail through the center of the base.

CANDLE HOLDER

Remove the end of a can. Cut out a back blade for a shield for the candle, leaving a rim for the base and to catch the tallow. Drive a small nail through the bottom and set a candle on it.

Other articles that can be made from tin cans are dishes, buddy burners or camp stoves, lamps, pins, cups, and jewelry.

Cartooning, Drawing, and Painting

CARTOONING

Needed supplies include a soft pencil and paper. Start with a familiar figure such as a circle or ball. Concentrate on heads. To indicate laughter put in cheeks up near eyes that are tilted upward and pull mouth corners up. Draw the rest of the figure from the head down by making circles of varying size.

Next try drawing the movement of arms, legs, hands, and feet. Begin with stick figures. Later draw the body proportions as accurately as possible for models.

Add for the final step drawings made from one basic figure such as a series of balls down to body scale showing various parts moving in correct patterns.

Start a cartoonist club and post the best work done each week.

DRAWING

Try drawing with a charcoal pencil, red or conte crayon, hard graphite lead pencil, black crayon, or pen and ink. Begin by drawing a human figure from a life model. Block off the drawing paper by drawing a line for the top of the head and one at the bottom for the feet. Think of the body as composed of three blocks (head, chest, pelvis). Draw these in curved lines and fill in the rest of the figure.

Draw other subjects such as scenes, buildings, still life, animals, etc., experimenting with charcoal, crayons, pencils and pen and ink. Keep all drawings to judge improvement. Mount the best ones in a frame of heavy white or colored cardboard.

PAINTING

Begin with tempera, and go on to water colors, then oils. Use large brushes first and paint with large movements. As you gain skill decrease both brush and stroke size. Paint pictures in a child's color book or draw your own. Master the art of staying within lines.

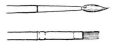

Use regular linen water color paper for water color painting. Keep the paper flat and stationary. Use a sable, flat-bristle, broad-wash, or camel's hair brush. Until you gain skill in recording impressions free hand, sketch the picture to be painted in pencil first. Begin by painting simple scenes and advance from there. The best colors to use first are:

orange vermilion	French blue
medium yellow	ivory black
yellow green	cadmium red
Antwerp blue	cadmium orange

Oil painting supplies can be obtained from art supply stores. Paint on a canvas of linen, hemp, cotton, or jute stretched on a framework. Use a variety of brush sizes, shapes, and degrees of stiffness. Paint from still life first — grouped cups, glasses, plates, fruit, a pile of books, etc. Arrange them in terms of contrasting colors, shapes, textures. Place them against a medium-toned background where contrasting light and shadow stand out. Paint under natural light. Study the subject and note that it has varying degrees of darkness and light, as well as a moderate intermediate shade between. Paint this intermediate first. Then fill in the lighter shades, and finally the most dominant ones. Use the least amount of paint for desired effect and develop techniques of shading darker tones over lighter ones and of painting both cool and warm halftones. Beginners can best work with these colors:

light yellow	yellow ochre
earth red	ivory black
permanent blue	white
burnt sienna	cadmium red

Metal Crafts

Types of metals best for this craft are pewter, copper, sterling silver, brass, and aluminium. From these ash trays, jewelry, belt buckles, bowls, trays, candle stick holders, and many other beautiful articles can be made.

To make any of these, first draw the desired pattern on paper. Transfer this to the metal and saw, clip, or file it out. To make ash trays, bowls, shallow dishes, or silver bread trays hammer them into shape over a hollow mold with a wooden mallet or ball peen-hammer. File off the rough edges, polish with fine steel wool and sandpaper.

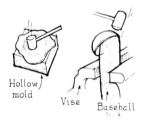

Mold for Bowl

Hollowing out bowls, or staking them, can best be done over a baseball bat held upright in a vise. Hammer the metal over this stake with a flat-faced mallet covered with leather, or a round-faced wooden mallet.

Jewelry, belt buckles or other articles require soldering. Clean the pieces thoroughly. Heat the soldering iron until it is hot, hold the tip of the iron vertically on a cake of sal ammoniac until it is coated. Next coat with flux both metal parts to be joined. Dip the hot iron tip into the solder and apply to one edge of the first piece, then to the second and allow to cool. Use a hard solder for silver, a soft one for pewter and aluminum.

To decorate metal you can:

Planish it with a ball-peen hammer to give it an uneven surface.

Flute it with the narrow end of a wedge-shaped hammer over a stake grooved in the shape of the desired flute.

Chase it with various kinds of chasing tools by striking the head of the tool lightly with a ball-peen hammer.

Etch it with acids by placing it in the proper solution for eating away the background of the design. To do this first clean the metal thoroughly. Cover all parts not to be etched with "resist" so that only those parts exposed are destroyed by the acids. Brush black asphaltum varnish over all parts not to be etched and allow it to dry. For copper and brass drop the article in a solution of one part nitric acid with two parts water. Keep the solution in a stone jar or enameled container. The mixture should be strengthened for silver, weakened for pewter. If the solution fails to bubble when the article is in it, it is too weak. If it shows too much action it should be diluted. When the surface has been etched to the required depth, run cold water over it. Dissolve the asphaltum varnish in turpentine. Polish the etched portions with fine steel wool.

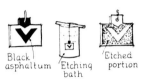

Black asphaltum   Etching bath   Etched portion

Additional Crafts

Additional popular and worthwhile crafts that might well be included in any recreational program at a school, center, club, camp, or playground are:

Amber craft
Archery craft (making bows and arrows)
Block printing (with potatoes and other vegetables, stencils,
    silk screen, and linoleum)
Book binding
Copper tooling
Etching (glass and metal)
Hooked rugs
Hat making
Jewelry craft
Camera craft
Leather craft (advanced tooling and lacing)
Magic craft (tricks, puzzles, gadgets)
Metal craft (advanced designing, engraving, spinning,
    plating, finishing)
Mounting (butterflies, insects, coins, stamps, etc.)
Needlework (embroidery, needlepoint, crocheting, stenciling)
Pottery (firing, glazing, decorating)

Painting (water colors, oils)
Paper folding and tearing
Poster design and lettering
Quilting
Weaving (harness and hand looms)
Wood inlay craft
Woodware craft

Consult the bibliography for selected references containing methods of construction, basic skill mastery, and needed supplies for each of these popular crafts.

Suggested Readings

Almeida, Oscar: *Metalworking*. Rev. ed. South Holland, Ill., Goodheart-Wilcox Company, Inc., 1968

Anderson, Edwin P.: *Home Workshop and Tool Handy Book*. Indianapolis, Ind., Theodore Audel, 1964

Anderson, Mildred: *Original Creations with Papier Mache*. New York, Sterling Publishing Company, Inc., 1967

Baker, Muriel L.: *Handbook of American Crewel Embroidery*. Rutland, Vt., Charles E. Tuttle Company, Inc., 1966

Baxter, William T.: *Jewelry, Gem Cutting and Metalcraft*. 3rd ed., New York, McGraw-Hill Book Co., 1950

Beitler, Ethel J.: *Create with Yarn*. Scranton, Pa., Intex Educational Publishers, 1964

Blumenau, Libi: *Creative Design in Wall Hangings*. New York, Crown Publishers, Inc., 1967

Boyd, Gardner T.: *Metalworking*. Rev. ed. South Holland, Ill., Goodheart-Wilcox Company, Inc., 1968

Butler, Anne: *Embroidery for School Children*. Newton Center, Charles T. Branford Company, Inc., 1970

Capua, Sarajean: *Jewelry Anyone Can Make*. Hollywood, Fla., Dukane Press, Inc., 1971

Cutler, Katherine N.: *Creative Shellcraft*. New York, Lothrop, Lee & Shepard Co., 1971

Fleming, Gerry: *Scrap Craft for Youth Groups*. New York, John Day Company, Inc., 1969

Fressard, M. J.: *Creating with Burlap*. New York, Sterling Publishing Company, Inc., 1970

Gaszner, George: *Working with Plastics*. New York, Drake Publishers, 1971

Hanauer, Elsie: *Art of Whittling and Woodcarving*. Cranbury, N.J., A. S. Barnes and Company, 1970

Horn, George F.: *Crayon*. Worcester, Mass., David Publications, Inc., 1969

Kampman, Lothar: *Creating with Clay*. New York, Van Nostrand Reinhold Company, 1971

LaCroix, Grethe: *Beads Plus Macrame: Applying Knotting Technique to Beadcraft*. New York, Sterling Publishing Company, Inc., 1971

Laskin, J.: *Arts and Crafts Activities Desk Book*. Englewood Cliffs, N.J., Prentice-Hall, Inc., 1971

Maloney, Joan: *Creative Crafts*. New York, Drake Publishers, 1971

Mattil, Edward L.: *Meaning in Crafts*. Englewood Cliffs, N.J., Prentice-Hall, Inc., 1971

Mell, Howard and Eric Fisher: *Modelling, Building and Carving*. New York, Drake Publishers, 1971
Newsome, Arden: *Spoolcraft*. New York, Lothrop, Lee and Shepard Co., 1970
Rothenberg, Polly: *Metal Enameling*. New York, Crown Publishing, Inc., 1969
Seyd, Mary: *Designing with String*. New York, Watson-Gumptill Publications, 1968
Shea, John G.: *Woodworking for Everybody*. 4th rev. ed. New York, Van Nostrand Reinhold Company, 1969
Shivers, Jay S. and Clarence R. Calder: *Recreational Crafts*. New York, McGraw-Hill Book Co., Inc., 1974
Villiard, Paul: *First Book of Leather Working*. New York, Abelard-Schuman, Ltd., 1971
Wright, Dorothy: *Baskets & Basketry*. Newton Center, Mass.: Charles T. Branford Company, 1959
Wright, Kenneth: *Woodworking*. New York, Emerson Books, Inc., 1970
Zechlin, Ruth: *Complete Book of Handicrafts*. Rev. ed. Newton Center, Mass., Charles T. Branford Company, 1968
Zimmerman, Fred W.: *Leathercraft*. South Holland, Ill., Goodheart-Wilcox Company, Inc., 1969

Suggested Periodicals

Art in America. Art in America, 115 Tenth Street, Des Moines, Iowa 50301
Better Homes and Gardens. Better Homes and Gardens, 1716 Locust Street, Des Moines, Iowa 50303
Ceramics Monthly. Ceramics Monthly, P.O. Box #4548, Columbus, Ohio 43212
Design. Design Magazine, 1100 Waterway Blvd., Indianapolis, Ind. 46202
Everyday Art Quarterly. Walker Art Center, Minneapolis, Minn.
Hobbies. Lightner Publishing Corp., 1006 S. Michigan Ave., Chicago, Ill. 60605
Industrial Arts and Vocational Education. Bruce Publishing Company, 400 North Broadway, Milwaukee, Wisc.
Junior Arts and Activities. Jones Publishing Company, 542 N. Dearborn Parkway, Chicago, Ill.
Metal Finishing. Metals and Plastics Publications, Inc., 99 Kinderkamack Road, Westwood, N.J. 07675
School Arts. School Arts, Printers Building, Worcester, Mass. 01608
Woman's Day. 19 West 44th St., New York, N.Y. 10036

Sources of Materials

American Crayon Company (Textile paint and clay products) 1706 Hayes Avenue, Sandusky, Ohio
American Handicraft Company, Inc. (Reed, raffia, and batik supplies) 45 South Harrison Street, East Orange, N.J.
Arts & Crafts Materials Corp. (General crafts supplies) 321 Park Avenue, Baltimore, Md. 21201
Boy Scouts of America (Methods and source materials) 2 Park Avenue, New York, N.Y.
Charles Toebe Leather Company (Leather, skins, tools, materials) 149 North Third Street, Philadelphia, Pa.
Contessa Yarn Company (Weaving materials) P.O. Box #336, 3-5 Bailey Avenue, Ridgefield, Conn.
Dennison Manufacturing Company (Paper crafts, methods and materials) Framingham, Mass.
E. W. Knapp (Handicraft yarns, chenilles, wefts) 442 Bourse Building, Philadelphia, Pa.

Favor Ruhl and Company (Modeling materials and tools) 425 South Wabash Avenue, Chicago, Ill.

Gordon's (Jewelry materials) P.O. Box #4073, Long Beach, Calif.

Grieger's Inc. (Jewelry materials) 1633 East Walnut Street, Pasadena, Calif.

Hook-Art Guild (Rug-making supplies) P.O. Box #57, Cumberland Mills, Maine

J. L. Hammett Company (Supplies, tools, materials for basketry, looms, and weaving) Cambridge, Mass.

Leisurecrafts (Jewelry materials) 941 East Second Street, Los Angeles, Calif.

Lester Griswald (Instructions, tools, materials) 623 Park Terrace, Colorado Springs, Colo.

Lily Mills (Yard products) Hand Weaving Department C, Shelby, N.C.

Norwood Loom Company (Looms) Baldwin, Mich.

Paternayan Brothers, Inc. (Rug-making materials) 10 West 33rd Street, New York, N.Y.

P. C. Hartung Company (Square knot materials, cord and cotton supplies) 121 Sands Street, Brooklyn, N.Y.

Remington Arms Company (Free materials on whittling and carving) Cutlery Division, Bridgeport, Conn.

S&S Arts and Crafts (General craft supplies) Colchester, Conn.

Sto-Rex Crafts (Enamels) Western Manufacturing Company, Inc., 149 Ninth Street, San Francisco, Calif.

Talens School Products, Inc. (School, club, and playground craft supplies) 76 Ninth Avenue, New York, N.Y.

The Handicrafters (Supplies, tools, instructions, materials) Waupun, Wisc.

Thomas Hodgson & Sons, Inc. (Yarns) Concord, N.H.

Universal School of Handicrafts (Supplies and tools) 2515 RKO Building, New York, N.Y.

W. A. Hall and Son (Leather tools, materials, and supplies) 99 Bedford Street, Boston, Mass.

W. B. Polloch, Jr. (Model kits, supplies and materials) 92 Lincoln Street, Worcester, Mass.

Western Ceramics Supply Company (Ceramic supplies) 1601 Howard Street, San Francisco, Calif.

Reference

1. Mitchell, Viola, and Crawford, Ida: *Camp Counseling.* Philadelphia, W. B. Saunders Co., 1976, p. 123.

chapter 9

Dance

*"Life is a dance over fire and
water."* —Havelock Ellis

Folk, social, and creative dance provide wholesome, satisfying recreation to millions. All three types of dance should be included in a recreation program and the latest dance "craze" included such as modern jazz, belly and hula dancing. Classes should be held for beginners and those more advanced. Hobby and club groups, such as a Square Dance Caller's Club or Folk Dance Group, should be interwoven into the overall program. Festivals, recitals, shows, and other types of public demonstration add richness and variety to the program as well as serve as a learning incentive to each participant.

Basic Planning

1. A survey of the interests, needs, and abilities of a group should precede actual planning of the inclusion of dancing in the total program.
2. Good leadership is imperative. The leader must like to dance as well as be able to dance well.
3. Set a definite meeting place and time. If a club is organized, keep membership open as long as possible.
4. Have all equipment ready for use at each session.
5. Use leaders from within the group to call squares, demonstrate, or assist in teaching.
6. Include all members in each session. Use arm bands or pinnies if there are more of one sex than the other.
7. Stress the importance of outside practice.

Facilities

The ideal location for dance activity is an unobstructed polished hardwood floor large enough to accommodate ten to forty couples. However, a smooth surface of any kind may be utilized for dancing—an asphalt tennis court, a multipurpose concrete surface, a plot of grass. Street dances are sometimes a solution to a space problem.

Public Address System

If it is at all possible, a public address system should be available. It should include two speakers, a turntable or phonograph that plays standard (78), 33⅓, and 45 r.p.m. records and has adjustable speed control, a microphone, and an amplifier. The amplifier should have connections for two speakers, two microphones, and the turntable, plus separate controls for the turntable and the microphone and separate controls for tone and volume.

Music

Although an orchestra or band is ideal, excellent phonograph recordings are available. Instructions and suggestions for teaching are often included with folk and square dance records and albums. Specialists in social dance and in creative dance have chosen and recorded music that is designed for teaching beginners as well as for dancing.

Records should be indexed, labeled, and stored either in albums or in metal carrying cases.

Folk Dance

Folk dance is a popular recreational activity. Beginners enjoy simple singing games, whereas skilled dancers respond to the challenge of learning intricate steps to difficult rhythms. It is important for the leader to use the fun approach when introducing any dance activity for the first time.

Before you lead the dance know the dance thoroughly yourself.

Analyze each part of it so that you can do it with and without the music. Be familiar with the music for the dance—rhythm, phrasing, melody, and character. Be able to do the pattern with the music. Learn all you can about the dance—its origin, the location of the country to which it belongs, the occupations and customs of the people, their costumes or typical dress, and the activity the dance is supposed to portray. Share this knowledge with the group.

TEACHING TECHNIQUES

Several approaches can be used to introduce a new dance. One is through the music itself. Telling the story of the dance is another. The dance may be related to any dance the group already knows or to a dance that the group has previously done, possibly one that includes some of the same steps as this particular dance. Whatever method is used, keep the introduction brief and begin dancing as soon as possible.

Start with a circle dance so that everyone will be doing the same steps and each person can see all the others in the group. Progress from the circle to couple dancing. Have an intermission before the group becomes tired. It is better to stop for rest than to let one couple after another drift away from the floor. Other suggestions include:

1. Stand where everyone can see you. Stand as part of the circle rather than in the center of a circle.
2. If you have an accompanist, stand where he can see you.
3. Give the name of the dance. The nationality may be mentioned at this time, or you may prefer to wait until after the music is played in order to give the group opportunity to guess the origin.
4. After listening to the music, discuss the kind of dance movements it suggests. (Skip, slide, walk, etc.)
5. Give some information concerning the background of the dance and any other facts of interest. Be brief and select interesting details.
6. Demonstrate the entire dance with music.
7. If the dance is short, use the whole method. If it is longer, use the whole-part teaching method. Teach with the music unless practice without it will speed learning.
8. Have the group walk through the first pattern. Use cue words to help them recall the steps and give these in rhythm with the music.
9. Select a signal with which to start both the dancers and the music. If you use a record, play the introduction at least twice so that the dancers will recognize the first measure of the dance.
10. Demonstrate with your back to the group. Arrange all in a line behind you. Demonstrate and give directions at the same time. (Step, hop, step, etc. Have all repeat and do step, hop, step with you.)
11. Dance the first pattern, then proceed to the next series of steps. Each time you dance with the music start from the beginning.
12. Be on the lookout for anyone who is having trouble. Analyze the way he is doing the steps and help him discover his mistake.
13. Have the dancers change partners often so that no one has to dance with a poor partner very long at a time and each has opportunity to dance with many others.
14. Select dances which are difficult enough to challenge the group.
15. Have everyone take part but do not insist that they do so.
16. Provide for review of familiar dances as well as for learning new ones in every session.
17. Progress as fast as is wise for your particular group.

A folk dance festival given as a climax to a class or club session does much to stimulate and sustain interest. Committees add to the working efficiency of the group. The duties of committees often used are shown below:

FOLK DANCE FESTIVAL COMMITTEES

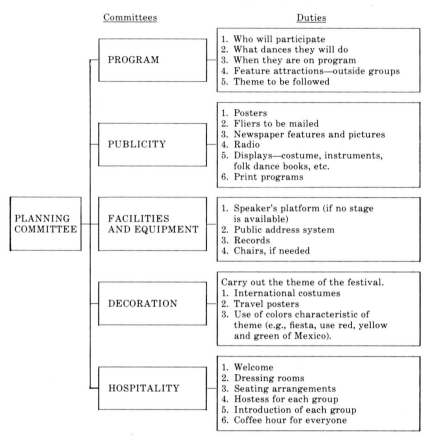

Committees	Duties
PROGRAM	1. Who will participate 2. What dances they will do 3. When they are on program 4. Feature attractions—outside groups 5. Theme to be followed
PUBLICITY	1. Posters 2. Fliers to be mailed 3. Newspaper features and pictures 4. Radio 5. Displays—costume, instruments, folk dance books, etc. 6. Print programs
FACILITIES AND EQUIPMENT	1. Speaker's platform (if no stage is available) 2. Public address system 3. Records 4. Chairs, if needed
DECORATION	Carry out the theme of the festival. 1. International costumes 2. Travel posters 3. Use of colors characteristic of theme (e.g., fiesta, use red, yellow and green of Mexico).
HOSPITALITY	1. Welcome 2. Dressing rooms 3. Seating arrangements 4. Hostess for each group 5. Introduction of each group 6. Coffee hour for everyone

(PLANNING COMMITTEE)

Dances popular with all age groups are:

DUTCH COUPLES DANCE (HOLLAND)

Music: Victor 22761

Beginning formation: Partners with inside hands joined in a circle facing counterclockwise. Men inside.

Main steps: Brush and waltz.

Figure:

Part I.   Men stamp L, brush right across, click R heel. Ladies stamp R, brush L, click L. Repeat.

Part II.   Hands on hips circle away from partner in 6 light running steps ending with partners facing. Bow with arms held at shoulder height, come back up and lower hands to sides; keep knees straight.

Part III.   Face partners. Men take 4 step swings backward and 4 step swings forward with hands on hips. Ladies follow. Begin on men's L, ladies' R. Step swing; step on L (one beat), swing R (2 beats).

Part IV.   Partners face with hands held at shoulder height. Waltz 8 steps in small circle.

RYE WALTZ (AMERICAN)

Music: "Comin' thru the Rye." Folk Dance Service, Nos. 398, 107.
Beginning formation: Couples. Closed social dance position.
Main steps: Point slide, and waltz.
Figure: (Directions given to the man; lady's part is opposite.) Music begins in 4/4 time.
Measures:

1.   Point left foot to side left; close back to right foot. Repeat.

2.   Two step-close steps left; then step left. (Step left, close right, step left, close right, step left again and rest weight on left.)

3.   Point right foot to right side; close to left foot. Repeat.

4.   Two side-close steps right. Step right.

5–16.   Music changes to 3/4 time. Begin left and waltz for 12 measures.

17.   4/4 time again. To the left: step, close, step, close, step.

Repeat as many times as desired.

NEBESKO KOLO (SLAVIC)

Music: Folk Dancer, 1003.
Beginning formation: Single circle with hands joined. No partners necessary.
Main steps: Running steps and stamps.
Figure:

Part I.   Begin on R foot. All take 4 series of 3 running steps clockwise in circle. Repeat going counterclockwise.

Part II.   Step forward toward circle center on R foot; place L along side R; step back R, place L along side R. Repeat.

Part III.   Starting R dance 4 series of alternating R, L, R, L, stamp R foot, bend R knee deeply.

MEXICAN WALTZ (MEXICAN)

Music: "Chiapanecas." Sonart M-301.
        Piano: Herman, Michael: *Folk Dances for All.* Chiapanecas, p. 16.
Main step: Waltz.
Beginning formation: Couples in a double circle facing clockwise. Man holds lady's left hand in his right. Outside hands are placed on hips.

Figure:
Measures:
1.   Step left; swing right foot forward across left.
2.   Step right; swing left.
3–4.   Stamp with left foot; pause 1 count. Clap own hands twice; pause 2 counts.
5–8.   Turn around (facing opposite direction) and join inside hands again. Begin right and repeat measures 1–4.
9.   Face partner, join both hands. Balance away from partner, stepping on left foot. Pause 2 counts.
10.   Balance forward, stepping on right foot. Arms are outstretched to the side at shoulder level.
11–12.   Balance away again, stepping left on count 1. Release hands; pause for count 2. Clap own hands on counts 3 and 1; pause for counts 2 and 3.
13.   Join both hands; balance forward on right foot, arms outstretched again.
14.   Balance away on left foot.
15–16.   Step forward on the right foot; release hands. (Count 1) Pause (Count 2) For counts 3 and 1, may encircle lady's waist with his arms; lady puts her arms around the man's neck, and both clap twice. Pause (Counts 2 and 3).
17–32.   Sixteen waltz steps. Closed social dance position.
Repeat the entire figure.

DANISH DANCE OF GREETING

Record—Victor 17158; Folkraft 1187.
Formation. Single circle; dancers facing the center with hands on hips.
Measures:
1–2.   Step 1. Clap hands twice; turn to partner and bow. Clap hands twice; turn and bow to neighbor.
3–4.   Step 2. Stamp right; stamp left; turn in place four running steps.
1–4.   Repeat measures 1 and 2.
5–8.   Step 3. All join hands and take sixteen running steps to right.
9–16.   Repeat to left. Repeat entire dance.

CHIMES OF DUNKIRK

Record—World of Fun Series, M 105 (French, Flemish, Belgian).
Formation. Double circle of partners facing each other; boys with back to center of circle.
Measures:
1–4.   Step 1. Clap three times; pause.
5–8.   Step 2. Partners join both hands and walk around circle in eight counts.

9–12.   Step 3. Partners join right hands and balance. Repeat.
13–16.   Step 4. Partners walk around each other once and boy moves on to his left to the next girl.

ACE OF DIAMONDS

Record—Victor 20989; World of Fun Series, M 102 (Danish).
Formation. Double circle; partners facing; boys with back to center of circle.
Measures:
1–4.   Step 1. Partners clap hands once; stamp foot once; hook right arms and swing around once.
5–8.   Repeat using left arm.
9–16.   Step 2. Girl puts hands on hips and moves backward toward center of circle with a step, hop. Step left; hop left; step right; hop right. Repeat. Boy follows with arms crossed on chest: step right; hop right; step right; hop right. Repeat. Return in reverse.
1–16.   Step 3. Polka—skating position, going counterclockwise.

TROIKA

Record—Kismet S112; Folkraft 1170 (Russian).
Formation. Groups of three facing counterclockwise. Center dancer is a boy; outside dancers girls. Hands are joined; free hands on hips.
Figure 1
Measures:
1.   Step 1. Four running steps forward diagonally to right.
2.   Step 2. Repeat diagonally to left.
3–4.   Step 3. Eight running steps forward around circle.
5–6.   Step 4. Hands still joined, the girl on the boy's right runs under arch, made by boy and girl on left, in eight steps. Other two run in place.
7–8.   Step 5. Girl on left runs under arch and back to place in eight steps.
Figure 2
Measures:
9–11.   Step 1. Each group of three joins hands in a circle and runs to left (clockwise) for twelve steps, beginning on left foot.
12.   Step 2. Stamp in place—left; right; left.
13–16.   Repeat Steps 1 and 2 running to right (counterclockwise).
16.   Release hands and repeat entire dance with same partners. Partners may change in measure 16. Girls raise outside hands to make an arch, release boy and he runs with fours steps to next group while girls stamp in place.

GREEN SLEEVES

Record (English)—Folk Fun Funfest (Dick Kraus) Educational Dance Recordings. P.O. Box 6062, Bridgeport, Connecticut.

Formation. Double circle in sets of two couples, numbered 1 and 2, facing counterclockwise; girls on right.

Step 1. Holding hands, walk forward sixteen steps.

Step 2. Form a star in sets. Man No. 1 gives hand to girl No. 2 and man No. 2 to girl No. 1. Walk clockwise eight steps; change to left hands and walk back to place counterclockwise.

Step 3. Couple No. 1 join hands and back under arch made by couple No. 2 who walk forward four steps, then walk backward while No. 1 makes the arch. Repeat entire dance.

TROPANKA

Folk Dancer Record—Disc Album 635 (Bulgarian stamping dance).

Formation. Single circle; little fingers joined.

Stamping step—cross foot over in front in ballet position with heel turned out.

Measures:

1–2.	Step 1. Beginning on right foot, take five running steps to right and stamp twice with left foot.
3–4.	Turn and run to left five steps and stamp twice with right foot.
1–4.	Repeat first four measures.
5.	Step 2. Facing center, all step on right foot, hop on right foot and swing left foot in front. Step; hop; swing; starting on left foot.
6.	Step on right foot; cross left foot over and stamp twice.
7–8.	Repeat measures 5 and 6, starting on left foot.
5–8.	Repeat measures.
5.	Step 3. Moving toward center of circle, all starting on right foot, step, hop right, step and hop left.
6.	Step right and stamp twice with left foot. (Arms raised high shout "Hey!")
	Repeat action of measures 5 and 6, dancing backward, starting with left foot. Gradually lower arms.
	Repeat measures 9 through 16 as in measures 1 through 9.

CHERKESSIA

Sonart Folk Dance Album M8 (Jewish).

Formation. Single circle, hands joined.

Teaching Suggestions. There should be quite a bit of bending backward and forward and swinging of joined hands as the dance progresses. On the verse the circle moves to the right; on the chorus the circle moves to the left.

Measures:

1–2.   Chorus. The dance begins with the chorus and is repeated after each figure.

Circle moves to the left. All leap on right foot across and in front of the left (ct. 1); step to the side with left foot (ct. 2); step across and behind left foot with right foot (ct. 1); step to side with left foot (ct. 2).

3–8.   Repeat first two measures three times.

9.   Bend forward on steps to the front and lean backward on steps to the back.

Figure 1. Circle moves to the right with sixteen steps. All step to the side on the right foot, extending the left leg to the side (ct. 1); place left foot behind the right and bend both knees slightly (ct. 2).

10–16.   Repeat seven times.

1–8.   Chorus

BROOM DANCE

Victor Record—20448 (German).

Formation. Couples form double circle facing counterclockwise. One child is left in the center of the circle with a broom.

Measures:

1–8.   Part 1. Couples march around the room to the music and the child in the center gives the broom to someone in the circle and takes his place. This one gives the broom to another quickly and takes his place, and so on for 8 measures.

9–16.   Part 2. The child who has the broom at the end of the eighth measure must dance with the broom in the center of the circle while the couples skip around singing Tra, la, la through 8 measures and the dance begins again with the center dancer passing the broom on.

THE CRESTED HEN

Folkraft 1194 (Danish).

Formation. Sets of three, one boy with a girl on either side.

Measures:

Step. The hop-step is done through the entire dance. Step on left foot on count one; hop on left foot; swing right foot in front of it on count two, keeping the knee bent. Reverse and step-hop on right foot; swing left foot to front.

1–8.   Figure 1. All sets of 3's join hands to form circles. Moving to left (clockwise) stamp left foot and do eight step-hops. Dancers lean back as they circle.

1–8.   Repeat measures 1 to 8, moving counterclockwise with eight step-hops.

9–12.   Figure 2. Girls release hands and place free hands on hips.
                Boy never releases the hands. Girl at the left of boy dances
                (step-hops) in front of him and under the arch made by
                raised hands of the boy and the girl on the right.
13–16.   Repeat same action with girl on the right, passing through
                arch.

MAYIM (Water)

Record—Folkraft 1108a (Israelian).
Formation. Students stand in circle facing center, hands joined and
down.
1. Four circasia combinations to the left. For each circasia combination:
   a. Place right foot in front and across left (accent right foot).
   b. Bring left foot along side right foot.
   c. Place right foot back, across left foot, to left.
   d. Hop on left foot along side right foot.
2. All take 8 steps toward center of circle, lifting hands gradually,
   accentuating first step by raising right knee.
3. All face left and take four walking steps toward left, starting with
   right foot.
4. While hopping on right foot, tap with left foot over right foot. Then
   tap with left foot to the left side. This combination is done 4 times.
5. While hopping on left foot, tap right foot over left foot. Then tap with
   right foot to right side. Slap hands on odd beat. This combination is
   done 4 times.
   This dance is supposed to convey the movement of water, of waves,
of going toward the well, and the joy of discovering water in an arid
country.

RAATIKKO

Folk Dancer Record—Scandinavian: 1123 (Finnish Polka—Old Maid's
Dance).
Formation. Couple; social dance position.
Step 1. Eight polka steps, turning clockwise.
Step 2. Four draw steps. Boy has girl by one arm pulling and girl moves
reluctantly toward rock.
Step 3. Eight slide steps away from rock.
Step 4. Repeat steps 2 and 3.
Repeat all.
Background. On the coast of Finland, there is a large rock close to the
beach. According to the story, if a boy succeeds in pulling a girl behind
the rock, she will be an old maid.

GIE GORDON'S

Beltona Record—BL-2455; Folkraft 1162 (Scotch—The Gray Gordons).
Formation. Couples in varsouvienne position.

Action.

Step 1. Both start on left foot. Take four walking steps forward. Reverse and take four walking steps backward, but continue in the same line of direction.

Repeat.

Step 2. Boy holds girl's right hand high with his right hand and polkas forward as girl does four polkas (clockwise) turning under boy's arm.

Step 3. In social dance position, do four polka steps turning clockwise. Repeat entire dance.

FINGER POLKA

Standard Record—2001A (Lithuanian).

Formation. Couples form double circle, facing counterclockwise; boys on inside of circle.

Action.

Step 1. Eight polka steps in open position (hold inside hands, starting hop on outside foot, etc., back to back and face to face).

Step 2. Eight polka steps in closed position turning clockwise.

Step 3. Drop hands and face partner. Stamp three times; clap own hands.

ROAD TO THE ISLES

Record—Imperial 1005A (Scottish).

Formation. Couples in varsouvienne position.

Measures:

1.	Step 1. Point left toe forward and hold. Grapevine step moving to right.
2–3.	Step left foot back of right foot; step right to side; step left foot in front of right foot and hold.
4.	Point right toe forward and hold,
5–6.	and grapevine to left stepping right, left, right and hold.
7.	Point left toe forward and hold.
8.	Point left toe backward in deep dip and hold.
9–10.	Step 2. Schottische forward diagonally to left, beginning on left foot—left; right; left; hop.
11–12.	Schottische forward diagonally to right, beginning on right foot—right; left; right; hop. On hop, in measure 12, half turn to right facing in opposite direction, keeping hands joined.
13–14.	Schottische, beginning on left foot. On hop, take half turn to left facing original direction.
15–16.	In place, step right; left; right; hold.

BLEKING

Record—Victor 20989; Folkraft 1188 (Swedish).

Formation. Partners face with both hands joined.

Measures:
1.   Step 1. Bleking (Ble-king): Jump lightly to left foot, placing right heel to floor—count 1.

See-saw arms by extending right arm forward with elbow straight and left arm backward with elbow bent. Reverse arms and jump lightly on right foot, placing left heel to floor—count 2.

2.   Repeat Bleking step three times in quick time—count 1 and 2.

3–8.   Repeat measures 1–2 three times.

9–16.   Step 2. Extend arms sideward and turn in clockwise direction with sixteen step-hops, alternately raising and lowering arms and kicking free leg to the side of the hops.

Repeat entire dance.

POLKA

2/4 or 6/8 Time Record—Basic Polka Steps, Educational Activities, Inc.
Starting Position. Social Dance—Girl on opposite foot. Skaters or varsouvienne position may also be used.
Basic Polka Step
Measure 1
Count "and"   Hop on right foot.
Count 1   Step forward on left foot.
Count "and"   Bring right foot to left foot (transfer weight to right foot).
Count 2   Step forward on left foot.
Measure 2
Count "and"   Hop on left foot.
Count 1   Step forward on right foot.
Count "and"   Bring left foot to right foot (transfer weight to left foot).
Count 2   Step forward on right foot.
Heel and Toe Polka
Measure 1
Count 1 "and"   Touch the heel of one foot forward and lean backward.
Count 2 "and"   Touch the toe of the same foot to the rear and lean forward.
Measure 2
Count 1   Step to the side (partners facing) or step forward on left foot (side by side).
Count "and"   Bring right foot to left foot (transfer weight to right foot).
Count 2 "and"   Step forward on left foot.
Face to Face—Back to Back (Partners facing girl on opposite foot).
Measure 1
Count "and"   Hop on right foot.
Count 1   Step to the side on left foot.

Count "and"   Close right foot to left foot (transfer weight to right foot).

Count 2   Step to the side again on left foot.

Measure 2

Count "and"   Hop on left foot, but while hopping pivot and be back to back with your partner.

Count 1   Step to the side on right foot.

Count "and"   Close left foot to right foot (transfer weight to left foot).

Count 2   Step to the side again on right foot.

SCHOTTISCHE

2/4 or 4/4 Time Record—Basic Schottische Steps, Educational Activities, Inc.

Starting Position. Social Dance—Girl on opposite foot. Skaters or varsouvienne position may also be used.

BASIC SCHOTTISCHE

Measure 1

Count 1   Step forward on left foot.

Count 2   Bring right foot to left foot (transfer weight to right foot).

Count 3   Step forward with left foot.

Count 4   Hop on left foot (right foot may be raised and knee bent during the hop).

Measure 2

Count 1   Step forward on right foot.

Count 2   Bring left foot to right foot (transfer weight to left foot).

Count 3   Step forward with right foot.

Count 4   Hop on right foot (left foot may be raised and knee bent during the hop).

RUNNING SCHOTTISCHE

Measure 1

Count 1   Step forward on left foot.

Count 2   Step forward on right foot.

Count 3   Step forward on left foot.

Count 4   Hop on left foot.

Measure 2

Count 1   Step forward on right foot.

Count 2   Step forward on left foot.

Count 3   Step forward on right foot.

Count 4   Hop on right foot.

LA RASPA (MEXICO)

Music: Methodist World of Fun Series, M-106

Main steps: Bleking step.

Beginning formation: Couples, facing each other holding both hands.
Measures, Part I:

1–4.	One Bleking step, beginning right.

Bleking step: Kick left foot forward and touch heel to the floor, hop on right foot.

Kick right foot forward and touch heel to floor, hop on left foot.

Repeat this action.

Hop on right foot; kick left foot forward touching heel to the floor.

Hop on left foot; kick left foot forward touching heel to the floor.

Repeat this action 3 more times.

5–8.	Turn so that right shoulders are together. Partners are facing opposite directions. Repeat measures 1–4.
9–12.	Turn left shoulders together. Repeat 1–4 again.
13–16.	Repeat 1–4 facing partner.

Measures, Part II:

1–4.	Hook right elbows; take 8 running steps; clap own hands on the eighth step.
5–8.	Turn to hook left elbow. Run 8 steps. Clap on the eighth step.
9–15.	Repeat measures 1 through 8.
Note:	Variation of measures of Part II is as follows: Skip 8 counts clockwise then reverse direction and skip 8 counterclockwise. Partners hold both hands; for the first 8 right shoulders are together and arms are extended to the right. Position is reversed for the next counts. Polka in skaters' position.

ST. BERNARD'S WALTZ (SCOTTISH)

Music: Victor 200FOB.
Main steps: Waltz and draw steps.
Formation:

Part I.	Beginning on man's L, lady's R, both take 3 slides and 1 stamp counterclockwise. Repeat going clockwise.
Part II.	Beginning on man's L, forward on lady's R, both take 2 draw steps toward center of room; take 2 draw steps away from center. Man takes 2 draw steps to L while lady turns under man's L arm with 2 waltz steps.
Part III.	Partners in social dance position and waltz counterclockwise in 4 waltz steps.

TEN PRETTY GIRLS (AMERICAN)

Music: Folkraft F1036B.
Main steps: Grapevine step and stamps.
Formation: Circle with hands held in skater's position with partner.

Figure:

Part I. Both point L toe across and in front of R. Point L toe sideward to L. Step L behind R, step sideward R, and bring L alongside R. Repeat starting with R.

Part II. Join inside arms with elbows high, walk forward 4 steps. Kick L forward, kick L back, and beginning on L stamp, stamp, stamp. Man moves forward to a new lady partner on stamps 2 and 3.

FINNISH SPINNING WALTZ (FINNISH)

Music: MacGregor 607 or Imperial 1036-A, Methodist World of Fun M-110.

Main steps: Step swing, waltz.

Beginning formation: Couples in a double circle. Men have their backs to the center; lady faces her partner. Hands are joined.

Figure:

Measures:

1. Step on outside foot (man's left, lady's right). Swing the inside foot across and point toe.

2. Repeat, stepping on inside foot.

3–4. Slide 2 steps to the left side—step, close, step. Repeat. Lady turns clockwise under the man's right arm.

5–8. Turn toward opposite direction. Repeat the figure with lady turning the man.

9–12. Join both hands; slide twice to the man's left, twice to his right.

13–16. Waltz, turning in clockwise circle.

Note: For a mixer, the man twirls this lady under his arm during the last two measures, then takes the lady behind him.

DANISH SCHOTTISCHE (DANISH)

Music: Methodist World of Fun Series M-102-B

Main step: Schottische.

Beginning formation: Skater's position.

Figure:

Measures:

1. Schottische step to the right, beginning right.

2. Schottische step to the left, beginning left.

3–4. Step-hop forward—right, left, right, left.

5–8. Repeat the figure in 1–4. On the last step-hop partners turn to face each other. Hold left hands.

9. Schottische to the right (away from partner).

10. Schottische to the left (back to partner).

11. Sweep right hand in a big circular motion over partner's head; place R hand on partner's back.

12. Partners look at each other and turn clockwise with step-hop four times.

Repeat from the beginning.

RUMNJSKO KOLO (YUGOSLAVIAN)

Music: Folk Dancer, Balkan 525.
Main steps: Walk, rocking steps, stamp.
Beginning formation: Single circle, joined hands held down.
Figure:
Measures:

1.	Moving backward, counterclockwise, take 3 steps beginning right, then hop.
2.	Turn to face the counterclockwise direction and repeat the 3 steps and a hop.
3–4.	Repeat measures 1 and 2.
5.	Face the center of the circle. Step right across left; rock back to left; step right again, then hop on right.
6.	Step left across right; rock back to right; step forward on left; hop on left.
7.	Repeat measure 5.
8.	Stamp 3 times with left foot.
9–12.	Repeat measures 5–8, beginning on left foot and finish with stamp on right foot.

Repeat from beginning.

Note: "Hissing" to express pleasure is characteristic of the Yugoslavian dances. Also, the feet are barely lifted from the floor.

EIDE RATAS (ESTONIAN) (SPINNING WHEEL)

Music: Folk Dancer MH-1018.
Main steps: Rocking steps, running steps.
Beginning formation: Couples in counterclockwise circle. Closed social
          dance position.
Figure:
Measures:

1.	Walk forward 2 steps, beginning on outside foot (man left, lady right), then hop in place on the inside foot. (Step, step, close.)
	On the first step, leap onto the outside foot, and bend forward. Then straighten with the hop on the inside foot.
2.	Repeat measure 1.
3–4.	Six running steps turning clockwise.
5–8.	Repeat measures 1 through 4.
9–16.	Repeat the entire figure.
17.	Partners face each other, men with their backs to the center of the circle. Hands are on hips.
	Partners take 3 steps away from each other, beginning on the left foot and turning right shoulder toward partner.
18.	Three more steps away, beginning right and turning left shoulder toward partner.
19–20.	Repeat measures 17 and 18.

21–24. Partners move toward each other with running steps; when they meet, they lock elbows and continue running for 12 more steps in clockwise direction. The lady now has her back to the center of the circle.

25–32. Repeat measures 17–24, hooking left elbows and finishing in original position.

PATCH TANZ (JEWISH) (CLAP DANCE)

Music: Folk Dance Service 137
Main steps: Walking step—step, then bend knee of stepping foot to the count "one and."
Beginning formation: Single circle, lady on man's right. Arms are bent at the elbow causing hands to be held at shoulder level.
Figure:
Measures:

1–4. Eight walking steps counterclockwise, beginning right.

5–8. Eight steps clockwise (to the left), beginning right.

9. Walk 2 steps forward into center of circle, beginning right.

10. Clap 3 times (3 counts). Pause (1 count).

11. Join hands again. Walk 2 steps backward; this time men begin left, ladies right.

12. Stamp 3 times with heel.

13–16. Repeat measures 9–12.

17–20. Partners face each other, join hands, then move to position with right shoulders almost touching, arms are outstretched to the right. Turn clockwise with 8 walking steps.

21–22. Turn to the right, counterclockwise, with 4 walking steps.

23–24. Release outside hands (lady's right, man's left). The lady walks in front of the man's left where she remains. Four walking steps.

LILI MARLENE (AMERICAN)

Music: MacGregor 310A.
Main steps: Walking and polka steps.
Beginning formation: Partners with inside hands joined facing counterclockwise.
Figure:

Part I. Walk 4 steps counterclockwise. Face partner, join both hands. Move in same direction with 4 slides. Turn to face clockwise with man still on the inside. Join inside hands and move clockwise with 4 walking and 4 slide steps.

Part II. Partners face, drop hands. Step R, swing L across and in front of R; step L and swing R. Join R hands and change places (man out and lady in) with 4 walking steps.

Part III.   Join L hands and go back to place. Face counterclockwise with inside hands joined and polka 4 steps forward alternating open and closed positions. Lady turns under joined inside hands and moves forward to next man in 4 walking steps.

Repeat from the beginning.

Social Dance

Social dance ranks as a top favorite recreational activity. Commercial and public schools, colleges and universities are increasingly offering more instructional classes in dance to increased numbers of pupils.

Classes for beginners, intermediates, and advanced students should include the dance walk, fox trot, waltz, tango, rumba, samba, mambo, and as many current variations of standard dance steps as possible.

LEADERSHIP HINTS

1. Begin with a small nucleus of those interested in learning to dance or improving their skills.

2. Plan with the group what they want to learn.

3. Use advanced class members to demonstrate and give assistance to those having difficulty.

4. Know each dance, the steps, the records to be used, and how to teach it before you begin.

5. See that the record player is in order and have the records you need available.

6. Organize the group into some formation that is best for teaching.

7. Introduce the dance walk as the basis of social dance; demonstrate the differences between "walking" and the dance walk. Use stick figure drawings on a blackboard or posters to show the difference.

8. Discuss the closed social dance position. First, teach the men to lead and then the women how to follow. (Leading and following techniques will need to be taught over and over.)

9. Progress through the fox trot and the waltz, then go on to the Latin dances. If they are appropriate, include the Lindy and the Charleston or other special dances.

10. Encourage the dancers to learn, practice, and go to dances.

11. Use key words to describe a step pattern. Review the patterns with the same key words. The group will learn faster if they repeat your directions as they do them.

12. Demonstrate each step.

13. Use mixers frequently to provide opportunity for each person to dance with many partners.

14. Enjoyment should be the primary objective. Improvements will come from a desire for improvement coupled with correct practice.

GROUP ORGANIZATION

1. Informal group, everyone facing in the same direction.
2. Lines facing each other. Men in one line, ladies in the other, so that each can practice his or her own part.
3. Double circle. Partners facing in opposite directions, hold hands. Ladies step backward, men forward, moving counterclockwise.
4. Single circle, everyone facing the center of a circle. Move into the center then out again.

The informal group is the best method of organizing a class which is all of one sex. Pinnies or arm bands may be used if the dancers want to identify themselves as leaders or followers.

THE DANCE WALK

The dance walk is a smooth, controlled natural walk that prevents each dancer from bumping into the knees of his or her partner and allows the dancers to take long, even steps, seemingly without bending their knees. The former is for safety and the latter for appearance. In the forward dance walk the weight precedes the step; for the backward dance walk the step precedes the weight. To do the forward steps: (1) Keep the feet in place; move or lean forward from the ankles; knees are slightly flexed. (2) Relax the left knee; swing the left foot forward *from the hip* without actually lifting the foot from the floor. (3) Step with the left foot, and transfer weight to left foot; right toe remains in place; right leg is straightened as weight is taken on left foot. (4) Relax right leg; bend knee, and swing right foot forward for another step.

To do the backward dance walk: (1) Take weight on the balls of the feet. (2) Swing the right leg backward *from the hip* until the leg and ankle are fully extended; "reach" backward with the toe. (3) Transfer weight to right foot. (4) Swing left leg backward; step, and transfer weight in the same manner. The backward walk requires that the dancer be perfectly balanced at all times. It is the basis for successful following.

All forward or backward steps should be long, smooth ones that let the dancers glide across the floor. The knee of the stepping foot should be bent slightly to swing the foot forward or backward. As the weight is transferred the knee should be flexed slowly to prevent jarring or jerking.

DANCE POSITIONS

The two dance positions most commonly used are the *closed position* and the *open position*. Both take on a different style with each dance, but, in general, the basic pattern is the same. Other positions are the conversation, the right reverse, and the left reverse.

THE CLOSED POSITION

1. Partners face each other, with their toes pointed directly forward, shoulders level.
2. The man places his right hand just below the lady's left shoulder blade. The lady *lightly* rests her left hand on the man's right shoulder or upper arm.
3. The man takes the lady's right hand in his left hand. Their palms are together. Hands should be cupped. Usually the most comfortable height is in line with the lady's right shoulder or slightly lower.
4. Partners look over each other's right shoulder.
5. The man begins dancing by stepping forward on his left foot; the lady steps backward on her right foot.

THE OPEN POSITION

1. The man turns his partner away from his right (to her right) until they are facing the same direction.
2. Positions of the hands remain the same as for the closed position.
3. Both partners step forward at the same time (man on his left foot, lady on her right).

THE CONVERSATION POSITION

1. The man leads into the open position, then drops his partner's right hand.
2. The lady's right arm and the man's left arm are dropped to their sides rather than extended sideward.

LEADING AND FOLLOWING

When dancers realize that the man must give the lead indication and that the lady follows an instant *later*, the couple will have an excellent start toward good dancing. Other suggestions are:

1. Know the basic steps and the variations of a dance.
2. Be conscious of the rhythm and the tempo of the music.
3. Begin on the proper foot: man steps forward left; lady, backward right.
4. Support your own weight. Have perfect balance at all times.

5. The lead indication is given immediately before the step is taken. It should be strong and definite. Timing is more important than method.
6. The man leads, then steps. The lady recognizes the signal, then steps. Therefore, the lady steps immediately *after* her partner transfers his weight into the step.
7. The lady must wait for her partner to step *first* if she is to follow successfully.
8. Lead indications are given through pressure of the hand, the arm or the upper part of the body. They are given by the man.

To move:

directly forward—press the upper body forward to begin moving in the line of direction.

backward—pull the right hand (and your partner) toward you.

into open position—turn partner away from you; press with the heel part of the right hand.

to the left—lower left shoulder slightly, press with right hand.

to the right—lower right shoulder slightly, press with fingers of the right hand.

THE FOX TROT

Fox trot music may be fast, medium, or slow. The medium or medium-slow dance is easiest to learn and the most popular, for bands play and record more music in this tempo than in any other.

Music for the fox trot is written in 4/4 time (four quarter beats in each measure); however, four steps are not taken during each measure. The dance is done in this step pattern:

Slow	.2 counts
Slow	.2 counts
Quick	.1 count
Quick	.1 count

Each complete step requires six counts or beats—the equivalent of one and one-half measures. The words *slow* and *quick* are especially descriptive of the step patterns.

The fox trot is characterized by its long, smooth, gliding steps. The quick indicates the time to be used in the transfer of weight and should not cause the dancer to jerk as he steps.

The rhythm pattern is:

$$\underline{1}\ 2\ \underline{3}\ 4 \qquad \underline{1}\ 2\ \underline{3}\ 4 \qquad \underline{1}\ 2\ \underline{3}\ \underline{4}$$
$$\overline{S}\quad \overline{S} \qquad \overline{Q}\quad \overline{Q}\ \overline{S} \qquad \overline{S}\quad \overline{Q}\ \overline{Q}$$

Groups can discover the accented first and third beats of each measure by clapping to fox trot music.

Arrange the group into a counterclockwise circle with the men moving forward and women backward. Call the slow, slow, quick, quick pattern and let the dancers follow. Practice this step in closed position. Introduce new steps as the group progresses. Demonstrate and practice several routines, and encourage all to make up their own.

FOX TROT STEPS

Basic Step
Step forward left ....slow
Step forward right ....slow
Step sideways left ....quick
Close right, transfer
   weight to right ....quick
Repeat beginning left again.
This step may be referred to as an "L" step to help the dancers remember the pattern.

Walking Step
Step forward left ....slow
Step forward right ....slow
Step forward left ....slow
Step forward right ....slow

Side Close
Step sideways left ....quick
Close right to left
   transfer weight ....quick
Step sideways left ....slow
(The right foot is closed to the left during the "slow" count, but weight is not transferred.)
To progress forward using Side Close Step:
Step sideways left ....quick
Close right to left ....quick
Step forward left ....slow
The steps and the transfer of weight in this step are the same as those of the basic quarter turns and half turns.

Dip
S Step left backward
S Step forward right, recovering the regular closed position
Q To add "side close," step sideways left
Q Close right to left
The man should step backward with a medium step, not extremely long, to insure smooth, continuous movement. The man's left knee is turned slightly out to allow his partner to bend her right knee as she steps forward.

Forward, Open Position
S Step sideways left
S Cross right foot in front of left, step right
   (Left foot should "brush" by right to be in place for next step.)

Q Step sideways left

Q Close right, transferring weight

This step may be varied by a "turn under": As the man steps sideways left, he turns the lady under her right arm. The lady pivots as she steps so that she completes a turn in time to take the second "quick" step, in regular closed position.

Turns

Quarter Turn

S Step sideways left

Q Close right to left, transfer weight

S Step forward left, turning toe out, pivot ¼ turn

Q Step sideways right

Q Close left to right

S Step back to right, turning toe in, pivot ¼ turn

Repeat this pattern to return to original position.

Half Turn Right

S Step forward left

S Step forward right turning toe out, pivot ¼ turn

Q Step side left

Q Close right to left

S Turn shoulders to the right, step back left, pivot ¼ turn

Q Step sideways right

Q Close left to right

S Step forward right

Half Turn Left

S Step forward left, toe out

Q Step sideways right

Q Close left to right

S Step back right, toe in

Q Step sideways left

Q Close right to left

S Step forward left

Combinations

Two Step

Q Step left

Q Close right

S Step left

S Step right

S Step left

Repeat pattern, beginning right.

Dance Walk with Side Close
Four dance walk steps, beginning left:
S Step left
S Step right
Q Step sideways left
Q Close right to left
Repeat routine.

Dance Walk, Side Close with Open Position
S Step left
S Step right
Q Step sideways left
Q Close right to left
Open position
S Step forward left
S Step forward right
Return to closed position
Q Step side left
Q Close right to left

Dance Walk with Turn Under
S Step 4 walking steps
Open position
S Step left
S Step right across or forward
Q Step left, turning girl under
Q Step right, returning to closed position.

THE WALTZ

Begin with clapping the rhythm, accenting the first beat of each measure. The words step, step, close, describe the waltz pattern much better than quick, quick, slow. The box waltz is the easiest for beginners to learn.

Music for the American waltz is in medium slow tempo. Fast waltz tempo has its own special step, the Viennese Waltz. Most dance groups will enjoy learning how to do this as a climax to a class.

Box Waltz
Counts
1 Step forward left
2 Step side right, "brush" by left making an angle
3 Close left to right, transfer weight
1 Step back right
2 Step side left
3 Close right to left, transfer weight
Repeat entire pattern.

Half-Squares to Progress Forward

Counts

1 Step forward left

2 Step side right

3 Close left to right, transfer weight

1 Step forward right

2 Step side left

3 Close right to left

Hesitation Waltz–for variation of pattern

1 Step forward left

2 Swing right forward

3 Touch right toe forward past left, leg extended

1 Step backward right

2 Swing left backward

3 Touch left toe to floor past right, leg extended

Actually the dancers step only on the first beat of each measure.

Left Turn

1 Step forward and to the side left, toe turned out

2 Step side right

3 Close left to right

1 (4) Step backward right, toe turned in

2 (5) Step side left

3 (6) Close right to left

Repeat counts 1 through 6 to complete turn.

Right Turn

1 Step forward and to the side right, toe turned out

2 Step side left

3 Close right to left

1 (4) Step backward left, toe turned in

2 (5) Step side right

3 (6) Close left to right

Repeat counts 1 through 6 to complete turn.

The Viennese Waltz

Characteristic of the Viennese Waltz is the continuous turning done by pivoting immediately after each step on the first and third beats of each measure. The key words are step pivot, side, pivot. Tempo of the Viennese Waltz is at least twice as fast as that of the American Waltz. Steps are small and weight is only half transferred because the steps are taken in such rapid succession.

Forward Turn

Counts

1 Step forward left, toe turned out, pivot ¼ turn
2 Step side right (short step)
3 Pivot on the balls of both feet ¼ turn, transfer weight to the left foot.

At the end of count 3, a half turn is completed.

Backward Turn

1 Step backward right, ¼ turn
2 Step back left (across right foot)
3 Pivot on the balls of both feet ¼ turn left, close left foot against right.

THE TANGO

Tango music is in 2/4 time with a special accent in rhythm that tells the dancer when to step and when to pause. First, play several tangos to let the group listen. Discuss the accents and the style of the music. Next, have them clap out the rhythm.

The basic step is the dance walk with slight variation. The dancer bends his knee as he steps and lifts his foot up off the floor to carry out the characteristic tango style. The steps are smooth, deliberate, and long.

Again the words slow and quick are valuable. The basic pattern of the dance is slow, slow, quick, quick, slow; the steps are forward, forward, forward, side, draw. In the draw, one foot closes to the other foot, but no weight is transferred to the closing foot. After the dancers have listened to music and have repeated slow, slow, quick, quick, slow several times, have them step in time with the words then progress to the basic step—the step, side draw. Variations are again introduced as soon as the group has practiced the first step in closed social dance position.

Tango Steps

Promenade

S Step forward left
S Step forward right
S Step forward left
Q Step forward right
S Step forward left

Repeat, beginning on right.

Side Close

S Step forward left
Q Step forward right
Q Step sideways left (short step)
S Close right to left, transfer weight

Side Draw

S Step forward left
S Step forward right
Q Step forward left
Q Step sideways right
S Draw left to right, weight remains on right

Pivot Turn Left

Open Position

S Step forward left (lady right)
S Step across right, lady steps left then pivots on left into closed
   position
Q Step forward left (small step)
Q Step sideways right
S Draw left to right

Pivot Turn Right (direction to man)

Open position as in left turn

S Step forward left
S Step forward right, pivot on right foot into closed position
Q Step backward left
Q Step sideways right
S Draw left to right

Step-Out with Sweep Pivot (directions to man)

Open position

S Step forward left
S Step forward right, swing left leg in a circle, cross left over
   right
Q Closed position, step left
Q Step side right
S Draw left to right

The Corte

Q Step forward left
Q Step back in place right
S Dip backward left
S Recover
Q Step forward right
Q Step side left
S Draw right to left

THE RUMBA

The rumba has the 4/4 time and key words "quick, quick, slow" in
common with the fox trot. However, special features of the rumba
definitely distinguish it from the smooth, even fox trot, so that the
dancer cannot fox trot a little faster and call his dance a rumba.

To do this Cuban dance move the upper part of the body only slightly while hip and knee action create a continuous, flowing movement from the waist down. Half-size steps are taken with the foot flat on the floor.

The step and the transfer of weight occur at different times. When one foot is moved, no weight is shifted until the other foot is in position to step. Always, one knee is bent in taking a step; the other is straight, holding the body weight. This delayed action causes the hips to move. The closed position is used with one variation. The man's left arm and the lady's right are bent at the elbow with their hands held at eye level.

Practice Pattern (two rumba steps)

Begin with feet together.

Counts

1 Shift weight to right foot; step left, foot flat on floor, knee bent, no weight.
2 Straighten left knee, take weight. Close right to left, right knee bent, no weight.
3 Straighten right knee, take weight; relax left knee, step forward.
4 Hold.

Rumba Box or Square

Q Step sideways left
Q Close right to left
S Step forward left
Q Step right sideways
Q Close left to right
S Step backward right

The Running Step

Q Step forward left; hips move to right
Q Step forward right; hips move to left
S Step forward left; hips move to right
(This last step and hip swing should be done slowly so that the movement will take two full beats, beats 3 and 4.)

The Turn (Lady)

Man leads lady into open position. He raises his left arm and turns lady to her right in a clockwise circle under his left arm.

Man continues to dance the rumba square in place, the lady dances the running step.

The Circle Turn (Lady)

Man retains lady's right hand in his left hand. Partners rumba away from each other until arms are straightened.

Man leads the lady to his right. When his hand is near his right side, he takes the lady's right hand in his right hand and transfers it to his left again behind his back.

As the lady returns to face her partner he raises his left hand and arm and returns to closed position.

THE SAMBA

The Samba is a delightful Brazilian dance in which the dancer rocks to a rhythm with an accented beat. As soon as a person learns the basic step, he can begin creating his own routines.

Samba music is written in 4/4 time, but actually the dance steps indicate that the time is quick, quick, slow, with the first quick step more heavily accented than the second. The characteristic movement of the dance is an up-and-down bounce, created by bending and straightening the knees on every step while the dancer sways or bends the body from the knees up in the opposite direction to the way the feet move.

Practice Pattern for the Basic Step
Q Step forward left, knee bent
Q Step forward right, closing right parallel to left foot; transfer weight, straighten both knees
S Step left in place, both knees bent
Q Step back right, knee bent slightly
Q Step back left, close to right, knees bent
S Step in place right, knees bent

As the dancer steps forward left, he sways the upper part of his body backward bending from the knees. He then sways forward as he steps backward. This basic step is done in closed position. Two popular variations are the butterfly break and the marcha or shuffle step. Routines should be done in fours or multiples of four. The lead indications should be given during the last step in a series of four.

The Butterfly Break–reverse open and open positions
(Reverse open—couples face man's right, lady's left)

Reverse Open
Q Step side left
Q Place right toe directly behind left heel and rock weight to toe
S Step in place left; transfer weight; return weight to left

Open Position
Q Step side right
Q Place left toe, behind right heel and rock weight to toe
S Step in place right, returning weight to right
In this break, the dancers bend from the waist in the direction that they step. Also, they should look over their shoulders toward the floor to lend style to their dance.

The Marcha or Shuffle–open or conversation position
S Step forward left, knees bent
S Straighten left knee quickly; shift weight momentarily to right foot; pull left foot slightly backward and in the same motion, bend left knee, taking all weight on left.

THE MAMBO

The Mambo has an off-beat rumba rhythm. The music is in 4/4 time but the accent is different from that of any other dance. The rhythm is slow, quick, quick, and the steps are draw, step, step, step. The pattern begins with the draw on the *fourth* beat of the measure; this draw and the first step are done during the slow count.

The step is heavy and definite. The dancer digs the ball of his foot into the floor as he steps. The basic step, a butterfly break, and the side-balance steps are described here to provide a beginning for creating original mambo steps. Actually any series of steps and stamps taken in the accent pattern will be considered the mambo; often partners do not even do the same step at the same time.

Introductory steps for counts 1, 2 and 3 of the first measure
Counts
Q 1 Step left to the left side
Q 2 Step back right
Q 3 Step forward left (in place)

Basic Step
Counts
S 4 Draw right foot to side of left, knee bent
  1 Step right, straighten knee
Q 2 Step forward left
Q 3 Step back right, in original place
S 4 Draw left foot to side of right, knee bent
  1 Step left, straighten knee, shift weight
Q 2 Step back right
Q 3 Step forward left, in place
Repeat pattern.

Side Balance Step
Repeat the three introductory steps or continue from the basic step.
Counts
S 4 Draw right foot parallel to left, knee bent
  1 Step right, straighten knee, shift weight
Q 2 Step side left, shift weight
Q 3 Step right in place, shift weight
S 4 Draw left foot to right, knee bent
  1 Step left, straighten knee, shift weight
Q 2 Step side right, shift weight
Q 3 Step left in place, shift weight

Butterfly Break

Continue from basic step or side balance step.

Counts

S 4 Swing right foot to right side

   1 Step right, toe forward, straighten knee, shift weight

Q 2 Step left behind right and across right; transfer weight

Q 3 Step right, in place, heavy step, transfer weight

S 4 Swing left foot to left side

   1 Step left, toe forward, straighten knee, shift weight

Q 2 Step right behind left and across left; transfer weight

CHA-CHA

4/4 Time Record—Basic Dance Steps, Educational Activities, Inc.

Starting Position. Social Dance—Girl on opposite foot.

Forward Basic Step

    Count 1.   Step forward on left foot.

    Count 2.   Step in place on right foot.

    Count 3–4. Bring left foot back to right foot; step in place three times (left, right, left).

Backward Basic Step

    Count 1.   Step back on right foot.

    Count 2.   Step in place on left foot.

    Count 3–4. Bright right foot back to left foot—step in place three times (right, left, right).

MIXERS

Dance games, or change-partner dances and elimination dances, should be an integral part of both dance classes and scheduled dance sessions. They serve to motivate the group to practice a particular step, emphasize important points to remember, and add interest.

Success of any mixer depends entirely upon the leader. He must constantly note the atmosphere as the game progresses. He should keep each moving in tempo with the reaction of the dancers toward it. Elimination dances should not be used too long or too much.

THE DOUBLE CIRCLE (PAUL JONES MIXER)

Ladies form in a circle facing away from the center, the men form a circle facing them. Both circles move with the music to the right until the leader gives a signal to dance. Then each man takes as his partner the lady directly in front of him. The signal may be simply the call, "Let's dance!" A sure way to attract everyone's attention is to stop the music until each person has a partner and then begin it again for the dance.

MULTIPLICATION

Three or more couples, depending upon the size of the group, are asked to begin dancing. When the music stops each chooses a new partner from those not dancing. The dancing with each new partner should be short until everyone has been included. Play one complete number dancing with the last partner chosen.

CHARACTERISTICS IN COMMON

Everyone with a certain characteristic or trait finds another with the same feature. For example, "All blonde ladies find a blond partner" or "Dance with someone whose birthday is in the same month as yours."

MATCHED SHOES

Each lady tosses one of her shoes into the center of a circle. At a given signal, all the men rush to pick up a shoe, then find its owner to be his partner for the next dance. This procedure may be reversed (the men take off their shoes). The similarity among men's shoes causes quite a scramble to find the right owners.

PUZZLES

Anything that can be divided into two parts when matched together again is a suitable prop. Two decks of cards can serve, a picture may be cut in half with a zig-zag edge, etc. Give each person half a song title or half a word and have him find his better half for the next dance.

BLIND DATE

The men form a line outside the room. Inside on the dance floor the ladies also form a line. As each man walks through the door, he begins dancing with the first lady in line.

BROOM DANCE

A broom is given to the person without a partner. He dances with it for a while then drops it as the signal for everyone to find a new partner. He then grabs a partner, leaving someone else to dance with the broom. Each partner of the broom should give time for new partners to dance a reasonable length of time before he drops the broom or there will only be a contest instead of a dance.

GRAND MARCH

The grand march is ideal for getting new partners. The ladies and men each form a line facing the same direction on opposite sides of the room. When the music begins, the first persons in each line move toward each other until they meet. They continue to march or walk down the middle of the floor until all others in the line have met dance partners.

ELIMINATION DANCES

"Cuttin' in." Each man without a partner is given some object that he can present to another man to "cut in." A lemon, a flower or candy that is well wrapped will be suitable. If you want to make something, cut out miniature phonograph records from cardboard, paint them black with red or yellow labels, and write on them titles of popular tunes.

This dance is even more interesting when there are extra ladies.

Balloon Dance. Tie a balloon to the ankle of each girl. The couple who protect their balloon longest and are the last on the floor are the winners. The leader may say that anyone may break a balloon provided that no one stops dancing to do it, or he may give each couple a number. When a number is called all other dancers rush to "kill" that couple. This dance is a lot of fun if the dancers do not become too rowdy.

Square Stop. Draw squares on the floor. When the music stops, the couples who are caught standing on a square are eliminated. The number of squares drawn will depend upon the space and the size of the group that will be dancing. The game is more exciting if the leader draws a new square for each couple that is eliminated.

Square Dance

Square dance is well established as a recreational activity. Even the drawback of providing a caller has been eliminated by recordings of both singing and patter calls that come complete with dance music and instructions.

Few people learn to square dance without good leadership; here again the recreation director must take on the role of teacher. A group may be interested and enthusiastic, but without skill they will soon settle down to watch others dance.

Only a sample of openers, endings, mixers, and patter calls has been included here, although hundreds are available. The dances selected are arranged in order from (1) simple dances, (2) through several from the intermediate level, to (3) more complicated figures.

SUGGESTIONS FOR THE LEADER

1. Discuss with your group the beginning of square dancing so that they will not get lost in a maze of terms. The first figures will soon be forgotten unless they are tied in directly with dancing. Explain briefly.

2. Demonstrate the step that is used during the dance. This is a smooth, shuffling step done with the knees flexed and relaxed. The dancers may add a two-step now and then for variety. Almost without exception, the beginner will either skip or jump with each step. Review the shuffle step over and over, and remind dancers individually to keep their dance smooth.

3. Begin with a grand march. Line the men up on one side of the room, the ladies on the other with both facing one end of the dance area. When

the music starts, the first "gent" in each line comes to the center of the room, meets his partner there with an elbow swing, and moves down the center of the room. Others in the lines follow. At the opposite end of the dance floor the first couple turns right, the second left, and so on to return to the other end of the floor. The couples next come down in groups of four, then in groups of eight. As soon as the last group of eight is complete, stop the music and explain how to "square your sets."

4. The Square: Explain the positions of the couples, partner, corner, home position.

5. Mention that calls are directed to the men.

6. Walk through the following: Circle left, allemande left.

7. Grand right and left, sashay and the promenade. Practice the two-step swing and the pivot swing.

8. Call these basic figures with the music.

9. Walk through a simple dance. Then dance it with the music. If you use a record with the call recorded with the music, go over the directions carefully and, in addition, tell the dancers the extra patter the caller includes. For the first experiences in dancing with the music, turn the speed of the record to slow tempo. If you have an accompanist, variation of tempo can easily be made.

10. Teach the do-si-do; practice it several times with various patter calls. Use it in a dance. Then review the allemande left pointing out the difference between it and the do-si-do.

11. Explain that each dance will begin with an *opener*, then the figure will be called until one couple has danced the figure with every other couple. After each figure, a *filler* or *mixer* may be included, and the last call is the *close* or *ending*.

12. Introduce a new dance. Walk through it at least once. Have one set dance through the figure if there is one that has previously learned it. Teach any part of the dance that is new to the group. Start the music, and dance. Review and begin again if the dancers become confused. Introduce another new dance. Review dances already learned People enjoy being exposed to the new, but they like best the old dances they can do well.

NOTES FOR THE CALLER

1. Learn the dance *first*, then memorize the call. It is impossible to read a dance from notes and expect it to sound like a call.

2. Practice listening to the rhythm of square dance music and repeating the call to yourself until you have the timing that is necessary.

3. Learn, explain, and demonstrate several openers, fill-ins or mixers, and closes or endings.

4. Be sure that you can analyze, explain, and demonstrate all calls that you include.

5. Practice calling into a microphone, if possible. Do not lean on the microphone or shout into it. Turn up the volume rather than yourself. Stand at least 6 inches away from the microphone so that your words will not be muffled.

6. All words must be clear and distinct. Singing calls are rarely as clear as spoken calls.

7. Give the dancers time to dance the figure, but remember that the call precedes the beginning of a figure. Since the dancers must hear directions before they can follow them, give each call during the last part of the preceding figure.

8. When one set is slightly behind the others, give them time to catch up. The other sets can clap hands during this pause. If, however, several sets are behind the call, stop the dance to walk through the pattern again. Then start over.

9. As soon as the group has passed the beginners' stage, use fill-ins and mixers for the element of surprise.

10. Call the dance as though you are telling the dancers when to do each pattern. Keep your voice pitched as low as is comfortable.

11. Have another person listen at the other side of the dance area to help you tune the tone and volume properly.

12. When the group of dancers is large, stand on a platform so that you can be seen and heard.

13. Add your own personality to your calling. Make up your own fill-in patter.

SQUARE DANCE TERMS

All Get Straight—The couples get in proper order (Couple 4 on right of couple 3, etc.)

Allemande Left—Give your left hand to your corner and swing one time around.

Allemande Right—Call that follows "allemande left." Swing your partner once around with your right hand.

Balance—Each partner steps two steps backward and bows, then takes two steps forward back to the original position.

Balance and Swing—Two steps backward, bow; forward again to swing your partner once around with a waist swing.

Bar—The position from which a dancer starts a figure.

Break—To release hands.

Break and Trail—Release hands, turn to the right and move single file back to home position.

Center—The middle of the square formed by the dancers.

Circle Eight—All four couples join hands, and move to the left.

Corner—The person across the "corner" of the square.

Corner Lady—The lady on the man's left.

Divide the Ring—One couple crosses the square to couple opposite them, passes between that couple. The lady turns to her right and the man to his left, and they move outside the square to return to their home position.

Do-Si-Do—Give your *partner* your *left* hand; swing her around. Give your corner your right hand, and swing her once around. Go back to your partner, and promenade home. When the call "one more turn" is given, repeat the figure: partner, left; corner, right; partner left again; corner right again then promenade home.

Dos-a-Dos—Partners face each other; advance, passing right shoulders. They step to the right without turning around, then move backward to starting position (facing partner).

Elbow Swing—Hook right elbows with the person you are to swing and swing once or once and a half around as the call directs.

Figure—The main part of the dance. A dance is identified by the name of its figure.

Forward and Back—Take four steps into the center and four steps back to place.

Grand Right and Left—Partners take right hands in handshake position, and pass right shoulders. They give the next person in the circle their left hands, and pass left shoulders, continuing weaving in and out around the circle until they meet at the opposite side of the square. The couples promenade home unless the call directs them to continue the Grand Right and Left until they are back to home position. This call usually follows "allemande left."

Head Couples—The first and third couples.

Home Position—The first position of each couple in the square. The man always returns to this first position at the call "Promenade home."

Honor Your Partner—Ladies' curtsy to their partners; men bow.

Honor Your Corner—Ladies curtsy to their corners; each man bows to his corner lady.

Ladies Chain—Two couples face each other. Each lady moves toward the other, they join right hands and pass right shoulders. Then the lady gives her left hand to the opposite man; he turns her once around. The ladies again join right hands and pass through back to their partners who turn them around to original position.

Lead Out—Call for one couple to move in some particular direction.

On to the Next—Call for couple or man to advance to the next couple to the right.

Opposite—The person or couple directly across the set from you.

Partner—The lady on the man's right; the man on the lady's left.

Promenade—Each man takes his partner in skater's position, and all the couples move counterclockwise around the circle. In this position, the partners stand side by side, lady on the man's right. The man takes his lady's left hand in his left hand, and her right hand in his right. His right arm is over her left arm.

Right Hands Across—Men join right hands and move clockwise. This call is also given to the ladies of the set.

Sashay—See Dos-A-Dos.

See-Saw—See Dos-A-Dos.

Set—See Square.

Side Couples—Second and fourth couples.

Square—Four couples in an arrangement that forms a square. Each couple makes one side of the square. The couple with their backs to the music is the number one or head couple. Couple two is on the right of couple one; three is opposite, and couple four is to the left of the head couple. The first couple begins each figure unless otherwise designated.

Swing—

> Two-Step Swing—Partners take closed social dance position then move to the left until their right sides are touching. The lady and the man both step forward on the left foot and continue moving in place, clockwise, by dancing a series of two-steps. Partners pull away from each other, making possible a "whirling" motion.

> Pivot Swing—Partners take position described above. The partners pivot around clockwise on their right feet, pulling away from the "center" of the pivot as in the two-step swing.

> Right or Left Hand Swing—The lady and man join right or left hands and swing around. Their arms are bent at the elbow; they extend their fingers up and catch hands at eye level. (This is in contrast to the handshake position.)

> Two Hand Swing—The couple joins both hands and swings around. The couple faces each other.

> Waist Swing—The man places his hands at the lady's waist; the lady rests her hands on the man's shoulders, and they swing to the right (clockwise).

Taw—Partner.

Twirl—The man holds the lady's right hand in his right hand; raises their right arms and turns the lady under his right arm until she is in promenade position.

OPENING CALLS

> Honor your corner, and the lady by your side,
> Now all join hands and circle out wide.
> Round and round and round you go,
> And you break that ring with a do-si-do, and a little more do,
> Chicken in the bread pan a'peckin' out dough.
> Grab your partner and home you go.

> All jump up and never come down. (Dancers yell as they jump.)
> Swing your little girl round and round,
> 'Till the hollow of your foot makes a hole in the ground.
> Promenade, boys, promenade.

> Honor your partner, and the lady on your left.
> All join hands and circle to the left.

Swing your corner like swingin' on a gate,
Right to your partner and right and left eight.
One foot up and the other one down.
Meet your partner as she comes down,
Swing her round and round,
And promenade home.

Honor your partner, honor your corner.
All join hands and circle eight.
And you circle eight and all get straight.
Allemande left with your left hand,
Right to your partner and right and left grand.
Meet ole Sal and meet ole Sue and
Meet that gal with a run down shoe.
All promenade, boys, promenade.

All eight balance,
All eight swing, and promenade around the ring.
Promenade!

All join hands and circle eight.
Break and trail along that line,
Ladies in the lead and gents behind.
Swing your partner and promenade home.

Note: These calls may be used also as mixers or fillers by omitting the
call "Honor your partner."

ENDING CALLS

Honor your partner,
Honor your corner,
Wave to your opposite,
That's all!

Promenade, and I don't care.
Take her to that high back chair.

Swing your partner,
Pat her on the head,
Take her out and feed her cornbread.

Swing your corner,
Swing your own,
And there you stand!

DO-SI-DO PATTER

Do-si-do and a little more do,
Hurry up boys, can't be slow.
You'll never get to heaven if you don't do so.
One more change, and home you go.

Do-si-do, and a little more do,
Chicken in the bread pan scratchin' out gravel.
Grab your gal, and home you travel.

Do-si-do—partner left—
Corner right—
Back to your partner, and home you go.

Do-si-do, and a little more do,
Aces high and deuces low.
One more change, and on you go.

Do-si-do, and here we go,
With a little bit of heel, and a little bit of toe,
Meet your partner and home you go.

DANCES

HOT TIME IN THE OLD TOWN
Music: Any recording of the song that is peppy.

All four girls, to the center of the ring.	Girls form center ring moving clockwise.
All four boys, promenade around the ring.	Boys circle in opposite direction.
Pass your partner, the next one you will swing,	Boys swing his right hand girl.
There'll be a Hot Time in the Old Town Tonight.	
Repeat three more times, until all boys are back to their original partners	Same as above.
All four boys, to the center of the ring,	Boys form center ring moving clockwise.
All four girls, promenade around the ring,	Girls circle in opposite direction.
Pass your partner, the next one you will swing,	Girls swing with next boy.
There'll be a Hot Time in the Old Town Tonight.	
Repeat three more times, until all boys are with original partners.	Same as above.
Use any ending call.	

OH! JOHNNY

Music: The Tune "Oh! Johnny" or the recorded singing call.

All join hands and circle the ring.

Circle 8 left.

Stop where you are and give your partner a swing.

Waist swing your partner twice around.

Now swing the girl behind you.

Waist swing your corner lady.

Swing your own if you think you have time to.

Swing your partner again.

Allemande left on your corners all.

Swing once around your corner lady, and face your partner.

And dos-a-dos your own.

Sashay your partner and turn to face your corner.

Then all promenade with that sweet corner maid.

Promenade your corner.

Singing, "Oh, Johnny, O, Johnny, Oh!!"

Promenade home—and sing!

Repeat three times until each man has his original partner.

SALLY GOODIN

(All Couples Dancing)

Music: "Sally Goodin"

Four men out, and swing Sally Goodin with your right hand.

Each man steps behind his partner, and moves to his right hand lady. He swings her once around with his right hand.

Now swing your taw.

Men return to partners and swing once around with left hand.

Swing that girl from Arkansas.

Man swings his corner lady with left hand swing, once around.

Now swing your taw.

Left hand swing with partner.

And don't forget to swing Grandmaw.

Men move to the right in the center of the square to the opposite lady.

With a two-hand swing.

Swing opposite once around.

Back to your partner,

Men again circle to the right to return home.

And everybody swing.

Everyone swings with a waist swing. The man should swirl his partner around the set to the next position, so that she will be ready to promenade.

And promenade your corner around the ring.

Promenade home.

Repeat three times, until the ladies are at their original home position.

UPTOWN AND DOWNTOWN

Music: Any square dance recording of "Golden Slippers."

Beginning pattern.

First couple up center and away uptown.

First couple, hands joined, walk to couple 3, bring them back to their home, to couple 3's home.

Bring that other couple down.
Pick them up and let them fall.
Here you go all around the hall.
Lady go gee and gent go haw,

Couple 3 separates, couple 1 walks through, dividing them.

Right elbow swing as you did before,

The first girl returns to her home position, her partner walks left. They meet and elbow swing.

Elbow swing as you go round.
And swing your corner lady.
Swing your corner lady, swing her round and round.
Now all promenade, go round the town, promenade around.
Tap your heel and save your toe,
Chicken in the breadpan scratching dough,
Places all and hear my call, ready, ready, here we go!

All boys swing their corner ladies.
Promenade with the corner back to boys' home.

The first boy repeats all above with a new partner.
Second boy does it twice. Third and fourth boys do it twice.
End with allemande left and grand right and left again.

Use any ending call.

TEXAS STAR

Music: Any square dance arrangement or "Cripple Creek."

Ladies to the center, and back to the bar.

Man takes his partner's right hand and twirls her into the center, then out again.

Gents to the center and form a star,
With your right hand across,
Now, back with your left, and don't get lost.
Meet your partner and pass her by,
Pick up the next girl on the fly.

Men catch right hands and move clockwise.

Men pivot, catch left hands, and move counterclockwise.
Each man passes his partner and hooks elbows with his right hand lady. He is still holding his opposite's left hand in the center.

Ladies swing in, and the gents swing out.
Turn that Texas Star about.

Now, do-si-do, and a little more do,
Swing your partner and promenade home.

Men drop left hands and swing the ladies to the inside. Ladies star with right hands across. The set is still moving.
The man releases the elbow hook. He takes his lady's left hand in his left hand and swings her until she faces the corner. The do-si-do continues as usual.

WAGON WHEEL
Music: Any square dance arrangement.

First couple, balance, first couple swing. Out to the couple at the right of the ring and circle four.
Leave that girl, go on to the next and circle three.

Self-explanatory.

Lady No. 1 stays with couple 2; Man No. 1 goes on to couple 3 and circles three. No. 2 man hooks elbows with his partner and lady 1; they stand facing center.

Steal that girl like honey from a bee, put her on your right.
And on to the next and circle four.
Leave that girl, and go home alone.

Lead man takes lady No. 3 as he advances to couple 4.
Man No. 1 and lady No. 3 circle with couple 4.
Man No. 1 returns to his home position alone. No. 4 gent hooks elbows with his partner and lady 3.

Forward six, and back to the bar.

End men forward and back like a shooting star.
Forward six, and sashay round as you cross over.

Men 2 and 4 and their ladies take 4 steps to the center then return to place.
Men 1 and 3 move forward, then back.
Men 2 and 4 again move to center, catch hands, and turn half way round; so that when they go back to place they will be on the opposite side of the square.

End men go on to Dover.

Men 1 and 3 meet at the center, twirl half around and back into place.

Now right hand up and left hand under.

Men 2 and 4 take the ladies' hands then raise right arms and twirl the right hand lady (partner) to the man on the left, and the left hand lady to the man on the right. The right hand lady moves first. Now men 2 and 4 become the "end men." The dance is continued three times until everyone has his original partner.

SIOUX CITY SUE

Music: The tune "Sioux City Sue" or the recorded singing call.

Swing, boys, swing. Everybody swing.
Promenade around the ring.
Promenade back home again,
Just like you always do.
Everybody swing, now swing Sioux City Sue.

Swing twice around.

Again swing twice.

First couple right and circle four hands 'round.
Dos-a-dos your opposite, the lady once around.
Dos-a-dos your partner, and you swing her too.
Both couples swing. Now swing Sioux City Sue.
On to the next, and your circle four hands 'round.

1st couple leads to 2nd couple and circles once around.
Sashay the opposite lady, returning to original position.
Sashay your partner.

Swing your partner twice around with a waist swing.
The figure is repeated until couple 1 returns home. Then the introduction is repeated, and couples 2, 3, and 4 each lead a complete figure.

ROSE OF SAN ANTONE

Music: The Tune of "San Antonio Rose" or the recorded singing call.

OPENER

Oh, you swing 'em, boys,
You swing 'em round and round.
Promenade that little lady
All around the town.
Promenade back home
With the one you call your own,
And swing with the Rose of San Antone.

Self-explanatory

FIGURE

First couple right, and you circle four and smile.
Now dos-a-dos your partner in that good ole mountain style.

Couples 1 and 2 circle once around.
Each man takes his partner's left hand in his right hand, leads her around in front of him and around him until she is back on his right. The man does not change the direction he is facing in and does not release his partner's hand. (The man may well pretend he is twirling a lasso.)

Swing with your opposites until you find your own.
Then swing with the Rose of San Antone.

Each man swings his opposite lady once around.
Each man swings his partner.

Couple 1 leads on to the next until they have danced with all the couples.
Between figures the following chorus is danced:

CHORUS

All gents swing your corners, the lady on your left.
Go back and swing your own; she's the one you love the best.
Allemande left your corners, And dos-a-dos your own.
Balance to your partner and weave that ring back home.
Now you weave that ring, Go 'round and 'round.
And when you meet your partner,
You will dos-a-dos around.
You weave that ring, until you find your own.
Then swing with that Rose of San Antone.

To "weave the ring" the dancers pass their partner's right shoulder, then continue around the set doing a grand right and left without touching hands. The men fold their arms across their chests, and the ladies catch their skirts in their hands.

Sashay your partner and continue moving in the same direction as before.
When you meet your partner, you will be at home position. Swing her once around.

Repeat the entire dance until all four couples have been the lead couple.

ALABAMA JUBILEE
Music: "Alabama Jubilee."

Four little ladies promenade
The inside of the ring.

Ladies go into the center and
move to the right until they
return home.

Back to your partner,
And give him a swing.
Dos-a-dos your corner,
Just once around.

Ladies sashay their corner men.

Bow to your partner, now,
Swing him 'round and 'round.
Four men promenade
The inside of the hall.

Men move in a circle to the
right.

Back to your partner,
And dos-a-dos all.

Men sashay their partners.

The corner girl will swing with
you.

Each man swings his corner
lady.

And promenade like an old
shoo-shoo
To the Alabama Jubilee.

Each man promenades his corner until the next call comes
for four little ladies to promenade. Couples should not try
to get home before the next
figure begins.

Repeat the figure three times until each person has his original partner.

MIXER (as called by Joe Lewis)

All join hands and circle left,
And form that big old ring.
Break the ring with a corner
swing,
Leave her on your right, and
you're gone again.
Ring, ring, a pretty little ring,
Break it again with a corner
swing.
Leave her on your right and
circle—
And don't you know.
Do-si-do, and a little more do,
Like a chicken in the bread pan
a'peckin' out do.
When you get back home this
time,
It's stop, you know.
Go all around your left-hand
lady,

See-saw 'round that taw.
Allemande left with that old left
  hand,
Partner right and a right and
  left grand.
Here comes Sal, here comes
  Sue,
And here comes the gal that
  came with you.
Take them home on the old
  shoo-shoo.
Promenade around that ring,
Get 'em happy, give 'em a swing.
To the Alabama Jubilee.

SWANNEE RIVER

(Only the opener of this dance is sung to the tune "Swannee River."
The dance is recorded as a singing call, but it may be used as a patter
call, with singing only during the opener.)

OPENER

Allemande left, and a grand
  right and left. SING:
"Way down upon the Swannee
  River
Far, far, away.
There's where my heart am
  longing ever,
Down where the old folks stay."

When partners meet half around
  the set, they hold right hands
  and step left and "kick," then
  step, kick right in time with
  the rhythm of the song. Then
  they pass right shoulders
  again with their partner and
  continue the grand right and
  left until they are back at
  home position.

FIGURE

First couple:
Lady go 'round the lady
And the gent go round the gent.

1st couple moves to face couple
  2. Lady 1 goes between couple
  2 and circles lady 2 without
  changing the direction she
  faces.
Man 1 follows his lady and circles man 2 back to place.

The gent go 'round the lady
And the lady 'round the gent.

The man moves in a circle
  around lady 2, then the lady
  goes around the man.

Circle half, and right and left through.

Swing your partner once around
And take her on with you.

And the lady go 'round the lady, etc.

Repeat figure until No. 1 couple has danced with couples 3 and 4.

The entire dance including the opener is danced three more times for couples 2, 3, and 4 to lead.

Circle four until couple 1 is facing the center of the set. (The couples simply change positions.) Each lady gives her hand to the opposite man. They pass right shoulders and meet their partners again.

Couples 1 and 2 swing. Couple 1 swings toward the center of the set to be ready to go on to the next.

GLORY, HALLELUJAH!

Music: "Battle Hymn of the Republic." Singing call recorded.

First lady, promenade the inside of the ring,

And when she is home again, Give her a great big swing.

Step right out, and face about.

Side couples fall in line.

Lady go right, gent go left, and march around the ring.

Note: The entire chorus is not used. See words below.

Lady 1 promenades to the right around the set, then goes home.

Man 1 swings lady twice around, and leaves her on his right.

Couple 1 faces away from the center.

Couples fall in line behind lead couple. When couple 1 is leading, the order is 2, 3, then 4. When 2 is leading, it is 3, 4, and 1, and when 4 leads, the order is 1, 2, and 3.

Lady 1 leads the ladies to the right in a half-circle; man 1 leads the men to the left. When couple 1 meets at the opposite side of the set they join inside hands and move up the center of the square to their home position. All the couples then drop hands and the two lines stand facing each other.

First couple, dos-a-dos, and dos-a-dos around.
Second couple, dos-a-dos, and dos-a-dos around.
Third couple, dos-a-dos, and dos-a-dos around.
Fourth couple dos-a-dos around.
Everybody forward and back
And I'll tell you the reason why.
Forward again, and pass right through,
And look your girl in the eye.
Then step right up and swing her,
And swing her till she cries.
Swing her back to home.
Sashay 'round your corner,
And your corner sashay 'round.
Sashay 'round your partner,
And your partner sashay 'round.
Allemande left your corner, and
Allemande right your own.
And a grand right and left around the ring.

As soon as the first couple returns to position the second couple advances to dos-a-dos, and so on.

All take three steps forward, then three backward to place.
Couples pass right shoulders and turn half way around; the lines exchange places.
Each man swings his partner back to their home position.

CHORUS: Everybody sing!
"Glory, glory, Hallelujah!
Glory, glory, Hallelujah!
Glory, glory, Hallelujah!
As we go marching on!"

Continue the grand right and left. When partners meet, they stop to bow and curtsy, then continue around the circle to home position where they waist swing twice around.

Creative Dance

Creative dance offers an exciting new recreational activity. The person learns established dance patterns and creates his own version of a mood, color, play, poem, word, etc. The leader who underestimates his influence in getting a dance group off to a good start is forgetting the most important single principle of leading—that enthusiasm is contagious.

His role is that of guiding father than of showing the group what to do to music after they have learned basic movement techniques. The leader should provide opportunity for experience in a variety of movements done to rhythm. Point out how these movements may be incorporated into a dance.

Creative dance is not limited to one sex or age or to those already dance minded. Anyone will usually be an enthusiastic participant if he joins a group voluntarily and is encouraged.

Dancers may be grouped according to age, sex, interests, level of skill, or according to any other standard suggested by the group. Small groups of from four to eight dancers are ideal for creative purposes. All should change groups often. When a group develops something interesting and valuable, this should be shown to the others.

The leader-teacher of creative dance should make a reference file of approaches that may be used. Include sheet music, poems, songs, records, words that suggest themes, and recordings. List the name of each on a separate card with such information as where to find it, the skill level for which it may be best used, and any notes that will be valuable in planning. Know the basic elements of music, such as measures, time, note symbols, where accents fall. Review these for yourself immediately before discussing them with a group, then make explanations clear. Move from the known to the unknown, trying to relate all dance techniques in some way to everyday living. Discussions, practice, and creative activity will thrive in an informal atmosphere. Again in creative dance as in every other phase of recreation, increased enjoyment is the main objective.

Any kind of comfortable costume that allows freedom of movement will be appropriate. If a club is organized, members may want to wear leotards. Dancers usually wear no shoes, but if the surface used for dancing is not smooth, suggest that the dancers wear dance sandals or soft shoes.

Dancers have the whole world and all that is in it from which to choose background or accompaniment as approach to a composition. An idea, a song, a drumbeat, interpretation of a single word are good to use at first. The group may choose to experiment with a series of movements then make a pattern and compose a particular rhythm to complement the pattern. In any case, knowledge of basic movement skills is necessary.

In creative dance there are (1) locomotor movements, (2) axial movements, and (3) a combination of these two.

Locomotor movements are done forward, backward, or sideward through space. Combinations of these forms are known as the traditional dance steps.

Axial movements are those in which all action takes place around a fixed base, as in a body swing, with the feet remaining stationary during the movement.

The three types of movement include:

Locomotor Movements	Axial Movements	Traditional Dance Steps
Walk	Flexion and extension	Waltz
Run	Bending and stretching	Polka
Leap	Swinging	Schottische
Hop	Twisting and turning	Mazurka
Jump		Two-step
Skip		
Slide		
Gallop		

These movements may be used in the following ways:

Locomotor Movement Combinations
1. Step, hop, step, hop.
2. Run, run, leap.
3. Run, run, run, run, walk, walk, walk, walk, run 4 steps, walk 4.
4. Hop on right foot 4 times; hop on left 4.
5. Hop 4 times, jump 4 times in place, hop forward 4 times.
6. Left foot: step, hop, slide to the left.
   Right foot: step, hop, slide to the left.
7. 4 small running steps, 4 long running steps.
8. Gallop with heavy step, then light step.

Axial Movements
1. Swinging:
   a. Arm swings.
   b. Body swing—1, 2, or 3 beats.
   c. Leg swings.
2. Sustained motion—smooth, even release of energy:
   a. Arm and torso movement.
   b. Sitting, stride position, raise slowly to knee. Support weight on knee and one hand.
3. Percussive—sudden explosion of energy with a definite beginning and a definite ending.
4. Vibratory—staccato movements in rapid succession.
5. Falls and recovery:
   a. Back fall—recovery to knees; to feet.
   b. Side fall—recovery to knees.

Rhythm (Move in any of the above mentioned ways to the following rhythms.)
1. Even and uneven.
2. Increase and decrease tempo.
3. Constant slow tempo; fast tempo; twice as fast.
4. Intensity—contrast loud and soft; heavy and light

Space
1. Moving forward, backward, sideward—diagonally, in a circle, zig-zag.
2. Change of direction—start one way, change and go a different way.
3. Levels—standing, kneeling, sitting, lying.
4. Focus—(direction of the gaze) up, down, sudden change from right to left, constant even as body turns.

Force
1. Pulling.
2. Repelling.
3. Striking.

Accompaniment
1. Music—piano, record, radio, voice.
2. Words—meaning or mood.
   (Party, Sailing, Miniature, Holiday, New Year's Eve, Giant.)
3. Poems—interpretation may set the mood for a dance and may suggest particular movement.
   Rhythym of poetry may be analyzed then used as dance rhythm.
4. Songs—words or theme may suggest type of composition.
   (Folk songs, Christmas carols, spirituals.)
5. Percussive instruments:
   a. Drums.
   b. Maracas.
   c. Gongs.
   d. Triangles.
   e. Two or more of these instruments.
   f. Sticks.

A RECITAL

Plan a recital for presenting compositions to the public and set a definite time limit toward which the group may work. Schedule the recital for late evening or night. More spectators can come at these times and special lighting adds much to the effectiveness of the program. The same surface that is used for the class can be the recital stage. Cheesecloth, sheeting, or some other cotton material makes suitable inexpensive curtains and backdrops. Tack one edge of this along a wooden pole three or four inches in diameter. Use clothesline rope to hang the pole horizontal to the floor from the rafters of the building. A tennis court or softball backstop covered with paper or cloth makes a suitable backdrop for outdoor demonstrations.

Use steps or risers, if possible, so that audience chairs will be graduated and all can see. Secure a spotlight or light the stage area, and turn off all other lights. Speakers of a public address system should be placed primarily so that the dancers can hear the music or narration.

Simple costumes, such as a long skirt over a leotard or a scarf tied at the waist, may be designed and provided by the group. To add special lighting effects for costuming, cover the face of the spotlight with cellophane of the desired color.

The show must have plenty of helpers. Select or have the group elect a person to be responsible for each of the following jobs:

Operate spotlights	Be responsible for costumes
Arrange for and set properties	Read the script
Print the program	Play the records and operate
Distribute programs and usher	the public address system

In order that the audience may recognize and understand the techniques and qualities of movement used in the compositions, present a brief lecture demonstration in which simplified versions of the techniques are explained.

Publicize this and other dance programs in local papers, on posters, or by other means. Add momentum to your efforts by enlisting volunteer leaders to help build a real dance program for all. Fan a spark of interest in dance into a flame.

RHYMES AND FINGER PLAYS

Preschool children will delight in doing the following activities:

HERE IS THE CHURCH

Here is the church (fingers interlaced, knuckles up),
Here is the steeple (index fingers point up and touch),
Open the doors (move thumbs to the side),
And look at all the people (turn hands over and wiggle fingers).

TEN LITTLE INDIANS

Ten little Indians standing in a row (hold fingers straight up),
They bow to the Chief, very very low (bend fingers),
They march to the left, then they march to the right (wiggle fingers to the left, then right),
They all stand up straight, ready to fight (straighten fingers again).

INSY WINSY SPIDER

An insy winsy spider climbed up the water spout (use fingers to represent climbing up).
Down came the rain (fingers wiggle downward like raindrops),
And washed the spider out (make sweeping motion with hands),
Out came the Sun (make large circle with arms),
And dried up all the rain (make sweeping motion with both hands in opposite directions),
So the insy winsy spider climbed right back up again (repeat climbing motion with fingers).

HEADS AND SHOULDERS

Touch head and shoulders, knees and toes, knees and toes,
Touch head and shoulders, knees and toes, knees and toes,
Touch head and shoulders, knees and toes,
Eyes, ears, mouth, and nose, mouth and nose (touch the body parts indicated as the melody is sung, repeat verses faster, or leave words out).

WHERE IS THUMBKIN?

Where is Thumbkin? Where is Thumbkin? (make a fist and hide thumb inside),

Here I am. Here I am (thumb pops up).

How are you today, sir? How are you today, sir? (thumb of one hand
   wiggles as if talking to the other thumb).

Very well, I thank you. Very well, I thank you (opposite thumb repeats
   action).

Now run away, run away (both thumbs run off together).

>   Repeat, using:
>   Pointer—index finger
>   Biggie—middle finger
>   Ringer—ring finger
>   Pinky—little finger

HANDS

I can knock with my two hands;
Knock, knock, knock.
I can rock with my two hands;
Rock, rock, rock.
I can tap with my two hands;
Tap, tap, tap.
I can clap with my two hands;
Clap, clap, clap.
>   (Do actions suggested by the words.)

TEN LITTLE GENTLEMEN

Ten little gentlemen standing in a row.
Bow, little gentlemen, bow down low;
Walk, little gentlemen, right across the floor,
And don't forget, gentlemen, to please close the door.
>   (Use fingers to simulate the action suggested by the words.)

FIVE LITTLE MICE

Five little mice went out to play,
Gathering up crumbs along the way;
Out came a pussy-cat
Sleek and black,
Four little mice went scampering back—
Four little mice went out to play, and so on.
>   (Use fingers of one hand for the mice and the other hand as the
>   cat.)

TEN GALLOPING HORSES

Ten galloping horses galloping through town.
Five were white and five were brown,
Five galloped up and five galloped down;
Ten galloping horses galloping all around.
>   (Use fingers as horses.)

Suggested Records

Childhood Rhythms, Vols. I, II, VI. Ruth Evans, 326 Forest Park Avenue, Springfield, Massachusetts.

Cowboy Dances (Calls by Lloyd Shaw). Decca Album A-524.

Honor Your Partner (Calls by Ed Durlacher). Square Dance Associates, 102 North Columbus Avenue, Freeport, New Jersey.

Herman, Michael: *Folk Dance Records*. Box 201, Flushing, Long Island, New York.

Methodist World of Fun Series: *Singing Games, Folk Dances, Couple Dances*, etc. Methodist Publishing House, Nashville, Tennessee.

Suggested Readings

Anderson, M., Elliot, M. E., and LaBerge, J.: *Play With A Purpose*. New York, Harper & Row, Publishers, 1966.

Andrews, G.: *Creative Rhythmic Movement For Children*. Englewood Cliffs, New Jersey, Prentice-Hall, Inc., 1960.

Bucher, C., and Reade, E. M.: *Physical Education in the Modern Elementary School*. New York, The Macmillan Co., 1972.

Clarke, H. H., and Harr, F. B.: *Health and Physical Education for the Elementary School Classroom Teacher*. Englewood Cliffs, New Jersey, Prentice-Hall, Inc., 1964.

Duggan, A. S., Schlottmann, J., and Rutledge, A.: *The Folk Dance Library*. New York, A. S. Barnes and Company, 1948.

Gilbert, C.: *International Folk Dances at a Glance*. Minneapolis, Burgess Publishing Company, 1974

Hall, J. T.: *Dance: A Complete Guide to Social, Folk and Square Dancing*. Belmont, California, Wadsworth Publishing Company, 1963.

Jensen, C., and Jensen, M. B.: *Beginning Square Dancing*. Belmont, California, Wadsworth Press, 1966.

Kraus, R.: *A Pocket Guide of Folk and Square Dances and Singing Games for the Elementary School*. Englewood Cliffs, New Jersey, Prentice-Hall, Inc, 1966.

Kraus, R., and Sadlo, L.: *Beginning Social Dance*. Belmont, California, Wadsworth Press, 1964.

Latchaw, M.: *A Pocket Guide of Games and Rhythms for the Elementary School*. Englewood Cliffs, New Jersey, Prentice-Hall, Inc., 1970.

Lidstir, M. D., and Tamburini, D. H.: *Folk Dance Progressions*. Belmont, California, Wadsworth Publishing Company, 1965.

Mynatt, C., and Kaiman, B.: *Folk Dancing For Students and Teachers*. Dubuque, Iowa, Wm. C. Brown Company, 1968.

Nielson, N. P., Van Hagen, W., and Comer, J. L.: *Physical Education for Elementary Schools*. 3rd ed. New York, The Ronald Press Company, 1966.

Spiesman, M.: *Folk Dancing*. Philadelphia, W. B. Saunders Co., 1970.

Stuart, F., and Gibson, V. L.: *Rhythmic Activities*. Minneapolis, Burgess Publishing Company, 1961.

Wakefield, E.: *Folk Dancing In America*. New York, J. Lowell Pratt Company, 1966.

PERIODICALS

Country Dancer. The Country Dance Society of America, 31 Union Square West, New York, New York 10003. Published irregularly.

Let's Dance. Folk Dance Federation of California, Inc., 1604 Felton St., San Francisco, California 94134. Published 10 copies per year.

Northern Junket. Ralph Page, editor, 117 Washington Street, Keene, New Hampshire 03431. Published monthly.

Resin in the Bow. 115 Cliff Street, Paterson, New Jersey 07522. Published quarterly.

Sets in Order, the Official Magazine of Square Dancing. 462 N. Robertson Blvd., Los Angeles, California 90048. Published monthly.

Square Dance (formerly *American Square*). Arvid Olson, editor, 1622 N. Rand Road, Arlington Heights, Illinois 60004. Published monthly.

Record References

Bowman Records: 4921 Santa Monica Blvd., Los Angeles, California, *Holiday Time Album,* No. 302.

Bowmar, Stanley Company: Burns, Joseph, and Wheeler, Edith: *Creative Rhythm Album.* (Visit to a farm, park and circus.) 12 Cleveland Street, Valhalla, New York.

Burns Record Company, 755 Chickadee Lane, Stratford, Connecticut.

Capitol Records, Sunset and Vine, Hollywood, California.

Childhood Rhythms, Vols. I, II, VI. 326 Forest Park Avenue, Springfield, Massachusetts.

David McKay Co., Inc., 119 W. 40th St., New York, N.Y. Rhythms for primary and intermediate grades, folk dances and social dances.

Decca Records: *Ye Old Time Night, Cowboy Dances.* Called by Lloyd Shaw. Book of instructions included. Decca Album A-524.

Durlacher, Ed.: *Honor Your Partner.* Square Dance Associates, 102 N. Columbus Avenue, Freeport, New York.

Educational Activities, Inc., P. O. Box 392, Freeport, New York 11520.

Folkraft Record Company: *Library of International Dances,* 7 Oliver Street, Newark, New Jersey.

Folkways: *Rhythms of the World.* 117 W. 46th Street, New York, New York. "Birds, Beats, Bugs and Little Fishes."

Henlee Record Company: Texas Square Dance Music (without calls), 2404 Harris B., Austin, Texas.

Herman, Michael: Folk Dance Records, Box 201, Flushing, Long Island, New York.

Hoctor Dance Records, Waldwick, New Jersey 07463.

Imperial Records: Square Dances (without calls), Jimmy Clossin.
Square Dances (with calls), Lee Bedford, Jr.
American Folk Dances, Russian Folk Dances, Baltic Folk Dances.

Israeli Music Foundation, Israeli Folk Dances (Direction book included), 731 Broadway, New York.

Kimbo Records, Box 55, Deal, New Jersey 07723.

Le Crone Rhythm Record Co., 9203 Nichols Rd., Oklahoma City, Oklahoma 73120.

MacGregor Records, 2005 Labranch, Houston, Texas.

Methodist World of Fun Series, Methodist Publishing House, Nashville, Tennessee. Singing Games, Folk Dances, Couple Dances, etc.

Phoebe James Products: *Creative Rhythms for Children.* Box 134, Pacific Palisades, California.

Playtime Records: These records are non-breakable, cost twenty-five cents and are found in most drug stores or record shops. Each contains a simple rhyme or singing game.

Radio Corporation of America. RCA Victor Division, Camden, New Jersey, *RCA Victor Record Library for Elementary Schools,* which includes: Music of American Indians with instructions and suggestions for sixteen dances; Rhythmic Activities, 5 volumes for primary and upper grades; Singing Games.

Rainbow Rhythms. Piano recordings, arranged and recorded by Nora Belle Emerson, edited by Thomas E. McDonough; 4 series 78 r.p.m. with instructions included in each set. P. O. Box 608, Emory University, Atlanta, Georgia.

Record Center, 2581 Piedmont Rd., N.E., Atlanta, Georgia 30324.

Rhythms Productions: Capricorn Records, affiliates of Woodcliff Productions.

Folk Dances from 'Round the World, Series I through V, Instructions included. Records LP—A 106–A 110.

Railroad Rhythms—Musical score by Ruth White, Instructions. Record AF 101.

Activity Songs—Facts, fancies and experiences of children. Record A 102.

Scandinavian Folk Dance Album, Michael Herman, Box 201, Flushing, Long Island, New York.

Shaw, Lloyd—Recording Company, Box 203, Colorado Springs, Colorado.

Square Dance Albums—Capitol, Disc, Keystone and others.

Square Dance Associates, 102 N. Columbus Ave., Freeport, Long Island, New York.

Sonart Folk Dance Album M-8, Sonart Record Corporation, 251 W. 42nd Street, New York. May order from Michael Herman.

Swiss Folk Dance Album M-8, Columbia Recording Company, Bridgeport, Connecticut.

Ultra Records—Jewish Folk Dances, Vols. I and II. New York City. Also available from Michael Herman, Box 201, Flushing, Long Island, New York.

Windsor Records—5528 N. Rosemead Blvd., Temple City, California.

Folk Dance Funfest (Dick Kraus), Educational Dance, FD-1, FD-2, FD-3, FD-4. David McKay Company, 119 W. 40th Street, New York, New York.

Living With Rhythms Series—Basic Rhythms for Primary Grades; Animal Rhythms; Rhythms and Meter Appreciation; Rhythms for Physical Fitness (Dick Kraus). David McKay Company, 119 W. 40th Street, New York, New York.

Visual Aids, Words, and Music

Bertail, I.: *Complete Nursery Song Book.* New York, Lathrop, Lee and Shephard Company, 1947.

Building Children's Personality Through Creative Dancing: Extension Dept., Bureau of Visual Instruction, University of California, Berkeley, California (film).

Durlacher, E.: *Honor Your Partner.* New York. The Devin-Adair Co., 1949.

Gomez, W. L.: *Merry Songs for Boys and Girls.* New York, Follett Publishing Company, 1949.

Lomax, J. and A.: *The 111 Best American Ballads, Folk Songs, U.S.A.* 2nd ed. New York, Duell, Sloan and Pearce, 1947.

Materials for Teaching Dance, Vol. III, Selected Visual Aids for Dance. Washington, D.C. National Section on Dance by the AAHPER, 1201 16th Street, N.W.

Wilson, J.: *Children's Pieces.* 56 Jane Street, New York, N.Y. Book I, six pieces, Book II, 8 pieces; Book III, 7 pieces. Include such as "Night Magic," "The Sick Lamb," "Early Morning Song," and "The Lost Balloon."

Suggested Records for Creative Movement Experiences

Available from: Educational Department, R.C.A. Victor Records, 155 E. 24th St., N.Y., N.Y.

Dance Me a Story
Little Duck
Noah's Ark
The Magic Mountain
Balloons
The Brave Hunter
Flappy and Floppy

Suggested Record Sources and Piano Music

Dance Records, Inc., Waldurck, New Jersey.
David McKay Co., 119 W. 40th St., New York, New York.
E–Z Records, Merrbach Record Service, 323 W. 14th St., Houston, Texas.
Folkraft Records, Folkraft Record Co., 1159 Broad St., Newark, New Jersey.
Hoctor Records, Hoctor Dance Records, Inc., Waldwick, New Jersey.
Israeli Music Foundation, 731 Broadway, New York.
Kimbro Records, Kimbro—U.S.A. Records, Box 55, Deal, New Jersey.
Lloyd Shaw Recording Company, Box 203, Colorado Springs, Colorado.
Rainbow Rhythm Records, Box 15116, Atlanta, Georgia.
RCA Victor Educational Records, 155 E. 24th (Dept. 300), New York, New York.
The Methodist Church, World of Fun Series, Nashville, Tennessee.
Victor Educational Sales, 155 East 24th Street, New York, New York.
Windsor Records, 5530 N. Rosemead Blvd., Temple City, California.
World of Fun Records, 150 Fifth Avenue, New York, New York.

chapter 10

Camping

"Now I see the secret of the making of the best persons,
It is to grow in the open air and eat and sleep with the earth.
Here a great personal deed has room,
  (Such a deed seizes upon the hearts of the whole race of men,
  Its effusion of strength and will overwhelms law
  and mocks all authority and all argument against it.)
Here is the test of wisdom,
Wisdom is not fully tested in schools,
Wisdom cannot be passed from one having it to another not having it,
Wisdom is of the soul, is not susceptible of proof, is its own proof —"
Walt Whitman

Camping is as old as man. Our primitive nomadic ancestors were campers who lived, slept, ate, worked and played under the big sky and close to the earth. They left behind them a rich heritage and love for the land.

Group camping is rapidly coming to be regarded as the birthright of every American child. The majority of our present camps are sponsored by youth-serving agencies. Private owners operate the second greatest number, whereas public camps make up the smallest group. However, public schools and local recreation and park departments are becoming increasingly active in a great drive to provide the opportunity for all to go camping, for it has been estimated that only about 10% of our American children go to camp. Many publicly supported agencies now conduct day, weekend, or two week camping periods for youth and family groups.

Under a broad classification of private, public, and organizational camps may be found:

Adult camps
Boy Scout camps
Brother and sister camps
Camps for delinquents
Co-educational camps
Camps for the physically and mentally handicapped
Camp Fire Girls' camps

Charity camps
Church camps
Day camps
Family camps
Farm camps
Four H camps
Girl Scout camps
Inter-racial camps
Speciality camps
School camps
Travel-on camps
Tutorial camps
Y.W.C.A., Y.M.C.A., Y.W.H.A., Y.M.H.A. camps
Work camps

Camping sponsored by a recreation department or local civic group should be started on a carefully planned small scale. Hiking trips, simple outdoor cooking, overnight trips, or all day campouts are ideal ways to begin. Gradually the program should be increased in scope and in the number of campcraft skills taught. If possible, each recreation department should own its own campsite. This may be on a vacant lot, in a wooded area, or in a farmer's field at first. However, real camping is possible only at a camp located in a wooded area far from crowded city streets.

Basic Skills

Those who most enjoy camping are skilled in campcrafts such as axe and tool craft, fire building, fishing, hiking, hunting, knotcraft, lashing, outdoor cooking, and shelter construction. Most of these skills can be taught at a community center, in a classroom, or on a playground. Those who have learned how to cook, whittle, use an axe, or do other needed tasks will be prepared to meet the challenge of camping with increased pleasure. The following basic skills should be included in a training program for camping:

FIRE BUILDING

A fire in camp is used for cooking, warmth, protection from animals, and companionship. Story telling, visiting with friends, special programs, and just plain day dreaming are experiences that come to mean more when a person is close to a campfire in a joyful outdoor living experience.

Select a campfire site away from trees and bushes. Build the fire with the wind at your back. Start with tinder of small dry twigs. Have your other wood gathered and ready for use. Add larger twigs gradually as the fire burns. Use soft wood (pines, spruces, cedars, aspen, etc.) for quick, hot boiling fires. Hard wood (oak, hickory, maple, etc.) makes the best slow burning fire.

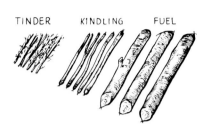

TINDER   KINDLING   FUEL

BEGIN WITH TEPEE
PLACED AGAINST
KINDLING

When building a fire remember to:

1. Build it so that air can reach the tinder and fuel. Air coming from the bottom or side is best.
2. Arrange the wood so that the flames will travel from piece to piece.
3. Use for tinder small, dry sticks, dried grass, or tree bark that snaps into small pieces readily.
4. Gradually increase the size of the wood, after getting the tinder started, to build the fire higher.
5. Use split wood for kindling, if possible, for it burns faster.
6. Have all fuel ready before you light the fire.
7. Use the same basic steps when building any of the many kinds of camp fires.
8. Be sure your campfire is out before leaving it. If you can hold your hands on the fire bed, it is safe to leave it.

OUTDOOR COOKING

Fire building progression should be linked with cooking more advanced than frying eggs or roasting wieners. Pit barbecue, clambakes, and baking chicken or cakes offer a challenge to both the novice and skilled outdoor chef. Types of outdoor cooking include:

COOK OVER COALS

ONE POT
MEAL

TIN CAN
STOVE

One-Pot Meals
  Chili
  Baked beans
  Stew
  Chowder

Baking
  Plank
    Steak
    Desserts
    Biscuits
    Fish
    Chops
  Bean hole
    Cooked cereals
    Beans
    Potatoes
    Baked meats

Coals
  Potatoes
  Corn roast
  Pig in a blanket
  Baked meats
Reflector oven
  Cookies
  Cake
  Biscuits
  Baked meat

For beginners, it is best to have each one cook one or two simple things for himself and to supplement the meal with sandwiches, fruit, or other dessert. Children enjoy progressing from toasting sandwiches to frying hamburgers on tin can stoves. Each camper, regardless of age, will thrill to cooking his entire meal on a tin can stove, tennis racket broiler, or green stick. Adults will favor progressing from fried bacon and eggs to broiled steaks, roast corn, or barbecues. Both groups should first cook individually, next in small groups of three or four, and finally prepare some food (clambake, barbecue, etc.) for ten or more people. Some will want to practice their skills at public outdoor grills provided by local parks or at roadside fireplaces built beside state highways.

EACH PERSON COOKS HIS OWN

COOK ON WIRE SCREEN

BROIL STEAKS

TOAST BREAD ON STICKS

HUNTER-TRAPPER

TRENCH FIRE

COUNCIL FIRE

STAR FIRE

REFLECTOR OVEN

TEPEE
FIRE

WAUGUN STICK

RECIPES

Campers will enjoy starting a collection of recipes for outdoor cooking as a hobby. Each leader who desires to teach others the fine art of outdoor cooking will find these recipes easy ones to learn:

Bread Twists. Add water according to directions to prepared biscuit dough or Bisquick. Mix in a paper bag until a stiff dough is formed. Wind this around a green stick or a broom handle covered with foil, browning it slowly. Stuff holes with butter, bacon, or jam.

Pancakes. Add water to prepared mix. Have pan hot and well greased. Pour a spoonful on the pan. Cook until bubbles appear, turn. Add cinnamon, cooked rice, blueberries, or a cup of whole kernel canned corn to the batter for variety.

Kabobs. Alternate cubes of beef (raw or partially cooked), potato, onion, carrot, and bacon on a green stick or pointed wire. Cook slowly over coals.

Roast Corn. Soak ears of corn in their husks in water for several hours. Cook in coals. Or wrap each water-soaked ear in aluminum foil after removing the husks. Cook in coals.

Chili Con Carne. Brown diced onions and hamburger. Add meat and cook until done. Season with chili powder. Add one can of Mexican chili beans, one can of tomatoes, two tablespoons of catsup and cook slowly.

Somemores. Make a sandwich of two white or graham crackers, add a piece of chocolate and one marshmallow. Toast slowly and sample. Judge for yourself whether you would like "Somemore."

Baked Fish. Wrap a piece of frozen fillet in aluminum foil with a piece of raw carrot, potato, onion, and celery. Cook over coals.

Baked Chicken. As above, wrap your favorite piece of chicken in the foil and cook with the vegetables.

Eggs in Mud. Cover eggs or potatoes with wet clay or mud. Cook eggs twenty minutes in hot coals, potatoes one hour.

Potatoes Baked in Tin Can. Scrub potatoes and rub with butter or wrap in wax paper. Put in a large coffee can that has five holes punched in the top. Place in coals and pile them around the sides. Cook about one hour.

Pioneer Drumsticks. Mix chopped beef with onions, two eggs, and one cup of crumbled corn flakes. Wrap this around the end of a green stick, squeezing it evenly in place. Cook over coals, turning frequently.

Camper's Stew. Have each person wrap the lower part of a large coffee can with foil. Put in alternate layers of chopped onions, carrots, celery, corn, and beef. Sprinkle tomato juice, canned tomatoes or catsup over the top. Put on lid. Wrap the entire can with foil. Cook in hot coals for fifteen to twenty minutes.

Camp Coffee. Use one cup of cold water for every tablespoon of coffee. Put coffee in cloth bag, tying it loosely with string. Add to briskly boiling water and leave in for several minutes.

Camp Cocoa. Use one teaspoon of cocoa to every two of sugar. Add one cup of milk for every person, or four tablespoons of powdered milk to every cup of water, or ½ cup of evaporated milk to every ½ cup of water. Mix cocoa and sugar with water in kettle and cook to a smooth paste. Add milk, a pinch of salt, and stir all together. Heat almost to a boil. Serve with a marshmallow for each cup.

AXE AND TOOL CRAFT

HAND AXE

Used for splitting firewood and cutting other small pieces of wood. Stand near a chopping block. Grasp the axe firmly. Slant the blade to chop a large piece of wood so that it makes a V-shaped cut. To split wood, bite the axe blade into one end of the piece of wood or log. Raise the wood and axe together and bring them down sharply on a chopping block. Twist the axe against the wood to split it. To point a stick, hold it upright on the chopping block, strike it at an angle and turn it around. Cut down each new edge until you have a point.

STEP I

STEP 2

STEP 3

AXE

Grasp the handle near the end with the left hand. Grip with the right hand about three-fourths of the way to the axe head. Raise the axe over the right shoulder. As you bring it down sharply, slide the right hand down to meet the left one. Both hands should be brought together as the axe hits the wood. Separate the hands again on the stroke back up over your shoulder. To cut a tree branch, make a sharp diagonal cut down first and follow with a second cut up. Repeat.

KNIVES

Grasp a single or double blade knife in one hand with the thumb around it. Whittle away from you. Turn a stick and cut each new edge to point it. Cut a V notch. Make fuzz stick for fire tinder by starting about two inches from one end and cut down making long, thin strips.

Things to make from native materials with axe, hatchet, and knife are:

Clothespins	Sign posts and bulletin boards
Candlesticks	Camp furniture
Belt buckles	Wooden buttons
Napkin rings	Letter openers
Book covers	Green stick cookers, broilers, pothooks, and other cooking aids

SHELTERS

Outdoor living is best when one is comfortable. It is vitally important to pick a good place to camp where there is access to water, fuel, shade, and drainage in case of rain.

A good bedroll is made of waterproofed canvas, a poncho, a plastic tablecloth, and as many blankets as needed. Wool blankets are superior to cotton. The bedroll should be made so that the camper has as much cover beneath as above him, for the ground gets cold during the night. The roll should be placed on a grassy spot free from rocks for sleeping. Pine needles, spruce, balsam, palmetto leaves, grass, ferns, and moss make an excellent mattress. A mosquito net supported by sticks and string will add to sleeping comfort. Beginners should sleep in some kind of shelter before trying an overnight trip. Sleeping bags can be purchased at most sporting goods stores and are also recommended.

Outdoor shelters such as pup tents, poncho tents, lean-tos, cabins, tepees, tree houses, and tents all make good shelters. A canoe turned on one side with the bottom facing outward can also be used. A brush den can be made and used as a last resort. Such a den can be quickly made by leaning a few poles against a log and covering them with boughs.

The most popular tent for permanent camps is the wall tent, named because of its upright canvas side walls. Guy ropes are used to tighten and loosen the tent; a clove hitch knot tied to a peg can be used if there are no tent adjustors.

A baker tent is recommended for winter use. With its front wide open to the warmth of a reflector fire it can be used by as many as four sleepers.

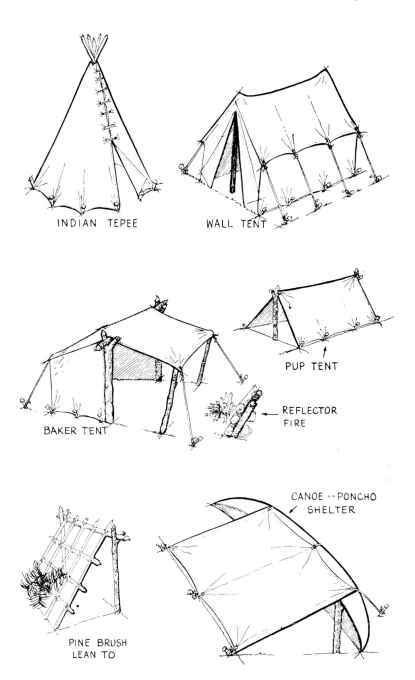

INDIAN TEPEE

WALL TENT

BAKER TENT

PUP TENT

REFLECTOR
FIRE

PINE BRUSH
LEAN TO

CANOE --PONCHO
SHELTER

HIKING

A hike is a walk with a purpose. It is one of our few remaining cost-free recreational activities as well as a good physical conditioner. There are many kinds of hikes ranging from bird walks to mountain climbing.

Hikes should be carefully planned and should end at a choice spot. This serves as a group incentive. Singing and round-robin story telling furnish fun along the way. Cook-outs add to the joy of the hike's end. These should be simple meals such as toasted sandwiches, fried eggs and bacon, etc. All hikers must wear comfortable clothing. Laced oxfords and heavy wool socks are recommended. Distances should be gradually increased as the group gains stamina. Photography, sketching, or impromptu dramatics can be interwoven into hiking trips for variety.

NEEDED EQUIPMENT

Enjoyable camping is comfortable camping. Having the proper and necessary equipment with you adds to the luxury of outdoor living and sharpens its pleasure. Suggested equipment for a camp of four to six persons includes:

For Cooking

1 pail for boiling water
1 kettle for sterilizing dishes
2 large cans with lids for
   drinking water and milk
4 kettles with lids
2 frying pans
1 dish pan
1 mixing bowl
2 large cooking spoons
1 pancake turner
1 butcher knife
2 peeling knives
1 salt shaker and 1 pepper
   shaker
1 complete table service for
   each camper

Miscellaneous

1 lantern
1 flashlight
1 jar of kitchen matches
1 first-aid kit
4 dish towels
2 dish rags
1 box of soap flakes or 2 bars of
   laundry soap
toilet paper
paper napkins
rope
rubber bands

Tools

1 large axe
2 small hatchets
1 short handled shovel
1 buck saw

CLOTHING

Jeans, dungarees or Levis are most suitable for camp. Other items to take along are:

Shorts
A wool or flannel shirt with long sleeves

A cotton shirt with long sleeves
Socks
Underclothing
Pajamas
Two pairs of comfortable hiking shoes — oxfords or laced heavy
    shoes preferred.
A rain coat and rain hat
A sweater
A wool or leather jacket
Bathing suit

Optional personal items to take along include:

Books
Toilet articles — comb, brush, mirror, etc.
Pencil, paper, envelopes
Toothbrush and paste
Pocket knife
Linen — sheets, blankets, pillow
A camera
A small musical instrument — harmonica, ukulele, etc.
A deck of cards

TELLING DIRECTIONS

The North Star always indicates north, and as long as stars are shining one need not lose his way in the woods. The sun marks east and west by day. When the sky is overcast, however, the camper must use woods signs to find directions. These are:

TREE MOSS

There is usually more of it on the north side. Also, the moss grows highest there. Look at several trees before reaching your decision as to direction.

TREE TOPS

The highest twigs of pines, spruces, and hemlocks usually lean a little east. Pick a tree in the open or the highest one in the area.

WHITE PAPER

Your finger nail will do, if no paper is available. Stand in a clearing, hold a match upright on the paper and watch where the shadow falls. This will tell you your direction east from west, depending upon the time of day.

WATCH

Hold the watch face up, place a match at the outer edge at the end of the hour hand. Turn the watch until the shadow of the match falls along the hour hand. In the a.m. south will be half way, clockwise, between the hour hand and twelve o'clock. At noon the hour hand will point straight south. In the p.m. south will be half way, counterclockwise, between the hour hand and 12 o'clock.

COMPASS

Every camper going into the woods should carry one. Directions telling how to use it come in the box.

FISHING

Casting, with both a rod and reel, can be taught to beginners of mixed age in a gymnasium or any other large room. A skilled leader who knows the value of group organization can teach as many as fifty persons arranged in sub-groups or squads. Each smaller group should be assigned to a specific safe place in the room; groups should be rotated at an interval so that each one casts. One squad can practice stringing the line, another casting, a third tying flies, a fourth studying pictures and charts showing the habits of certain fish. Everyone should be doing something to learn about this fascinating, exciting, and soul-satisfying sport.

Skilled casters should assist the leader, be organized into casting clubs, taken on fishing trips, shown how to improve their skills, or encouraged to compete in local, state, or national contests.

Targets best suited for beginners meeting inside can be made from heavy white cardboard cut into solid circles. These should be supported behind by wooden blocks or in some other way. Those learning outside at a pool, lake, or stream will find suitable targets in white painted bicycle or car tires, wood or plastic rims. If possible, each person should furnish his own equipment. Each should also be instructed in how to buy and care for his own gear.

Bait casting is done with live, artificial, or fresh bait. Worms, spoons, or pork rind are often used. The rod is made from wood, steel, glass, or bamboo.

Hold the rod easily in one hand with the thumb on the spool where it feels best as you apply pressure to control the speed of the lure. Do the overhead cast on three counts:

Count One — Hold the rod almost horizontal.

Count Two — Bring it back to an imaginary twelve, then eleven o'clock.

Count Three — Snap your wrist, bringing the rod back down slightly above your original horizontal position.

Practice to develop a smooth, relaxed, accurate cast. Use the rod tip for aiming and whip the line straight ahead each time. Avoid back casting too far or tensing up. Stand squarely, or with the opposite leg forward in a stride position (right leg forward for a left handed person and vice versa for a right handed one).

Fly casting is done with artificial or live bait. Artificial flies are multi-colored and have colorful names such as the royal coachman, grizzly bear, etc. Live bait includes salmon eggs, worms, grasshoppers, and minnows. The rod is made from tubular steel, split bamboo, or glass.

Hold the rod easily in one hand with the thumb on top or at one side (whichever is more comfortable). Learn to cast on these four counts:

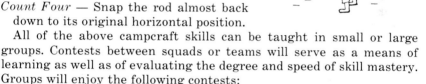

Count One — Hold the rod horizontal. Take up the line slack with an outward pull of the opposite hand.

Count Two — Snap the line back over your head to one o'clock.

Count Three — Make a momentary pause until the lure completes its backward movement.

Count Four — Snap the rod almost back down to its original horizontal position.

All of the above campcraft skills can be taught in small or large groups. Contests between squads or teams will serve as a means of learning as well as of evaluating the degree and speed of skill mastery. Groups will enjoy the following contests:

Water boiling
Fire building — with or without matches
Wood chopping
Lashing camp tables, bridges, etc.
Whittling
Making functional crafts from native materials

Pie, cookie, or cake baking contests
Casting to targets placed at varied distances
Biggest fish caught
Fishing for the most fish
Knotcraft displays
Tent pitching and ditching for speed
Trail blazing

Organized Camping

Camping conducted by good leaders offers an invaluable educational experience. Some educators claim that children can learn as much, if not more, at a camp in eight weeks than they can in a whole year in school. Here in an informal, relaxed environment the child learns through direct experience from nature, his peers, and counselors. A lessened social distance between the adult and youth is made possible in a real living situation. The reduction of outside influences and simplicity of life produce a rich group living experience.

Group camping for recreational purposes is of three types: (1) short term (three to seven days), (2) long term (two or more weeks), and (3) day camping. The greatest expansion in public camping has been in the latter. The Recreational Division of the Chicago Park District operates public day camps. The cities of Pittsburgh, Pennsylvania; Grand Island, Nebraska; Decatur, Illinois; Cleveland, Ohio; San Francisco, Los Angeles, Oakland, and San Diego, California, accommodate thousands of children yearly in their city-sponsored day camps. The Girl Scouts, who introduced this type of camping in 1922, accommodate many youth yearly in their day camps.

A day camp is operated usually from 9:00 a.m. to 5:00 p.m. The campers do not stay overnight but are transported daily to and from camp. Each pays a small fee. He may or may not be asked to supply his own lunch. It is a common practice for each child to bring his own sandwiches and for the camp to furnish milk and dessert.

Since the turn of this century there has been a rapid increase in the number and types of camps, both publicly and privately sponsored. Travel-on-camps, inter-racial camps, co-educational camps, family camps, camps for handicapped children, and camps sponsored by industry for family groups are only a few indications of this growth. Church camps, school camps, and work-experience camps are rapidly expanding.

THE PROGRAM

Camp programs should be geared to fit all age groups. Young adults, middle age groups, and even the aged are becoming increasingly enthusiastic about camping. Although program activities they find most enjoyable are less strenuous than those for children, they should be largely camp activities revolving around food, shelter, and recreation in the out-of-doors.

Campers should camp is a good motto to follow when planning any camp program. The best programs are camper-counselor made. Care should be taken not to duplicate activities the campers could do just as easily at home or on a playground. Recreational sports such as baseball and tennis belong more to the city, whereas canoeing and outdoor cooking are best suited for camp. Since camping offers a unique kind of recreational opportunity, great care should be taken to build the program around activities which can be done better at camp than elsewhere.

Suggested program areas include:

Astronomy	Lashing
Explorations	Nature hikes, trails, study
Excursions	Map and compass reading and
Cook-outs	construction

Carpentry
Fire building
Fishing
Hiking
Hunting
Gardening

Outdoor cooking and menu
  planning
Overnight hikes
Outdoor shelter construction
Use of camp tools

If the camp is conducted on the basis of overnight, weekend, weekly, or longer duration, the evening recreational program should be made up of activities not done during the day. These might include:

Amateur night
Banquets
Masquerades
Pageants
Community business
  camp post office
  camp bank
  camp store
Discussion groups
Firelighting ceremonials
Hobby clubs
World friendship nights

Parties
  birthday
  costume
  seasonal
Game nights
Indian pow wows or council
  rings
Moonlight hikes
Scavenger hunts
Square and folk dancing
Tournaments
Treasure hunts
Corn roasts or clam bakes

The camp program should be adventurous and fun and should be composed of new as well as traditional activities. In reality, the program consists of everything that happens at camp. Rest hours, clean-up duties, swimming help make up this entirety; each is equally important from an educational and recreational standpoint.

The complete program may be broken up into the following areas and their sub-groups:

1. The daily program:
   a. Athletic Activities
       team sports
       individual sports
       aquatics
       land sports
   b. Health Protective Activities
       camp feeding
       clean-up duties
       health and safety measures
       rest hours

    c. Creative Activities
        arts and crafts
        dance
        dramatics
        music
    d. Campcraft Activities
        hiking
        outdoor cooking
        outdoor living
        map construction and reading
        land conservation
        nature lore

2. The evening recreational program
        competitive games
        parties, plays, and pantomimes
        clubs, hobby groups
        free time to follow individual interests

3. Special events
    a. Out of Camp Trips
        canoe trips
        cookouts
        hikes
        boat trips
        mountain climbing
        pack-mule or horseback trips
        trek cart trips
        sailing trips
        visits to local places of interest
    b. Guest Speakers or Outside Entertainers
        visiting days

4. Moral or religious program
    a. Daily Worship or Ceremonials
        grace before meals
        group discussions
        flag ceremonials
    b. Weekly Worship Programs

There are three types of program possibilities: (1) those which are highly scheduled and compartmentalized, (2) those which are selective choice, and (3) those which are built around out-of-door living.

The highly scheduled program chops up the campers' day into hourly activities. Bells or bugles signal the end of one "class" and the beginning of another. Little choice is given to campers to elect to do their most appealing activities. Each unit or age group moves as a group and everyone must go with his group. This type of program is easy to schedule and carry out. However, it is often too patterned after a school schedule.

Selective choice programs are found in more progressive camps. Here campers can select one or more activities in which they wish to participate. Definite times are set for retiring, meals, and rest hours. Swimming is usually required of all.

Programs built around learning to live in the out-of-doors contain set times only for rising and retiring, resting, and meals. Within these limits activities are built by campers and their counselors around the program that arises from group living. All activities are designed to provide purposeful experiences in which learning is achieved through life situations.

Factors determining which type of program each camp will use as a pattern are: (1) the philosophy and objectives of the camp, (2) surroundings and climatic conditions, (3) centralization or decentralization of camp organization, (4) camper age range, (5) campers' experience and home background, and (6) leadership skills.

Programs which are camper-counselor planned offer opportunities for adults and youth to contribute, share, and respect each other. However, it is necessary that the director and staff plan beforehand program possibilities to present to the campers or their chosen representatives. The staff or the selected committee should discover what campers wish to do, decide who are to take part and when, and determine what can best be done in that particular camp setting.

Principles to keep in mind when planning group camp activities are:

1. Select things that are fun to do and can best be done at camp.
2. Campers and counselors should both assume responsibility for doing the chosen activities.
3. Base the offering upon the needs, skills, interests, and capacities of the group.
4. Select activities which will lead to a better use of present and future leisure time.
5. Choose activities which will develop individual and group creativity.
6. Choose activities which will develop moral and ethical values.
7. Make the best use of time, facilities, groups, community resources, and leadership.
8. Arrange activities so that there is a tapering off with less strenuous ones near the end of the day.
9. Keep all plans elastic and modifiable.

SURVIVAL CAMPING

Survival skills are ideal for inclusion in the camp program for older youth and adults. Basic survival skills must be mastered before individuals are left alone in the woods for a 24-hour period or longer and must survive by finding their own food and making their own shelters. These basic camp skills include the following:

Demonstrate the ability to:

Erect some type of temporary shelter

Extract water from the earth

Find five edible plants or nuts found in the region

Constructing two types of temporary shelter

Trail blaze by using bits of cloth or plants

Catch fish using a safety pin or trap an animal with vines

Start a fire using a magnifying glass or by using the Indian fire drill method

Make a tennis racket broiler and other cooking devices from tree branches

Purify water

Treat sprains or protect broken bones

Make a variety of improvised shelters

I. *Ways to Avoid Being Lost*
   A.
      1. Leave your destination and approximate time of return with a friend, ranger, or law officer.
      2. Know the hazards (rapids, ski slopes, etc.) of your area.
      3. Make sure you have all necessary equipment before leaving a camp (first aid kit, knife, poncho, extra paddles if canoeing, matches, etc.).
   B. After deciding you must be lost or are in trouble, *relax* and fight off feelings of panic and think about your predicament.

II. *Signaling*
   A. First make your position known as soon as possible, since aircraft or others may be looking for you.
   B. Ways of signaling:
      1. Best in *daytime* is smoke. Have a comfort fire with wet or green leaves, grass, or moss nearby which can be added if an airplane is heard coming.
      2. At *night* the light of a campfire is best signal.
      3. Mirror or piece of shiny metal.
      4. Some type of flag which will be distinct from its surroundings and readily visible.
      5. Write out S.O.S. on ground with rocks, in snow, or by using clothing.

III. *Fire*
   A. If you have difficulties starting a fire
      1. Matches wet — run end through hair; dip match in wax.
      2. If you do not have matches, use flint, quartz, hardrock and steel and strike them together to get sparks to land and

glow on tinder (dried grass, leaves), blow until flame appears.
3. Flashlight batteries and steel wool — scratch against battery to start a spark.
4. Use a magnifying glass (convex lens from camera, binoculars, etc.). Hold it over tiny pieces of thin wood, dried grass and leaves.

IV. *Shelter*
  A. Make some kind of shelter for protection from the wind, sun, heat or rain.
  B. Some types of lean-tos:
    1. Stretch poncho or clothing over cut tree branches.
    2. Tree branches covered with leaves.

V. *Protection from area hazards*
  A. Biting or stinging insects
    1. Smoke will deter them.
    2. Crushed ferns or wild onions can be used as a repellent.
    3. Scorpion and spider bite — lie down till pain eases (always check clothes and shoes for them).
  B. Sunburn — can make you feel nauseous and very tired, if extreme.
    1. Seek shade and stay clothed.
    2. Wear some kind of hat.
  C. Wet feet — cripple feet, if they are constantly wet for several days or longer time. At 50° F., wet feet react as if frostbitten. Must keep feet dry, and wear dry socks and shoes. (Note: In freezing conditions, let socks freeze then beat out crystals.)
  D. Make boots from canvas or a blanket to keep snow or sand out of low top shoes.
  E. Carbon monoxide poison — make sure close quarters are well ventilated.

VI. *Water*
  A. A human being needs about 2 quarts average per day (includes water in food as well as drink).
    For average efficiency in hot climates — a gallon per day is needed. In 50° F. — can last 10 days without water if conserving energy.
    In 120° F. — can last 2 days without water if energy is conserved.
    Death from dehydration is possible and remember that you can live around 30 days without food but only a few days without water.
  B. Don't drink:
    Sea water (it has too much salt)

Urine

Alcohol

Battery water (could contain toxic amounts of lead)

Fish fluids

Glacier ice

Anything milky, salty, or soapy (coconuts excepted)

Conserve your existing amount while trying to find new water sources. Avoid loss of body water through wind and sun dehydration (wear clothing and stay in the shade).

C. Sources of water

Ground water

Rain water

Dew — make a dew pit of canvas, plastic, shiny objects, pots, etc.

Snow — make into chunks and heat

Ice — melt in the sun or on flames

Mud — squeeze or mop moisture out

Plants — cut and squeeze out cactus juice

Vines — cut at top, then bottom and allow the fluid to run into a cup

D. Purification

Strain

Boil for 1 minute

Water purification tablets

For taste, add pinch of salt

VII. *Food*

A. If you have no more than 1 pint of water per day, don't eat, and try to conserve your energy. Unless you have up to 10 pints water per day, don't eat proteins for too much water is needed for digestion. Can stay alive *several weeks* without food.

B. Eating Plants (General test)

Plant must not irritate skin, smell, or have milky juice.

Bite off small piece.

Hold piece inside lower lip for five minutes.

Eat if not soapy, bitter, or has a hot, burning taste.

If no ill effects occur within 10 hours, plant is safe to eat.

C. Plants you can eat

Nuts

Inner layer of tree bark

Seeds of grasses (roast or boil)

Ferns (boil)

Dandelion leaves (boil)

Seaweed clinging to rocks or floating, if it looks fresh and firm

Berries, if they pass the test (B)

D. Hunting

Doing this on foot can make you hungrier, so conserve your energy as much as you can.

Methods:

Spearing or gigging frogs (for rear legs) or large fish

Traps and snares for small game made from tree branches and vines.

E. Fishing

Use shoelace for line

Use stone for sinker

Make gorges of wood on bone

Make hooks from claws, thorns, nails, wood

Generally use live bait (insects, worms). Once you catch a fish, check its stomach to see what it has been eating, then use these stomach contents or stomach parts for bait. Fresh water fish may contain parasites, so do not eat it if raw. The flesh of salt water fish can be a good source of water.

SUGGESTIONS FOR IMPROVING CAMP PROGRAMS

If camping is to realize the educational potentialities it holds for youth, it is necessary that serious consideration be given to the type of program the camp is to offer, how it is to be planned and conducted, and how it is to be evaluated.

If one accepts the thesis that camping is a unique type of group living and education that takes place while living close to nature in the out-of-doors, it becomes apparent that directors, counselors, and campers must seriously consider those things that are the unique offerings of the camp environment and that are the most useful in education. In this respect, Dr. Lloyd Sharp has declared that those things that can best be learned in the classroom should be learned there, but those things that can best be learned only out in the open should be fully utilized while in the camp environment. Directors who follow Sharp's thesis that camping is learning to live in and use the out-of-doors often include in their programs the activities of conducting weather stations, marking trails, exploring, outdoor cooking, excursions to nearby points of interest, making things from natural resources, spiritual appreciations and experiences, and evening get-togethers.

It would be a drastic course if all camps followed the same standardized type of program. Directors, counselors, and campers must plan together what they wish to learn and do while at camp and how they can best utilize their own particular camp environment.

LEADERSHIP

The key person in camp is the counselor. He must be a combination of parent, friend, social worker, and teacher. Above all he must be a good practicer and rarely a preacher, realizing his important role as a character pattern youth will copy.

DeMarche, who secured data on 433 counselors in 33 camps in six different states, has isolated four factors descriptive of the most successful counselor. He is:

1. Twenty years of age or older
2. A college graduate or a graduate student
3. One who has been out of college 2 years or more
4. One who has had 4 or more years' experience as a group leader

Qualities, both professional and personal, necessary for camp counselors are:

1. Basic understanding of self, others, and principles of group living
2. Resourcefulness, emotional stability, and creativity
3. Sense of humor, responsibility, and values
4. A belief in people and desire to work with them
5. Youthfulness in spirit with a zest for life, and the ability to capitalize and use constructively the enthusiasm and idealism of youth
6. Enjoyment of and adaptability to outdoor life and group living
7. Basic camping skills

The total camp staff should include a director, unit or sub-group leaders, general and specialty leaders, junior and/or counselors-in-training, health personnel, and maintenance men. The number of leaders will depend upon the size of the camp.

Camp directors are becoming increasingly aware of the importance of training their own staffs. Although many counselors have received general camp training elsewhere, each director should give specific training to his staff. Actually their training begins with the first interview and continues throughout the season. The content of the training program depends upon the task to be done, where the training is given, the length of the period, facilities, and ability and background of each staff member.

This complete training program should contain five elements: (1) the before-camp training, which takes place away from camp during three or more months prior to camp opening, (2) the pre-camp training at the camp before the campers arrive, (3) the in-service or continuous training, which goes on throughout the season, (4) the post-season evaluation period, and (5) the counselor-in-training program for older youth.

All training programs should be built around the broad areas of (1) the philosophy, aims, and objectives of the camp, (2) camping as a means of education and worthy use of leisure time, (3) health and safety rules and procedure, (4) individual and group guidance techniques, (5) methods of democratic leadership, (6) job analysis, and (7) campcraft skills.

PROGRAM PLANNING

Counselor-camper planned programs offer opportunities for adults and youth to learn to contribute, share, and respect each other. It is necessary, however, that the director and staff plan program possibilities before they present them to the campers. Here children gain valuable experiences in learning the techniques of group planning; because they share in selecting and conducting what they wish to do, activities are done *with* them, not *for* them.

So that the greatest benefits may accrue from counselor-camper planning, the committee should explore program possibilities together by discovering what they wish to do, deciding who are to do it, and determining what activities can best be done in the camp environment. Factors this joint committee might well keep in mind when exploring program possibilities together are:

1. Are the selected activities fun to do?
2. Can both campers and counselors assume responsibility for carrying out the selected activities?
3. Are the selected activities based upon the needs, interests, and capacities of the group?
4. What opportunities are provided in carrying out the activities for growth in skills and appreciations?
5. How will the selected activities lead to a better use of present and future leisure time?
6. What are the opportunities for the development of individual and group creative expression?
7. Will the selected activities develop moral and ethical values?
8. Will the selected activities contribute to the development of each individual and group who take part?
9. Will the selected activities make best use of time, facilities, groups, community resources, and counselor staff?
10. Are the activities scheduled or arranged so that there is a tapering off with less strenuous ones near the end of the day?
11. Is the program elastic, flexible, and modifiable?

DAY CAMPING

Most recreation departments offer summer programs for children in day camping. Many hold these programs on their own playgrounds; others take the children to nearby lakes, mountains, or wooded areas for a day of outdoor fun and challenges. Typical programs begin at nine o'clock and end in mid-afternoon. The best of such camps provide children with exciting and adventurous activities they can best do in a camp setting. These include instructions on how to build fires and cook their own meals, blaze trails, use axes, saws, and hatchets for building protective shelter, trap and care for animals, canoe, and swim. They also introduce the child to the many mysteries of the world of nature. The most successful day camp directors believe in planning with children a program that omits the many activities they can do elsewhere and includes only the ones they can best do through a day camp program.

Such programs are greatly needed in large metropolitan areas where many children are missing the thrill of being close to nature and growing things. However, many living in rural small towns can profit greatly from being, working, and playing with other children through such a camp program.

Best teaching and learning results will accrue in the summer camp:

1. If the program activities are child-centered.
2. When the individual camper's needs, interests, and capacities are fully considered.
3. When counselors aid children to explore and discover things for themselves.
4. When campers are free to create their own responses in a situation.
5. When campers cooperatively plan with counselors what they are to learn.
6. When campers are guided by sympathetic counselors who believe in them.
7. When campers believe that what they learn is personally valuable to them.
8. When what is learned will increase the camper's power to make intelligent choices.
9. When what is learned will build and refine new meanings.

THE COUNSELOR AS AN EDUCATOR

Counselors must realize the importance of the basic principles of learning, and think through for themselves wherein those principles may be fully applied in the camp. When they grasp the significance that their chief function as a leader is to teach children *through* activities, they will select with campers those activities that are fun, educationally challenging, and satisfying for each person and each group. To best utilize the camp environment the counselor must know and enjoy campcraft skills. Mastery of the following techniques will help the counselors replace city recreational games and sports with real camp activities:

1. Use of tools — knives, axes, hatchets, saws, shovels, picks, hammers.
2. Fire building — types and kinds of wood best suited for outdoor cooking.

3. Outdoor cooking — menu planning, packing food for hikes and excursions, protection of food, disposal of waste.
4. Hikes and outings — organization and planning, camp making and breaking, accident prevention.
5. Selection, use, construction, and care of outdoor camping equipment — tent pitching, ditching, and striking, bed rolls, ponchos, sleeping bags, knapsack packing, light camping equipment.
6. Nature and wood lore — plant, insect, and animal life, star gazing, land conservation, trail blazing, map reading, weather chart construction.
7. Improvised shelter construction — lean-to-camps, outpost camps, tree houses, shacks.

EVALUATING THE RESULTS

The daily, weekly, and seasonal programs should be carefully evaluated by campers, counselors, and the director. This may be done by group discussions, individual conference, and observations. The best evidence of the effectiveness of the program will be gathered from observing the campers. If they are happy and have been challenged to become better and totally functioning individuals and group members, if they exhibit changes in behavior, attitudes, and interests, and if they are aware of their importance as a citizen in the camp community, the camp program has been effective and, no doubt, has been educational.

TYPES OF BEHAVIOR PROBLEMS FOUND IN CAMPS

Behavior problems often found among children in camps include the following:

Boredom	Homesickness
Bullying	Inconsideration for others
Cheating	Lying
Crushes	Masturbation
Defacing and destroying camp property	Nonconformity
Disturbed sleeping	Poor sportsmanship
Disturbing others during quiet hours	Prejudices
Eating problems	Running away from camp
Enuresis	Self-consciousness and acute shyness
Exaggeration	Showing off to an excess
Excessive daydreaming	Surliness
Fear	Teasing
Friendliness	Temper tantrums
Griping	Timidity
	Withdrawal

Although the preceding list is imposing, one equally as long could be compiled listing behavior problems common among adults. Certainly both groups share many of the same difficulties. The number of children in camp whose behavior is atypical is small when compared with those whose behavior is average or normal for their age range. Counselors should be aware that those who possess behavior problems move in two directions — toward people or away from people. If they move toward people, they become aggressive, resentful, and overbearing. If they move away from people, they withdraw from the group, become excessively shy, take on needless fears and worries.

It would be unwise if camp counselors became amateur psychologists who would try to analyze every child's moves. Counselors need, however, to become more skilled in understanding children and in distinguishing between typical and atypical behavior. They must be able to recognize defense and escape mechanisms when they see them. They should realize that daydreaming, fantasy, reverie, compensation, aggression, rationalization, temper tantrums, homesickness, overcritical behavior, and hysteria are danger signals an unwell child flashes out calling for help.

PRINCIPLES FOR WORKING WITH CHILDREN

Counselors should be aware that there is no one overall method for dealing successfully with children. They must master a variety of techniques and become skilled in recognizing the failure or success of each technique. The best way to help children to learn to help themselves is based upon sound principles. These principles are:

1. All behavior is caused; atypical actions occur when needs or drives clash.
2. All human beings are totally unique; since no two children are alike, a method that works with one child may not necessarily be successful with another.
3. When children are busily engaged in activities they have selected to do and when they have a feeling of success from taking part in that activity, they are less likely to develop problems.
4. Conflicts and personalities are not changed overnight nor by advice; since changes are gradual, each child must be *patiently* aided to learn to help himself.

When aiding, playing, and working with children, a counselor will obtain the best results if the following suggestions are kept in mind:

1. Always be fair, considerate, and display a genuine liking for all children.
2. Never show favoritism.

3. Be sympathetic and understanding of children's problems even though the difficulty may seem absurd, unimportant, and small from the adult viewpoint.
4. Never be shocked at a child's actions.
5. Give each camper a genuine feeling of belonging and security.
6. Give children increased opportunities to assume responsibilities of real worth.
7. Remember that every human being reacts favorably to praise and that everyone resents being criticized or blamed.
8. Be consistent in offering help and suggestions to others.
9. Become more sensitized to children — their hopes, fears, and tensions.

CAMP DISCIPLINE

There are times at camp when children misbehave either knowingly or not and should be punished. Although camp rules and regulations should be few, some are necessary for the safety and well-being of all. Regulations pertaining to the swimming areas or other such hazardous places must be strictly enforced at all times. Campers who disobey these rules and regulations must be corrected immediately. Since the best discipline is self-directed, all punishments should be given with this end in mind. When punishing campers, it is recommended that the adult leader:

1. Take away the things the child likes most to do.
2. Be fair and point out to the offender where he has made a mistake so that he will clearly understand why he is being punished.
3. Have the punishment follow the offense as soon as possible; delayed punishment is practically worthless from an educational point of view.
4. Relate the punishment to the offense.
5. Never use work as a form of punishment.
6. Use punishment as a last resort when other methods have failed to reach the desired solution to the problem.
7. Never use physical punishment.

It has been said that children, like plants, grow best in a favorable environment. Camp life is a rich soil in which boys and girls can thrive abundantly. Both plants and children suffer from neglect as well as from over-nourishment. Smothering, babying, and excessive sheltering damage and retard all human growth and development. Skillful, wise handling can aid all growing things to find the best that life contains.

It has been said that youth is a bank where adults deposit their most precious treasures—their hard-won wisdom and their dreams of a better, happier, more secure world. All the accomplishments of tomorrow will be judged by the type of education youth has had today. The summer camp, be it operated on a short or long term basis, be it publicly or privately owned, has taken its rightful place beside our other recognized educational institutions—the home, school, and church. It is imperative that counselors realize that their role through camping is to help youth and adults live more abundantly, now and tomorrow. As leader-teachers they deal with America's most precious possession, our children and our future parents.

Suggested Readings

American Camping Association. *Resident Camp Standards; Day Camp Standards; Family Camp Standards.* Bradford Woods, Martinsville, Indiana. Every camp carrying the A.C.A. approval seal must meet the Association's standards in the areas of facilities, leadership, program, health and safety, and administrative policies as judged by a visiting expert evaluation team. Anyone concerned with camping should know about and adhere to these protective standards.

Boy Scouts of America. *Camping; Conservation in Camping; Firemanship; Forestry; Knots and How to Tie Them; Pioneering; Hiking; Orienteering; Boy Scout Field Book; Whittling; Woodcarving; Cooking; Weather; Signaling; Surveying.* New Brunswick, New Jersey. Excellent campcraft materials can be found in each of these highly recommended materials.

Burton, Maurice. *Curiosities of Animal Life.* New York: Sterling Publishing Company, 1960. This fascinating book is a must for any camp library and a nature specialist concerned with helping children learn to love and care for animals.

Girl Scouts of America. *Girl Scout Handbook; Flip Charts of Campcraft Skills; Compass and Maps; Toolcraft; Knife and Ax; Let's Start Cooking.* 830 Third Ave., New York, N.Y. Many valuable campcraft materials other than these are also available from the Girl Scouts. Write for a publication list.

Loughmiller, Campbell. *Wilderness Road.* Austin, Texas: The University of Texas Press, 1965. Unlike any book or camp program in America, this book tells how year-round camping is used to rehabilitate emotionally disturbed boys. It is an amazing success story, showing what leadership and nature can do to help heal the sick.

Macfarlan, Allan. *Living Like the Indians.* New York: Association Press, 1960. This fascinating book contains excellent materials for those interested in Indian lore and activities as part of a camp program or theme.

Mitchell, Viola, and Ida B. Crawford. *Camp Counseling,* 5th ed. Philadelphia: W. B. Saunders Co., 1976. This textbook, written for the would-be camp counselor, is used by most schools and colleges offering a camp leadership course. The materials are cleverly presented. Especially valuable are the chapters on campcraft and nature activities.

Pohndorf, Richard. *Camp Waterfront Programs and Management.* New York: Association Press, 1960. A book primarily for camp administrators and the waterfront staff.

Shuttleworth, Dorothy. *Exploring Nature with Your Child.* New York: Greystone Press, 1957. A must for every camp library and anyone interested in bringing the exciting world of nature into the lives of children for their lifelong enrichment.

Smith, Julian. *Outdoor Education for the Youth of America.* Washington, D.C.: American Association for Health, Physical Education and Recreation, 1958. Written by America's foremost authority on outdoor education, this book is especially valuable for those city folks having to use park facilities for day camping.

chapter 11

Nature

What is this life, if full of care,
We have no time to stand and
stare?

No time to stand beneath the
boughs,
And stare as long as sheep or cows.

A foolish life, this, if full of care,
We have no time to stand and stare.
—William H. Davies

Nature is relatively an undiscovered gold mine of stimulating recreational activities. A program in this area can be conducted almost anywhere and everywhere—at a pond, city playground, or college campus. Our world is teeming with life. History is ever being recorded in rocks, trees, and streams. War, birth, death, and family life ever abound in the grass beneath our feet and in the sky above our heads. Literally the whole world is at the leader's doorstep and nature is *always* available.

Almost everyone is interested in one or more of nature's countless facets. The leader's role is to uncover and develop this interest.* Some few can be lured through crafts to a quickened interest by copying nature in clay, charcoal drawing, water colors, jewelry craft, leather work or finger painting. Some others can be led through physical activity such as a field trip or hike and gradually be slowed down to stop, look, listen, and marvel at the world which they and others share. Boys, particularly those who like airplanes, can be led into an accelerated nature interest by making a comparison and variation study of aircraft and bird flight patterns. This simple beginning offers rich possibilities for later explorations, such as the cultivation of the new hobby of bird watching, counting, banding and recording the mysteries of migration.

Any leader untrained in this area can learn about it with his group. The nearest public library is an information storehouse. The tenderfoot

---

*Read the exciting book *Pilgrim At Tinker Creek* by Annie Dillard, New York, Harper's Magazine Press, 1975 for many suggestions for ways to discover the wonderful world of nature.

naturalist should choose a child's book. As he progresses in understanding reading sources he should likewise be graduated. Too frequently the timid novice selects reference materials that squelch his enthusiasm because they are far beyond his level of comprehension. Other sources of local help are:

> Nature hobbyists
> Florists
> Veterinarians
> Farmers
> Science teachers in schools and colleges
> Leaders in the YWCA, YMCA, Boy Scouts, Girl Scouts, Camp Fire Girls, 4-H
> Forest rangers
> Museum, aquarium, zoo, or other such nature directors or employees
> National, state, county or local park naturalists

Free and/or inexpensive printed materials are available upon request from the following governmental departments or agencies:

> *National*, Washington, D.C.
> United States Forest Service, Department of Agriculture
> National Park Service, Department of the Interior
> *State*
> State and city park departments
> State fish and game commissions
> Extension service of state universities and agricultural colleges
> State conservation commissions

PRINCIPLES

Principles around which the leader should build a nature program, be it on a short or long term basis, include a desire to conduct a program that is:

1. Fun to carry out; is adventurous.
2. Done through first hand experiences; studying and learning about the real bird rather than the stuffed birdie in a cage. The program must revolve around *living* things.
3. Geared to quicken and broaden an initial nature interest.
4. Built around local materials and the common everyday passed over and unseen miracles of nature.
5. Begun with one or a few specific things to study and slowly graduated to include more. (For example, study the feeding habits of one animal before making a broader study of the differences between the feeding habits of dogs and goats.)

6. Based upon seasonal and timely opportunities. (For example, study trees and flowers in the spring when they are budding or watch animals prepare for winter.)

7. Geared to the age and interest level of each group, yet broad and varied enough to include all age groups. (Young children tend to favor gardening and pet care as well as art and dramatic activities centering around nature. Teen-agers often prefer service projects such as working as assistant nature leader, forest and land conservation projects, and a more detailed study through club activities of a few things in nature by means of an Astronomer's Club, a Woodcrafter's Club, etc. Adults are attracted to activities which lead to the improvement of their own environment through garden, flower arrangement, or similar clubs. Both sexes enjoy illustrated lectures on birds, flowers, animals, rivers, or other areas of nature.)

ACTIVITIES

PROGRAM POSSIBILITIES IN NATURE INCLUDE:

Aquariums
Making and laying nature trails
Hikes and excursions
Map making
Collections

Flowers	Tree cross sections	Seaweed
Leaves	Seeds	Rocks
Twigs	Insects	Minerals
Wood	Bird nests	Shells
		Others

Gardening

Flowers	Indoor gardens
Vegetables	Miniature plants
Transplanting	Rock gardens
Landscaping	Others

Weather Study

Barometer making, reading, recording	Hygrometer making, reading, recording
Weather charts	Weather flags
Forecasting	Cloud photography and study
	Others

Crafts

Barkcraft	Cloud, tree, flower
Seashell crafts	photography
Dyeing materials from native	Plaster molds
fruits and vegetables	Leaf prints
Wood carving	Mounting insects
Sketching, painting	Fly tying
	Others

Drama

Story reading and telling of ancient legends and myths about the sun, moon, stars, clouds, etc.

Original plays about nature or any phase of it.

Costume making, copying nature's colors or figures.

Others

Music

Instrument making from gourds, hollow logs, reeds, corn stalks, bamboo.

Singing favorite songs about nature.

Original song contests around a specific part of nature, such as the moon, stars, clouds, etc.

Listening to classical music about rivers, birds, the sea, etc.

Recording bird calls.

Recording nature's sounds heard during the day or at night, or each month or season.

Dancing

Creative dance built around one specific theme in nature such as the willow tree, or the moods of nature such as a storm, etc.

Indian dancing: the dance of the thunderbird, the corn dance, etc.

Club Activities

Junior naturalist

Junior museum

Gardening

Astronomy

Bird watcher's club

Dog or other pet caring and training clubs

Native material craft club

Nature photography club

Explorer's club

Hiking club

Bicycling and/or youth hosteling club

Indian Lore

Katchina dolls	Sand painting
Archery	Jewelry craft
Bow and arrow craft	Miniature villages
Drums, tom-toms, and Indian drama	Headdress and costume making
Songs of Indians	Dancing
Rattles	Native dyes
Bead craft	Totem poles

NATURE GAMES

Wise is the leader who has a large supply of carefully selected nature games to add zest and sparkle to his program, or variety and surprise during adverse weather conditions. Even adults enjoy testing their wits or newly acquired nature knowledge in a game similar to Twenty Questions. Each selected game should add to the effectiveness of the total program and not be a tacked-on unnecessary fringe to an already attractive garment. The leader might well make a large collection of such games, writing each on a separate card based upon the pattern used below to describe each of the following active and passive games:

ONE FOOT SQUARE

Outdoor—Quiet

1. Divide the group into teams.
2. Place a book or other object over a piece of ground approximately one foot square.
3. Give each group 5 minutes or less to collect as many living things as possible in that square.
4. Reward the winning group with the privilege of choosing the next activity.

RETRIEVING

Outdoor—Active

1. Divide the group into teams.
2. The leader holds up one specimen (rock, maple leaf, etc.) and says "Go!"
3. Award one point to the group which returns first with a similar object.
4. Play for ten or fewer points.

I SAW

Outdoor or Indoor—
Active

1. Arrange players in a circle.
2. One acts out what animal, fish, or bird he saw recently.
3. He remains inside the circle if anyone or all fail to guess what he saw.
4. The winner remains in the circle longest.

TRAILING

Outdoor—Active

1. Leader goes cross country into the woods, marking his trail by bending twigs, footprints, or similar signs.
2. The group tries to find him 10 to 15 minutes later.
3. The first to find him is winner.

TRUE OR FALSE

Outdoor or Indoor—
Active

1. Divide the group into two teams, naming one side True and other False.
2. The leader reads a statement which is either true or false, such as "Dogs fly."
3. Each side runs behind own safety line depending upon the statement. If true the True group runs while the False chases.
4. Winning team ends up with the most players.

TOUCH

Indoor—Quiet

1. Place bird nests, leaves, fruit, etc., into a paper sack.
2. All players close their eyes and each handles all articles inside the bag.
3. When all have removed blindfolds, the winner is the one who records the largest correct number of articles.

KIM'S GAME

Indoor—Quiet

1. Place a nut, vegetable, leaf, etc., into an uncovered box.
2. Have all players look into the box for 2 minutes.
3. Winner has recorded the largest correct number of articles.

SOUNDS

Outdoor—Quiet

1. Give each player pencil and paper.
2. All remain silent for 5 minutes, noting down all natural sounds heard during that period.
3. The winner is the one who has recorded the greatest number.

SHARP EYES

Indoor—Quiet

1. Show all a bird or animal picture for two minutes.
2. Have all record the answers to specific questions such as "What color was the bird's left wing?" etc.
3. Winner has recorded the greatest number correctly.

DRAW

Indoor —Quiet

1. Divide into teams.
2. Call one from each team to see the name of a bird or beast you have written down.
3. Each goes back to his own group and without talking must draw a picture of the bird or animal.
4. Winning team guesses correctly first and is given 1 point.
5. Play to 5 points.

BLIND AS A BAT

Outdoor—Active

1. Leader blindfolds and ties rope to wrist of one representative from each team.
2. Leader holds rope ends and allows each 5 feet of rope.
3. All walk around and call out the identity of as many objects as possible in 5 minutes.
4. Winner has named most objects correctly.

FLASH NATURE GAME

    Outdoor or Indoor—
      Quiet

1. Give each player a number and divide into two teams.
2. Leader has ten or more specimens from wide variety of nature objects in a bag.
3. Holds each one above his head, turning it around slowly, allowing all to see.
4. Calls a number and player with that number guesses what object is.
5. Award one point to team member who correctly identifies object.
6. Play for 10 points.

CHANGING COVER

    Outdoor—Active

1. While leader counts ten all players hide themselves 30 feet away.
2. Leader eliminates anyone he can see.
3. Leader closes his eyes and he counts to nine while players move closer.
4. Continue counting one less each time and eliminate all those seen as they all move closer each time.
5. Winner gets closest to the leader at the most reduced count.

NUMBER ONE MAN

    Outdoor—Active

1. Leader arranges hikers in single file behind him.
2. He sees an object of nature and asks person behind him (the Number One Man) to identify it.
3. Failure to do so means that player goes to the end of the line and second person has chance to move up if he can answer. If he fails, he goes to the end of the line, too.
4. Winner remains in first place longest.

HARE AND HOUNDS

Outdoor—Active

1. Divide group into Hare and Hound teams.
2. Hares hide in groups of three and must remain in this group.
3. Hounds search until all groups are found.
4. Hares become Hounds and game continues.
5. Team finding others in shortest time wins.

CURIO COLLECTION

Outdoor—Active

1. Leader names an oddity of nature such as a tree with red leaves, a tree bent by a strong wind, etc.
2. Players search until the curio is found.
3. Winner finds the greatest number.

FETCH IT

Outdoor—Active

1. Divide the group into two lines, each player numbered so that opposite players have the same number.
2. Leader asks any two with same number to "fetch" (bring him) a certain object, such as a milkweed, etc.
3. Line scoring 10 points first wins.

WHO AM I?

Outdoor or Indoor—
Active

1. One player pretends to be some character in nature.
2. He tells brief facts about himself but conceals his identity, such as "I live along the seashore and am an animal."
3. The one guessing correctly becomes the new leader.

FIND ME

Outdoor—Active

1. Divide the group into teams.
2. Give each team a list of various nature objects to find with points given according to difficulty for each article.
3. First group to make 15 points wins.

I SPY

Outdoor—Active

1. Hike with a group.
2. Leader says "I spy a robin." (Or any other nature object.)
3. All who also see the object sit down.
4. Others remain standing until they see it.
5. Award points to each of the first three in the group who see the object named.
6. Play until one wins 10 points.

MATCH IT OR KNOW IT

Outdoor—Active

1. Divide group into two teams.
2. Allow each team 15 minutes to collect objects of nature (leaves, twigs, seeds, nuts, etc.) and to take them back to their side.
3. One representative from each goes to opposite side with an article.
4. If opposing team can name it, award one point; if they can match it from their collection, award 2 points.
5. Play for 15 points.

NATURE SCAVENGER HIKE

Outdoor—Active

1. Divide group into teams of six to ten on each.
2. Give each a list of nature objects to find within a given time.
3. Winning team finds the greatest number within the allotted time.

NATURE SCOUTING

Outdoor—Active

1. Divid group into teams and send each on a 15 to 30 minute hike going East, West, North, or South.
2. Representative from each team tells most interesting things seen by the group.
3. All vote which team saw the most interesting things.

TREE TAG

Outdoor—Active

1. "It" tries to tag players.
2. Designate one kind of tree which players are safe when touching.
3. Tagged players assist "It" until all are caught.

SCRAMBLE

Indoor—Active

1. Arrange twenty or more nature objects in a pile.
2. Divide players into teams, giving each corresponding numbers.
3. Call out all number two's to find the bird nest (etc.) and to bring the object to their teams first.
4. Winning team has secured the most objects.

NATURE BASEBALL

Indoor—Quiet

1. Arrange nature questions on cards.
2. Divide players into two teams.
3. Draw baseball diamond on floor with chalk.
4. Leader asks batter a question. If he answers correctly he goes to first base; if he fails he is out.
5. Play according to regular baseball rules.
6. Play four innings or for 10 to 15 minutes.

PROVE IT

Outdoor—Quiet

1. Arrange players in a circle.
2. One says "From where I sit I see a tree with moss on it." (Or any other natural object in sight.)
3. If anyone challenges his seeing the tree, he must prove it by touching the tree.
4. If challenged and unable to prove what he saw he must drop out; if he can prove it, his challenger must leave the game.

STRING BURNING CONTEST

Outdoor—Active

1. Stretch two strings between stakes, one twelve inches above the ground, the other eighteen inches above it.
2. Contestants must collect tinder kindling and build a fire to burn the upper string.
3. No wood may be piled higher than the twelve inch string.
4. Each one tries to burn the upper string apart first.

Nature Crafts*

Nature crafting is like junk or scrap art and it can be done with almost any kind of nature object. Care must be taken not to alter the original shape or color. An insertion of toothpicks in a squash can make a wonderful bird. Yarn, feathers and other materials can transform one interesting object into another—thus a pecan plus pipe cleaners, a toothpick and two little feathers can magically become a Texas roadrunner, that fast moving creature who "beep beeps" his way swiftly along. A potato, with imagination, can turn into a warty witch's head or a squatty, fat frog. Sticks, driftwood, and tree roots can become a giraffe, an arm, a gun, or a snake. Squash, corncobs, potatoes, or dried pods make wonderful wrinkled faced puppets. Sand dollars, shells, bamboo sticks, and even thin slabs of rocks can make sweet sounding, tinkling wood chimes. Sticks tied or lashed together make attractive toys, initials, or figure and even whole scenes, such as an Indian village with horses, teepees, etc. Pictures and frames for sharing and showing found treasures such as insects, rocks, flowers, or even bones can be attractively arranged on cardboard covered with burlap and put in a lashed frame with a see-thru protective lid from a discarded Christmas card box. Bracelets and necklaces can be made by stringing beans, sticks, bones, feathers, rocks or shells. Trumpet vines make fantastic boats that really sail by glueing a thin twig in the center of the pod and attaching a leaf for a sail. Driftwood, dried flowers, pods, and almost anything else found in nature's bountiful cupboard can make attractive room decorations upon which to feast your eyes later after a trip through the woods or on the beach searching for treasures.

*The author is grateful to Ginny Inge, student in the class, Recreation Leadership, at S.M.U. for these suggested activities.

Motivating Suggestions

Microscope, magnifying glasses, telescopes
nature books with lots of color pictures
nature slides
biology, anatomy books, and slides
large nature pictures hung around the room
display of African, Indian and other primitive art pieces
nature displays in the room that the children can observe, handle
and care for

ant farm	sprayed spider webs
aquarium	bird nest and eggs
terrarium	wasp nests, bee hives
living plants	field trips
dried plants, pods	zoo
driftwood	museum
rocks	park, woods
shells	creek, pond

MATERIALS THAT CAN BE USED

Sticks, branches, tree knots, driftwood, bark,
leaves, moss, fern
seeds, beans, berries, nuts, acorns, pinecones
dried pods and flowers
feathers
bones, teeth
hide, horse hair
shells, coral, sea urchins
rocks, sand, dirt, charcoal, small fossils
bird nest
snakeskin
butterflies, moths, any insect
grasses, raffia, Johnson grass, jute, hay, corn husks
spider webs, wasp nest, honey comb
potatoes, squash, corncob

USES

assemblage, collage, mosaic	pictures, frames
sculpture	toys
painting, printing	gifts
jewelry	mobiles
weaving	garden decorations
wall, table or party decorations	windchimes

PLACES TO FIND MATERIALS

flowerbed, gardens   beaches
wood pile   shell and rock shops
fields, woods, forests   farm, nursery
ditches, creeks, river-   zoo, aquarium
    beds
piles of wash and flood
    debris

Suggested Readings

MAGAZINES

American Forests. The American Forestry Association, 919 Seventeenth Street, N.W., Washington, D.C. 20006.
Audubon Magazine and *Audubon Nature Bulletin.* National Audubon Society, 1000 Fifth Avenue New York, N.Y.
Bird Lore, National Association of Audubon Societies, Harrisburg, Pennsylvania.
Camping Magazine. American Camping Association, Bradford Woods, Martinsville, Indiana 46151.
Junior Natural History. American Museum of Natural History, Central Park West at 79th Street, New York, N.Y. 10024.
National Geographic Magazine. National Geographic Society, Sixteenth and M Streets, Washington, D.C. 20036.
Natural History Magazine. American Museum of Natural History, Central Park West at 79th Street, New York, N.Y. 10024.
Nature Magazine. American Nature Association, 1214 Sixteenth Street, N.W. Washington, D.C. 20036.
Recreation. National Recreation Association, 315 Fourth Avenue, New York, N.Y. 10014.
Science Digest. 631–43 St. Clair St., Chicago, Illinois 60611.
Science Newsletter. 2101 Constitution Avenue, Washington, D.C. 20037.
The World Is Yours. Smithsonian Institute, Washington, D.C.

GENERAL

Comstock, Anna Botsford: *Handbook of Nature Study.* Ithaca, New York, Comstock Publishing Co., 1947.
Devoe, Alan, and Berry, Mary: *Our Animal Neighbors.* New York, McGraw-Hill Book Co., 1953.
Gaudette, Marie: *Leader's Nature Guide.* Girl Scouts of America, 155 E. 44th St., New York, 1942.
Nesbitt, Paul: *Nature Games.* 711 Columbia Road, Colorado Springs, Colorado, 1952.
Price, Betty: *Adventuring in Nature.* New York, National Recreation Association, 1951.
Pettit, Paul: *Book of Nature Hobbies.* New York, Didier Press, 1947.
Stevenson, Elmo: *Nature Games Book.* New York, Greenberg, Publisher, Inc., 1941.
Vinal, William: *Nature Recreation.* New York, McGraw-Hill Book Co., 1940.

SPECIFIC

Anthony, H. E.: *Animals of America.* New York, Doubleday and Co., 1937.
Blanchon, Neltje: *The Bird Book.* New York, Doubleday and Co., 1932.
Brown, Vinson: *Amateur Naturalist's Handbook.* Boston, Little, Brown and Co., 1948.

Cormack, Maribelle: *First Book of Stones.* New York, F. Watts Co., 1950.
Ditmars, R. L.: *The Reptiles of North America.* New York, Doubleday and Co., 1936.
Fabre, Jean-Henri: *Animal Life in Field and Garden.* New York, D. Appleton and Co., 1921.
Kaehele, Edna: *Training the Family Dog.* New York, Lantern Press, 1953.
Lemmon, Robert: *Our Amazing Birds.* Garden City, New York, Doubleday and Co., 1952.
Mason, George: *Animal Sounds.* New York, William Morrow and Co., 1948.
Pope, Clifford: *Snakes Alive and How They Live.* New York, Viking Press, 1951.
Sperisen, Francis: *The Art of Lapidary.* Milwaukee, The Bruce Publishing Co. 1953.
Teale, Edwin: *The Junior Book of Insects.* New York, E. P. Dutton and Co., 1953.
Walcott, Mary, and Platt, Dorothy: *Wild Flowers of America.* New York, Crown Publishers, 1953.
Zim, Herbert, and Baker, Robert: *Stars: 150 Paintings in Color.* New York, Simon and Schuster, 1951.

Visual Aids

SOURCES OF FREE AND INEXPENSIVE NATURE CHARTS, SLIDES AND FILMS

Audubon Society, 1776 Broadway, New York, N.Y. 10019
American Museum of Natural History, Central Park West at 79th Street, New York, N.Y. 10024.
Association Films, 347 Madison Avenue, New York, N.Y. 10002.
Boy Scouts of America, 2 Park Avenue, New York, N.Y.10016.
Girl Scouts of America, 155 E. 44th St., New York, N.Y. 10017.
National Geographic Society, Washington, D.C.
U.S. Department of Agriculture, Washington, D.C.
U.S. Forest Service, Washington, D.C.
U.S. Superintendent of Documents, Washington, D.C.
Wild Flower Preservation Society, 3740 Oliver Street, Washington, D.C.

OUTDOOR EDUCATION

American Association for Health, Physical Education and Recreation (AAHPER): *Casting and Angling; Outdoor Education.* Washington, D.C. AAHPER, 1958.
Benson, Kenneth R. and Frankson, Carl, E.: *Nature Crafts.* Englewood Cliffs, N.J., Prentice-Hall, 1968.
Brehm, Shirley A.: *A Teacher's Handbook for Study Outside the Classroom.* Columbus, Ohio, Charles E. Merrill Publishing Company, 1969.
Brown, Robert E. and Mouser, G. W.: *Techniques for Teaching Conservation Education.* Minneapolis, Burgess Publishing Company, 1964.
Donaldson, George and Goering, Oswald: *Perspective In Outdoor Education.* Dubuque, Iowa, Wm. C. Brown, 1972.
Garrison, Cecil: *Outdoor Education: Principles and Practice.* Springfield, Charles C Thomas, 1966.
Hammerman, Donald R. and Hammerman, William, M.: *Teaching in the Outdoors.* Minneapolis, Burgess Publishing Company, 1964.
Hug, John W. and Wilson, Phyllis, J.: *Curriculum Enrichment Outdoors.* New York, Harper & Row, 1965.
Frankel, Lillian and Frankel, Godfrey: *101 Best Nature Games and Projects.* New York, Gramercy Publishing House, 1974.
Jaeger, Ellsworth: *Wildwood Wisdom.* New York, The Macmillan Co., 1957.
Mand, Charles L.: *Outdoor Education.* New York, J. Lowell Pratt & Company, 1967.

Milliken, Margaret, Hamer, Austin, F., and McDonald, Ernest C.: *Field Study Manual for Outdoor Learning*. Minneapolis, Burgess Publishing Company, 1968.

Smith, Julian W. and others: *Outdoor Education*. Englewood Cliffs, N. J., Prentice-Hall, Inc., 1963.

van der Smissen, Betty and Goering, Oswald, H.: *A Leader's Guide to Nature-Oriented Activities*, 2nd ed. Ames, Ia., Iowa State University Press, 1968.

Suggested Films

Beyond the Chalkboard. Northern Illinois University, DeKalb 60115.

Nature's Classroom. Division of Conservation, Department of Natural Resources, Madison, Wisconsin 53701.

Outdoor Education. AAHPER, 1201 Sixteenth Street, N.W., Washington, D.C. 20036.

chapter 12

Athletic Sports and Games

Play for children is the gaining of life.
Play for adults is the renewal of life.
                    —Joseph Lee

Ours is a sports loving nation. The manufacture and distribution of sports equipment is one of our leading industries and plays a vital role in our national economy. The rapid expansion of commercially operated bowling alleys, ice and roller skating rinks, golf courses, archery ranges, tennis, racquetball, platform tennis courts and swimming pools indicates that the public is becoming increasingly interested in participating in these activities. Commercially owned sports facilities greatly outnumber those operated by public agencies. Spectator attendance at football, basketball, baseball, boxing, and wrestling matches is astonishingly large.

The greatest participation increase in sports has been in tennis, swimming, bowling, jogging, skiing, and golf. Millions watch on television screens or in the stands professional tennis and golf matches, as well as football, baseball and hockey games. Scuba diving, surfing, and deepsea fishing appeal to both the young and older sets. Now the physically handicapped are enjoying games and sports in rapidly increasing numbers. Popular activities are wheelchair basketball, bowling, archery and track and field events. Swimming, bowling, archery, simple games, and field events are favored activities among the blind, deaf, and mentally retarded. Senior citizens now are jogging, playing golf, tennis, bowling, and going on fishing trips.

Participation in competitive sporting events among women and girls is at an all time high, thanks to the momentum given to this trend by the efforts of those in the women's lib movement and the government ruling, Title IX, which gives females opportunity to participate in sports on an equal basis to that which has always been given to men in our nation. Billie Jean King and Chris Evert in tennis, as well as Olga Korbutt and Nadia Comaneci in gymnastics, are idols for the thousands of would-be female competitors in a wide range of sports.

Recreation departments throughout the nation have not enough tennis courts, ball fields, golf courses, swimming pools and other facilities to accommodate the vast number of people throughout the community who want a place to enjoy doing active sports in their free time after work or school hours, or over the weekend and holiday period.

People of all ages are flocking to classes held at community recreation centers in which the basic skills of such lifetime sports as tennis, badminton, golf, racquetball, and the self-defense activities of judo and karate are being taught.

The recreation leader's responsibilities in athletic sports and games lie in (1) organizing and conducting classes or clubs for beginners, intermediates, and advanced players, (2) devising policies and regulations regarding competition, (3) drawing up leagues and tournaments, (4) conducting, officiating, and supervising competitive events, and (5) providing facilities. In large cities these duties are usually assumed by a special athletic council in the municipal recreation department. In smaller communities, the recreation leader includes athletics and sports as one part of his complete program. His job is that of stimulating and promoting an interest in competitive sports. This is often done by sponsoring exhibition matches or demonstrations by local or outside experts. A diving exhibition by an AUW champion or a demonstration of correct batting by a visiting big league player can do wonders toward building interest in a particular activity. The leader must also provide for adequate safe playing areas. He should constantly search for more courts, fields, and playing facilities within the community and should seek to increase the number of hours games can be played on them through the use of night lighting. Additional player participation and spectator interest should lead to the acquisition of more and better facilities.

Teaching Motor Skills

Teaching motor skills to others is far from an easy task, even though the instructor may be a skilled player in a sport himself. It is imperative that the leader-teacher knows that the teaching-learning situation must be a controlled one. The instructor who tries to speak without the attention of the group is wasting both time and energy. The inability to get and hold the learner's attention is characteristic of the beginning leader and also the poor one. One has only to observe someone teaching a child successfully to realize the role the following play in getting fast and sure results: (1) complete attention, (2) firmness of voice, (3) repetition or conditioning by using the same pattern of movement and voice repeatedly, and (4) a reward in the form of verbal praise for the student. It is recommended that all those who desire to become master leaders gain experience and increase their greatly needed patience by practicing on pet animals or birds before teaching human beings. There are many elements common in teaching all age groups. One must learn to be a teacher, for it is impossible to become a superior one without hard work and capitalization on past errors. Just as the way to *learn* is to start learning, so the way to teach is to *teach*. The time to learn is now, not when one gets a job as an instructor in one, two, three, or four years. To practice, evaluate mistakes, and learn how as you go along is the only magic formula for obtaining success as an educator.

In teaching any skill the leader should:

1. Briefly explain what he is doing and how to do it.
2. Show others how to do it by means of demonstration.
3. Give individual assistance to all who are having difficulty copying the movements.
4. Help each evaluate the progress made.

Some teachers prefer to explain and demonstrate simultaneously by first facing the class lined up in a single line, so he has good eye contact with the group, doing each movement to count, and then having the class repeat, through mimetics, with him both the movement and the count. The entire class again watches him demonstrate with his back to the group as they say the count, followed by all of them counting and doing the movement with him. For example, when teaching the softball throw the instructor should have the group, on count one, hold the ball in both hands in front of the body, on count two bring the hand and arm holding the ball down below the waist, on count three move the hand and arm up and around, making almost a complete circle, and release the ball on count four.

Regardless of how the teacher drills class groups in new skills, all skills should be used in a game as soon as possible. Movement accuracy should precede the development of agility, speed, timing, and body flexibility.

It is important that teachers demonstrate skills correctly, for students learning through trial and error and insight may copy an incorrect movement pattern and develop a habit that is difficult to break. Drills, relays, and novelty games are all valuable for skill practice purposes, but *only* when done with the specific goal of assisting the student in mastering the needed skills for successful game play. Movement accuracy should be acquired first, followed by the development of speed, correct timing, and the ability to change direction suddenly.

When the learner, with the teacher's help, gains an understanding of what he is doing incorrectly and can avoid doing it, he has learned. Skill polish results when movements are done correctly and become easy, rhythmic, automatic responses. Thus, teaching is both remedial and diagnostic. It is imperative that the teacher pick out faulty movement patterns, and know how to correct them. Just as the patient quickly loses confidence in the physician who declares, "Now your trouble *may* be this" or "I *think* your difficulty may be" so students tend to disregard the guesses of teachers who cannot immediately spot what is being done incorrectly. One has only to watch the face of any student with its glow of triumph as he hits the target after making the movement correction his teacher recommended to realize the tremendous value correct diagnostic ability plays in learning. Likewise, one has only to note the expression of frustration in any student as he tries this, that, and many more teacher suggestions for improvement (and none of them works) to comprehend the importance of the teacher helping the student discover *what* is wrong, *why* it is wrong, and *how* to avoid repeating the same mistake again and again.

Teaching Game Rules

The best way to teach game rules is in relation to skills to be mastered. For example, the rules for serving a volleyball and the techniques for doing so correctly should occur simultaneously, just as would the teaching of the basketball free throw and the reason a player is awarded it. All players must know and understand that game rules are necessary for safe but fast play. Teacher or student demonstrations showing how rules are broken and what happens when they are afford splendid ways to help players learn them. Pencil and paper tests aid the instructor to spot quickly those who have a hazy or false concept of the laws of any game. All such tests should be discussed with the group and the correct answers given for all questions. Oral review, for several days, of certain test sections may be followed successfully by another revised written rule test.

The instructor should help his group know each rule and why it is a rule, as well as the penalty for breaking it. When players discover that rules have been devised for their protection and for the improvement of the quality of the game, they are often more interested in learning them. The use of student officials increases a desire for rule mastery especially when it is considered an honor among peer groups to be chosen for such a leadership position. Physical education majors are usually required to complete an officiating course for many sports as part of their professional training and must call many games in the intramural program in order to fulfill requirements of the course. Both such younger and older students often help teams and classmates learn game rules more quickly than can the teacher.

All practice and competitive games should be played according to the rules. The game should be stopped in classes or at practice periods at teachable moments when rule infractions occur. In class situations the teacher may ask the group what someone did incorrectly rather than call out the penalty or award the offended player his earned privilege. Inferior instructors tend to answer such questions themselves and then go on automatically with the calling of the game. Thus they deprive their students of many fine learning experiences.

The use of clinics and workshops is also often a successful way to teach rules to large groups. Since most of our learning comes through our eyes and ears actual demonstration with explanation of all rules is superior to the use of movies or slides. The latter, however, may be successfully used as a means of summarizing materials for a class, a clinic, or other groups.

Teaching Game Strategy

The techniques of offensive and defensive play may be taught by first helping groups discover the object of the game, how scores are made, what each score counts and how to prevent the opponent from scoring. Since the object of most team games is to advance a ball, the offensive team should help develop skills for doing so through defensive territory. A player without the ball tries to move into a free area to be in a receiving position. A player with the ball tries to pass into an open space to a free teammate.

There are numerous ways to teach the techniques of offensive and defensive play The use of magnetized boards is highly recommended. The teacher can use them to show almost every kind of play possible in a game situation. Such boards are relatively inexpensive and can be purchased from companies advertising them in the monthly *Journal of Health, Physical Education, and Recreation.* Chalk talks, movies, filmstrips, and still pictures have proven successful also. Drills of set plays and variations to use when the first-learned combinations fail are valuable techniques for teaching advanced game tactics to players. However, no team or individual player should be drilled to excess so they become "burned out" from the experience to the extent that skill in actual game play is destroyed or game enjoyment damaged.

Suggested Sport Activities

Suggested sport activities for inclusion in this part of the recreation program include:

Individual	*Team*
Archery	Baseball
Badminton	Basketball
Bait and fly casting	Field ball for girls
Boxing	Hockey (ice, floor, field)
Bowling	Football
Fencing	Lacrosse
Golf	Lead-up games
Lead-up games	Polo (field, water)
Racquetball	Soccer
Shooting (skeet, rifle,	Speed-a-way
pistol)	Speedball
Skating (ice and roller)	Swimming
Skiing	Touch football
Squash racquets	Volleyball
Tennis	Wrestling
Track and field	
Wrestling	

Self-testing activities
Acrobatics
Apparatus
Obstacle course
Rebound tumbling
Rope climbing
Stunts
Trampoline

Fitness activities and gymnastics
Body conditioning
Gymnastics
Slimtrim clubs
Weight lifting

Aquatics
Boating and canoeing
Sailing
Scuba diving
Senior lifesaving
Skin and scuba diving
Speedboat racing

Surfing
Swimming
Synchronized swimming
Water ballet
Water games
Water safety instruction

Recreational activities
Box hockey
Camping and outing
Card games
Checkers
Chess
Croquet
Dart ball
Duckpins
Fly and bait casting
Games of low organization
Hiking
Hopscotch
Horseshoes
Rope jumping
Shuffleboard

Guidelines for Conducting
A Successful Program

Being a skilled player in a sport is no guarantee that one will be a skilled instructor in this area of the total recreation program. Found below are suggestions which will prove helpful for the teacher-leader in becoming so:

1. Select only those activities to include in the program which are best suited for the age, skill level, and physical condition of all players. (Young boys age 6–10, for example, are not physically ready for rugged competition in tackle football. Those over 50 years of age should not participate in a jogging program without their physician's permission.)
2. Play all games according to the rules and be sure that all players wear protective gear. (Game rules have been made for each player's protection. Require all participants to wear protective gloves, helmets, shin guards, etc. Such measures will protect you from being involved in a costly law suit in case of player injury.)
3. Stress good sportsmanship, team effort, obeying game rules and be an example of one who lives by these concepts.

4. See to it that every player gets an equal opportunity to play in competitive events and avoid playing only your best players in every game of tournament play.
5. Have many round robin and winner-loser tournaments and few single elimination ones. This will provide less skilled players with additional chances to keep on playing. Remember that your goal is to help all become more physically fit by playing a game or a sport for a longer time period.
6. Be sure that girls and women have equal opportunity to take part in all phases of the program as do boys and men.
7. When teaching any game or sport be sure that you know the rules of each and how to demonstrate and teach the basic skills involved in it. Have all equipment needed at hand and be sure that all playing areas are in good condition.
8. Modify games and sports for the handicapped. Use beep balls for the blind, shorten running or walking distances for crippled, simplify playing rules for the mentally retarded, etc.
9. Only play with the group occasionally yourself, for when involved in playing with the group, it is harder to detect and correct each player's weaknesses.
10. Keep equipment attractively displayed and encourage greater use of it by providing practice and free play time in your program scheduling.

Competition Possibilities

Youth as well as adults thrill to competition, either as individuals or as team members. Enjoyment of the activity through skill mastery, individual personality and character growth, as well as improved physical fitness is an objective to be sought. Taking part in a game, league, or city-wide tournament should be the means through which this goal is accomplished. A diversified program can be built around the motto "A sport for all and everyone in a sport." The program should reach girls and women as well as boys and men. Each group should have equal opportunity to use all equipment and facilities. The program should offer simplified contests for children, rugged competitive sports for teen-agers and young adults, as well as less strenuous activities for older persons. Such a program might include:

Competitive sports for children

Baseball throw for
distance
Box hockey
Circle soccer
Croquet
Darts
Field ball

Hopscotch
Jackknife contests
Jacks
Jumping
Kickball
Kite flying
Lariat roping contests

Long base
Marbles
Model airplane flying
Mumblety peg
Newcomb
Punch ball
Races
  Bicycle
  Coaster wagon
  Hoop-rolling
  Hurdle
  Ice skating
  Obstacle running

Running
Sack
Scooter
Sledding
Stilt walking
Tin can stilts
Rope jumping
Rope spinning
Scout signaling
Snowball rolling contests
Tether ball
Top spinning contests

Competitive sports for teen-agers and older youth

Archery
Archery golf
Badminton
Baseball
Basketball
  Foul shooting
  Spot shooting
  Twenty-one
Bowling
Curling
Fencing
Fly and bait casting
Football
Golf
Gymnastics
Handball
Hockey
  Ice
  Field
Horseshoes
Lacrosse
Paddle tennis
Ping Pong
Riflery
Rowing
Shuffleboard
Skiing
Soccer

Speedball
Squash racquets
Swimming and diving
Tennis
Touch football
Track and field events
  Sprints
    100, 200, 440 yard dashes
  Hurdles
    High, low
  Distance running
    Half-mile, mile, two mile
  Relay races—baton
    passing
     shuttle hurdles
  Weight events
    Shot put
    Discus throw
    Javelin throw
  Jump events
    Running high jump
    Pole vault
    Running broad jump
    Running hop, step, and
     jump
Trap and skeet shooting
Water polo
Wrestling
Volleyball

Competitive sports for older persons

Archery	Lawn bowling
Bicycling for distance	Ping Pong
Bowling	Shooting (skeet, rifle, pistol)
Croquet	Shuffleboard
Curling	Swimming
Fly and bait casting	Table tennis
Golf	Tennis
Horseshoes	Track and field
Jogging	Weight lifting

VALUES

True sport brings a rewarding satisfaction from meeting and responding to a challenge. To defeat an opponent brings forth one's best effort. Wholesome athletic contests offer a socially approved way to blow off steam and rid oneself of a need for destruction, aggression, hostility and daring adventure. The social values inherent in individual and team competitive play are numerous; they center largely around gaining more understanding, appreciation, and tolerance of others. The individual, spurred on by a desire to belong, joins a team and thus learns social skills necessary for successful group participation. Through activity he learns the true meaning of loyalty, cooperation, democracy. Under desirable leadership, good sportsmanship and character growth will accrue. Athletic contests can improve physical fitness, build strength and endurance and increase total body flexibility, coordination, and control.

Units of Competition

These units vary according to the type and objectives of the organization sponsoring the events. On the college level, units of competition for men are grouped into tournament entries representing fraternities, independents, classes, individuals, dormitories, clubs, and departments. Class, dormitory, sorority, independent, and individual representatives make up competitive entries for college women. In public schools, teams or individuals competing in any tournament may be from a homeroom, grade, physical education class or section, chosen teams or players selected by a teacher or student captain, interest groups, color team, or club group. In city recreation, competing units usually represent a playground, community center, club, organization, church, a certain section of the city, or interest group.

There are many methods of classifying competitors for fair tournament play. Age, height, sex and weight are commonly used. Physical examinations or sport skill tests can also be used.

If a large number of teams are entered for competition, leagues should be formed of those with equal ability. This is done by arranging four or eight teams in several preliminary elimination tournaments. Those placing first in each tournament should be placed in the First or A League, those who were next in the second or B League, etc. Essential factors to consider in league formation are the sport to be played, the number and skill of teams entered, eligibility requirements, available facilities, and a playing schedule best suited for the majority of players. Players may also be grouped into leagues according to age. These include:

1. Midgets   — — 10 years or under
2. Juniors   — — 11 to 14
3. Seniors   — — 15 to 17
4. Adults   — — 18 years or over
5. Senior citizens — — 50 years or older

For safety reasons, boys and girls should compete separately in those rugged contests that require strength, skill, and endurance such as soccer, field ball, kickball. However, opportunities should be made for the two sexes to compete on the same teams for social reasons. Suggested activities suitable for mixed teams of children include capture the flag, croquet, marbles, relays and other similar simple games of low organization.

Tournaments

The leader's ability to organize and conduct tournaments successfully is of paramount importance. Care should be taken to organize competition fairly and to conduct all games impartially. Good sportsmanship and playing for fun as well as to win should be stressed. All games should be supervised and officiated, if possible. Strict insistence upon playing according to the rules will help eliminate accidents.

The total athletic program should be organized around seasonal sports and games. Kite flying, marbles, jacks, and jump rope contests are best for young children in the spring. Football, soccer, speedball, and hockey are more suited for older groups and should be played largely during the fall. Basketball, ice skating and other traditional winter sports are best played in that season. Swimming, tennis, track, and archery are ideal for the summer months. Simple games that use the basic skills of running, throwing, catching, jumping, hopping, creeping and hanging should be stressed for youngsters. More advanced games and sports into which these fundamental skills are integrated are best for older groups.

Types of tournaments most commonly used include the round robin, elimination, winner-loser, and ladder.

ROUND ROBIN TOURNAMENT

In this type of competition a revolving column is the simplest for pairing opponents. Numbers are given to teams or individuals. "Bye" is used in the place of teams or individuals if there is an uneven number of competitors. Pairing of competitors is done by placing them in two columns. Once teams or individuals are given a number and these appear on the tournament chart, that order must be maintained. Competitors are arranged in the following manner:

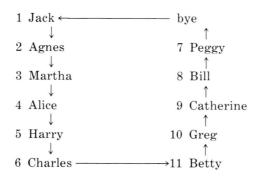

Players are moved either clockwise or counterclockwise to meet their opponents. If there is a "bye" it remains stationary, each number jumping over it to the next place.

One round fewer is played than the number of teams or individuals entered. The pairings and series for a round robin tournament for eight teams are given below:

First Round	Second Round	Third Round	Fourth Round
1 — — 8	1 — — 7	1 — — 6	1 — — 5
2 — — 7	8 — — 6	7 — — 5	6 — — 4
3 — — 6	2 — — 5	8 — — 4	7 — — 3
4 — — 5	3 — — 4	2 — — 3	8 — — 2

Fifth Round	Sixth Round	Seventh Round
1 — — 4	1 — — 3	1 — — 2
5 — — 3	4 — — 2	3 — — 8
6 — — 2	5 — — 8	4 — — 7
7 — — 8	6 — — 7	5 — — 6

The pairings will be different in each round. The team winning the most games is declared the winner. The above procedure may be followed for any number of teams if a "bye" is used for an uneven number. The tournament is completed when all players have played each other in each round.

ELIMINATION TOURNAMENT

In this type of tournament competing teams should be a perfect power of two (i.e., 4, 8, 16, 32, 64, etc.). A "bye" or "byes" are added to make the number of entries equal these powers. If there are only seven players, one "bye," plus seven entries are made; if there are thirty players, two "byes" are added. A "bye" enables a player to move automatically into the next bracket without playing against another. Teams are paired as shown below:

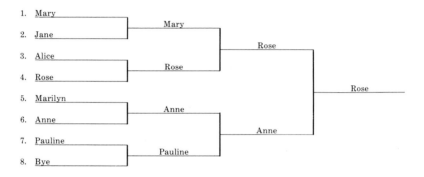

WINNER-LOSER TOURNAMENT

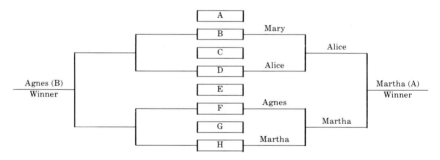

The principle of adding byes in this type of tournament is the same as in the elimination tournament. Winners move out to the right of the chart; losers move out to the left in the second round, and winners continue to move out to the left or right in all continuing rounds.

LADDER TOURNAMENT

Individuals or teams are arranged in ladder formation. Any player may challenge another player directly above. If the challenger is successful in defeating the opponent his name takes the place of the defeated one. The final winner has remained in the first position longest at the completion of the tournament.

This type of tournament is practical for tennis, badminton, handball, horseshoes or other similar games. One advantage of it, like that of the round robin, is that it gives players an opportunity to continue playing with a large number of others. This social value coupled with the desirable results of increased physical fitness through continued participation makes both kinds of tournaments highly desirable for all age groups.

Team 1
Team 2
Team 3
Team 4
Team 5
etc.

Purchase and Care of Equipment

The recreational leader will usually have the responsibility of buying and caring for athletic equipment. His goal should be to provide the best and safest equipment to all players from a budget allocated for this purpose. In order that he may gain the greatest good from these funds, the following suggestions are made for purchasing equipment:

1. Buy from reputable sporting goods companies.
2. Buy the best equipment possible. Equipment cannot be judged as expensive or less expensive by its initial price. Often the more expensive model will wear many times longer than the cheaper one.
3. Consider climate, playing areas, age, and skill of those using the equipment.
4. Do not accept gifts from salesmen. Know reputable company representatives and buy according to their recommendations.
5. In buying sportswear consider:
   a. the nature of the activity
   b. local conditions—purpose, climate, age, frequency of use, facilities for care and repair
   c. appearance
   d. comfort
   e. wearing quality of fabric
   f. stability

    g. safety

    h. guarantee and testing

6. Investigate several sporting goods companies in order to get the best equipment as economically as possible.
7. Buy multi-purpose equipment.
8. Buy a few extras if your budget allows. You always need them and many things are cheaper by the dozen.
9. Exercise caution in buying new and different equipment (for example, hard rubber softballs).
10. Use every cent of your budget.
11. Begin any awards system on a small scale, for it can soon consume the entire budget.
12. Price is poor index to the value or appearance of a trophy. Choose trophies from samples, if possible, or order them without engraving so that they may be returned if they are not satisfactory.
13. Always provide for left-handed players.
14. Be sure that ample safety devices are provided (masks, glasses, guards, knee pads, shin guards, canvas bases for softball, first aid supplies, etc.).

In buying books one should:

1. Purchase those books that contain a great deal of information. For example, buy a book including the rules of many individual or team sports rather than buying an official rulebook for each sport.
2. Buy those books that have been endorsed by national organizations, individuals who are experienced in recreation, or authorities in the field.
3. Write the National Recreation Association for a list of their publications. Also, consult bibliographies, reading lists, and current publications for recommended source material given in those books available to you.
4. Know the publishers who are particularly interested in the field of recreation and ask to be placed on their mailing lists for announcements of new books.
5. Be sure you know what a book contains before you invest in it.

In caring for equipment and sportswear properly, one should:

1. Urge all who use it to do so with care since it does not belong to them.
2. Store equipment properly (i.e., racks for tennis rackets, stands for arrows, separate shelves for baseballs, etc.).
3. Try to insure longer life of equipment (i.e., remove all dirt from leather goods and oil them, etc.).

4. Repair all equipment at the first signs of wear.
5. Train all players to report damaged equipment and to help care for and repair what things you have.

Suggestions for the care of specific kinds of equipment include:

I. Leather

   A. *Methods of Tanning:*
   1. Vegetable—action of liquors or extracts from tree bark.
   2. Chrome—chemical action while skins are in rotating-tumbling drums.
   3. Alum—for white leather (baseballs).

   B. *Kinds of Leathers, Their Properties and Uses:*
   1. Cowhide—heavy, durable (baseball gloves, shoes, footballs).
   2. Calfskin—importance in appearance of grain (volleyballs, basketballs).
   3. Kidskin—from young goat, has qualities of cowhide and of calfskin.
   4. Sheepskin—loose, spongy texture (boxing gloves and bindings, football pads).
   5. Horsehide—scuff resistant (baseball covers, mitts and gloves).
   6. Kangaroo—suppleness, toughness, extremely thick grain, moisture resistant; will not crack or peel; 17 times stronger than any other leather (football shoes).

   C. *Care of Leather Goods:*
   1. Keep dry—dry at normal room temperature, oil with mineral oil or vegetable oil.
   2. Clean *only* with saddle soap, apply with moist cloth and rub into leather, wipe dry.
   3. Store in low humidity and normal room temperature to prevent green mold rot.

II. Woods

   A. *Classifications:*
   1. Very hard—hickory, Osage orange, persimmon, dogwood.
   2. Hard—oak, beech, black walnut, yew, hard maple.
   3. Medium hard—birch, red gum, hackberry, soft maple, chestnut, elm.
   4. Soft—willow, Douglas fir, hemlock, spruce, red cedar.
   5. Very soft—cypress, redwood.

B. *Defects to Note:*
1. Brashness—not as hard as type should be, dries too fast.
2. Knots—cause weak spots.
3. Shakes—splits between annual rings.
4. Flecks—dark streaks.
5. Checks—small breaks caused by unequal shrinkage (vaulting poles).
6. Warping—unequal shrinkage or swelling.

C. *Care:*
1. Protect against moisture. Apply hot linseed oil every two weeks as a sealer.
2. Remove small dents by moistening them to allow swelling, then dry.
3. Store where temperature and relative humidity are moderate and consistent.

III. Plastics

A. *Types, Properties and Uses:*
1. Thermoplastics—helmets, golf club heads, celluloid materials, coating for fabric, as in golf bags.
2. Thermosetting plastics—like thermoplastics except in manufacture; "Bakelite" is the trade name (whistles, football thigh guards).

B. *Care:.*
1. Wash with plain or soapy water, dry.

IV. Rubber

A. *Types, Characteristics and Uses:*
1. Vulcanized—strong, waterproof, frictional resistance. Used for cores in golf balls, cleats, tennis shoe soles, covers for balls.
2. Foam—does not shift or mat like wool or kapok but breaks down with continued shock or moisture. Wears much longer than sponge rubber. May be purchased in sheets (½"–1" thick) used for protection and safety.

B. *Care:*
1. Keep in cool place away from heat and light.
2. Keep dry.
3. Wash with water only. Cleansing agents such as gasoline, alcohol, dry cleaning fluid will injure rubber.

V. Light Metals

    A. *Types, Characteristics, and Uses:*
1. Aluminum—tennis nets, vaulting poles, golf clubs. Aluminum offers strength, light weight, permanence, safeness, durability. Metal strings in rackets, however, are not recommended.
2. Magnesium—baseball bats.

    B. *Care*
1. Apply light coat of oil before storing.

VI. Textiles

    A. *Types, Characteristics, and Uses:*
1. Cotton—staple fiber for sports clothing and for much equipment.
2. Wool—also staple, high elasticity, excellent moisture absorbing properties. Used to pad baseball bases, mitts and gloves, shin guards, boxing gloves. Look for labels to judge type: virgin wool is new wool; reprocessed is not used but has been fabricated; remanufactured wool is used by the consumer, returned and reused.
3. Rubber covered thread—elastic used in football pants, boxing shorts, straps, for chest protectors, masks, lacings for balls.
4. Nylon—quick drying, light weight, holds shape well, non-moisture absorbent.
5. Rayon—used for sheen satin uniforms, always marked "Rayon."

    B. *Care:*
1. Since all fibers, except acetate rayon, weaken in prolonged sunlight, do not let fabrics remain in sun. All fibers should be washed or dry cleaned to remove perspiration odors.
2. Use insect repellent to protect the fabric from moths and other insects.
3. Strong bleaches are injurious.

Water Sports

No recreation program would be complete without water sports. Swimming, whether conducted at a camp or public beach during the summer months only or at a YMCA or athletic club throughout the whole year, has long been a favorite activity. Classes should be held for beginners and pool facilities made available for those more advanced to swim for recreation, work toward life saving certification, or qualify for competitive swimming and diving meets. Exhibitions, life saving classes, learn to swim or dive campaigns, water pageants, synchronized swimming shows, fancy diving exhibitions, and canoeing races are suggested ways for creating and maintaining interest in this sport.

The swimming program should be directed by only those qualified by the American Red Cross as instructors or life savers. The fun approach should be used to teach all beginners. This connotes that the instructor must first gain the confidence of the learner. Counting one's fingers with his face under the water, picking up pebbles from the bottom of the pool are easy-to-do skills that help lessen water fear. Learning to breathe properly, moving through water while relaxed as a sleepy kitten, floating as though you were coasting on a sled, circling your arms like a car wheel, kicking your feet up and down dog paddle fashion while lying prone are quickly learned movements of the crawl, the most popular and basic swimming stroke. Each instructor should strive to find expressive words to describe vividly the movement he expects his pupils to do. "Float like a log" is an expression beginners easily understand. Word pictures quickly clarify instruction and speed learning. All beginners should master the crawl, back, side, and breast strokes before attempting more advanced skills.

There should be few pool regulations, but all of them must be strictly enforced at all times. These rules may include:

1. No admission to pools for those having contagious disease, infectious colds, or conditions that appear to be infections (ringworm, pink eye, athlete's foot, etc.). Persons with excessive sunburn, unhealed abrasions, corn plasters, bunion pads, adhesive tape or rubber bandages should not be admitted.
2. No food, drink, gum, or tobacco allowed in the enclosed pool area.
3. Soap and water showers are required of all before entering the pool. Anyone leaving the area for any reason must shower before returning.
4. Bathing caps must be worn by all with long hair.
5. The personal conduct of all must be such that it does not jeopardize the health and safety of oneself or others. Expectorating, roughness, rowdyism are forbidden.
6. Those people wearing street clothes are not allowed in the pool area.
7. No running or fast walking allowed.

Pool sanitation conducted along those lines required by local and state laws will increase pool use. Normally the floors around the pool and in dressing rooms should be disinfected at least twice daily. Several methods are standard:

1. Mopping with hot soapy water, followed by application of chlorine, creosol, or copper sulfate.
2. Using a combined cleaner and disinfectant.
3. Mopping with hot strongly alkaline soapy water.

4. Hosing the floors, applying with a stiff brush a solution of one-half of a thirteen ounce can of lye dissolved in one bucket of hot water followed by a hose rinse.
5. Alternating any of these methods.

Slippery concrete can be eliminated by the frequent use of strong non-acid cleaning powder. Diving board mats should be regularly inspected for safety and should receive daily treatments of a strong disinfectant. The required use of protective footbaths will help reduce athlete's foot, prevent bathers from tracking dirt into the pool, and keep all those wearing street shoes from entering the swimming area.

Swimming has long been the favorite camp activity. The H dock has been found to be the best type of facility for the camp waterfront from the standpoints of safety and increased teaching efficiency:

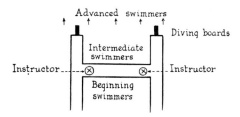

Numerous safety devices are possible when supervising and teaching large groups. These include:

1. Buddy system—each person is paired with and is made responsible for another swimmer of equal skill.
2. Colored caps—red for beginners, yellow for intermediates, and white for advanced swimmers.
3. Checkboard—each swimmer turns his number over when he enters the water and back again when he comes out.
4. The assignment of specific swimming areas for beginners, intermediate, and advanced swimmers.

Modifications of these classifications often include the Tadpoles, Paddlers, Swimmers; Minnows, Fish, Whales; Sandpipers, Cranes, Gulls; Corkers, Lifebuoys, Lifesavers; Turtles, Fish, Marlins.

The camp waterfront staff should be qualified by the American Red Cross, American Camping Association, the national Girl or Boy Scouts or any one of these. They should assist each camper to grow in swimming skills as well as to gain an appreciation of animal, plant, and marine life, fishing, sand modeling, and how to use various kinds of water craft including kayaks, surfboards, rowboats, canoes, war canoes, sailboats. Techniques for teaching these activities are relatively

standardized and accessible. Only those campers who can pass requirements such as swimming 100 yards, tipping over a canoe and getting
back in it, treading water for five minutes, or other similar tests should
be allowed to use such equipment.

Water Pageants

Water pageants will increase interest in the total swimming program
in the city as well as in camp. Suggested committees are: publicity,
business, stage, costume, and program content. Each group should work
closely with the water pageant director. Simple costumes are most
desirable. Cheesecloth, oilcloth, and cambric are practical materials to
use. Flexible cardboard or heavy oilcloth can be used for belts, hats, or
boots. Colored sealing wax effectively dripped into a design creates the
effect of jewels. A ribbon here and a bow or piece of raveled rope there
can produce a desired effect or character. Suggested themes are a
nursery rhyme, fairy story, seasonal event, or place to go, such as a
circus, etc. First, music should be selected, script written, parts
assigned, swimming routines learned, narrator selected, scenery and
lighting added, rehearsals held and then, finally, the actual production
given. Throughout it all the leader should be a guide who is working
toward his objectives to produce group and individual creativity, a
feeling of we-ness among the members, and increased physical skills and
body control.

Suggested patterns for pageants and synchronized swimming shows
include the following:

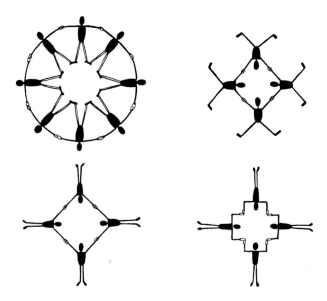

Music, which can be used to teach rhythmical swimming strokes to individuals for fun as well as to groups for demonstration purposes, include:

CLASSICAL

Bridal Procession	(Edvard Grieg)
Rondino	(Fritz Kreisler)
Faust Ballet Waltz	(Charles Gounod)
In the Hall of the Mountain King	(Edvard Grieg)
In a Persian Market	(Albert Ketelby)
Indian Lament	(Anton Dvorak)
Golliwogs' Cake Walk	(Claude Debussy)
Moonlight Sonata	(Ludwig Van Beethoven)
Blue Danube Waltz	(Johann Strauss)
Humoresque	(Anton Dvorak)
Marche Slave	(Peter Tschaikowsky)
Wild Horseman	(Robert Schumann)
Elfentanz	(Felix Mendelssohn)
Gavotte in E Major	(Johann Sebastian Bach)

COLOR THEME

Deep Purple	Over the Rainbow (Finale)
Blue Tango	Black Magic
Mood Indigo	Blue Moon
Jet	Red Sails in the Sunset
Serenade in Blue	Blue Champagne
Flamingo	

CALENDAR THEME

September Song	Autumn Nocturne
Shine On, Harvest Moon	My Valentine
Autumn Leaves	Easter Parade
White Christmas	June is Bustin' Out All Over
April Showers	

CHRISTMAS THEME

White Christmas	Here Comes Santa Claus
Sleigh Ride	Rudolph, the Red Nosed Reindeer
Winter Wonderland	
Frosty, the Snowman	Oh, Holy Night
Toy Trumpet	Jingle Bells

OLD SOUTH THEME

Alabama Jubilee
Arkansas Traveler
Carolina in the Morning
Georgia
Moon Over Miami
Old Man River

Tennessee Waltz
Way Down Yonder in New
    Orleans
Deep in the Heart of Texas
Carry Me Back to Old
    Virginny

FLOWER THEME

Sweet Violets
When You Wore a Tulip
Orchids in the Moonlight
Flower Song Finale

Blue Gardenia
Red Roses for a Blue Lady
Sunflower from the
    Sunflower State

GIRLS' NAMES

Dolores
Charmaine
Ida
Mary Lou
Harriet
Sweet Sue
Dinah
Laura
Amanda
Marie

Rose, Rose I Love You
Ruby
Jeanie with the Light Brown
    Hair
Margie
Louise
Sweet Lorraine
Mary
Good Night, Irene

MISCELLANEOUS

Music Box in Blue
Sophisticated Lady
Album—Music for Dreaming

Stormy Weather
When Day Is Done

THEME SUGGESTIONS

Moon theme
Names of rivers
Names of states

Names of countries
College days

Games

Games and stunts add to the spirit of fun and adventure for those who are learning or perfecting swimming skills or who are learning how to use water craft. Adventurous activities suitable for camp, beach or pool are:

Tug-of-War: Form two teams and play as on land. The winner pulls the other team past a stationary player or land mark.

Nail-Driving Contest: Give each player a board, nail, and hammer. The winner is the first to drive his nail while in two or more feet of water.

Buoy Touch: Players circle the buoy by holding hands. All try to make others touch the buoy with some part of their body. Eliminate until there is a winner.

Dog and Cat: Blindfold one as the Dog. Select a Cat. Others form circle around him. Dog says, "Cat, where are you?" Cat answers, "Meow." Dog swims to find the Cat. Replace with new players.

Retrieve: Divide into two teams. First in each line swims to bring back to his line one article (stick, rock, cork, etc.) that has been thrown into the water. Winner scores one point. Next two in line compete. Play for ten points.

Mamma and Baby: Players pair off. Each pair has a diaper, pins, and bonnet on opposite bank. All pairs try to dress one partner as the child and carry this "baby" back to the starting point first.

Hot Ball: "It" tries to tag person with a ball. The ball must be handed to another, not thrown. Tagged player holding the ball becomes "It."

Fish and Net: All join hands and try to encircle the "fish" in their net. Caught players become part of the net. Continue until all are captured.

Shoe Scramble: Each puts his pair of tennis shoes in a pile in waist-deep water. The winner finds his shoes, puts them on, and swims back to shore first.

Inner-Tube Race: Each player paddles with his hands as he sits in an inflated tube to reach the finish line first.

Water Golf: Divide into couples. One player stands on shore and tosses a ball into inflated bicycle tires. His partner returns the ball each time. He must play each hole in turn. Winner plays all six in the least "strokes." Couple change roles and game continues.

Foot Tag: A swimmer can be tagged only on his feet.

Bubble Burst: Each carries a balloon, which others try to break. The winner has his inflated balloon the longest.

Water Baseball: Anchor floating bases. All but the outfielders stand in water waist deep. A base runner may dive under water to avoid being put out. Play regular baseball rules.

Keep Away: Divide into two teams. Give each group a team color, which must be visible at all times. Each team tries to work the ball to its end of the pool for one point. Play for 10 points.

Candle Race: Divide into two teams. Each in line must swim to end of the pool and back carrying a lighted candle. He must return to starting point to relight the candle if it goes out. Winning line finishes first.

Thread the Needle: Each swimmer tries to thread his needle first with his head ducked under the water.

Touch: Divide into teams facing the leader. "It" calls out an object. All must swim to and touch it, and then return to their exact places in line. First team to do so scores one point.

Water Dodge Ball: Played as on land except that all players tread water and may duck to avoid being hit. Those eliminated join the outer circle to help hit those remaining inside.

Shark's Teeth: Divide into teams and line each up on opposite ends of the pool. Throw three or more corks for each team member into the center. Each must retrieve corks with his teeth without aid of his hands and swim with them back to his team's collecting spot. Score 1 point for the team collecting the most corks every 2 minutes.

Square Dance: Form into sets of eight in deep water. Couple number one have their backs to the leader, who calls the dance to recorded square dance music such as "Round That Corner Take a Little Peek" or "Birdie in the Cage."

Four Standing Canoe Race: Four stand on the gunwales of each canoe and paddle with brooms or regular paddles to finish line.

Variations: Four squat and handle paddle; four pie pan paddle; four hand paddle; four doing any of these in a rowboat; two players for each event.

Capsize Race: Each paddles his canoe to given area, turns it over, and swims back with it capsized. Next swimmer in each line repeats this until all have taken turns.

Canoe Fencing: Each couple in their own canoe challenges others to fence. One guides the canoe while his partner, balanced on the gunwales, tries to knock his opponent into the water using a broom handle or longer stick with a boxing glove fastened to the end.

Sailing Races: For distance, for speed, or for rigging and sailing away first in competing group.

Canoe Bobbing: Each player stands on the gunwales near rear seat. He pumps the craft toward the finish line by bending and straightening his knees and circling his arms. Winner crosses the finish line first.

Suggested Readings

American Association for Health, Physical Education and Recreation and the Athletic Institute: *Equipment and Supplies for Athletics.* Physical Education and Recreation, Washington, D.C., 1970.

Bunn, John: *Scientific Principles of Coaching,* 2nd ed., Englewood Cliffs, N.J., Prentice-Hall, Inc., 1972.

Vannier, Maryhelen and Poindexter, Hally Beth: *Individual and Team Sports for Girls and Women,* 3rd ed., Philadelphia, W. B. Saunders Co., 1976.

Vannier, Maryhelen, David Gallahue and Mildred Foster: *Teaching Physical Education in Elementary Schools,* 5th ed., Philadelpia, W. B. Saunders Co., 1973.

Vannier, Maryhelen and Fait, Hollis (Editors): *Physical Activities Series.* Philadelphia, W. B. Saunders Co.

This series of sport booklets are available from the above publisher. Each was written by a national authority and college teacher of that sport. The series includes the following:
GOLF
    Billye Ann Cheatum, Western Michigan University
GYMNASTICS FOR GIRLS AND WOMEN
    Betty Maycock Roys, Bowling Green State University
TENNIS
    Robert E. Gensemer, University of Denver
TRACK AND FIELD FOR GIRLS AND WOMEN
    Virginia Parker, Westport, Connecticut and Robert Kennedy, University of Connecticut

TUMBLING
  Vannie M. Edwards, Centenary College
FOLK DANCING
  Mildred C. Spiesman, Queens College
POWER VOLLEYBALL
  Thomas Slaymaker, Central Missouri State College, and Virginia H.
    Brown, Shawnee Mission Kansas School District
JOGGING FOR FITNESS AND WEIGHT CONTROL
  Frederick B. Roby, Jr. and Russell P. Davis, University of Arizona
SOCCER
  C. Ian Bailey and Francis L. Teller, Eastern Illinois University
BOWLING
  Carol Schunk, University of Cincinnati
TRACK AND FIELD FOR COLLEGE MEN
  Robert E. Kennedy, University of Connecticut
FOIL FENCING
  Waneen Wyrick, University of Texas
ARCHERY
  Lorraine Pszczola, San Bernardino Valley College
HANDBALL
  Thomas Yukic, Chico State College
GYMNASTIC ROUTINES FOR MEN
  William Vincent, San Fernando Valley State College
BADMINTON
  M. L. Johnson, Southeastern Louisiana University
SWIMMING
  Joanna Midtlyng, Ball State University

chapter **13**

Social Recreation

A man would have no pleasure in
discovering all the beauties of the
universe, even in heaven itself,
unless he has a partner with whom
he might share his joys.   Cicero

Social recreation includes parties, luncheons, suppers and banquets, guessing games, puzzle, tricks, stunts, dances, family fun nights, trips, watching sports, music, and drama events, and table games. Some authorities also include clubs under this general heading.* Although most recreation is social in value, these activities are used most often by the director when he searches for games that will provide increased opportunities for people, both strangers and old friends, to share good fun and fellowship. Directed social recreation helps everyone feel welcome and wanted. It gives immediate pleasure, seeks to entertain rather than educate, and accepts people as they are without attempting to help them become someone else who could do bigger and better things elsewhere.

Parties

Successful party leadership depends upon careful planning. Wisely selected activities must be balanced with active and passive games presented to reach a climax. The party should be held in a cleverly decorated room large enough to accommodate the crowd comfortably. Committees, appointed or elected, should plan the program, refreshments, decorations, and clean-up details. As a group they should determine the object of the party (to recruit members, fellowship, build unity, etc.), and set the time and place of the event. Invitations may be sent individually by mail or be extended collectively by posters or other forms of public announcement. All invitations, decorations, and refreshments should be built around a theme, as illustrated on page 278.

*See Chapter 15, Clubs, for information regarding leadership suggestions for these groups.

DECORATIONS

Natural setting, Indian blankets, small campfires, one large campfire.

ACTIVITIES

War dance—Folk dance
Roping the wild horses—Relays
Throwing the tomahawk—Baseball throw for distance
Cooking the wild turkey—Water boiling contests
Trailing the enemy—Scavenger hunt
War chants—Group singing

REFRESHMENTS

Bear grub (roast beef sandwiches)
Wild roots (carrot and celery strips)
Sassafras tea (punch)
Wild rice (ice cream)
Corn (popcorn)

Easy-to-do mixers, unusual entrances (a gang plank for a shipwreck party, through the witch's den for a Halloween party), and name tags help early arrivals become acquainted quickly and feel at ease. Informal group singing around the piano, guessing the number of rubber bands in a quart jar, fortune telling wheels, couple stunts and find your partner games are also suggested.

Successful parties have an attention-snatching beginning and ending. The first directed activity should be active, easy to do, and should include everyone. The right beginning sets the mood and stage for all play that follows. The ending, likewise, should be skillfully planned and the party stopped at the climax, when fun and group spirit are at a peak. The ending should be the cherry on the top of an ice cream sundae. The rest of the program, like a sandwich filling, to be pleasurable is made up of carefully blended ingredients. All games should be given in logical order. Care should be taken to move groups gradually from one end of the room to the other, for people resent being shepherded. Follow mixers with small group games (relays, team charades, etc.) before presenting the activities for the group as a whole.

Party themes are numerous. Favorite ones are:

General	*Seasonal*
Baby party	New Year's Eve party
Circus party	Lincoln's Birthday party
Gay Nineties party	Valentine's Day party
Hard times party	April Fool party
Hobo party	June Bride's party
Kids' party	Fourth of July party
Indoor beach party	School Day party
Rodeo party	Halloween party
Sailor or nautical party	Thanksgiving party
Scavenger hunt party	Christmas party

Eating Together

Good food, an excellent speaker and/or entertainment plus a capable leader form the basis upon which a successful luncheon, supper party, or banquet rests. The director, aided by committees, must plan and provide a program, a skilled toastmaster or host, an appropriate theme, favors, and other extra touches to make the occasion memorable. Those attending the party should be made to feel welcome. Seating arrangements should provide opportunities for individuals to become better acquainted and should separate often seen business associates. Nonsense stunts, special music, and group singing help add to a spirit of gaiety. Suggested themes are:

Athletics	Books
Honor awards	Circus
Indians	Deepest Africa
Pilgrims	Mother-daughter
Pioneers	Father-son
Mother Goose	Hearts or Valentines
Characters from famous plays, books, movies	Aboard ship
Colleges	Men from Mars
Treasure hunts	George Washington
Nations (round the world tour)	Abraham Lincoln
Thanksgiving	Victory dinner
Christmas	Gay Nineties

Guessing Games

Mental or pencil and pen games can be played by individuals or by teams. The director should call out the score each time a point is made, thus urging the players on. Team competition, played according to spelling bee rules, can be both exciting and hilarious. The leader should select questions easily answered yet challenging enough to interest all. Standard radio quiz show questions, newspaper items or current events, and game books are splendid material sources. The group should play for fun and not to win superior intelligence honors. The type of questions chosen helps determine which it will be. Several short quizzes are better than a few long ones. Teams should be re-grouped often. Prizes, inexpensive but clever such as a ribbon decked tin cup, add to the enjoyment.

Types of suitable questions can be seen in the variety of samples below:

What Country
Expresses anger?	Ireland.
Suggests a cocktail?	Iceland.
Is thought of at meals?	China.
Etc.	

Know your Alphabet
What letter suggests
a bird?	J.
an insect?	B.
a horse command?	G.
to look?	C.
part of the face?	I.
Etc.	

Pans
What pan suggests
a piece of clothing?	Pants.
an imitation?	Pantomime.
a flower?	Pansy.
a favorite food?	Pancake.

Quotations
"War is hell."	General Sherman.
"God's in His heaven And all's right with the world."	Robert Browning.
"The British are coming."	Paul Revere.
"Know thyself."	Socrates.
Etc.	

What State?
(Use abbreviation for the answer.)

Is a physician?	Md.
Is unwell?	Ill.
Is strike one?	Miss.
Is clean?	Wash.
Etc.	

Spell
Spell these in two letters.

Not full.	MT.
Indian's house.	TP.
Comfortable.	EZ.
Etc.	

Food for Thought
What is the appropriate food for

A couple?	A pear.
A boxer?	Punch.
An actor?	Ham.
A jeweler?	Carrots.
Etc.	

Slogans

Fly the friendly skies	United Air Lines
The pause that refreshes.	Coca-Cola
When you're having more than one	Schaeffer beer
What has _____ done for you lately?	Sheraton Hotels
Good to the last drop	Maxwell House coffee

Proverbs
Complete the sentence.

Blood is thicker ____	than water.
A stitch in time ____	saves nine.
For want of a nail ____	a shoe was lost.
Too many cooks ____	spoil the broth.
Etc.	

Sports Quiz
Who was known as

Juice	O. J. Simpson
Broad Street Bullies	The Flyers
The Big Dipper	Wilt Chamberlain
Say Hey Kid	Willie Mays
Broadway Joe	Joe Namath

A Tree Love Story

Fill in the blanks with names or parts of a tree.

The girl's name was (Olive). His name was (Red Bud). When he asked for a (date) she said perhaps. He said he would be on the (beech) at ten o'clock and hoped she would meet him there. He waited in vain. She never arrived. He got in his boat and drifted far out into the (bay), realizing sadly he could never be the (apple) of Olive's eye. Etc.

Authors

Best with eggs?	Bacon.
A high wind?	Gale.
An animal?	Wolfe.
Loud?	Noyes.
Etc.	

Famous Numbers

These numbers are used in famous quotations or are well known in other ways. How are they used?

0	The Zero hour.
10	The Ten Commandments.
5	5th Avenue, New York.
1,2	One, two buckle my shoe.
Etc.	

Puzzles and Tricks

The leader who has mastered several tricks and puzzles can, like Pied Piper, draw people to him. The technique is to perform and puzzle others by supposed special skills or magical powers. Success depends upon keeping the trick a secret as long as possible. The role of the leader is to both entertain and help others learn the secret of and how to do each mysterious trick. Care should be taken while doing so not to show off or act superior to the group. Timing is of the utmost importance. The trick should come off at the right moment, just as the rabbit is *slowly* drawn out of the hat when *all* eyes are focused there. Tricks and puzzles offer entertainment to individuals as well as groups. Anyone can learn to do them by following directions carefully step by step, practicing and improving upon past mistakes.

The following ones challenge others to want to do them.

Match Square

Make three squares using ten matches.
Take away two matches, leaving two squares.
(Remove matches 1 and 2.)

Of What Are Matches Made?

Make four separate squares with sixteen matches.

Move three and take away four to spell out what matches are made of. (Love.)

Match Pick Up

Stand with your back and heels against a wall.

Put a match or coin in front of either foot.

Pick it up without moving your heels off the floor.

The Captive Dime

Place a dime on a tablecloth. Put a nickel on either side of the dime so that when a drinking glass is inverted over the dime, the rim of the glass rests on the two nickels. The trick is to remove the dime from under the glass without touching the dime, nickels, or glass.

This is done by short, fast scratches on the tablecloth with a fingernail of one hand.

Wall Stand

Try to stand with shoulder, arm, leg and foot against a wall.

Bring your other foot in parallel to the one against the wall.

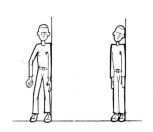

Hand Balance

Hold a pencil in each hand and bring them together so that their points touch.

Do so without touching hands or having arms or elbows resting on anything.

Through the Wall

Draw a continuous line through each wall, outside as well as in, without passing through any wall twice.

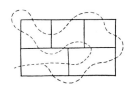

Water, Gas, and Electricity

Three newly built houses each needed to be connected to water, gas, and electricity stations.

Draw a line from each station to each house without crossing any line.

(The line for water for House 3 goes through House 1.)

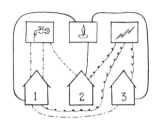

The Cut Up T

Prepare the shape of a T cut into four pieces.

Have others put them together again.

Scrambled Famous Men

Rearrange the letters in each group to form the last name of a famous American: 1. Oniclnl (Lincoln). 2. Erowheisne. 3. Kanacgso. 4. Eomrs. Etc.

The Two Trains

One train leaves New York for Washington, travels at a speed of 25 miles per hour. At the same time a second train leaves Washington for New York and speeds along a parallel track at 50 miles an hour. When the trains meet, which is nearer New York?

Answer: Neither. When the trains meet they are each at exactly the same distance from New York.

Three Coins

Arrange three coins in a row. Change the position of the middle one without touching it.

Answer: Move the left coin to the right end of the row. This changes the position of the original middle coin, for it is now at the left end of the row.

Glass Stand

Stand balanced on one foot on an over-turned glass tumbler.

Place a cigarette and match or a pocket comb in front of you.

Bend one knee with the other leg extended in front of you.

Pick up and light the cigarette without falling off the glass or putting one foot on the floor, or pick up the comb and comb your hair in this position.

Take the Dollar Away

Balance four pennies on the lip of a glass almost full of water.

Lift them up slowly and tuck a dollar bill under them.

The pennies will remain balanced with the bill projecting horizontally.

Remove the bill without touching the coins or upsetting them or the glass.

The trick is to strike the dollar sharply so fast that the coins stay put.

Head and Wall Balance

Stand facing a wall arm's length away.

Bend at waist with body held at right angle, the forehead touching the wall.

Fold arms, put feet together, and try to come upright again.

Keep your heels flat on the floor.

Sock Kick

Roll up a sock into a ball.

Toss it in the air and keep it off the ground, kicking it using alternate feet.

Reward the one who can keep the sock going the longest without missing.

Over the Stick

With the left hand hold perpendicular to the floor a broomstick which is almost waist high. One end of the stick touches the floor. Throw the right leg over the stick, letting go of it with the left hand and catching it with the right. Repeat with right hand and left leg.

Keep the movement going as long as possible without dropping or failing to catch the stick.

Bottle Balance

Sit cross legged on an upside down quart milk bottle with one heel on the floor.

Thread a needle or sew on a button while sitting in this position.

Pencil Balance

Point your fourth and first fingers out with your hand held horizontal to the floor.

Place a pencil or smooth stick over them.

Bring your second and third fingers up over, and back down under the pencil without dropping it.

Stick Hop

Arrange ten sticks one foot apart in a straight row.

Each player takes his turn hopping over all them one by one on the same foot.

He must pick up the tenth stick, hop back to the starting point, then the ninth, etc.

The winner picks up the most sticks without losing his balance or putting both feet on the ground.

Pigs in Pens

Use matches to build pens and coins to represent pigs.

Put nine pigs in four pens so that there will be an odd number in each.

Answer: Put three pigs in each of three pens and build a fourth pen around the other three.

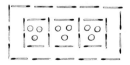

Clothes Puzzle

List all the types of clothing found in this puzzle.

Use a letter twice if you desire.

Play in partners or alone. Set a time limit.

R	A	T	E
H	O	M	E
D	O	W	N
W	O	R	D

Envelope

Draw the envelope shown here with one continuous line without lifting your pencil from the paper and without retracing any line.

Start

Egg in a Bottle

Have several present try to insert a peeled hard boiled egg through the neck of a milk bottle without breaking the egg.

Later show them how to do it.

Drop a piece of lighted paper inside the bottle.

Set the egg in the bottle neck while the paper still burns.

Watch the egg drop through.

The Arrest

A newly married couple went to Paris on their honeymoon.

The young, beautiful, and wealthy wife died suddenly.

Her husband, upon returning home to America, was arrested in the railway station from which they had left for their trip.

How was he found to be guilty of premeditated murder?

Answer: He had bought only one round trip ticket and one one-way ticket.

Cahoots

Two are needed for this trick.

One leaves the room while those remaining choose one of their group whom the returning person must name.

The trick is that the magician's partner assumes exactly the same position as the person selected.

Stunts

The demand for clever stunts is growing rapidly among civic, conference, church, camp, and other groups. However, since sheer nonsense remains just that, stunts should be used in moderation and only to relieve tension and to add variety or fun. The leader should avoid using them among those shy or sensitive. Care should be taken not to embarrass anyone but to help the group share laughter.

Suggested stunts include:

The Beans

Give each person ten beans.

Any person must forfeit one of his beans to anyone hearing him use the words "I", "me," or "mine" during the first part of the evening.

The winner has collected the most beans.

Known by His Nose

Cut a triangular hole in a large sheet of wrapping paper.

Have different people hold the paper in front of themselves so that only their noses show through the hole.

The rest of the group tries to identify the person concealed behind the paper merely by seeing his nose.

Variations: eye, ear, mouth, hair.

I Don't Want to March with the Infantry

Sing and act out these words as directed to the tune of "The Old Gray Mare, She Ain't What She Used to Be."

I don't want to march with the infantry
   (march in place),
Ride in the cavalry, shoot with artillery
   (ride in place, extend one arm as a
   gun).
I don't want to fly over enemies (flap
   arms).
I want to be friendly (shake own hands).
I want to be friendly (shake those of left
   neighbor).
I want to be friendly (shake those of
   right neighbor).
Repeat.

Do Your Ears Hang Low?

Tune: "Turkey in the Straw."
Do your ears hang low? (Wave hands
over your ears and down.)
  Do they wobble to and fro? (Wave
hands back and forth.)
Can you tie them in a knot? (Tie a big
knot under your chin.)
  Can you tie them in a bow? (Tie a big
knot on top of your head.)
Can you throw them 'cross your shoulder
Like a Continental soldier? (Throw
hands over your left shoulder.)
Do your ears hang low? (Touch both ears
of the person on your left.)

Picture Taking

"Take" a picture of each guest upon
arrival.

Give them all comic pictures of animals
or people cut from magazines later with
each person's name written below.

Track Meet for Teams

Shot put: Throw inflated balloons for
distance.

Discus throw: Throw paper plates.

Javelin throw: Throw paper straws.

High jump: Blindfold two contestants at
once after both have seen a rope stretched
knee high. Take away the rope. Award a
prize or team point for the "highest
jumper."

100 yard dash: Tie four people together
above the ankles. Race to end line.

Hurdles: Relay over upturned waste
baskets or people in leap frog position.

50 yard dash: Scooter or roller skating
race, or race on hands and knees.

Banana Relay

Form teams. Give each player a banana.

He must keep his right hand behind him
while he peels and eats his banana.

When he is able to sing the first line of
"America" the next in line may start.

Card Throw

Place a man's upturned hat ten feet in front of each small group.

Give each player on each team five cards.

Score one point for each card tossed into the hat.

Have them add up their team scores.

Potato Golf

Use a small potato and pencil for ball and club.

Mark "holes" with chalk.

Award a prize to the one playing five or nine holes with the lowest score.

Table Games

Table games can be played individually, by couples, or by groups. They offer excellent opportunities for people of all ages to share activity, for they provide rich entertainment for oldsters and youngsters, family groups and even for strangers. Number spinning activities, checkerboard type games, finger snap games, or those similar to tiddledy winks offer challenging competition. Some groups enjoy making their own games. A pencil, ruler, poster material, colored crayons or paints are basic tools with which children and adults can spend many profitable hours fashioning games they and others can share.

The following are some favorite table games:

Baccarat	Hearts
Backgammon	Twenty-one
Dominoes	Last In
Bridge	I Doubt It
Cribbage	Euchre
Canasta	Five Hundred
High Card Pool (Red Dog)	Napoleon (Nap)
Dutch Bank (Banker Poker)	Pinochle
Lottery	Poker
Put and Take	Piquet
Faro	Roulette
Old Maid	Rummy
Authors	Skat
Slapjack	Solitaire
War	

All games should be played according to rules. Tournaments increase interest. Lessons in the more difficult games should be made available and those eager to learn to play urged to attend.

Hobbies

All hobbies can be classified into four main groups: (1) collecting, (2) creating, (3) educational, and (4) performing. However, they range wide in variety all the way from collecting antiques to newspaper recipe clippings with coins, books, clocks, china, dolls, matchbooks, travel postcards, shells, stamps, Indian arrowheads, cartoon books and a host of other exciting activities in between. Children begin it all. Their pockets quickly become treasure storehouses soon after they start to wear dresses or pants with magical creases in them in which to keep all kinds of wonders, including string and bottle caps. Often even an old rock found when one was only a wee laddie or lassie can start a child on a path of lifelong joy. In some cases this path even leads to a vocation centering around a hobby started "long ago."

The best hobbies are those which lead to many things, including travel, adventure, new friends and further and further study that is fun, and never "stuffy" or "hard to do." Some examples of hobbies which attract and bring joy to people of all ages are:

Collecting
(See paragraph above)

Creating

Arts and crafts	Painting
Gardening	Sewing
Knitting	Textiles
Model airplane building	Woodcarving
Music	Woodworking
Needlework	Etc.

Educational

Chess, bridge, and other advanced table games	Learning new skills in any activity including sports, dance or playing a musical instrument
Reading	
Study and care of animals	
Study of the heavens	
Study of trees	Photography
Study of plant life	Travel
	Etc.

Performing
Doing any sport, dance, or
  dramatic activity
Survival camping, backpacking
  and mountaineering
Etc.

LEADERSHIP SUGGESTIONS

The best hobby groups are often those which attract people of all ages. Here is one program activity in which the young can participate with adults, including the aged. It is best to start with a small, enthusiastic group, even though this may only attract two or three people. From this nucleus a new "fad" can become a reality. Publicity, coupled with a display of things made (such as model airplanes or leatherwork), by the group will help attract others into the program. Volunteers are usually easy to find to serve as leaders or assistants, for anyone who is really keen about his hobby can, by his own enthusiasm for it, attract others to join him to share in all the fun and excitement of it.

Suggested Readings

Borst, Evelyn and Mitchell, Elmer: *Social Games for Recreation.* New York, Ronald Press, 1959.

Burns, Lorell Coffman: *Instant Fun For All Kinds of Groups.* New York, Association Press, 1964.

Carlson, Adelle: *4 Seasons Party and Banquet Book.* Nashville, The Broadman Press, 1965.

Corbin, H. Dan and Tait, William: *Education for Leisure.* Englewood Cliffs, N.J., Prentice-Hall, 1973.

Duran, Clement: *The New Encyclopedia of Successful Program Ideas.* New York, Association Press, 1967.

Edwards, Myrtle: *Recreation Leader's Guide.* Palo Alto, California, The National Press, 1967.

Harbin, E. O.: *The Fun Encyclopedia.* New York, Abingdon Cokesbury Press, 1940.

Hindman, Darwin: *Complete Book of Games and Stunts.* Englewood Cliff, N.J., Prentice-Hall, 1956.

MacFarlan, Allan and Paulette: *Fun With Brand New Games.* New York, Association Press, 1961.

Millen, Nina: *Children's Festivals From Many Lands.* New York, Friendship Press, 1964.

Opie, Iona and Peter: *Children's Games in Street and Playground.* London, Oxford University Press, 1969.

Reiley, Catherine Conway: *Group Fun, Games and Activities for Girls.* New York, Dodd, Mead and Company, 1955.

Tillman, Albert: *The Program Book For Recreation Professionals.* Palo Alto, California, The National Press, 1973.

Wackerbarth, Marjorie and Graham, Lillian: *Successful Parties and How to Give Them.* Minneapolis, T. S. Denison & Co., Inc., 1962.

Yukic, Thomas: *Fundamentals of Recreation.* New York, Harper & Row, 1963.

chapter 14

Special Groups

*The purpose of any recreation
program should be to develop each
person as he enjoys what he is
doing in directed activity, and to
improve society as the result of
what each group does.*

Maryhelen Vannier

Through play the child and the adult are revitalized, refreshed, and recreated. All adequate recreational programs must be built to meet the basic needs and interests of people. These may be social, physical, creative, mental, a desire to serve or to be with others. Each program should reach all ages from the young to the aged. It should be conducted in those places where people live or gather—in remote rural areas as well as in the large city, at the church as well as on the playground. It should include both active and passive activities and should vary according to seasonal and environmental conditions. Such a program would reach young children, teen-agers, young adults, the aged, the family, and the handicapped.

The home, school, church, state and youth-serving agency have important and unique contributions to make in providing positive recreation for all. Each should be cognizant of its own special contribution. All need to work more closely together to avoid duplication of program offerings and to make fuller use of existing facilities.

The leader must recognize the differences in the interests, needs, skills, and purposes of all who take part in the program. Methods of leadership and materials to be shared with each group vary widely. No one activity will be likely to serve the entire group, so that a large variety of offerings is necessary. On a playground people of varied age may be found doing the following different things:

Children—Sand crafts, wading, relays, creative play.
Teen-agers—Swimming, crafts, tennis, softball, box hockey.
Adults—Sketching, handball, swimming, table games.
Aged—Table games, lawn bowling, fly and bait casting, toy
repairing.

The successful play leader is aware of (1) the characteristics of each age group, (2) individual backgrounds, (3) environmental conditions where the activities are to be conducted, and (4) how to provide for his ever-changing recreational population a wide-reaching program that will lead to continuous growth and development.

Games for Children

The interest span of children is short. The leader can best work with this group by introducing several new games during an allotted time rather than only one or two. He should introduce a new game when he senses a climaxed interest rather than a lagging one. Other suggestions are to:

1. Give directions as simply as possible.

2. Demonstrate as you describe how the game is played. Or as the children say, "Show me how."

3. Get the game started as quickly as possible.

4. Choose games best suited to the needs, interests, and abilities of the group. Volleyball is not for a group of six-year-olds, whereas "Catch the Fish" (found below) is.

5. Rotate often the opportunities to be "It."

6. Let children gradually develop their own leadership. Ask, "Who would like to teach us to play his favorite game next?" Help the child learn to direct the group, remembering that a real leader makes more leaders.

7. Remember that those on the fringe of a crowd will voluntarily join a group that is having great fun. Forcing the child to play is usually wasted effort.

8. Create an air of expectancy. It will aid in keeping group control.

9. Talk quietly to a formed group of eager players. Inexperienced leaders shout at a scattered group. You have just so much energy. It is too precious to waste.

10. Discover your own best method for getting the group to listen to your directions. Some people use the voice, a whistle, piano chord, upraised or clapped hands.

11. Play with the group.

Children of ages 5 to 10 will find delight in the following games:

SIMPLE GAMES

CATCH THE FISH

Players divide into two teams—the fish and the net.

Each group stands behind a goal line—50 to 75 feet apart and parallel.

Players of one group join hands to form the net. On signal both groups move forward—fish trying to reach the other goal.

Fish can only go around ends. Net must make circle around the fish.

Those caught are out of the game. This continues till all are caught. Teams reverse—fish become the net.

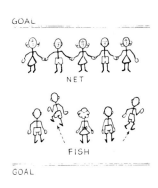

OLD MOTHER WITCH

One player is witch and walks in front of the group.

Players follow calling, "Old mother witch fell in the ditch. She picked up a penny and thought she was rich."

Witch turns around and asks the leader of the group, "Whose children are you?"

Leader says any name, and they start on again, but if he says "Yours," the witch chases them.

The first child caught is the new witch. Or the witch catches as many as she can and then chooses a new witch.

CATCH THE CABOOSE

Form groups of four in line, each clasping arms around the player in front. The last in line is the "caboose," and the head player is the "engine."

"It" tries to hook on to the last player, while each line tries to prevent this.

If "It" succeeds in hooking on to the file, the first in line becomes the new "It" and tries to join another line.

Several "Its" add interest and skill to the game. Begin with one and add the others gradually.

FLOWERS AND THE WIND

Divide into two equal parties—with home bases at opposite sides of the room.

One party is the wind.

Other party represents different flowers—two or three of each kind.

Flowers advance and play near home of the wind.

Wind tries to guess what flowers they are. As soon as the right name is said, the flowers of that name run home with the wind chasing them.

Any players caught join the winds.

Remaining flowers repeat their play—continuing till all flowers are caught.

TAG

No bases or goals. "It" attempts to catch or tag any of the players.

The one tagged holds up his hand and calls "It" to show other players that he is the new "It."

Variations

Squat Tag

Players save themselves from being caught by assuming a squat position.

Tiptoe Tag

All players must walk on tiptoes instead of running. A goal is marked for resting.

Ankle Tag

A player may be saved by touching his hands to his ankles.

Nose and Toes Tag

Player must save himself by touching his nose with one hand and toes with his other hand.

Partner

All players but two take partners.

One of odd players is "It" and tries to catch the other.

The runner may save himself from being tagged by taking the hand of any one of the other players.

The third one of the group which the runner joins must take off and try to join another group before "It" catches him.

Cross

One player is "It." One being chased can be saved only by a third player running between him and "It." The "It" then chases the third player.

Reverse

"It" attempts to catch any one of the players. All must run or walk backwards. First one caught changes places with "It."

Stiff Knee

Runners must touch the ground without bending the knees to be safe.

Stork Tag

Runner must stop and stand on one foot to save himself.

Dumbbell Tag

Players scatter about the room and pass a dumbbell from one to another. One tagged holding the dumbbell is "It."

RUN FOR YOUR SUPPER or THE FLYING DUTCHMAN

Form circle and join hands.

One person is "It" and stands outside.

"It" touches hands of two players and says, "Run for your supper."

The two players take off, running in opposite directions (pass on the right side always).

"It" takes place of one runner.

Whichever one of the two runners fails to get back in first is "It."

FOX TRAIL

Circle 15 feet to 30 feet in diameter (stamp it out in the snow) with spokes and a smaller second circle about 10 feet inside. Den in center and outside at each spoke.

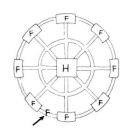

Hunter takes position in center den.

Foxes get in all dens—one fox has no den.

Foxes try to change dens (on signal) without being caught by the hunter. Odd player tries to get a den.

All must stay on the lines.

Any player tagged by the hunter (any time he is out of a den) becomes a hunter. Several hunters add interest.

RED LIGHT

Two parallel lines are drawn 50–75 feet apart to mark the playing field.

"It" stands in the center of the field with his back to the group. Other players on the line behind him.

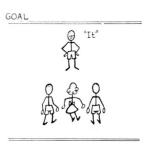

"It" counts to ten and calls out, "No talking, no laughing, no moving. Red Light." On "Red Light," he faces the group.

During counting the other players go as far toward the opposite line as possible, but must stop and obey "It's" command. "It" sends the violators back to the starting line and counts over again.

First one to reach opposite line becomes "It" for the next game.

MIDNIGHT

Markings: Two long lines at end of room parallel and 3 feet apart. At opposite end—50 to 75 feet—another line is drawn parallel to these.

Fox stands behind the double lines. Mother hen and her chicks stand in front of the double lines.

Mother hen asks the fox, "What time is it, Mr. Fox?" He might answer any hour, but if he says "Midnight," the hen and chicks must run to the other end of the room.

Those caught become foxes. Only the Old Fox answers the hen's question. Game continues until all are caught. Last child becomes the fox for the next game. If hen is caught, another one is chosen.

ANIMAL BLIND MAN'S BUFF

One player blindfolded stands in center with a cane or stick.

All the players skip around in a circle until "It" taps three times with the cane. All stand still.

"It" points to a player who then takes the opposite end of the cane in his hand.

"It" asks him to make a noise like a cat, dog, cow, sheep, lion, parrot, duck, etc. "It" tries to guess who the other player is.

If correct, "It" goes to the circle and the other player takes his place. If wrong, he is "It" again.

ANIMAL CHASE

Two pens on opposite corners of playground.

One player is called a "chaser."

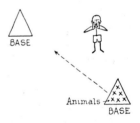

Other players make teams, calling themselves by animal names—two or three of each kind. All in one pen.

Chaser calls out animal names (one at a time).

All animals of that name run to reach other pen before the "chaser" catches them.

The one caught takes the chaser's place and the game continues.

BLACK AND WHITE

One person is leader and stands facing the other players.

Others divide in two teams. Whites tie hankies around arm; others are Blacks.

Whites and Blacks mingle and stand anywhere around the ground.

Leader spins disk—white on one side, black on the other. (Hang on a short string or let it fall to the ground.)

Whichever side shows, the players of that color try to tag the others before they can stoop down.

Any player tagged is out.

Winning team puts out all opponents.

GRASS BLADE

Each child takes a handful of grass and makes a loop out of one blade.

Another child loops a blade of grass through this and the two pull.

One whose blade breaks loses and gives pieces to winner.

Winner goes on to next person until his own blade breaks.

When his blade breaks, the next person starts around.

One with the most pieces at end wins.

CIRCLE RACE

Players form a circle around the leader.

Upon his signal, all run around the outside of the circle. Each tries to pass the runner in front of him on the outside. Any player passed must go to the center of the circle. The last remaining runner wins.

The leader may reverse the runners for added fun and variety.

HOT POTATO

Players form a compact circle.

"It" stands outside the circle with his back turned to the group. On his signal, players start handing a ball around to the right. When "It" says "Stop!" the person having the ball drops out of the circle, joins the leader and continues to call the signals for the rest of the game.

Continue until all are eliminated. Last one left is the winner.

BLACK TOM

The players are divided into two groups.

Each group lines up behind one of two goal lines at opposite ends of the playing area.

"It" stands in the middle of the playing area.

"It" calls "Black Tom" which is a signal for the players to change goals.

Anyone tagged before reaching the opposite goal becomes "It."

"It" may call "Blue Tom," "Green Tom," etc., in order to trick the players into running for the opposite goal.

PLUG

A file of three to five players forms Plug, the old tired horse. He has a head, body and tail.

"It" tries to hit Plug in the tail with a volleyball. The line swings away to prevent the horse from being hit.

Child who is Plug's tail becomes "It" if legally hit with the ball below the waist.

The successful thrower joins the line as the new head. The rest of the players move back in line until each becomes Plug's tail.

FROG IN THE POND

The Frog sits with crossed feet. All players circle around him.

Players tease him while chanting, "Frog in the middle, can't catch me." The Frog, who must remain seated, tries to tag the rest.

The tagged player becomes the new Frog and the old one joins the circle.

Add two or more Frogs as the players become more skillful.

BALL GAMES

TETHER BALL

Tie a tennis ball in a sock or net and attach it to a long heavy cord suspended from a pole 10 to 13 feet long.

Two players, each with a tennis racket or paddle tennis racket, alternate hitting the ball while standing at opposite sides of the pole.

Each must stay in his own area and try to hit the ball to wind it completely around the pole above the 6 foot mark.

The server may hit the ball in any direction. His opponent must always hit it in the opposite direction.

A point is scored when the ball rests against the pole above the mark. The point is given to the player in whose direction the cord is wound. Alternate serves after each point. Play for 10 points.

THROW IT AND RUN

The THROWERS line up in a single file to one side of home plate.

The FIELDERS arrange themselves in a semicircle in the field.

To begin the game, one of the throwers steps to home plate and throws the ball out into the playing field. He then runs to first base and back to home.

The game continues until all the throwers have been at bat. Then the throwers become fielders.

A person is out if the fielders catch the ball on the fly or throw to the catcher at home plate before the thrower gets back to home.

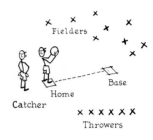

KICK IT AND RUN

Played similar to "Throw It and Run" except:

The throwers are KICKERS.

A pitcher is used by the fielders and the ball is kicked rather than thrown.

Three fouls (outside the boundaries) constitute an out.

DOUBLE CIRCLE BALL

Form two circles. Each has a volleyball or basketball.

Players in each circle throw the ball to anyone on their circled team.

Score a point each time the ball is caught. Add these together.

The winning team scores the most points in 3 minutes.

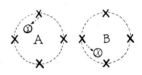

PRISONER'S BASE

Two teams are chosen and each is in a designated area at opposite ends of the playing area.

Each team has a "prison" (see diagram). In each prison are located three objects (balls, blocks, etc.)

The object of the game is for one team to steal the blocks from the opposing team's prison.

Players may be tagged if they are caught in enemy territory, in which case they are put in "prison."

Prisoners may be freed only by being tagged by members of their own team.

TUMBLEBALL

Play on a regular baseball diamond. One team is at bat, the other in the field.

Regular baseball rules are played except that each batter must do a forward roll before reaching first base, a cartwheel and a backward roll before reaching second, a backward roll before reaching third, and stand on his head before reaching home.

Use less difficult stunts for younger players.

OVERTAKE

All players line up and count off by twos.

The "ones" are one team and the "twos" the other.

Each team chooses a captain and these captains stand in the center of the circles formed by their teams.

Each captain is given a ball.

The game is started by the balls being tossed by each captain to one of his team, back to the captain, then to the next one on his team, etc.

The team which passes the ball completely around the circle and finishes with the ball in the hands of the captain first, wins.

LONG BALL

This game is similar to softball except:

There is only one base and that base is about 60 feet from home plate.

The pitcher uses a volleyball.

The batter catches the ball and hits it with his fist.

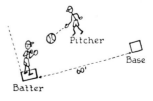

PIT BOWLING

Play up to four individual players or in teams of three.

Each player rolls four croquet or softballs toward three pits dug in the ground 20 feet away.

Score 3 points for each ball that lands in a hole. Play for individual or team points.

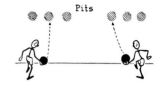

JACKS

One-sy, Two-sy

Toss ball up, pick up one jack, catch ball on first bounce. Repeat for each jack.

Next—2 at a time.

Next—3 at time—until all jacks have been picked up.

Up Cash

Pick up jacks one at a time in hand that threw ball, catch ball, and then throw up again and transfer jack to other hand, and catch ball.

Quick Up Cash

Same as Up Cash except the second jack is picked up when the first is transferred to the other hand.

Shoo Fly

Play One-sy by picking up jacks with the same hand which threw the ball and changing jacks to other hand before catching the ball on first bounce.

Pigs in the Pen

Make left hand (with little finger on the floor) into a cup. Slide jacks into hand instead of picking them up.

Over the Pen

Hand is in fist form and jacks are thrown over it.

END DODGE BALL

All players form circle except six players.

Six players line up, hands on hips of next person—all inside the circle.

Players forming circle pass ball around and toss it trying to hit the player at the end of the line.

Player is out when he is hit.

When one is left, choose another six.

Head man in line moves around facing person who holds ball—as quickly as he can move. All try to keep end man from being hit.

INDIAN CLUB GUARD BALL

Team A forms as small a circle as possible about three upright Indian clubs—team faces outward.

Team B, facing inward, standing in a large circle about 10 feet away throws two basketballs or volleyballs through team A to knock over all three clubs. All balls may be retrieved near team B but must be thrown while standing on the circle.

Teams change places when all three clubs are down. Compare times to determine the winner.

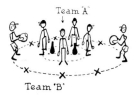

Team 'A'

Team 'B'

CIRCLE PASS BALL

All players form circle—3 to 5 feet between players.

Toss ball rapidly from one player to another—any player.

TIN CAN GOLF

Sink tin cans in the ground for holes. Players use improvised sticks and old tennis balls.

Variations

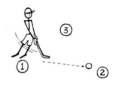

Use croquet mallets and balls.

Use hockey sticks and balls.

Use pencils and ping pong balls on a smoother, shorter course.

Arrange the cans like a clock face with each hole across the circle from the preceding one, i.e., 1, 3, 5; 7, 9, 11; 6, 8, 10.

Use posts that extend about a foot above the ground instead of holes. Each hole is made when the ball hits the proper post.

CENTER BASE

All players but one form circle—20 feet in diameter.

"It" stands in the center and throws ball to a player and immediately runs out of the circle.

Player catches the ball, returns it to the center of the circle or a marked spot, and then chases the "It."

"It"can be saved only by touching the ball. Running must be near the circle.

"It" when caught or saved, chooses another "It" and the game starts over.

CURTAIN BALL

Divide into two teams of six each.

Seat players on each team on either side of an improvised court. String a rope between two trees and cover it with a blanket, so that neither team can see the other.

Play for 10 points. When the serving team wins a rally, score a point. When it misses, the serve goes to the other side as in volleyball. Only one serve is allowed unless the server scores a point for his side. The ball may be played only three times (once by each of three players) before going over the net.

Play for time or for points.

RELAYS

STICK RELAY

Each team forms parallel lines with 5 or 6 feet between players from front to back.

Each team has stick, rope, or belt which is held in front of team by the first two players.

At signal, first two run with stick held close to floor, to the rear of team. Players jump over the stick.

First man stays at the end, second goes to front where number 3 takes end of stick, and they take it down the line.

No 2 stays at end, No. 3 takes stick to front where No. 4 takes the other end, etc.

Last one in line when the end is reached runs up to the head of the line. First team through wins.

NEWSPAPER RELAY

Equal teams stand behind starting line. Mark a goal about 10 feet away.

First person on each team starts at signal, lays two sheets of newspaper on floor in front of him—one ahead of the other, and puts one foot on each.

He keeps one foot on the paper ahead, picks up paper behind, places it in front and steps on it. He keeps going like this to the goal.

He picks up papers and runs back to second person.

First team finished is winner.

KANGAROO RELAY

Equal teams, starting line, and goal about ten feet away.

Player places volleyball between his knees and hops to the goal like a kangaroo.

Removes ball and runs back giving it to next player in line.

First team finished is winner.

MY STATE RELAY

Divide into two teams.

The leader gives two players on opposite teams the name of the same state.

When each player's state is called he runs to an end line, touches the leader, and returns to place.

Winning team is the one with the most individual winners.

BASKETBALL BOUNCE RELAY

Divide into two teams.

Set a waste basket 4 feet in front of each team.

Each player toes a mark in front of team and bounces the ball on the floor ahead so that it goes into the waste basket. He continues until successful, then tags off the next in his line.

Winning team finishes first.

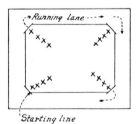

FACE THE CORNER RELAY

Running lane: around the room 3 feet from wall.

Starting line: 4 feet from corner.

Players: four equal teams who line up facing each corner.

Each leader has a hankie. On signal leaders of all teams run to the right, return to home, and hand hankies to next players.

Last player on each team to reach home yells "Home!" First team to yell "Home!" is the winner.

Players may go outside the lane to pass but must return to lane immediately.

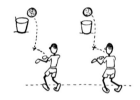

THROUGH THE STICK RELAY

Divide into two teams.

Each leader has a stick about 3 feet long.

On a signal each first player runs to an end line, puts the stick behind his back with his palms turned outward, brings the stick up over his head with both hands, jumps over it while still grasping it, then runs back and tags off next player.

Winning team finishes first, or has the most who were not disqualified. It is illegal not to keep both hands on the stick at all times or to jump through the stick without first bringing it up over the head.

STUNTS

CATCH THE CANE

All in a circle except "It." All have numbers.

"It" stands a cane on the floor with one finger on top.

"It" calls a number and raises finger from the cane.

Number called must catch cane before it hits the floor. He is "It" if he succeeds.

(This can be done also by having "It" call out simple addition or subtraction problems. Player whose number is the answer must catch the cane.)

SPIN THE PLATE

Same as above except that a tin plate is used.

FOLLOW THE LEADER

Leader starts any activity (jump, roll, chin). All must follow.

Those missing must go to the end of the line.

Second person in line starts an activity, etc.

ALPHABET

Each team has cards with letters of alphabet; each player holds one.

All line up facing a line drawn half way between the teams.

"It" calls a simple word (using letters which players hold), and players with letters rush to the line and spell the word with the cards.

First side to get it right wins.

JUMP THROUGH YOUR FOOT

Grasp the left toe with the right hand.

Jump over left leg with the right foot without letting go of your toe. Try to jump back over it without releasing your toe.

HAND PULL APART

Two players face each other. "A" folds her hands together as in prayer with all fingers and thumbs touching. "B" tries to separate "A's" fingers by pulling on her wrists. She succeeds when "A's" fingers are no longer all touching. The two change roles.

CIRCLE PULL

Draw a large circle around two players. Each tries to pull the other out of it. One is considered out if his foot touches any part of the circle.

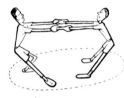

SHOULDER SHOVING

Fold arms against the body in front and hop on either foot. Object is to knock your opponent off balance or out of a ring 6 or 8 feet in diameter.

UNDER-HAND SLAP

Players stand holding hands out in front of them—one's hands on top of the other's (palms touching). Stare each other in the eyes. Underneath hands withdraw quickly and try to slap opponent's hands. Alternate. Score two points for both hands slapped, one for one.

STANDING BROAD JUMP

All players line up behind a line. On a signal all jump forward on both feet and land on both feet. The one who jumps the greatest distance and lands on both feet without losing his balance is the winner.

BASKET WRESTLE

Players stand in boxes (or circles) about one foot apart, facing each other, and try to knock each other out of the box or circle by holding hands and pulling or by pushing off balance.

COMMAND RESPONSE

Players form a circle around the leader. He calls out commands such as "Forward roll," "Touch the back wall," etc. All must respond quickly. The last one to do so each time is eliminated.

DO JUST THE OPPOSITE

Players must do just the opposite to the leader's command. His order, "Touch your left toe," really means "Touch your right toe," "Roll forward" means "Roll backward," etc. Last to respond to each command is out.

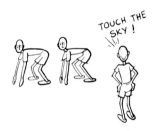

HOW LONG IS A MINUTE?

Players stand with eyes closed. When they think a minute has passed they sit down. (This is harder to judge than it seems.)

TRAINED SEAL

All lie face downward, fingers on back of neck, elbows extended to side.

Count one: Lift head and shoulders off floor.

Count two: Return to starting position.

Repeat 5 times, increasing gradually to 10 times as each improves.

HALF SIT-UP

The children work in pairs. One child lies on his back with knees bent, feet flat on the floor, hands resting on thighs. The second child holds the first child's ankles, helping him to keep feet on floor.

Count one: The first child raises head and shoulders, keeping chin in, and curls forward slowly, sliding hands to touch knees.

Count two: Returns slowly to starting position.

Repeat 3 to 5 times; increase number as strength increases. Pairs alternate positions and repeat the exercise.

PUSH-UP FROM KNEES

All rest on their hands and knees, with their toes held off the floor, their hands slightly more than shoulder width apart. The fingers are turned in, hips bent at right angles, with the knees directly under the hips.

On "one": Bend elbows, touch chin to floor.

On "two": Return to starting position.

Repeat five times, increasing number gradually, as the children improve. As strength develops, each child should continue as long as he can.

ANIMAL WALK

Each player imitates the way his chosen animal walks. The player who gives the best imitation or the most difficult but accurate one wins.

SPIN

Couples grasp hands, touch toes, and lean away from each other until arms are straight. Spin around taking small steps.

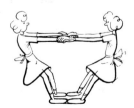

WOODEN MAN

Two players stand three feet apart. A third person stands rigidly between them. He is pushed back and forth. If he fails to remain straight he must exchange places with the one who pushed him.

THE TOP

Standing with his feet together, the child springs into the air, and attempts to turn completely around before landing. Arms may be extended sidewards for balance and impetus in the swing.

ONE O'LEARY

Children take turns bouncing a ball on the ground with the palm of the hand. Count how many times each bounces the ball without missing.

When some skill has been attained, try this: On every third bounce as "O'Leary" is repeated swing one leg over the ball without touching it and without missing the bounce.

>One, two, three, O'Leary,
>Four, five, six, O'Leary,
>Seven, eight, nine, O'Leary,
>Ten, O'Leary, Postman.

JUMP THE SHOT

All players but one form a circle.

Odd player holds one end of a rope and swings it around, so that a weight attached to the other end skins the ground.

Other players jump over the rope as it swings past them. Any player who fails to jump over the rope is eliminated.

Those missing could have points scored against them. The one with the least points would be the winner.

TIP-UP

Child squats, places his hands on the floor between his legs with his elbows pressed hard against his knees. He leans forward, slowly placing his weight entirely on his hands, until his feet swing clear.

THREE LEGGED BOX RACE

Two groups of three compete. Numbers one and three of each group stand with each foot in a box. Player two has one foot in each of their boxes. Players advance by scooting boxes forward, being careful not to step out of the boxes. Team crossing finish line first wins.

POISON CLUB

Two opponents face each other, grasping each other's shoulders. Between them an Indian club stands on the ground. Each person tries to cause the other to touch the Indian club with any part of his body. The winner succeeds in getting his rival to "touch poison."

DUCK FIGHT

Each opponent squats and grasps his ankles.

Each tries to push the other over by butting him on the shoulder.

COIN CATCH

Place several coins in a stack on your right elbow, holding it level with the shoulder in a bent position. Drop the elbow suddenly and try to catch the coins in the right hand.

CRISS CROSS

Squatting, cross the left leg over the right. Grasp the left ankle with the right hand and the right ankle with the left hand. Uncross the legs without breaking the grip of either hand.

BEAN ROLL

Give each player a bean and a toothpick.

Each must roll his bean to the end line, trying to do so first.

THROW AWAY

Players line up on the end line.

Each throws a basketball held over his head while standing in a stride position without moving his feet.

The winner throws the greatest distance.

For variation, have the players throw the ball back over their heads for the greatest distance.

FORWARD ROLL

Stand with the feet well apart, knees bent.

Place hands on the ground close to the feet.

Lean over and tuck the head under so that the chin is on the chest.

Taking the weight first on the hands, go over carefully until the back of the neck and shoulders can take the weight.

Then roll over; do not let the head take any of the weight.

Keep the back rounded throughout the roll.

ANGELS

The bottom person, A, stands in a stride position with knees bent.

B with his back to A, steps up on the thighs of A.

A catches B just below the knees, while B arches his back and holds his arms sideways.

A and B can lean as far from the midline as it is possible and still maintain balance.

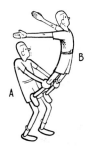

MEASURING WORM

The child places his hands on the floor as close to his toes as possible. With his weight on his hands as well as on his feet, he walks forward with his hands, keeping his feet stationary, until his body is stretched out straight, supported by hands and toes. Then he walks his feet toward his hands until he has assumed his original position. The entire process is repeated as many times as possible.

With two or more players of nearly equal strength, it is possible to have measuring worm races.

SEAL CRAWL

Body is in a face-downward position with all the weight on the hands.

Walk on the hands, dragging the rest of the body.

PLAY EQUIPMENT FOR YOUNGER CHILDREN:

Sandboxes and tools.

Wide and narrow horizontal planks and boards several inches off the ground for running and balancing.

Barrels, kegs, and hoops for rolling.

Inclined boards for running up and sliding down on.

Stairs built with varied step heights to climb up and over and jump from.

Wheelbarrows.

Small tables and work benches.

Large wooden boxes and cartons.

Telephone poles laid flat on the ground for climbing on and jumping from, and others holed securely in the ground for vertical climbing.

Numerous tires and wheels of varying sizes for rolling with hands or a crossed T-shaped board.

Pipe tunnels of reinforced concrete sewer pipe, arranged in units of three, set at different angles three feet apart.

A "Whatnot," or small platform of 9 × 6 feet, surrounded on three sides by a low wall and reached on the fourth open side by steps.

Tables and benches.

As many box hockey sets as feasible.

The school administrator, assisted by a committee of classroom teachers and the physical education teacher and/or supervisor, should give serious consideration to the following factors regarding playground facilities and their use: location, arrangement for the protection of all pupils but especially the youngest ones, regular safety inspection forms and procedures, fencing and marking hazardous zones, care of the ground underneath apparatus, instruction in its correct use, and necessary safety rules.

Courts and playing fields laid north and south should be designated as permanent play areas and marked with paint or whitewash. Dry slaked lime or tennis tape markers can be used on turf or dirt areas. Fixed posts are superior to moveable standards for paddle-type games. Iron nets are better and cheaper in the long run than oil-treated ones, substituted wire fencing, or ropes. Track and field facilities should be laid out according to the recommendations made at the National Facilities Conference sponsored by the Athletic Institute.[1]

Multiple purpose courts of cement or macadam should be laid and marked on all permanent play areas. A tennis court can also be used for paddle tennis, volleyball, badminton, shuffleboard, basket shooting, hopscotch, ice and roller skating. Electric outlets, if provided, will make it usable for dancing or showing films at night. Lighted courts and play areas increase participation to such an extent that they are wonderfully inexpensive investments.[2]

Standard game areas that should be established are:

Outdoor badminton courts	Softball and baseball
Basketball courts	diamonds
Croquet courts	Speedball court
Handball courts	Speed-a-way fields
Shuffleboard courts	Tennis courts
Soccer fields for both boys and girls, if possible	Touch football field
	Volleyball court
Lawn bowling courts	Paddle tennis courts

Outdoor equipment, other than balls of varying size, includes:

Aerial darts	Individual and long jump
Badminton sets	rope sets
Basketball or Goal Hi standards	Jumping standards and crossbar
Bat-O-Net sets	Lawn bowling sets
Box hockey sets	Marbles
Croquet sets	Putting game sets
Deck tennis rings	Shuffleboard sets
Horseshoe sets	Tennis equipment
Hurdles	Tether ball sets

Activities for the playground should add to the pleasure of the moment and enrich the recreational life of the child so that he uses new activities in his leisure time away from school. By teaching obedience to rules and regulations, games help teach children to get along with others. Activities should be selected that are suitable to sex, playing space, clothing and weather, as well as age level.

Some suggestions to assure proper conduct on the playground are to:

1. Provide a varied program appealing to all.
2. Have a few concise rules and enforce them.
3. Make frequent tours of the playground with pupils, looking for hazards and having the children paint these hazards bright yellow.
4. Always maintain a spirit of fairness and justice.
5. Foster a spirit of self-government by giving children a share in the making of conduct rules on the playground, and have them help supervise and officiate at activities.
6. Use pupil-game rotation plans so that all get equal use of the best facilities and equipment.

SUPPLIES AND EQUIPMENT NEEDED

The materials listed below are minimum essentials needed to conduct an adequate program in elementary schools. The amount and variety to be purchased will be dependent upon class size. Rubber balls are cheaper than leather ones and may prove to be just as serviceable.

Supplies

Balls:
  Basketball, official
  Basketball, rubber
  Football, official
  Football, rubber
  Indoor, 12″
  Rubber, 5″, 6″, 8″, 10″
  Soccer, official
  Soccer, rubber
  Volley, official
  Volley, rubber
Baseball gloves, balls, bats,
  protective equipment
Beanbags, 6 × 6, and targets
Broomsticks of various
  lengths
Chalk

Deck tennis rings
Five-pin bowling sets
Hoops
Hula hoop rings
Indian clubs
Jump-off boxes
Jump ropes, 3′8″ sashcord
  Individual, 6′, 7′, 8′
  Long, 12′, 15′, 20′, 25′
Phonograph needles
Phonograph records
Shuffleboard sets
Squad cards
Tape measure, 50′
Tempera paint

Equipment

Balance beams of varying
  height from the floor
Ball inflator
Bases
Bats
Bicycle racks
Blackboard, portable and
  permanent
Bulletin board
Cabinet, steel
Canvas bags in which to
  carry balls
Chinning bars
Equipment box
Flying and stationary rings
Game nets
Hurdles, 12″, 15″, 18″, 20″
Jump and vault standards
Jungle gym
Junior jump standards
Landing nets
Lime and markers
Low parallel bars
Mats, 33″ × 60″, 3′ × 5′, 4′ × 6′
Microphone and speaker
  system
Net standards
Percussion instruments
Portable phonograph
Recreational games
  (checkers, horseshoes, etc.)
Slides
Stall bars, vertical and
  horizontal bars
Stop watch
Storage cabinets or lockers
Surplus parachutes
Swim fins, unsinkable
  boards, hair dryers
Swings
Table hockey
Targets
Teeter boards
Tin can walkers
Traveling rings, vaulting
  buck and horse, Swedish
  box, springboard, parallel
  bars, climbing stairs
Wooden stilts of varying
  heights
Whistles, timers

Activities for Teen Agers

Teen agers enjoy activities for mixed groups as well as those primarily for one sex. The leader will find the following suggestions helpful in working with this particular age group:

1. Begin social activities with easy-to-do icebreakers. Avoid games that are too easy or that might be called babyish.
2. Provide a wide variety of active and passive games.
3. Delegate responsibilities to committees; develop strong leadership from within the group.
4. Conduct activities in several places such as at a ranch, community center, park, church, etc., rather than at the same place each time. Youth is restless, craves adventure, and wants to do new things in new places.
5. Provide opportunities for partners to change often, but see that

each boy has ample opportunity to be the partner of the girl he brought.

6. Give everyone an opportunity to serve his own or some other recreational group. Youth is idealistic and anxious to help others. Service projects are recommended.

SUGGESTED ACTIVITIES INCLUDE

BIRDIE ON A PERCH

Active

Couples form a circle with boys on the inside.

Girls walk counterclockwise to music while boys walk clockwise.

When the music stops, each boy kneels on one knee and a girl sits on his other.

Last girl to sit and the boy acting as her perch are eliminated

Continue until one couple wins.

SPOON

Active

Not more than 13 players sit in a circle on the floor. All but one put a spoon into the center.

A pack of playing cards is dealt out among them.

Each player tries to get four cards of a kind (four aces, four nines, etc.) by passing one card at a time to the person on his left as he receives one from the person on his right.

When a player gets four cards of a kind he takes a spoon from the center and stops playing.

Round continued until all spoons are taken.

All those without spoons are eliminated. The rest resume play, there being one less spoon in the center than there are players in the game.

Game continues until one player wins.

SHOE PING PONG

Active

Seat couples on the floor; each has his legs stretched out in front.

Play ping pong across a drawn chalk line, each person using his shoe as a paddle.

One serves and continues to do so as long as he wins a point. Score only on points won.

Player loses his serve when he fails to win a point.

Play for 11 points.

RHYMES WITH

Quiet

Players sit in a circle.

One stands in the center and says a word that rhymes with the one of which he is thinking (thinks of "cat" but says "rat.")

Each acts out his guess of the leader's word.

No one but the leader may speak.

Winner becomes the leader.

PATCH SEW-ON RELAY

Active

Divide the group into couples and into two teams.

Each couple in each team races to a chair at the head of their line

The girl threads the needle the boy holds.

She sews a patch on the seat of his trousers.

They tag off the next couple, who repeat the process with new patch, needle, and thread.

Winning team finishes first.

SONG SCRAMBLE

Active
Icebreaker

Give each person one line of a song.

All must find the rest of the lines of their song.

The group that sings a completely found whole song first wins.

BROOMSTICK DANCE

Active
Icebreaker

Arrange groups in couples for dancing. One person dances with a broomstick.

When the music stops, he drops the stick and everyone changes partners.

Person unable to find a partner dances with the broomstick.

MAGNETISM

Active

Divide into teams and give each first player a Kleenex.

Without using his hands, he must keep the tissue on his nose by inhaling.

First person passes Kleenex to next in line by placing it on his nose without the use of hands. Second player retains the tissue by inhaling.

Tissue is passed along the line in this way.

If tissue falls to floor it must be picked up by inhaling.

First team finished wins.

Variations
(a) Without using the hands, pass an orange or a lemon to the next player by tucking it under the chin.
(b) Pass a Lifesaver on a tooth-pick.

NEWSPAPER RACE

Active

Divide into teams by couples.

First in each line steps on a newspaper, one foot at a time, that his partner puts down for him.

Couples change duties at a turning point and the other one puts the paper down for his partner.

Winning team finishes first.

ROLE PLAY

Quiet

Divide group into couples.
Give each couple a role to play
    such as Our First Date, The
    Day the Mortgage Was Due,
    Our Vacation Trip, etc.
Each couple act out their role.
Group selects the best.

CHOO-CHOO TRAIN

Active

All form a circle.
One asks another, "What is
    your name?"
She tells her name and stands
    behind him with her arms
    around his waist.
These two move their feet and
    arms with elbows bent, in
    rhythm to the name given
    (i.e. "Jane," (pause), "Jane,"
    (pause), "Jane," "Jane,"
    "Jane").
Pick up each player as he gives
    his name. All move in rhythm
    until everyone is part of the
    train.

PUSH BALLOON

Active

Give each player a small
    inflated balloon.
On a signal, each tries to kick
    his balloon over the finish
    line 20 yards away.
First to do so wins.

APPLE TIE

Active

Suspend apples on strings
    around the room.
On a signal, all try to eat their
    apples with their hands be-
    hind their backs.
Winner does this first.

TAXI

Active

Divide into teams by couples.

Give each couple first in line two suitcases.

Fill the boy's case with feminine apparel, the girl's case with men's clothing. Give the girl an umbrella.

Upon a signal, each couple in each line races to a goal. The boys put on the clothing in their bags, the girls, in theirs. The boy helps the girl climb upon a chair to call a taxi.

The taxi (the next couple in line) races down and runs back to the line with the first couple.

Couple two runs and dresses, etc.

Winning team finishes first.

RED, WHITE, OR BLUE

Quiet

Group sits in a circle.

Leader in the center points to one player saying one of the colors and counts rapidly to ten.

Player must name an animal or tree starting with the color (for example, white whale) or becomes "It."

PENNY PICK-UP

Active

Give two toothpicks to each player.

Place a penny for each one on a line 25 yards away.

On a signal, first one who successfully picks up his penny with the toothpicks and deposits it in a basket back at the starting line wins.

SWAT THE CRACKER

Active

Choose a representative from each team. Tie a cracker on each person's head and give each a rolled up newspaper.

Winner is the first to break the cracker on his opponent's head.

LEG HOP TANDEM RACE

Active

Divide group into couples behind a starting line.

Boy grasps left foot of his girl
with his left hand as she
extends it backward.

Boy grasps his own right foot
with his right hand.

At a signal, each couple races,
in this fashion, toward finishing line to determine the
winner.

Other suggested activities for teen agers include:

Active relays, games, and contests.
Camping, outing, and outdoor activities.
Club activities.
Craft and musical activities which culminate in a show or concert.
Folk and square dancing.
Fund raising activities and other service projects.
Individual, dual, and team (including co-recreational) sport tour-
naments.
One-act plays and other dramatic activities.
Social dancing.

Activities for Young Adults

Too often young married couples are neglected in organized recreation programs. In reality, this group greatly needs outside interests and
stimulating social contacts with others. Today, more than ever before,
however, adults everywhere are coming to regard play as a necessary
emotional, mental, and physical cathartic. The adult seeks more than
just fun during his leisure time; he searches for activities with meaning
and purpose to them.

Types of activities appealing to this group (ages 24–35) include:

1. Physical activities—swimming, volleyball, handball, tennis,
   badminton, hiking, skating, golf, archery, sailing and boating,
   horseback riding, mountain climbing.
2. Social recreation—dinner parties, folk and square dancing,
   social dancing, social games.
3. Dramatics—play acting and production, minstrel and stunt
   shows, play reading, fashion shows, going to plays or making it
   possible for other groups to go, collecting hobbies.
4. Music appreciation clubs—participation in glee clubs, choral
   groups, orchestras, and bands; listening to and discussing radio,
   television, or "live" concerts; collecting hobbies related to music.

5. Literary and general cultural clubs—collecting and discussing such material as rare books or poetry; current events, debates, public forums, guest speakers.
6. Art appreciation clubs—china painting, woodcraft and machine shop activities, water color and oil painting, metal craft, photography, collecting hobbies.
7. Table games—bridge, canasta, hearts, backgammon, poker, checkers, dominoes, Scrabble, Ping Pong.
8. Outdoor recreation—picnics, outdoor cooking, hiking, nature lore, gardening, collecting hobbies.
9. Family fun—picnics, family trips, at-home nights, birthday and other parties.

Techniques for successfully leading recreational activities with this group stress:

1. Basing the initial program upon an interest finder chart (see pp. 70–71).
2. Working with a small committee of four to six persons to set up a sample program.
3. Forming other committees and giving as many people responsibilities as possible. This leads to individual identification with and support of the group.
4. Introducing new activities in the program gradually.
5. Forming hobby clubs. (Toy Makers Club, Fly and Bait Casting Club, etc.)
6. Creating new interests. A hobby show, demonstrations, visits to community centers, etc., will help groups see the vast number of recreational activities possible.

The Aged

In early Roman times the average life span was only 23 years. By 1850 it had extended to 40 in the United States. During this century it has increased to 65 years for men and to 68 for women. By 1945, over 11% of all Americans were over 60 years of age. It has been estimated that 20% of all Americans will be beyond the age of 60 by 1980. Thanks to scientists, doctors, physical educators, and other professional groups we have more people living longer and, consequently, have more new problems—housing, unemployment, and an increase in certain diseases, to mention but a few. Our success in adding years to life must be now coupled with a concentrated, united drive to add life to years.

WHO ARE THE AGED?

"They are people like all of us. They are educated and they are simple. They are wealthy and they are on welfare. They are part of life and they are isolated. They are well and they are desperately ill. They are productive and they are dependent. They are warm and they are mean. They give of themselves to others and they withhold themselves totally from the world.

They are human. Many of them fight for that humanness. As they begin to grow forgetful or to suffer from loss of competence, they battle for that quality which says they are alive, they are real, they are remembered, they are cherished. Some are concerned about what constitutes "living," and they beg their physicians to end their physical lives if their minds deteriorate to such an extent that they are unknowing animals instead of feeling human beings."[3]

Providing stimulating activities for the aged is a community task and responsibility. Agencies and institutions should work together in this program. A survey should be made of how many aged people reside in the area, who and where they are, what they do during a 24-hour period, and what they would like to do in the way of recreation or fellowship with others. A program based upon these data should be made available. Factors to consider in starting such a program are: organization, personnel, budget, facilities, program, publicity, and community relations. A full or part-time director is necessary for success. His qualifications should include:

1. A genuine interest in and understanding of older people.
2. The ability to plan and carry out a program that will benefit and stimulate all members.
3. A belief in and knowledge of how to direct programs leading to interest, growth, and happiness among this group.

The meeting place for the group when organized should be centrally located, easily accessible, attractive, well lighted and heated, and if possible, it should have a kitchen where the members can make tea, coffee, or sandwiches.

Program areas are:

1. Card games—bridge, canasta, pinochle, backgammon, cribbage, hearts, whist, rummy.
2. Table games—checkers, chess, billiards, others.
3. Outdoor games—croquet, bowling on the green, shuffleboard, archery, horseshoes, others.
4. Dancing—ballroom, folk, square, waltz, and other contests.
5. Instruction in handcrafts—sewing, knitting, millinery, jewelry making, violin making, junk crafts, toy making, others.
6. Classes in charm, current events, Americanization, dramatics, music, china painting, others.
7. Picnics, camping, and outings.
8. Birthday and seasonal parties.

9. Hobby groups—poetry lovers, stamp and coin collectors, picture postcard collectors, others.
10. Trips to historic landmarks, county fairs, rodeos, state parks, others.
11. Service projects—knitting and sewing for welfare groups, toy repairing, others.
12. Visits and conducted tours to places of local interest (to a bakery, the zoo, the automobile factory, others).
13. Travel films, free and rented movies. Homemade slides and travel films.
14. Guest speakers.
15. Dramatics, music, and art activities.
16. Fishing, hunting, hiking.
17. Gardening, flower arrangements, transplanting, others.
18. Nature activities—bird walks, care and training of animals, weather forecasting, hobbies, others.

Suggested techniques for successfully leading this group are to:

1. Realize that the best approach is through fellowship and service. Organize clubs around hobby interests and service projects.
2. Use volunteer leaders from the group or outside oldsters of the same age.
3. Plan a program with officers the group elects.
4. Develop new hobbies that are easily done and inexpensive. (More than 70 per cent of all people over 65 live on investments, savings, pensions, charity, or family support.)
5. Arrange for transportation to and from the meeting place.
6. Provide opportunities for each person to take part in organized recreation as well as in leisure time activities of his own choice. (For example, toy repairing and reading a magazine, both done at the center.)
7. Serve refreshments at every party and meeting if possible. Food brings much pleasure to this age group.
8. Observe all birthdays and seasonal occasions with colorful parties.
9. Help provide a recreational program for shut-ins by using volunteers from the group. Capitalize upon their desire to serve others.
10. Avoid discussions of controversial issues, such as religion, sex education, racial prejudice, and politics.
11. Work toward health and happiness as worthy goals to be realized at any age.
12. Provide opportunities for the group to be with young people and children.

13. Give everyone a feeling that he has found real friends and that he is much needed in the club and community.
14. Personalize the program to the utmost.

Family Fun

It has been said that the family that plays together is the family that *stays* together. Increasingly, churches, agencies, and community centers are recognizing their responsibilities to provide recreation for families in their groups. Home and neighborhood parties are long cherished in the minds of children and parents.

The purpose of Family Fun Night is to help the family develop stronger bonds of unity through play and discover the vast number of activities available that they can continue to do in their own home. The community center, church, school, or city playground can profit greatly by providing a game library. Cards, checkers, balls, and other kinds of equipment may be checked out overnight for a family party or evening of fun at home and be returned the next day. This is not only ideal publicity for the institution but may draw many more people of varying age into the program. Unfortunately, agencies (including the school) too often decry spectatoritis and misuse of leisure time and too rarely keep their buildings open for use or share what equipment they have when the majority of people have free time available in which to use them.

In directing family recreation at a church, center, or elsewhere the leader should:

1. Start with an icebreaker type of activity in which all family members take part. (Song Scramble, etc.)
2. Provide for father-son, mother-daughter, father-daughter, and mother-son couple activities.
3. Have several games in which only one family member competes to represent the group. (A cracker eating-whistle blowing contest for mothers, a button sewing contest for fathers, a balloon blowing contest for brothers, a nail driving contest for sisters, etc.)
4. Separate all the adults for some games at one end of the room and direct this group in the games while all the children are directed in games at the opposite end of the room. Exchange leaders and activities so that eventually the entire group plays the same games.
5. Provide some time for everyone present to join a group and some activity of his own choosing. (The son may want to play Ping Pong, the daughter to throw darts, the parents to play bridge.)
6. End the evening's activities at a successful climax with a game in which all the family takes part and have everyone feel that the evening went all too fast.

Teaching activities that can be played at home should be the ultimate goal of family recreation conducted by any agency or institution. Home recreation possibilities include:

Yard games—croquet, badminton, horseshoes, etc.
Table games—dominoes, snap, canasta, rummy, etc.
Astronomy and homemade telescopes
Birthday and seasonal parties
Book and daily news discussions
Clay modeling
Entertaining guests
Gardening
Informal dramatics
Puppetry
Puzzles
Reading aloud
Story telling
Tricks
Weather forecasting

The Handicapped

All atypical persons fall into two groups: (1) those physically handicapped, and (2) those socially handicapped. Within each of these classifications each person differs greatly, for no two are alike, just as no two normal persons are identical.

Types of physical handicaps are:

1. Postural
2. Crippling
3. Visual
4. Hearing
5. Speech
6. Respiratory
7. Cardiac
8. Nutritional

Types of social handicaps are:

1. Mental retardation
2. Delinquency and/or deep emotional difficulties

Techniques for successful activity leadership with this group are largely the same as those used with the normal. The leader, however, will need increased patience, knowledge of what is the cause of difficulty and how to help the individual work around his handicap, and a real desire to work with each individual to guide him to a world of new interest.

Suggested activities for those with marked postural defects are:

Lead up games to basketball, football, softball, volleyball, soccer, and speedball
Hand and Indian wrestling
Individual stunts including leap frog, chinning, rope climbing
Hiking, camping, fly and bait casting
Relays
Shuffleboard
Swimming
Tether ball
Bicycling

Those persons suffering from heart diseases can safely play, upon the recommendation of a physician, activities from the following list:

Archery	Mild roller or ice skating
Circle games	Rope spinning and tricks
Bag punching	Social dance
Croquet	Swimming and light
Camping	water games
Fishing, hunting, trap	Shuffleboard
shooting	Ping Pong
Juggling and balancing	Paddle tennis
stunts	Ring toss
Horseshoes	Volleyball

The deaf or hard of hearing often develop needless fears, frustrations, and feelings of loneliness. Actually many of them can take an active part in almost all games and sports. Individual stunts, gymnastics, tennis, archery, badminton, bowling, and golf are highly recommended for this group. Even social dancing, basketball, softball, and football can gradually be included in their program.

The blind and partially sighted enjoy body building stunts, self-testing activities, camping, dancing, and dramatics. Some who become skilled in using their hands creatively have been known to enjoy clay modeling, wood and chip carving.

Suggested activities for those with crippled bodies confined to wheel chairs are:

Table games	Archery
Darts	Swimming
Fly and bait casting	Crafts

Those wearing leg braces might well take part in:

Archery	Horseshoes
Shuffleboard	Individual stunts
Camping	Crafts

Activities for those with paralysis of one arm are:

Social dancing	Swimming
Relays	Individual stunts
Camping	Roller skating
Rope spinning and jumping	Hiking

Persons with brain injuries, such as the victims of cerebral palsy, often are highly intelligent and educable. Often they are too carefully shielded and become spoiled or maladjusted. Play takes an increased importance with this group for it is the magic ticket admitting them to sharing with normal groups. Since play provides desirable outlets, it is important that this group learn to do a number or even a few activities with average or above skill. Highly competitive games and relays should be avoided, for under stress the person may be hurt more than helped.

Suggested activities (other than corrective exercise done to music) and techniques in recreation include:

Crafts	Camping
Simple folk dances and	Simple games
singing games	Horseshoes
Social dance	Shuffleboard
Swimming	Target throwing
	Table games

A physician usually encourages epileptics to take part in almost all phases of recreation. The leader should present the doctor with a list of proposed activities for this or any other handicapped group, for approval. Activities many victims of this malady can engage in profitably call for concentration, such as learning to do an intricate tap dance routine. A controlled epileptic may benefit greatly from competitive relays and minor team sports which require conditioning. Swimming, rope climbing, or other activities in which the child would be in danger if an attack occurred should be always avoided.

Victims of lowered vitality, diabetes, height and weight abnormalities, congenital deformities, speech defects, hernia, low intelligence, and emotional disturbances should pursue physician-recommended modified recreational programs followed by increased opportunities for securing better balanced diets, sleep and rest. For this group, pleasure can be found in:

Archery	Jacks and other sidewalk
Bait and fly casting	games
Building toys	Table games
Hiking	Sketching and painting
Camping and outing	Musical activities
Simple games	Social, folk, and square
Dramatic activities	dances
Crafts	Swimming

The Disadvantaged

Although every group needs recreational outlets, not every group has equal opportunity to find them. Poor people living in our decaying inner cities are the most deprived of all in relationship to those residing in other more affluent community areas. Approximately 30 million Americans are classified as poor people, with yearly incomes of around $3,500 per family. The majority of these poor people are from racial minorities.

This group suffers from lack of employment, education, and vocational skills. Thousands of them have lost hope or are discouraged and no longer try to better themselves or their lot in life. Many have rarely been outside of their own ghetto areas, and so are ignorant or have a distorted picture of how other people live and/or the many cultural advantages available within the city in which they live. The gap between the affluent and the poor (the have and the have nots) has always been wide in all nations of the world. It is particularly so in America today.

Few poor people have recreational skills or have developed habits of seeking city-sponsored recreational opportunities nearby or at parks or centers elsewhere. Since few can afford the luxury of commercial recreation, most of them "just hang around" or frequent cheap bars and joints. Consequently, greater services to these people must be provided by local, state and national recreation agencies. These services must be year round and far more than hastily drawn up programs to keep crime rates down among minority groups during "long, hot summers."

The following guidelines suggested by one recreational authority might well be used when approaching the problem of providing recreation for the disadvantaged:[4]

1. "Recognizing ethnic and cultural differences in program offerings.
2. Providing services in public housing developments.
3. Creating much-needed jobs in the economically depressed areas.
4. Coping with social ills in community life with positive action programs.
5. Instilling a sense of purpose in the lives of disadvantaged people.
6. Establishing mutual trust between the department staff and the public being served.
7. Establishing a compensatory recreation program, in which disadvantaged areas are often given more funds than the city as a whole.
8. Providing a decentralized recreation program that can serve various geographic areas.
9. Recruiting, training, and employing indigenous leaders and encouraging them to broaden their education.
10. Personalizing recreation and bringing it down to the neighborhood level."

THE CHANGING ROLE OF RECREATION SERVICE

Recreation service to the poor has until recently been isolated and superimposed, for in the past programs consisted largely of "fun and games" directed by white leaders who came into ghetto recreation centers to conduct recreational programs and then returned to their own more affluent neighborhood after the completion of their working hours. Many of these leaders had little real knowledge of or concern for the many problems of blacks, Chicanos, and other subordinated groups for whom their programs were conducted. Today, however, the delivery of leisure services for the poor is being seen in a much larger perspective as part of the whole field of human services in which health, education, job placement, and consumer protection are included. Such services can hopefully lead to the improvement of human welfare and environmental conditions. Minority groups in many inner-cities today are gradually beginning to plan and conduct their own recreation programs with the assistance of professional leaders. Although new, this pluralistic approach to leisure service is already proving to be far more productive than techniques used in the past.

NEW PROGRAM EXAMPLES

1. In Los Angeles ghetto youth participate in a sports program several days a week in which competitive sports are combined with an educational program. Youth engaged in this program compute their scoring averages and game points in both individual and team sports.
2. Seattle, Washington's, "Pitch-In" programs include a mobile library, bookmobiles, creative writing, little theatre interest groups, as well as a beautification project.
3. Many communities are now conducting Encampment For Citizenship programs in which the fun approach to education is used. Workshops stressing the development and uniqueness of the black and Mexican-American cultures attract participants from all age groups. Interest groups made up largely of adults and older teen-agers meet regularly to bring about needed changes in education, school busing programs, employment, and civil rights.
4. In Reading, Pennsylvania, work-recreation programs provide youth with work during the morning and a well-rounded recreation program for the rest of the day.
5. Louisville, Kentucky's, program, "Project WORC," combines recreation, work-orientation, and culture programs in an endeavor to help youth gain realistic self-concepts. The group, assisted by educators and recreation specialists, has an active recruitment and training program for the development of young leaders from their own neighborhoods.
6. Many cities now are conducting summer youth services programs sponsored by the President's Council on Physical Fitness and Sports.
7. The Boston Recreation Department has a free bus travel program in which ghetto youth are taken on fishing trips to a large recreation area.

8. Cincinnati, Ohio, Recreation Department provides a wholesome recreation program for transients and the unemployed.
9. San Francisco, Dallas, and numerous other recreation departments in many cities now conduct recreation programs in housing projects.
10. Junior League volunteers conduct storytelling hours, toy lending centers, charm school programs for teen-agers, and educational programs including classes in citizenship, reading and the English language for the foreign born in slum areas.

Thus, it is evident that through the mention of only a few types of recreation-education programs for the deprived now in existence, that progress is now being made not only to meet the critical recreational, cultural, vocational, and educational needs of people of all ages in slum areas, but also to help these citizens learn how to help themselves in breaking the chain of poverty for their own betterment.

PROGRAMS IN NURSING HOMES

For the more than 900,000 aged found in nursing homes, care ranges from excellent to horrible. National concern about providing good nursing home care is increasing rapidly, largely due to the inspection teams of a variety of nursing homes by congressional committees, Ralph Nader, and others.

Some "model" nursing homes look and are like resort hotels. Others, reeking of odor, are filled by sad, family-rejected old people neglected and often lying unattended for hours in their urine and feces. The senile wards of most state hospitals are ugly, overcrowded and understaffed, and the atmosphere as cheerless as most of the patients. Recreation activities are few. Yet there are some bright spots emerging from this dismal picture, as found in the state hospitals in Big Springs, Texas, Topeka, Kansas, and Ypsilanti, Michigan, to mention only a few.

SUGGESTED SUITABLE ACTIVITIES

The following suggested recreational activities for the aged in nursing homes include:
1. *Arts and Crafts*
   Activities such as knitting, quilting, scrapbook making, toy repairing, and other similar simple crafts which do not require much money or equipment.
2. *Music*
   Group singing, rhythm bands, playing instruments, and listening to records.
3. *Dramatics*
   Role playing, skits, stunts, dramatizations, recitations, and pantomime activities.

4. *Dance*
Social, folk, and square dance lessons and special dance parties for those able to take part. Wheelchair square dancing and simple rhythmic exercises done to recorded music for those who are bedridden or too crippled to take a more active part.

5. *Religious Services*
Bible reading, discussion groups, hymn singing, rosary, and other similar programs for interest groups. Personal visits by volunteers affiliated with local churches, as well as guest speakers from within the community.

6. *Films*
Slides and home movies shown in an auditorium-like setting or privately to those who are bedridden. Travel films (especially to the Holy Land) are highly recommended as are nature films.

7. *Card and Other Table Games*
Bingo parties, checker, bridge, and chess tournaments, as well as old favorite card games such as hearts or I doubt it.

8. *Physical Activities*
All games should be modified according to the limitations of the patients including lawn bowling, shuffleboard, horseshoes, darts, golf, and gardening.

9. *Social Programs*
Birthday parties especially, all seasonal holiday, hobby displays, and small club interest groups.

LEADERSHIP

The recreation program should dovetail with the other treatment activities such as doctor's visits, physical and occupational therapy. It is imperative that the leader have a love for old people and is dedicated to helping them find joy in their lives. Volunteer assistance is a must if the program is to provide opportunity for the happiness and involvement of all patients. Increasingly in institutions of higher learning recreation major students are required to gain practical experiences by leading activities for people of all ages in a variety of recreational settings, including nursing homes. Their youthful zest for life and eagerness to serve well will add much sparkle to any nursing home recreation program.

Recreation in Correctional Institutions

Although recreational outlets for juvenile delinquents in detention homes and adults behind prison bars are increasing, in far too many of these institutions programs lack variety, are used as a privilege or denied as a punishment or are hastily added as a means of preventing impending riots.[5] Far too many correctional institutions are over-crowded and under-staffed and are merely places to put law breakers behind bars for the protection of the rest of society. The prison or detention center seemingly does more to increase crime than to decrease crime, for the majority of those who are behind bars (over 60%) soon become lawbreakers again and commit around 70% of all crimes when released from jail. Then, too, in many institutions recreation is an added frill and is the first area to be eliminated when money is scarce.

RECREATION'S ROLE

Recreation can be and is a therapeutic rehabilitative experience wherein human joy, dignity, creativity, and emotional outlets that are positive in nature can be found. The program should consist of individual, team and combative sports, outside attendance of sports and other events, movies, musical performances, arts and crafts, reading, writing, discussion groups, debate clubs, photography, and radio and television programs.

Most prisons have their own newspaper written by the inmates, intramural sports, and table games such as checkers or chess, as well as educational self-improvement programs such as public speaking, radio, television or auto repairing. Many prisoners work toward the completion of their high school certificate and a few complete correspondence courses and graduate from institutions of higher learning while serving term. However, the need for improvement of recreation programs in prisons is great. Public attitudes must change, more money be allotted to support programs, and above all, leadership must be provided which will provide recreation programs that are rehabilitative in nature and conducted in a rehabilitative rather than a punitive environment.

RECREATION IN YOUTH INSTITUTIONS

Increasingly recreation programs in juvenile detention homes are being used to help troubled youth find ways in which to express hostility and aggression in legitimate ways through boxing, soccer, art or other means. Some state correctional institutions such as found in Gatesville, Texas, offer a variety of services which include vocational education, medical and dental care, religious and psychological counselling. Large institutions throughout the nation are increasingly becoming subdivided into small cottage units wherein emphasis is placed upon group living and the attainment of rehabilitation goals sought by each individual therein. Facilities at the institutions often include a gymnasium, swimming pool, combined all weather outdoor courts for basketball and volleyball, a baseball playing field and a running track.

The program, which is often under the direction of a recreation specialist, consists mainly of sports conducted on the intramural basis, weekly movies, birthday and special occasion parties, crafts, hobby and other interest groups, and a variety of musical activities including talent shows.

THE CAMPING APPROACH

One of the most successful rehabilitation problems for emotionally disturbed pre and delinquent youth in America is conducted by the Salesmanship Club of Dallas in a large, wooded area at Hawkins, Texas. Here boys between the ages of 8–14 live in tents year round in a rustic camp setting. They do not go to school, instead, the camp environment is used to its fullest extent to educate as well as rehabilitate each boy. As Campbell Loughmiller, the founder of this camp has said:[6]

> "Life in this setting provides for the maximum variety, freshness, and intensity in the daily experience of each boy. Whether the boy is on a canoe trip, climbing over southwest Texas mountains, camping in east Texas forests, or enjoying everyday experiences such as catching a snake, wading a stream, feeding the birds, catching a fish, cooking a meal—there is novelty, excitement, adventure, and exploration that lend zest and enthusiasm to living."

Each group of ten boys at this camp live close to the land, build their own shelters, provide their own food and recreation, and share all the experiences and problems of creative group living. Groups plan and go on canoe, float, hiking and camping trips to Colorado, the Gulf of Mexico, and elsewhere throughout the nation. They may be away as long as 4 to 10 weeks. As they plan each day and long trip they learn to work together and solve immediate problems. They learn mathematics by figuring out allotted canoe space for food and gear storage or by buying, cooking and sharing the food they eat at the camp provision store, as well as other subjects traditionally taught in schools, which most of them hate and from which almost all have been expelled as failures.

At this camp there is no competitive sports program, no footballs, balls or bats, etc. Instead, everything in nature is utilized to its fullest, including fishing, crafts made from native materials, trapping animals, or collecting such treasures as rocks or found animal horns. There are no planned recreation programs, yet everything is recreation and education.

The majority of the boys are rehabilitated (around 92%) through this unique program.* Its success is due to the wonderful leadership of the dedicated young men, two of which live, play, and work with a small group of ten boys. One leader has the group alone while the other is off duty. The boys are with the same two leaders all of the time. Although educationally, the program is "life wide," its success is due to their dedication as a teacher-helper-friend playing a supporting role in assisting the group achieve its goals and each boy in it to reach his own determined self-developmental objectives.

*It is estimated that less than 3% of all youth sent to correctional juvenile institutions become rehabilitated. The majority of them become adult criminals.

The Salesmanship Camp for Emotionally Disturbed Boys has been so successful in rehabilitating troubled boys that a similar camp for pre and delinquent girls was opened outside of Palestine, Texas, early in 1976. A former director of the boys camp now directs two camps, patterned after the Salesmanship Camp, outside of Tampa, Florida, one for boys and one for girls.†

†For further information regarding this outstandingly successful educational experiment accomplished through camping, write to the director at Hawkins, Texas, or read the previously mentioned book, *Wilderness Road*.

Suggested Readings

Cleaver, Eldridge: *Soul On Ice.* New York, McGraw-Hill Book Co., 1968.

Gold, Seymour: *Urban Recreation Planning.* Philadelphia, Lea & Febiger, 1973.

Jones, Le Roi: *Blues People.* New York, William Morrow and Company, 1963.

Kando, Thomas M.: *Leisure and Popular Culture in Transition.* St. Louis, The C. V. Mosby Co., 1975

Kramer, Larry: "Alcoholism: New Victims, New Treatment," *Time Magazine,* (April 22, 1974).

Kraus, Richard: *Therapeutic Recreation Service.* Philadelphia, W. B. Saunders Co., 1973.

Loughmiller, Campbell: *Wilderness Road.* Austin, Texas, The Hogg Foundation, 1965.

Moran, Joan May and Leonard Harris Kalakian: *Movement Experiences for the Mentally Retarded or Emotionally Disturbed Child.* Minneapolis, Burgess Publishing Company, 1974.

Mouckley, Florence: "Cars, Liquor and Youth—Lethal Trio," *The Christian Science Monitor,* October 10, 1973.

Murphy, James: *Recreation and Leisure Service.* Dubuque, Iowa, Wm. C. Brown Company, 1975.

National Council on Aging: *Publication List,* 1828 L Street N.W., Washington, D.C., 20036.

Roszak, Theodore: *The Making of a Counter Culture.* New York, Doubleday and Co., 1969.

Smith, Bert Kruger: *Aging in America.* Boston, Beacon Press, 1973.

Stein, Thomas and H. Douglas Sessoms: *Recreation and Special Populations.* Boston, Holbrook Press, 1973.

Stone, Joseph and Church, Joseph: *Childhood and Adolescence.* New York, Random House, 1973.

Toffler, Alvin: *Future Shock.* New York, Random House, 1970, and *The Futurists.* Random House, 1972.

Tomlin, Janice: "Teen-age Drinking Studies Reveal Alarming Boos," *The Dallas Times Herald,* August 18, 1974.

Vail, David: *Dehumanization and the Institutional Career.* Springfield, Charles C Thomas, 1967.

Vannier, Maryhelen, David Gallahue and Mildred Foster: *Teaching Physical Education in Elementary Schools,* 5th Ed., Philadelphia, W. B. Saunders Co., 1974.

Vannier, Maryhelen and Fait, Hollis: *Teaching Physical Education in Secondary Schools,* 4th Ed., Philadelphia, W. B. Saunders Co., 1975.

Vannier, Maryhelen: *Physical Activities for the Handicapped.* New York, Prentice-Hall, 1976.

References

1. Athletic Institute: *A Guide for Planning Facilities for Athletics, Recreation, and Physical and Health Education.* Revised ed. Chicago, Illinois, 1970.
2. Vannier, M. and Fait, H.: *Teaching Physical Education in Secondary Schools,* 3rd ed. Philadelphia, W. B. Saunders Co., 1968, pp. 123.
3. Smith, Bert Kruger: *Aging in America.* Boston, Beacon Press, 1973, p. 9.
4. Weiskopf, Donald C.: *A Guide to Recreation and Leisure.* Boston, Allyn and Bacon, Inc., 1975, p. 208.
5. Garland, Wollard: "Recreation in a Prison Environment," *Therapeutic Recreation Journal,* 6:115, 1972.
6. Loughmiller, Campbell: *Wilderness Road,* Austin, Texas, The Hogg Foundation For Mental Health, The University of Texas, 1965. p. 1.

chapter 15

Clubs

No man is an island, entire of its
selfe; every man is a piece of the
Continent, a part of the Maine.
                    John Donne

Man is both a copy cat and a joiner. His behavior is a carbon of those he most admires. The groups he voluntarily joins are made up of those he strives most to imitate. His need to belong is a dynamic pull down a two-way path; the group with whom he unites can get him into serious trouble or keep him out of it. Few are like Thoreau, the famous New England hermit author, and can find a companion so companionable as solitude. Fewer still want to be far from "the clank of the crowd," as Walt Whitman called it, too often or too long. Our best times seemingly are those spent with others, for life's happiness is largely found and shared with people. To belong to, feel secure in and wanted by a group is essential to human joy and well being.

Club activities have an important place in the well-rounded recreational program. They provide opportunities for all age groups to:

1. Learn new skills.
2. Perfect old ones.
3. Form new bonds of friendship.
4. Gain new knowledge and appreciation of other people, places, ideas, and things.
5. Be of service to others.
6. Further a cause, conviction, or way of life.
7. Have fun.

The value of some clubs lies in a combination of several opportunities. A Toy Repair Club composed of golden agers over 70 can provide an answer for a need to perfect old skills, be of service to others, further a way of life, and forge new bonds of friendship.

TYPES

An organized club has officers, a written constitution, keeps attendance records, sets up membership qualifications, and meets regularly in a specific place. There are numerous kinds of clubs. Each of the broad recreation program areas (dance, music, dramatics, sports and games, etc.) offers many possibilities. Popular types of clubs are:

Airplane	Garden	Rock
Archery	Glee	Radio
Athletic	Health	Riding
Bicycling	Hiking	Rifle
Bird	Hobby	Safety
Book	Homemakers'	Science
Book Review	Hosteling	Service
Bowling	Golden Age	Sewing
Camera	Leathercraft	Skating
Card	Magic	Skeet Shooting
Charm	Men's	Sketch
Checker	Mother and	Skiing
Chess	Daughter	Sky diving
Choral	Model Train	Social
Church	Music	Square dancing
Clay Modeling	Nature	Stamp
Dads'	Needlework	Swimming
Debate	Orchestra	Teen
Discussion	Opera	Women's
Dramatic	Painting	Woodwork
Father and Son	Photography	Yacht
First Aid	Playground	Youth
Fly and Bait	Puppet	
Casting		

Procedure

THE NUCLEUS

A group of five or more people interested in starting a club is a large enough nucleus. This initial group should discuss the tentative name, purpose, time and meeting place, and possible sponsor for the activity. Next, a time and place should be set for a gathering of all others who might be interested in joining. Attendance at this meeting can be promoted by telephone, posters, bulletin board notice, newspaper items, or word of mouth. One of the initial organizers should preside at this first meeting. The agenda would probably include the following items for discussion:

1. The purpose of the club.
2. Membership.
3. Proposed name.
4. Time and place of a regular meeting.
5. Dues.
6. Officers needed. Elect a president, vice president, secretary and treasurer at this meeting, or the temporary chairman should appoint a nomination committee to submit candidates' names at the next meeting.
7. A sponsor.

A temporary secretary should be appointed to serve the group until an elected one takes over. Ice breakers, name tags, or having each person give his name and hobby interest will help all to become acquainted and feel welcome.

THE SPONSOR

The sponsor chosen by the group should democratically guide rather than autocratically rule them. Leadership is influencing others to cooperatively reach a goal they establish. It is a group phenomenon. One can lead only if he has followers and, ironically enough, is at times a follower himself. Democratic leadership is based upon cooperation; it demands self-control and self-direction. Under it all contribute and all benefit. The club sponsor who gives his group a feeling of belonging, worthwhileness, and a deep satisfying knowledge that each has something of worth to contribute is wise indeed. Groups like leaders best who are:

1. Agreeable, friendly, approachable.
2. Strict and can maintain order.
3. Able to participate in activities with them.
4. Sympathetic and understanding.
5. Fair to all and have no favorites.
6. Efficient in their assigned work.
7. Athletic.
8. Not overbearing, bossy, or conceited.
9. Not unnecessarily severe.

The sponsor as the leader behind the elected club president should set the example for all other officers and club members to follow. If he is a model worth emulation, membership in the club will be a rich social experience. To be consistent with this ideal, his approach should be positive and should appeal to another's sense of worth as a dignified human being. Dexterity in using objects and in sports and games will help this leader to catch the envious eyes of others. Proficiency in a number of things will lengthen and broaden the bridge over and with which he can touch and enter his followers' world.

Some of the sponsor's hardest tasks will be to develop leadership skills in others, to let groups learn through their foolish fumbles, or to allow them to dally along an experience journey at a snail's pace, taking unnecessary time-consuming detours rather than accomplishing what they wanted to by "just getting up and going."

The club should be regarded by this more mature and skillful leader as a miniature cooperative society. It should be a learning laboratory where the ideas, ideals, and techniques of democracy can be proved, adopted, and mastered.

It has been said that culture is getting something for nothing. No newborn infant inherits the social ideas and patterns of the society in which he has been born. He will not follow or adopt that way of life unless he is educated to do so. Consequently, if American democracy is to be perpetuated, all must learn and practice its true meaning. The home, the church, the state through its educational institutions, as well as the sponsored recreation club, must deliberately plant, foster, and strengthen this ideal in the behavior patterns of its citizens—youth and adults alike.

THE OFFICERS

All club officers should be selected and elected because of their qualifications and willingness to serve the group. Youth needs to learn how to choose its leaders wisely. Too often those most popular are selected rather than those most capable. The sponsor can assist in helping the group select leaders wisely by serving on the nominating committee and indirectly guiding his followers to submit the best slate of officers possible.

The president, vice president, secretary and treasurer should each have the ability to organize and get things done, as well as to choose capable committee assistants and attract volunteers. The president, especially, should have the strong leadership trait of setting goals within the reach of the group. He should be dependable and energetic, like people, have ideas and ideals, like and want to be the leader, and be able to speak well. His job is to conduct meetings, delegate duties to others and help them carry them out, as well as to coordinate the efforts and talents of all members. The vice president should be able to perform the duties of the president in his absence. The secretary should record the minutes of all meetings, handle all club correspondence, keep a written copy of all reports made, keep an up-to-date membership roll, and send out meeting notices. The treasurer should receive and deposit all funds, pay all bills, and be able to make a financial report to the group when called upon to do so.

THE CONSTITUTION

When club groups formulate and understand their aim and purpose, they should next write a constitution—the written laws by which they wish to abide. These governing rules may be preceded by a preamble, although this is often omitted. Separate articles to be included in the constitution are:

Article I. Name	Article IV. Officers
Article II. Purpose	Article V. Meetings
Article III. Membership	Article VI. Amendments

It is usually wise procedure to appoint a small committee to write a sample constitution. This pattern document can then be tailored, approved, and adopted to fit the specific needs of the club.

Adopting the constitution should take careful thought. Each article should be read through slowly aloud, discussed, and changed if the majority present vote to do so. To avoid hasty and numerous changes later, it is customary that two readings and two-thirds majority vote be necessary to amend any part of the original document.

PARLIAMENTARY TECHNIQUES

All meetings should be conducted in a business-like way. *Roberts' Rules of Order* is commonly used as a guide. This book on parliamentary procedure is based upon the principle that the majority rules but that everyone has equal rights of opinion and voice. Each meeting should follow a plan or an agenda which includes:

1. The call to order.
2. Reading of the minutes of the last meeting.
3. Committee reports.
4. Old business.
5. New business.
6. Announcements.
7. Adjournment.

The following simplified parliamentary procedures for conducting business should prove helpful:

1. *Motions.* One member suggests action by standing and saying, "Mr. Chairman, I move that we . . ." If another present agrees, he stands and seconds the motion. It is passed by two-thirds majority vote. All motions should be given in the affirmative, such as "I move that we meet Saturday at 10 a.m." instead of "I move that we do not meet Wednesday at 2 p.m." Once a motion has been defeated, it cannot be brought up or voted upon again at that meeting.

2. *Voting.* The vote may be taken orally by having all those in favor of a motion say "Aye," those opposed "No." The president announces whether the motion has been carried or lost by the volume of sounds heard. In case of doubt, a standing vote is taken, and those in favor of or opposed to a motion are counted. A third method of voting is by written ballot. A motion can be carried by majority or plurality vote. In the former, over half of those voting is considered a majority (for example, 5 to 4). In the latter, in order to be passed a motion must receive more votes than any one of two or more others (for example, 9 to 7 to 4 out of a total of 20).

3. *Amendments.* A motion is amended, or changed slightly, by inserting or deleting words or phrases, striking out, or substituting words or phrases. The president should read the main motion and the amendment so that the club will understand the suggested change. If there is no discussion following this reading, and if the group calls for the question, or that the amended motion be voted upon, the vote is taken in the same manner as that used for any other motion.

4. *Tabling a Motion.* This means postponing a decision until a later date. It often eliminates hasty, unwise group action. In order for a motion to be reconsidered later, a new motion must be made, seconded, and agreed upon by the group.

BASIC TERMS

1. The Chair—Means the presiding officer.
2. The House—The League or Club.
3. The Meeting—A gathering of the society's members.
4. Addressing the Chair—To speak to the presiding officer.
5. Obtaining the Floor—Securing the right to speak.
6. Motion—It is a proposal that certain action be taken by the organization.
7. Seconding a motion—Shows that another member approves of the motion.
8. Amending the motion—To change or modify it.
9. Put the question—Take the vote.
10. The Question—Means business before the house.
11. Minutes—Official report or record of the proceedings of a deliberative assembly.
12. Quorum—The number of members that must be present so that business may be legally transacted.
13. Proxy Vote—A vote cast for an absent member by someone authorized to do so.
14. Pro and Con—Usually applied to arguments for and against.
15. Pro Tem—For the time being. Acting during the absence of another.
16. Lay a Question on the Table—To put a motion aside. May be considered later.

17. Ex-Officio—By virtue of office.
18. Unfinished Business—Business that has been carried over from a previous meeting.
19. New Business—Business that has been brought before the assembly for the first time.
20. Adjourn—To close a meeting.

STEPS NECESSARY TO OBTAIN ACTION OF THE BODY

Four essential steps should be observed by members, and four by the president.

MEMBERS

1. A member should rise and address the chair.
2. He should await recognition (unless he offers a motion with the high privilege of interrupting another member).
3. He makes the motion.
4. Another member seconds it. Some motions do not require a second.

THE CHAIR

1. The president states the motion.
2. If the motion is debatable the president says, "It is moved by ... and seconded by ... that we. ... Are you ready for the question?" But if he thinks members are not familiar with parliamentary procedure he had better ask, "Are there any remarks?" If the motion is undebatable, he puts it to vote at once without asking if members are ready for the question, unless he is interrupted by higher motions.
3. He takes the vote.
4. He announces the result. "The motion is adopted." If he is in doubt, he says, "The ayes seem to have it." If no one calls for a division, he continues, "The ayes have it; the motion is adopted." If the motion is not approved he says, "The motion is lost."

TO OBTAIN THE FLOOR

When a member wishes to make a motion or to address the assembly, it is necessary for him to rise after the floor has been yielded, and to address the chair by his official title, as "Mr. President," or "Mr. Moderator." A temporary presiding officer with no special title is addressed as Mr. ... or Madam. ...

The presiding officer recognizes a member by announcing his name, but in small clubs where members are acquainted with one another, by bowing to him. In a large assembly a member rises, and when he catches the president's eye, he says "Mr. President, Mr. ... speaking." The presiding officer assigns the floor to him by saying "Mr. . . ." IT IS OUT OF ORDER TO STAND WHILE ANOTHER HAS THE FLOOR. One must wait until the floor has been yielded.

POINTERS FOR MEMBERS

Do not say "I make a motion," but instead "I move."

Do not remark "The mover of the motion"; rather say "The maker of the motion."

In amending motions, use the motion "to insert," "to add," "to strike out," "to strike out and insert," or "to substitute."

Do not say "The president put the motion." He puts the QUESTION to vote.

Do not offer a motion to "reconsider" unless you voted on the prevailing side.

MOTIONS THAT DO NOT REQUIRE A SECOND

Call to order

Question of order

Objection to the consideration of a question

Question of privilege

Call for a division of the question (under certain circumstances)

Call for a division of the assembly (in voting)

Nominations

Permission to withdraw a motion or to modify it

Filling blanks

Inquiries of any kind

Call up motion to reconsider

Call for orders of the day

Requests of any kind

COMMITTEES

Good leadership, interesting programs, and democratic committee organization form the tripod upon which successful club operation rests. Every club member should, at some time, serve on numerous committees. Members of committees can be appointed by the club president or committee chairman, or committees can be made up of volunteers. Working on a committee helps each member to identify with the group as well as to find an answer to his basic need to serve others and create or do something of value. Dr. Karl Menninger, the world famous psychoanalyst, calls this a love need and claims that emotionally healthy people have a balance between this creative drive and a destructive force, or hate need. Both needs, he claims, are constantly struggling for supremacy in all human beings.

Important committees necessary in most clubs are the:

1. Constitution committee.
2. Program committee.

3. Food committee.
4. Clean-up committee.

The role of the chairman of each of these subgroups is to stimulate individual and group action and to help all pool their talents and energies to get a job done. Often young leaders need to be taught that it is *not* simpler or easier to do all of the work of the committee themselves, but rather that taking on the tasks of others is in reality robbing them of a rich educational experience and is usually done for martyr reasons.

THE PROGRAM

All club programs should be based upon interests and needs of the group. Both can be discovered by simple check-list questionnaires, word of mouth expressions of things to do that would be fun, surveying the community to find out what interesting things there are to do in it, gathering program materials and ideas from books, magazines, or other printed sources, and inviting guest speakers to meet with the club to present new interest fields.

The program committee, after gathering information on what the group wants, can, and might do, should present a list of these suggestions to the group. After the month's, season's, or year's program has been blocked out and accepted, the program committee should next contact those whose help they will need to make their activity desires become a reality and should work out details of financing program areas. All meeting plans should be kept flexible. A sunny day and a stormy day program should be planned for all meetings usually held out of doors, so that a club date need not be cancelled in case of bad weather.

Refreshments, decorations, and guest speakers perk up interest and keep club attendance high. The meeting place or club room should be attractive and well ventilated, have comfortable chairs, and look inviting. Teen age centers usually have special names such as The Ranch House, Funteen, Swing Inn, Co-Ed. Inc., Junior Junction. Ideas for decorations and programs naturally follow the selected clubhouse name. The Ranch House, for example, can have a refreshment center called the "Chuck Wagon" or a dance floor called "The Corral."

EVALUATION

The sponsor, officers, and club members should evaluate yearly, or more frequently, the job they have done or failed to do in the light of their aim and purpose as stated in the constitution. A simple check-list questionnaire, such as the one below, can be used to obtain this information from all members. It is suggested that no person sign the paper and that all be encouraged to use the provided blanks for writing in their suggestions of how the club might be improved.

Club Evaluation Questionnaire

	YES	NO
1. Did you enjoy most of the meetings?	----	----
2. Did you feel that everyone had a chance to serve on a committee or be of assistance to the group in some way?	----	----
3. Was the meeting time convenient for you?	----	----
4. Have all our officers done a good job this year?	----	----
5. Does the club cost too much, or do you think the dues are too high?	----	----
6. Did you feel that we have accomplished our aim and purpose as stated in the constitution?	----	----
7. Do you wish we had been of more service to our community?	----	----
8. Do you hope the club will follow along the same organizational and program patterns next year?	----	----

9. List ways in which you think our club can be improved.

_____
_____
_____

10. List the new program ideas you have for next year.

_____
_____
_____

Suggested Readings

Creative Graphs of the School of Speech: *Parliamentary Procedure; A Pictorial Presentation of Roberts' Rules of Order.* Denver, Colorado, University of Denver Press, 1950.

Hoogestraat, Wayne and Sikkink: *Modern Parliamentary Practices,* Minneapolis, Burgess, 1974.

Kraus, Richard: *Recreation Today–Program Planning and Leadership,* New York, Appleton-Century-Crofts, 1966.

Kraus, Richard: *Recreation Leader's Handbook.* New York, McGraw-Hill Book Co., 1955.

Letton, Mildred, and Ries, Adele: *Clubs Are Fun.* Chicago, Science Research Associates, 1952.

McDowell, Nancy: *Your Club Handbook.* Chicago, Science Research Associates, 1951.

National Recreation Association: *Clubs in the Recreation Program; Teen Age Centers.* New York, 1947.

Steiner, Ivan: *Group Process and Productivity.* New York, The Academic Press, 1972.

Weiskopf, Donald A.: *A Guide to Recreation and Leisure.* Boston, Allyn and Bacon, 1975.

chapter 16

Evaluating the Results

Learning is mastery over experience. It is the refusal to repeat past mistakes to the extent that one adopts new tactics to reach desired goals. In the final analysis, it means changed behavior. We learn when we discover new ways to do things from our old attempts and errors. Maryhelen Vannier

Evaluation is a method of thinking through an accomplishment so that one can revise purposes and procedures for new or renewed effort. It means checking up on your progress and taking stock of where you are in the light of where you want to go. Old timers called this getting the lay of the land. We all do it to a small degree when replying to the question "How are you doing?" On a larger scale this process of thinking through a project, and appraising our mistakes and success is the valuable tool with which to build new and clearer blueprinted plans for better recreation programs.

Learning means changed behavior. One learns when he acts differently and when he profits from his own and the errors of others. We learn largely by doing or by experience, from success as well as failure, and from discovering what we did that caused us to succeed or fail.

Unfortunately, educators and recreation leaders have not been too well trained in using evaluative techniques on themselves or their work. Many of them, however, are skilled in using measuring scales to appraise others, in keeping attendance records, and in inventorying supplies or equipment. Knowing yourself is a tremendous task. On the other hand, self-understanding is the only key to understanding others. Judging the results of one's work is almost equally difficult, for intangible objectives such as character education or the development of social consciousness are hard to detect, let alone measure. But as Erasmus believed long ago, "We cannot accept what we are without striving for something better." This applies to analyzing our accomplishments critically as well as seeing ourselves objectively.

Man, history shows, is a slow learner in some areas. These areas are largely individual and social. They are concerned with finding how to live peaceably with others, discovering happiness and purpose in life, and other similar treasure hunts. History, we claim, repeats itself. Indeed, history itself has been compared to the record of the slow progress of a drunken man on horseback, weaving from one extreme to the opposite, forever failing to move very far forward, because he cannot learn to "sit his saddle" or see clearly where he is or the path ahead.

Values

1. *Evaluation checks on the degree to which objectives are being realized.* Critical appraisal is the primary requisite for change, growth, and progress. Every organization, staff, and individual must have definite objectives well in mind in order to accomplish a purpose. Often such objectives are unknown to the individual worker, the entire staff, and in some cases even to the organization itself. Frequently, avowed purposes are far from being reached. Hartshorne and May discovered in a study of honesty, for example, that there was more stealing going on in a school where the development of honesty was the primary objective than in any other. Thrasher, the famous research pioneer in juvenile delinquency, discovered that playgrounds and community centers were often the very breeding places of crime. This came as a jolt to a public convinced that delinquency could be reduced by providing more space for directed play. Sheldon and Eleanor Glueck have found that often the community center becomes the gang hangout where plans are laid for future destruction. Numerous studies show that prisons breed rather than eradicate crime. Sanders, in a camping study, found that instead of being healthful or safe, camps sometimes were the breeding place of illness and accidents. He discovered that, in some cases, the longer the child stayed in the camp the more liable he was to become ill or have an accident. Many studies made of the reading habits of Americans show that, in spite of the fact that more people are going to school than ever before, more are reading trash instead of good books. This is hard to understand in an age in which one avowed purpose of education is to teach us how to live a fuller, happier, more abundant life by improving ourselves mentally, physically, socially, and morally. Objectives must be well thought through, believed in, worked toward, and results critically analyzed before progress becomes a reality. Careful evaluation of our work can be alarming and disappointing; it can also serve as an incentive for renewed effort and challenge us to improve.

2. *Evaluation aids in interpreting our work to others.* People support the things they believe in, things they see and understand. Figures do talk when presented in charts, graphs, and other forms the public understands. These can be used to help the community become aware not only of how many are being reached through a recreation program but of what has happened to each one while participating in it.

3. *Evaluation leads to new ways for obtaining better results.* Leisure time leaders must rely upon principles, theories, and techniques used before by others. Some of these are outdated and ineffective. New and better ways of leading others must be found if we are to serve more productively the increased numbers taking part in our ever-expanding program.

Like the farmer, we must separate the wheat from the chaff if we are to discover from the vast number of theories and techniques available the new and better methods for leading others successfully. We need to discover ways for ourselves to judge what activity does for a person, not what a person does in an activity.

Types

There are four types of evaluation. Each may be done by the individual leader, a group of staff members, outside experts, a joint committee composed of layman and professionals, as well as participants in the program.

Periodic evaluation is done seasonally or at regular intervals. The best time to judge the results of the winter program is at the beginning of spring. Evaluation of some kind goes on all the time and is done unconsciously as well as consciously. General evaluation is made in the light of stated objectives and their relationship to the entire program. Special evaluation, on the other hand, is done in one specific area or event. Regardless of which type the leader uses, he must consider all factors that have bearing upon the material collected and recorded for study.

Tools

Both subjective and objective data are collected for analysis. Objective or quantitative data are easier to collect and record, such as attendance records, equipment inventories, etc. They are often considered more reliable than subjective or qualitative data. The latter attempt to measure attitudes, opinions, feelings, and emotions—intangibles hard to peg down by words. These subjective appraisals are made through interviews, questionnaires, check lists, reports, and surveys.

Too often recreational programs are evaluated only in terms of attendance. The important question is not how many came to the square dance party but what happened to them through the activity as individuals and group members. Americans have fallen into a trap by thinking that something is worthwhile because hundreds do it. Does the movie that millions see entertain, amuse, enlighten, or serve as an escape from boredom? Is it artistically acted and filmed? These are the important factors to consider, not how many saw the spectacle. Padding attendance figures in order to impress or convince others is a common practice. Some claim that although figures do not lie, liars will play with figures for a long time to come.

Evaluators must determine what they want to appraise, how to do it, and how to use the findings to their best advantage. Statistical data can be used to conceal as well as reveal, like the modern bathing suit: what is seen is interesting but what is hidden is often vital. A committee should be formed to devise appraisal questions, methods of tabulating the results, and ways of using the categorized and interpreted results most fruitfully.

Areas

Broad areas to be studied are the participants, program, leadership, and use of facilities. Questions to consider in studying participation are:

1. Who takes part in the program? What percentage are there of each sex, age, race, religious, and socio-economic background?
2. What changes are evident in the interests, knowledge, skills, and appreciations of the group? Of individuals in the group?
3. Have there been changes in character development? In what ways? How permanent were these changes?
4. Has each member found adventure, love, security, and recognition? To what extent?
5. Has each individual learned to get along better with others in his group?
6. How many have become democratic leaders among their own peers?
7. Are the majority of the members growing into good citizens?
8. Is a conscious attempt made to teach individuals through activity?

The participants should also be given opportunity to appraise what they have gained from taking part in the program. This evaluation can be made by observing their reactions to what they are doing, to the group, and to the leader. Successful groups radiate happiness. Another method of evaluating results is to check how many and what activities learned in the program are continued during free play or leisure hours. Questions used to test individual reactions should concern each person and the program. These might include:

1. Do you enjoy this group? Why?
2. How many new things have you learned to do? What are they? Have you taught anyone else away from here to do them with you?

3. Whom do you like best in this group? Why?
4. What qualities do you most admire in others? Why? How many of these qualities do you have?
5. What did you learn here that will help you become a better citizen? A better member of your family?
6. Are you accomplishing what you wanted to by being here? Why? In what ways?
7. How can we make what we are doing be of more value to us as individuals and group members?

Program evaluation can be done by the leader, his supervisor, and the participants. Both the leader and the supervisor should judge the program in light of its:

1. Relation to sought objectives
2. Balance of activities from active to passive, creative to athletic, social to individual, flexible to stereotype, new to old
3. Leadership effectiveness, professional as well as volunteer, superimposed as well as natural
4. Degree of democratic methods used in planning, conducting, and evaluating the program
5. Adequacy of facilities and equipment in view of health and safety objectives
6. Carry-over value for better use of leisure time

The attitude of each individual toward the program can be gained through observation, interviews, opinion polls, check-list questionnaires, and unsigned written answers to specific questions. Suggestions for improvement can also be gained through individual and group discussion. This method brings best results if there is good rapport between the leader and his group and all feel free to express themselves. As children we learn early in life to give back to adult questioners the answers they expect or want. The skillful leader will, however, be able to gain valuable information from groups through the use of discussion.

Successful recreation leaders, professional as well as volunteer, have a clear understanding of their own agency's objectives and knowledge of the community and its resources. They understand people of all ages and can work well with them. They know the techniques of group leadership, how learning or behavior change can best accrue, how to plan and conduct programs. And they can objectively evaluate results. Each leader's evaluation should include appraisal in all of these areas.

The following suggested evaluation sheet can be filled out by the supervisor or individual worker. The findings should be used as a means of in-service training in a supervisory conference. Such meetings are best when carefully prepared for by the supervisor, conducted in a friendly helpful manner, and held at regularly scheduled intervals.

EVALUATION OF RECREATION LEADERS

Name of leader_____ Professional____Volunteer____
Date of rating_____ Rated by _____

Instructions: Using a scale of 1–3, rate the leader on each item appearing below. Rate 3 for above average, 2 for average, 1 for below average.

	1	2	3
Understanding of objectives			
1. Shows a working understanding of the purpose of the agency and of the objectives of the organization.	___	___	___
2. Uses available resources in the community to reach desired goals.	___	___	___
3. Uses available co-workers or assistants or volunteer leaders to help carry out a program to reach avowed purposes.	___	___	___
4. Has his own objectives clearly in mind and works toward them.	___	___	___
Understanding people:			
1. Recognizes individual differences in people	___	___	___
2. Is sensitive to each individual's need for affection, recognition, belonging, and security.	___	___	___
3. Has a deep feeling and love for people and desires to help them grow as citizens.	___	___	___
4. Realizes that self-understanding is the key to understanding others.	___	___	___
5. Understands group behavior.	___	___	___
6. Has formulated objectives to help each person in the group and is working toward reaching those goals with each individual.	___	___	___
7. Can deal with discipline problems skillfully.	___	___	___
8. Realizes all behavior is caused, that a problem boy is a child with a problem.	___	___	___
9. Respects people as individuals and seeks to help each develop along his own growth pattern.	___	___	___
10. Sees maturation and developmental levels in skills, physical, social, mental, and moral growth.	___	___	___

Understanding the group process:
1. Helps groups plan, conduct, and evaluate their own program.
2. Uses democratic methods.   ___ ___ ___
3. Knows how to build group unity.   ___ ___ ___
4. Can develop a sense of group pride and club cohesiveness in the right amounts.   ___ ___ ___
5. Develops leaders from within the group.   ___ ___ ___
6. Helps the group grow in ability to work together.   ___ ___ ___
7. Helps the group and individuals to rid themselves of prejudices.   ___ ___ ___
8. Develops group discipline through directed self-discipline.   ___ ___ ___
9. Is well liked and respected by all.   ___ ___ ___
10. Is professional in his dealings with others.   ___ ___ ___

Understanding of how learning takes place:
1. Knows how to teach individuals through group instruction.
2. Can demonstrate well.   ___ ___ ___
3. Can diagnose and correct the mistakes of others.   ___ ___ ___
4. Recognizes individual skill differences.   ___ ___ ___
5. Teaches all group members efficiently, the moron as well as the genius.   ___ ___ ___
6. Realizes the value of experience in learning.   ___ ___ ___
7. Realizes that teaching is more than telling.   ___ ___ ___
8. Has clearly in mind what he hopes each group will accomplish and is working toward that goal.   ___ ___ ___
9. Has a clear understanding of how to motivate the leader and recognizes the place of success in the learning process.   ___ ___ ___
10. Safeguards the health and safety of all.   ___ ___ ___
11. Realizes that good character is caught rather than taught.   ___ ___ ___
12. Provides a warm, friendly learning environment.   ___ ___ ___

13. Realizes that a real teacher becomes progressively unnecessary by developing independence and skill in each group member. ___ ___ ___
14. Can measure the learning of others and profit from his mistakes in teaching them. ___ ___ ___

Understanding of programming:
1. Provides a well-balanced program for all ages. ___ ___ ___
2. Stimulates individual and group projects. ___ ___ ___
3. Seeks to develop new interests, skills, and appreciations by offering new activities often. ___ ___ ___
4. Makes the best use of available facilities and equipment. ___ ___ ___
5. Helps each group to make short- and long-range plans and to carry them out. ___ ___ ___
6. Has a wide variety of special events and program extras for each age group. ___ ___ ___
7. Uses true rather than false motivation to reach desired goals. ___ ___ ___
8. Includes many activities high in carry-over value. ___ ___ ___
9. Makes the best use of community resources. ___ ___ ___
10. Can evaluate and profit from his work with each age group. ___ ___ ___
11. Seeks to do more than entertain others through the program. ___ ___ ___
12. Helps each group to become responsible for their equipment, safety, and social conduct. ___ ___ ___
13. Keeps adequate records and realizes their importance. ___ ___ ___
14. Uses a wide variety of techniques to build better programs, including guest speakers, movies, discussions, forums, trips, and the various media of communication. ___ ___ ___
15. Publicizes the program well. ___ ___ ___
16. Makes the best use of program resources from the National Recreation Association, current events, magazine articles, and books. ___ ___ ___

A suggestion form for the leader's evaluation of his own work follows. This material should remain confidential and should serve as a basis for self-improvement.

LEADER'S EVALUATION OF HIS WORK IN RECREATION

	Always	*Frequently*	*Seldom*	*Never*
1. Do the majority of group members enjoy working with me?	_____	_____	_____	_____
2. Am I sure that every person leaves the group feeling he has accomplished something valuable?	_____	_____	_____	_____
3. Are the majority in my groups growing into better citizens?	_____	_____	_____	_____
4. Am I patient enough with slow learners?	_____	_____	_____	_____
5. Do I enjoy my work?	_____	_____	_____	_____
6. Do I utilize all my provided space fully?	_____	_____	_____	_____
7. Do I have enough activities that are high in carry-over value?	_____	_____	_____	_____
8. Do I tend to under-plan my work?	_____	_____	_____	_____
9. Do I keep my plans flexible?	_____	_____	_____	_____
10. Do the majority have real fun in the program?	_____	_____	_____	_____
11. Am I patient with all?	_____	_____	_____	_____
12. Do I sincerely try to discover the interests, needs, and individuality of each person?	_____	_____	_____	_____
13. Do I have definite objectives clearly in mind for each individual and group?	_____	_____	_____	_____
14. Do I handle discipline problems well?	_____	_____	_____	_____

15. Do I develop leaders from within the group?

   _____   _____   _____   _____

16. Do I accept criticism well?

   _____   _____   _____   _____

17. Do I evaluate my work and try to profit from my failures?

   _____   _____   _____   _____

18. Am I able to control each group without using threats or physical force?

   _____   _____   _____   _____

19. Am I using democratic methods most of the time?

   _____   _____   _____   _____

20. Am I trying to learn new activities or brush up on program areas in which I am weak?

   _____   _____   _____   _____

Things I must do to improve my work are:

a. _____   e. _____
b. _____   f. _____
c. _____   g. _____
d. _____   h. _____
   Date: _____

My progress on this so far has been:

a. _____   c. _____
b. _____   d. _____
   Date: _____

A survey of the use of all facilities is most profitable and should include a record of the number of people that use each available space and the total peak enrollment figures for each day. Each leader should make a careful study of all available play areas in order to use them to the greatest advantage. Boys and men should not be allowed to monopolize the baseball diamonds or other play space but should rotate with those of the opposite sex the privilege of using all marked areas. A weekly schedule of all space assignments should be carefully drawn up. Leaders should also be on guard not to allow or plan for a few to play while many watch but should use a wide variety of activities many can enjoy doing. It is as foolish for 20 to dance in a large room and for 200 to watch them at a community center party as it is to plan a playground program only for children.

All supplies and equipment should be carefully selected, kept, and repaired. Those using sports equipment can be taught to assist in storing it properly as well as repairing it. All things on hand should be inventoried at least once yearly or at the beginning and end of the season of their greatest use. Worn out equipment should be replaced, and those items that are discarded should be sent to charitable institutions if they are good enough to be repaired or enjoyed by others. The leader should teach groups to respect the property of others. Definite procedures and rules for handing out and returning all things will aid in developing this trait.

Using the Results

Evaluation is time consuming. To be of value the gleanings of each study should be put to use. When this is done there should be a marked improvement in three major areas: facilities, program, leadership.

FACILITIES

An enlightened public usually supports the things they believe are worth while. Facts gathered from research on population trends, available physical resources, and what people do or want to do in their leisure time should be used in a drive to obtain more play space for all. After a careful study has been made of the use of available facilities already existing in schools, churches, youth-serving organizations, industries, libraries, community recreation centers and private clubs, long-range plans should be formulated for expanding both the services and usefulness of each for the increased benefit of all. Recent studies show, for example, that school buildings are closed a large part of the time, especially during those periods when most people have leisure time, such as after 5 p.m. and over the weekends.

A careful check of all existing facilities will also help leaders make fuller use of those physical resources already available.

NEIGHBORHOOD PARKS AND PLAYGROUNDS

Parks should be built near schools and within walking distance of every home in the area as determined by population density, residential lot size, and safety of access. There should be one acre for every 1000 people for parks and one acre allotment for neighborhood playgrounds for every 800 people. This provides a standard for a combined park and playground of one acre for every 500 people in a neighborhood. The neighborhood park should include:

1. Shelter building with game room, meeting room, storage and toilet facilities, and small kitchen, *or* access to comparable facilities in the elementary school building
2. Grassed open area for informal games

3. Multi-purpose, all-weather courts with games standards and basketball goals, night-lighted for play of older children
4. Spray basin or wading pool
5. Landscaped neighborhood park area for passive recreation and nature study
6. Family picnic area

THE COMMUNITY PLAYFIELD

There should be two acres of community playfield space for every 1000 people. The minimum size for a community park playfield is 10 acres. There should be one such facility for every 10,000 people. Desirable facilities of the community park should include:

1. Area for game courts (tennis, volleyball, handball, basketball, etc.)
2. Athletic fields (softball, baseball, football, soccer)
3. Open turfed lawn area
4. Picnic area
5. Landscaped park area
6. Children's play area
7. Fieldhouse
8. Parking area

The service radius for a community playfield should not be greater than one mile.

CITY-WIDE PARKS

The park should be in a beautiful natural setting. The facilities should include:

1. A golf course
2. Woods
3. Winter sports center
4. Adequate off-street parking areas
5. Picnic areas
6. Athletic fields
7. Gardens
8. An outdoor theatre bandshell
9. A public library

The size of such an area depends upon the need for balancing out the facilities in the entire park and recreation system. A minimum of four acres for every 1000 people is essential.

REGIONAL PARKS AND RESERVATIONS
(usually forest preserves and state parks)

These are usually located outside the city limits. Their purpose is to preserve an area of natural landscape, supplement other existing recreational facilities of the city, and act as a greenbelt separating cities or regions in large metropolitan areas. Two acres for every 100 people is a minimum standard.

SPECIALIZED RECREATION AREAS AND FACILITIES

Golf Courses—One hole for every 3000 people where private courses also exist in a city. The ratio should be less if no other course is available so that there is one full course for every 54,000 people.

Swimming Pools—Enough pools are needed to service 3 to 5 percent of the total population at one time. The minimum standard is 27 square feet of water surface per swimmer, with deck space provided on a ratio of 2 square feet of deck area for each square foot of water area.

ATHLETIC FIELDS OR STADIUM

Although often located near a secondary school, some cities have such facilities available in more separated areas. The athletic field should have lighted football fields, plus running track and space for field events. It should include adequate parking lots and seating accommodations. The area should not be less than ten acres.

BASEBALL AND SOFTBALL DIAMONDS

There should be one of each type of playing area for every 3000 people.

PUBLIC TENNIS COURTS

There should be one court for every 2000 people, built in a battery of two, three, or more courts within a fenced area.

RECREATION BUILDINGS

Public provision for indoor recreation should be made in view of available indoor public school facilities for community recreational use. Care should be taken not to over-service one group or duplicate facilities. The following rooms should be made available for recreational purposes in buildings regardless of where they are provided:

1. A multiple-use room for every 4000 people or less
2. A gymnasium for every 10,000 people or less
3. An auditorium or assembly hall for every 20,000 people or less
4. A social room or playroom for every 10,000 people or less
5. An informal reading and quiet game room for every 10,000 people or less
6. An indoor game room for every 10,000 people or less
7. An arts and crafts room for every 10,000 people or less
8. An indoor swimming pool for every 50,000 people or less

Ways to Evaluate Facilities Quickly

Discovering the answers to the following questions will enable anyone to evaluate any recreational facility quickly:

1. Are the facilities planned, located, and laid out, or modified and oriented, for functional recreation use? Are they geared to program needs?

2. Is the recreation facilities planning integrated with comprehensive city planning?
3. Does the facilities planning consider long-range as well as immediate recreation needs? Is there included a schedule of priorities for acquiring property and improving it?
4. Are standards applied intelligently? Is space sufficient?
5. Are the facilities accessible to those who use them?
6. Are they planned to keep to a minimum costs of construction, improvement, and maintenance?
7. Are the facilities aesthetically attractive and comfortable?
8. Is supervision, control, and leadership made easy?
9. Are the facilities designed for multiple use?
10. Can maximum use be obtained around the clock and calendar?
11. Are the health and safety of the users protected?
12. Does pedestrian and vehicle traffic flow freely and are adequate accommodations provided without hazard?
13. Are natural resources used to the best advantage?
14. Are the facilities planned and operated so as not to constitute a nuisance to adjacent property owners?
15. Do the facilities lend themselves to maintaining cleanliness and proper sanitation?
16. Are the "service" facilities well arranged?
17. Are acoustical conditions good?
18. Are crowding of facilities and over-use of equipment avoided?

Program

Any recreation program might be compared to a mirror, a good book, and a tool. As a mirror it reflects what is happening to people and to how many of them—whether they are having a positive, radiant experience or a negative, dull one. Like a good book a valuable program can change the pattern of a person's life. It is the tool the leader uses to reach people and to share with them some of the good things in life. People will come often to take part in an interesting, adventurous, meaningful, well-planned program. The number of those attending will steadily increase under the guidance of a skilled leader. Even he cannot be magnet enough to draw or hold people to a haphazard ill-planned program.

A functional program is built with regard to the population, age, sex, needs, socio-economic status, racial and religious background, and geographical location. It should be the result of citizen-leader planning. It must contain balance and at the same time must satisfy the desires and interests of the people.

Plans should be made for program improvement after suggested changes and constructive criticisms have been analyzed and understood. The ultimate purpose of a recreational program is two-fold: (1) to develop the person's enjoying what he is doing is directed activity, and (2) to improve society as a result of what each group does.

Leadership

Quality leaders, experienced as well as professionally trained, form the foundation for any worthwhile recreational program. Leadership implies more than providing places for people to play and merely throwing out the ball. A real leader influences and helps others reach socially approved goals for the betterment of the individual and society.

Leaders are both born and made. Even those who already possess that magic "x" quality that draws others to them can learn to increase their effectiveness for the benefit of mankind. A desire to succeed has been found to be a more potent force for human improvement than superior intelligence or ability. A dynamic drive to do one's best, to learn, to win is the spur that hastens our journey toward accomplishment.

In-service training for recreation leaders can often be as important as the pre-employment or professional training program. Carefully planned staff meetings, frequent personal conferences with each worker at regularly scheduled times, books, mimeographed materials and visual aids, visits to see what others are doing, attending conventions, enrolling in short training courses in known weak areas, and job effectiveness rating scales followed by personal conferences are suggested ways of helping leaders develop the ability to lead others successfully. In spite of the vital and dynamic role the recreation leader plays in shaping the lives of others and in spite of the awareness of his unique worth among educators, in reality scanty attention has been given to the pre-employment or in-service training necessary for this important work. Leaders need to be better selected, better trained in school and colleges as well as on the job, and helped more to view themselves and their work objectively. Appraisal is the royal road to improvement. It can lead to richer, more meaningful recreation programs for all people. It can produce more effective leaders who are fully aware of their important role as teachers, friends, and guides to the good life.

Suggested Readings

Hjelte, George, and Shivers, Jay: *Public Administration of Recreation Services.* Philadelphia, Lea & Febiger, 1972.

Kraus, Richard and Curtis, Joseph: *Creative Administration in Recreation and Parks.* St. Louis, The C. V. Mosby Co., 1973.

Rodney, Lynn: *Administration of Public Recreation.* New York, Ronald Press, 1967.

Shivers, Jay: *Principles and Practices of Recreational Service.* New York, The Macmillan Co., 1967.

Standards and Evaluative Criteria. Report of The National Recreation Education Accreditation Project. New York, National Recreation Association, 1962.

Van der Smissen, Betty: Evaluation and Self-Study of Public Recreation and Park Agencies: A Guide With Standards and Evaluative Criteria. Arlington, Virginia, National Recreation and Park Association, 1974.

Appendix

Interest Finder of Activities for Program Leaders

Directions: Check those activities you most like to do in your leisure time. Double check new activities you would like to learn how to do. Write in any activities you would like to learn to do that have been omitted.

Activities	Activities You Like To Do	Activities You Would Like to Learn How To Do
Sports and Games		
Baseball	-------------------	-------------------
Basketball	-------------------	-------------------
Box hockey	-------------------	-------------------
Boxing	-------------------	-------------------
Bowling	-------------------	-------------------
Handball	-------------------	-------------------
Horseback riding	-------------------	-------------------
Horseshoes	-------------------	-------------------
Kickball	-------------------	-------------------
Lacrosse	-------------------	-------------------
Life saving	-------------------	-------------------
Model airplane making and flying	-------------------	-------------------
Roller skating	-------------------	-------------------
Skiing	-------------------	-------------------
Tobogganing	-------------------	-------------------
Sailing	-------------------	-------------------
Swimming	-------------------	-------------------
Trap shooting	-------------------	-------------------
Social Activities		
Bridge	-------------------	-------------------
Canasta	-------------------	-------------------
Party leadership techniques	-------------------	-------------------
Pencil and paper games	-------------------	-------------------
Social dancing	-------------------	-------------------
Square dancing	-------------------	-------------------
Table Games		
Anagrams	-------------------	-------------------
Backgammon	-------------------	-------------------
Caroms	-------------------	-------------------
Chess	-------------------	-------------------
Checkers	-------------------	-------------------

Activities	Activities You Like To Do	Activities You Would Like To Learn How To Do
Dominoes	-------------------	-------------------
Monopoly	-------------------	-------------------
Skip across	-------------------	-------------------
Music Activities		
Glee clubs	-------------------	-------------------
Opera groups	-------------------	-------------------
Singing games	-------------------	-------------------
Whistling groups	-------------------	-------------------
Harmonica playing	-------------------	-------------------
Mandolin, guitar or ukulele playing	-------------------	-------------------
Rhythm band	-------------------	-------------------
Orchestra (dance)	-------------------	-------------------
String quartets or ensembles	-------------------	-------------------
Symphony orchestra	-------------------	-------------------
Victrola concerts	-------------------	-------------------
Making musical instruments	-------------------	-------------------
Arts and Crafts		
Basketry	-------------------	-------------------
Beadcraft	-------------------	-------------------
Carving wood, soap, brick, bone	-------------------	-------------------
Ceramics	-------------------	-------------------
Costume design	-------------------	-------------------
Etching	-------------------	-------------------
Finger painting	-------------------	-------------------
Home decorations	-------------------	-------------------
Jewelry making	-------------------	-------------------
Millinery	-------------------	-------------------
Model airplanes, cars, trains, villages	-------------------	-------------------
Painting—oils, water colors	-------------------	-------------------
Photography	-------------------	-------------------
Pottery	-------------------	-------------------
Sandcraft	-------------------	-------------------
Sketching	-------------------	-------------------
Tin can craft	-------------------	-------------------
Weaving	-------------------	-------------------
Woodwork	-------------------	-------------------
Drama Activities		
Charades	-------------------	-------------------
Costume design	-------------------	-------------------
Fashion shows and modeling	-------------------	-------------------
Impersonations	-------------------	-------------------
Marionettes	-------------------	-------------------

Activities	Activities You Like To Do	Activities You Would Like To Learn How To Do
Mask making	-------------------	-------------------
Minstrel shows	-------------------	-------------------
Musical comedies	-------------------	-------------------
One act plays	-------------------	-------------------
Play reading	-------------------	-------------------
Play writing	-------------------	-------------------
Puppetry	-------------------	-------------------
Radio and television plays	-------------------	-------------------
Shadow plays	-------------------	-------------------
Stagecraft	-------------------	-------------------
Storytelling	-------------------	-------------------
Three act plays	-------------------	-------------------
Vaudeville acts	-------------------	-------------------
Dancing Activities		
Acrobatic	-------------------	-------------------
Ballet	-------------------	-------------------
Clog and tap	-------------------	-------------------
Folk	-------------------	-------------------
Modern	-------------------	-------------------
Square	-------------------	-------------------
Social	-------------------	-------------------
Tap	-------------------	-------------------
Nature and Camping Activities		
Astronomy	-------------------	-------------------
Birdhouse building	-------------------	-------------------
Bird walks	-------------------	-------------------
Campcraft	-------------------	-------------------
Cooking	-------------------	-------------------
Firebuilding	-------------------	-------------------
Lashing	-------------------	-------------------
Crafts for outdoor living made from native materials	-------------------	-------------------
Tent pitching and ditching	-------------------	-------------------
Caring for and training of pets	-------------------	-------------------
Explorations	-------------------	-------------------
Fishing	-------------------	-------------------
Gardening	-------------------	-------------------
Hiking	-------------------	-------------------
Hunting	-------------------	-------------------
Mountain climbing	-------------------	-------------------
Nature study		
Plants	-------------------	-------------------
Animals	-------------------	-------------------
Minerals	-------------------	-------------------
Insects	-------------------	-------------------
Trees	-------------------	-------------------

Periodicals in Recreation
Published In the United States

Adventure, 205 E. 42nd St., New York, N.Y. 10017.

Air Trails, Hobbies for Young Men, 304 E. 45th St., New York, N.Y. 10017.

All American Sportsman, Pioneer Globe Printers, Inc., 420 S. 6th St., Minneapolis, Minn. 55415.

All Pets, 18 Forest Ave., Fond Du Lac, Wis. 54935.

Amateur Book Collector, W. B. Thorson, 903 Wrightwood Ave., Chicago, Ill. 60614.

Amateur Athlete, 733 Broadway, New York, N.Y. 10003.

American Artist, Watson-Guptill Publ., 24 W. York St., New York, N.Y. 10018.

American Bicyclist and Motorcyclist, Cycling Press, Inc., 461 8th Ave., New York, N.Y. 10001.

American Bowman Review (National Archery Assoc.), News-Reporter Publishing Co., McMinnville, Ore. 97128.

American Canoeist (cruising, camping, sailing etc.), American Canoe Assoc., 45 Duchess St., Roosevelt, N.Y. 14620.

American Chess Bulletin, H. Helms, 150 Nassau St., New York, N.Y. 10007.

American Fencing, W. L. Osborn, Grand Central Terminal, New York, N.Y. 10017.

American Field: The Sportsman's Journal, American Field Publishing Co., 222 W. Adams St., Chicago, Ill. 60606.

American Glass Review, Commoner Publishing Co., 7th St., Pittsburgh, Pa. 15222.

American Horseman, Phoenix Hotel, Lexington, Ky. 40509.

American Motel Magazine, Patterson Publishing Co., 5 S. Wabash Ave., Chicago, Ill. 60603.

American Photography, American Photographic Co., 353 Newberry St., Boston, Mass. 02215.

American Record Guide, Peter Hugh Reed, 155 Reed Ave., Pelham, New York 14610.

American Rifleman, National Rifle Assoc. of America, Inc., 1600 Rhode Island Ave., N.W., Washington, D.C. 20006.

American Roller Skater, American Skater, 110 E. 42nd St., New York, N.Y. 10017.

American Squares (record review), Charles Thomas, 121 Delaware St., Woodbury, N.J. 08096.

American Woodsman, American Woodsman, Inc., Fort Loudon, Pa. 17224.

Antiques: A Magazine for Collectors, 40 E. 49th St., New York, N.Y. 10017.

Archer's Magazine, 1200 Walnut St., Philadelphia, Pa. 19107.

Archery (hunting and field), 121 N. Broadway, Los Angeles, Calif. 90012.

Arkansas Round Up (square dance journal), Box 15, Little Rock, Ark. 72203

Arts and Crafts (leather, copper, ceramics, woodworking, diversified arts), Pacific Arts & Crafts, 2431 W. Manchester Ave., Inglewood, Calif. 90305.

Audubon, National Audubon Society, 1006 5th Ave., New York, N.Y. 10028.

Athletic Journal, Athletic Journal Publishing Co., 6858 Glenwood Ave., Chicago, Ill. 60626.

Baseball Magazine, Baseball Magazine Co., 175 5th Ave., New York, N.Y. 10010.

Beach and Pool and Swimming, Hoffman Harris, Inc., 425 4th Ave., New York, N.Y. 10016.

Better Homes and Gardens, 1714 Locust St., Des Moines, Iowa 50309.

Billiards, 836 Agatite, Chicago, Ill. 60640.

Billiard Player, Billiards Assoc. & Control Club, Ltd., Cecil Chambers, 107 Fleet St., London E. C. 4, England.

Bowhunter, 28 E. Jackson St., Hartford, Wis. 53027.

Bowling, American Bowling Congress, 2200 N. 3rd St., Milwaukee, Wis. 53212.

Braille Chess Magazine (text in Braille), National Institute for the Blind, Great Portland St., London W. 1, England.

Bridge World, Bridge World, 39 W. 94th St., New York, N.Y. 10025.

Camera, The Camera, Inc., 306 N. Charles St., Baltimore, Md. 21201.

Camping Magazine, American Camping Association, Martinsville, Indiana, 46151, 8 issues yearly.

Canadian Fisherman, National Business Publications, Ltd., Gardenvale, Quebec.

Canadian Nature, Whitmore Pub. Co., 177 Jarvis St., Toronto, Ontario.

Canadian Sports Magazine, Canadian Lawn Tennis & Badminton Co., Ltd., 1551 Bishop St., Montreal.

Chase (fox hunting), Chase Publishing Co., Inc., 152 Walnut St., Lexington, Ky. 40507.

Chess, Correspondence Chess League of America, 2826 Correctionville Rd., Sioux City, Iowa 51106.

Chess Review, 250 W. 57th St., New York, N.Y. 10019.

Children's Activities, Child Training Association, Inc., 1018 S. Wabash Ave., Chicago, Ill. 60605.

Coin Collector's Journal, Wayte Raymond, Inc., 654 Madison Ave., New York, N.Y. 10021.

Contest Magazine, A. D. Freeze and Sons, Upland, Ind. 46989.

Country Dancer, Country Dancer Society, Inc., 63 5th Ave., New York, N.Y. 10003.

Craft and Hobbies, Fox-Schulman Publications, 30 E. 29th St., New York, N.Y. 10016.

Craftworker: A Magazine of Crafts at Home, Craftwork Publications, 3 Albion St., Broadstairs, Kent, England.

Crockery and Glass Journal, Haire Publishing Co., 1170 Broadway, New York, N.Y. 10018.

Cryptogram (puzzles), American Cryptogram Association, Burton, Ohio 44021.

Dance, 231 W. 58th St., New York, N.Y. 10019.

Dance Observer, 55 W. 11th St., New York, N.Y. 10011.

Debater's Digest, E. P. Han, 364 Main St., East Orange, N.J. 07018.

Design: The Creative Arts Magazine, 337 S. High St., Columbus, Ohio 43215.

Deltagram (simple things to do), Delta Mfg. Co., Milwaukee, Wis.

Design, Design Publishing Co., 243 N. High St., Columbus, Ohio 43215.

Dog World, Judy Publishing Co., 3323 Michigan Blvd., Chicago, Ill. 60616.

Downbeat (dance bands and modern music), Downbeat Publishing Co., 203 N. Wabash Ave., Chicago, Ill. 60601.

Dramatics, National Thespian Society, College Hill Station, Cincinnati, Ohio 45224.

Dude Rancher, Box 1363, Billings, Mont. 59101.

Educational Music Magazine, Educational Music Bureau, Inc., 30 E. Adams St., Chicago, Ill. 60603.

Educational Screen, Educational Screen, Inc., 64 E. Lake St., Chicago, Ill. 60601.

Everyday Art, American Crayon Co., Sandusky, Ohio 44870.

Field and Stream, Field & Stream Pub. Co., 515 Madison Ave., New York, N.Y. 10022.

Fisherman, Oxford, Ohio 45056.

Flower Grower: the Home Gardener's Magazine, Williams Press Inc., 99 N. Broadway, Albany, N.Y. 12202.

Folk Dancer, Box 201, Flushing, Long Island, N.Y.

Fur, Fish and Game, A. R. Harding Pub. Co., 174 E. Long St., Columbus, Ohio 43215.

Gamecock, D. C. Marburger, Hartford, Ark. 72938.

Game Fowl News, Box 483, Asheville, N.C. 28802.

Golf Digest, Box 629, Evanston, Ill. 60204.

Golfing, Golfing Publications, Inc., 407 S. Dearborn, Chicago, Ill. 60605.

Gourmet, Gourmet, Inc., 768 5th Ave., New York, N.Y. 10019.

Handweaver and Craftsman, 246 5th Ave., New York, N.Y. 10001.

Hobbies, Buffalo Society of Natural Science, Buffalo Museum of Science, Buffalo, N.Y. 10011.

Hobbies: The Magazine for Collectors, Lightner Publishing Co., 2810 S. Michigan Ave., Chicago, Ill. 60616.

Home Craftsman, Home Craftsman Pub. Corp., 115 Worth St., New York, N.Y. 10013.

Home Movies, Ver Halen Pub., 1159 N. Highland, Hollywood, Calif. 90038.

Hot Rod, Trend, Inc., 5959 Hollywood Blvd., Los Angeles, Calif. 90028.

Hounds and Hunting, Greenfield, Ohio 45123.

House and Garden, Condec, Boston Post Rd., Greenwich, Conn. 06830.

Hugord's Magic Monthly, J. Haggard, 2634 E. 19th St., Brooklyn, N.Y. 11235.

Hunting and Fishing, National Sportsman, Inc., 275 Newberry St., Boston, Mass. 02116.

Industrial Arts and Vocational Education (shop), Bruce Pub. Co., 540 N. Milwaukee St., Milwaukee, Wis. 53202.

Industrial Sports Journal, 202 S. State St., Chicago, Ill. 60604.

Journal of Health, Physical Education and Recreation, American Alliance of Health, Physical Education and Recreation, Washington, D.C., Published monthly.

Journal of Leisure Research, National Recreation and Park Association, Arlington, Va., Published quarterly.

Journal of Living, 1819 Broadway, New York, N.Y. 10023.

Just Buttons, for Pleasure, Pastime, and Profit, Sally Lewis House, Southington, Conn. 06489.

Leisure Today, American Alliance of Health, Physical Education and Recreation, Washington, D.C., 6 issues yearly.

Let's Dance, Folk Dance Federation of Calif., 420 Market St., San Francisco, Calif. 94111.

Lifetime Living, 22 E. 38th St., New York, N.Y. 10016.

Living Wilderness, Wilderness Society, 1840 Mintwood Place, Washington, D.C. 20009.

Maryland Conservationist, Game and Fish Commission, Munsey Bldg., Baltimore, Md. 21202.

Mechanix Illustrated, Fawcett Publications, Inc., 1501 Broadway, New York, N.Y. 10018.

Missouri Conservationist, Conservation Commission, Jefferson City, Mo. 65101.

Model Airplane News, Air Age, Inc., 551 5th Ave., New York, N.Y. 10017.

Modern Builder (mechanical models), Lionel Corp., 15 E. 26th St., New York, N.Y. 10010.

Modern Photography, Automobile Digest Pub. Corp., 22 E. 12th St., Cincinnati, Ohio 45210.

Modern Needlecraft Knitting, Needlecraft Publications, Inc., 247 Park Ave., New York, N.Y. 10017.

Monthly Evening Sky Map: A Journal for the Amateur, 244 Adams St., Brooklyn, N.Y. 11201.

Motor Boating, Hearst Magazines, Inc., 572 Madison Ave., New York, N.Y. 10022.

Motorcyclist, Western Journal Co., 1035 E. Green St., Pasadena, Calif. 94303.

Movie Makers, Amateur Cinema League, Inc., 420 Lexington Ave., New York, N.Y. 10017.

Music Educators Journal, Music Educators National Conference, 64 E. Jackson Blvd., Chicago, Ill. 60604.

Music Courier (review of the world's music), Music Periodicals Corp., 119 W. 57th St., New York, N.Y. 10019.

Musical American, Musical American Corp., 113 W. 57th St., New York, N.Y. 10019.

National Bowler's Journal, 506 S. Wabash, Chicago, Ill. 60605.

National Parks, National Parks Asso., Washington, D.C.

Nature Magazine, American Nature Assoc., 1214 16th St., N.W., Washington, D.C. 20006.

North Dakota Outdoors, State Fish and Game Dept., Bismarck, N. Dak. 58501.

Numismatist, American Numismatic Assoc., 95 5th Ave., New York, N.Y. 10003.

N.W.A. Official Wrestling, 1472 Broadway, New York, N.Y. 10036.

Outdoor America, Isaak Walton League of America, Inc., 31 N. State St., Chicago, Ill. 60602.

Outdoor Life, Popular Science Publishing Company, Inc., 353 4th Ave., New York, N.Y. 10010.

Outdoorsman, Outdoorsman Publications, 814 N. Tower Court, Chicago, Ill. 60611.

Our Dogs, H. Clay Glover Co., 101 W. 31st St., New York, N.Y. 10001.

Outdoor Sportsman, 109 Commerce, Little Rock, Ark. 72201.

Opera and Concert, Montgomery Bldg, San Francisco, Calif. 94111.

Pack-O-Fun (scrapcraft), 205 E. 42nd St., New York, N.Y. 10017.

Parks and Recreation, American Institute of Park Executives, 327 W. Jefferson St., Rockford, Ill. 61101.

Parks and Recreation, National Association and Park Association, Arlington, Va., Published monthly.

Photography, Ziff-Davis Pub. Co., 366 Madison Ave., New York, N.Y. 10017.

Playthings, McReady Pub. Co., 71 W. 23rd St., New York, N.Y. 10010.

Plays: The Drama Magazine for Young People, Plays, Inc., 8 Arlington St., Boston, Mass. 02116.

Playshop, Division of Dramatics, Pennsylvania State University, State College, Pa. 16801.

Poetry, Poetry, 232 E. Erie St., Chicago, Ill. 60611.

Popular Gardening, Gardening Publications, Inc., 90 State St., Albany, N.Y. 12207.

Popular Homecraft; Home Workshop Magazine, General Pub. Co., 814 N. Tower Court, Chicago, Ill. 60646.

Popular Mechanics, Pop. Mech. Co., 200 E. Ontario St., Chicago, Ill. 60611.

Popular Science, Pop. Sc. Pub. Co., Inc., 353 4th Ave., New York, N.Y. 10010.

Post Card Enthusiast, Orville C. Walden, 130 W. 66th St., New York, N.Y. 10023.

Professional Tennis and the Tennis World, 321 Broadway, New York, N.Y. 10007.

Profitable Hobbies, Modern Handicraft, Inc., 24th and Burlington, Kansas City, Mo. 64116.

Promenade, American Square Dance Group, 550 Riverside Drive, New York, N.Y. 10027.

Puppetry Journal, Puppeteers of America, Ashville, Ohio 43103.

O.S.T. (devoted entirely to amateur radio), Amer. Radio Relay League, 38 LaSalle Rd., West Hartford, Conn. 06107.

Racquet (formerly Am. Lawn Tennis), Allegheny Pub. Corp., 35 W. 53rd St., New York, N.Y. 10019 (tennis, badminton, and squash).

Railroad Model Craftsman, Model Craftsman Pub. Corp., Ramsey, N.J. 07446.

Recreation Management, National Industrial Recreation Association, Chicago, Ill., Published monthly.

Recreation, National Recreation Association, 315 4th Ave., New York, N.Y. 10010.

Recreation World, Recreation World Co., 1170 Broadway, New York, N.Y. 10001.

Ring, Ring, Inc., Madison Square Garden, 307 W. 49th St., New York, N.Y. 10019.

Road and Track, Enthusiast's Publications, 540 W. Colorado Blvd., Glendale, Calif. 91204.

Rosin the Bow (for folk and square dancers), Rod La Forge, 115 Cliff St., Holedon, Paterson, N.J. 07522.

Rudder, Rudder Pub. Co., 9 Murray St., New York, N.Y. 10007.

Saddle and Bridle, Midwest Publishers, Inc., Hotel Chase, St. Louis, Mo. 63108.

Safety Education, Nat'l Safety Council, 20 N. Wacker Dr., Chicago, Ill. 60606.

Scholastic Coach, Scholastic Coach, 72 E. 12th St., New York, N.Y. 10003.

Sets in Order (for square dancers), 462 N. Robertson Blvd., Los Angeles, Calif. 90048.

School Activities, Sch. Act. Pub. Co., 1515 Lane St., Topeka, Kan. 66604.

School Arts, Davis Press, Inc., 44 Portland St., Worcester, Mass. 01608.

Ship Models, Robt. A. Nash, 228, Baldwin Ave., Sierra Madre, Calif. 91024.

Skating, U.S. and Canadian Figure Skating Assoc., S. Hungington Ave., Boston, Mass. 02116.

Skating News, Box 857, Detroit, Mich.

Ski Magazine, National Skiing Assoc. of Amer., Hanover, N.H. 03755.

Skiing, Golden Press, Inc., 7301 Colfax Ave., Denver, Colorado 80215.

Skin Diver, Box 128, Lynwood, Calif. 90262.

Social Service Review, Univ. of Chicago Press, 5750 Ellis Ave., Chicago, Ill. 60637.

Sport, 205 East 42nd St., New York, N.Y. 10017.

Sport Life, Official Magazine Corp., 270 Park Ave., New York, N.Y. 10017.

Sporting News, J. G. T. Spink, 2012 Second Ave. S., Minneapolis, Minn. 55404.

Sports Afield, Sports Afield Pub. Co., 401 Second Ave. S., Minneapolis, Minn. 55401.

Sports Illustrated, 9 Rockefeller Plaza, New York, N.Y. 10020.

Stamps, H. L. Lendquist, 2 W. 46th St., New York, N.Y. 10019.

Story Art: A Magazine for Story Tellers, Nat'l Story League, 5835 Martel Ave., Dallas, Texas 75206.

Survey, Survey Associates, Inc., 112 E. 19th St., New York, N.Y. 10003.

Tennessee Folklore Society Bulletin, Dr. P. J. Parr, Tennessee Polytechnic Inst., Cookeville, Tenn. 38501.

Theatre Arts, 208 S. LaSalle, Chicago, Ill. 60604.

Therapeutic Recreation Journal, National Therapeutic Recreation Society (NRPA), Arlington, Va., Published quarterly.

Texas Game and Fish, State Game and Fish Commission, Austin, Texas 78701.

Tourist Court Journal, Tourist Court Journal Co., 107 S. 1st St., Temple, Texas 76501.

Town and Country, Hearst Corp., 572 Madison Ave., New York, N.Y. 10022.

Toy Trains, Penn. Publication, Inc., Route 17, Ramsey, N.J. 07446.

Travel, 115 W. 45th St., New York, N.Y. 10019.

Turf and Sport Digest, Montee Publishing Co., Inc., 511 Oakland Ave., Baltimore, Md. 21212.

U.S. Camera, U.S. Camera Pub. Corp., 420 Lexington Ave., New York, N.Y. 10017.

West Virgnia Conservation, Conservation Commission, State Capitol, Charleston, W. Va. 25311.

Woman Bowler, Women's International Bowling Congress, Inc., Spencer Walker Press, Inc., 32 Warren Street, Columbus, Ohio 43215.

World Theatre, Olivier Perrin, 198 Boulevard Saint Germain, Paris.

World Youth, World Youth, Inc., El Quinto Rd., Los Gatos, Calif. 95030.

Wyoming Wild Life, Game and Fish Commission, Capitol Bldg., Cheyenne, Wyoming 82001.

The Writer, The Writer, 8 Arlington St., Boston, Mass. 02116.

Yachting, Yachting Pub. Corp., 205 E. 42nd St., New York, N.Y. 10017.

Youth Leaders, Youth Leaders, Inc., Putnam Valley, New York 10579.

Youth's Instructor, Review and Herald Publ. Assn., Takoma Park Station, Washington, D.C. 20012.

Addresses of Agencies Concerned with Recreation

Amateur Athletic Union, 505 Broadway, New York, N.Y. 10012.

Amateur Bicycle League of America, 108 W. 45th St., Brooklyn, N.Y. 11232.

American Association for Adult Education, 41 E. 42nd St., New York, N.Y. 10036.

American Association for Health, Physical Education and Recreation, 1201—16th St. N.W., Washington, D.C. 20036.

American Bowling Congress, 2200 N. Third St., Milwaukee, Wis. 53212.

American Child Health Association, 370 Seventh Ave., New York, N.Y. 10001.
American Country Life Association, 105 E. 22nd St., New York, N.Y. 10010.
American Federation of Labor, Washington, D.C.
American Forestry Association, Washington, D.C.
American Home Economics Association, Mills Bldg., Washington, D.C.
American Institute of Park Executives, Rockford, Ill.
American Legion Headquarters, Indianapolis, Ind.
American Library Association, 520 N. Michigan Ave., Chicago, Ill. 60611.
American Nature Association, Washington, D.C.
American Olympic Association, Washington, D.C.
American Social Hygiene Association, 450 Seventh Ave., New York, N.Y. 10001.
American Youth Hostels, 14 W. 8th St., New York, N.Y. 10011.
Association for Childhood Education, 1201 16th St. N.W., Washington, D.C. 20036.
Athletic Institute, 209 S. State St., Chicago, Ill. 60604.
Big Brother Movement, Inc., 200 Fifth Ave., New York, N.Y. 10010.
Big Sister Movement, Inc., 122 E. 25th St., New York, N.Y. 10010.
Boy Scouts of America, 200 Fifth Ave., New York, N.Y. 10010
Boys Club Federation, Inc., 3037 Grand Central Terminal, New York, N.Y.
Bureau of Education, Dept. of Interior, Washington, D.C. 20242.
Camp Fire Girls, Inc., 31 E. 17th st. New York, N.Y. 10003.
Children's Bureau, U.S. Department of Labor, Washington, D.C. 20214.
Drama League of America, The, 59 E. Van Buren St., Chicago, Ill. 60605.
Girl Scouts, Inc., 352 Fourth Ave., New York, N.Y. 10003.
International YMCA, 347 Madison Ave., New York, N.Y. 10017.
Jewish Welfare Board, 352 Fourth Ave., New York, N.Y. 10003.
Library of Congress, Washington, D.C.
National Amateur Athletic Federation (Men), 6 N. Michigan Ave., Chicago, Ill.
    60602.
National Amateur Athletic Federation (Women), 2 W. 46th St., New York, N.Y.
    10036.
National American Red Cross, Washington, D.C.
National Board of YMCA, 291 Broadway, New York, N.Y. 10019.
National Board of YWCA of USA, 600 Lexington Ave., New York, N.Y. 10022.
National Bureau for Advancement of Music, 105 W. 45th St., New York, N.Y.
    10036.
National Catholic Welfare Council, Washington, D.C.
National Child Welfare Association, 70 Fifth Ave., New York, N.Y. 10011.
National Congress of Parents & Teachers, 1201 16th St. N.W., Washington, D.C.
    20036.
National Education Association, 1201 16th St. N.W., Washington, D.C. 20036.
National Golf Association, 804 Merchandise Mart, Chicago, Ill. 60654.
National Horseshoe Pitchers' Association, London, Ohio 43140.
National League of Girls' Clubs, 465 W. 23rd St., New York, N.Y. 10011.
National Physical Education Service, 315 Fourth Ave., New York, N.Y. 10003.
National Recreation Association, 315 Fourth Ave., New York, N.Y. 10003.
National Rifle Association, Woodward Blvd., Washington, D.C.
National Ski Association, Washington, D.C.
National Storyteller's League, Washington, D.C.
National Vocational Guidance Association, 425 W. 123rd St., New York, N.Y.
    10027.
Russell Sage Foundation, 120 E. 22nd St., New York, N.Y. 10010.
U.S. Dept. of Agriculture, Washington, D.C. 20251.
U.S. Golf Association, Washington, D.C.
U.S. Lawn Tennis Association, 130 Broadway, New York, N.Y. 10019.
U.S. Public Health Service, Washington, D.C.
Women's International Bowling Congress, 85 E. Gay St., Columbus, Ohio 43215.

Sources for Equipment and Supplies

Large Indoor Equipment

Atlas Athletic Equipment Co.
2339 Hampton Ave.
St. Louis, Missouri 63139

Gym Master
3200 So. Zuri Street
Englewood, Colorado 80110

Jayfro Corp.
1 Bridge Street, PO Box 50
Montville, Conn. 06353

Lind Climber Co.
807 Reba Place
Evanston, Illinois 60202

Nissen Corporation
930 27th Avenue S.W.
Cedar Rapids, Iowa 52406

Trampoline, Inc.
247 West Sixth Street
San Pedro, California 90733

Large Outdoor Equipment

The J. E. Burke Co.
Fond du Lac, Wisconsin 54935

Game-Time Inc.
Litchfield, Michigan 49262

Jamison Manufacturing Co.
510 East Manchester Ave.
Los Angeles, California 90003

Northwest Design Products, Inc.
1235 South Tacoma Way
Tacoma, Washington 98409

Otto Industries PTY., Ltd.
309–313 South Road
Mile End South
Sth. Australia 5031

Playground Corporation of America
29–16 40th Avenue
Long Island City, N.Y. 11101

W. J. Voit Rubber Corp.
29 Essex Street
Maywood, New Jersey 07607

*Hand Manipulative and
   Games Equipment*

Adirondack Industries, Inc.
Dolgeville, New York 13329

American Seating
Grand Rapids, Michigan 49502

Childcraft Education Corp.
PO Box 94
Bayonne, New Jersey 07002

Cosom Corporation
6030 Wayzata Blvd.
Minneapolis, Minnesota 55416

General Sportcraft Co. Ltd.
140 Woodbine Street
Bergenfield, New Jersey 07621

Interstate Rubber Products Corp.
908 Avila Street
Los Angeles, California 90012

Lojen Apparatus, Inc.
Box 785
Fremont, Nebraska 68025

Mid-Valley Sport Center
5350 No. Blackstone
Fresno, California 93726

Oregon Worsted Co.
8300 S. E. McLoughlin Blvd.
Portland, Oregon 97202

Physical Education Supply
   Associates Inc.
PO Box 292
Trumbull, Connecticut 06611

Playskool, Inc. Dept. E.
Division of Milton Bradley Co.
3720 North Kedzie Ave.
Chicago, Illinois 60618

Program Aids, Inc.
161 MacQuesten Parkway
Mt. Vernon, New York 10550

R. E. Titus Gym Scooter Co.
Winfild, Kansas 67156

Wolters Co.
9250 So. Buttonwillow
Reedley, California 93654

Ed-Nu, Inc.
5115 Route 38
Pennsauken, New Jersey 08110

School Tech, Inc.,
745 State Circle
Ann Arbor, Michigan 48104

Index

Page numbers followed by t refer to tables.